OK, GOD, NOW WHAT?

Do You Need Answers?

- Why can't I seem to change? Why does it not change when I pray and pray? I feel so frustrated, helpless and unloved.
- How many times do I have to go to the altar to get my life changed and free from these sins, doubts and problems?
- Why do I keep worrying? How do I stop?
- How do I get a calm heart in the midst of the storms of life?
- The Bible says I am to walk in joy, yet I have so little. Why?
- I quit going to church because it didn't seem to make any difference. I did all they said, and still I'm not changed. Why?
- I go up for every altar call, for every evangelist, for every revival, and still I can't get free. Why?
- I go to church because I know it's good for me, but I don't see how it fits into the rest of my life in a major way. Why?
- I want to grow in God, yet I seem to be getting nowhere. Why?
- I fast, I pray, I tithe, I give to the poor, I repent, I read the Bible daily and do good deeds, yet I see no results. What is going on?
- Why can I not hear God for myself?
- I am making progress in God, but there is so much more. How do I get it? How do I grow in knowing Jesus?
- I want to be healthy, yet I've tried all the fads and still I'm sick. Where is God in all this?
- Every sermon I hear seems to go into a vast tank, never to be remembered again. Why?

OK, God, Now What? gives effective Bible answers to these questions in the light of the findings of modern science on how the brain works, combined with God's ancient secrets.

With the basic tools in this book, you can start on a program to grow in grace with God and man, and see dramatic changes in your life and in the lives of those around you, all by knowing who and what you are because of the sacrifice and resurrection of Jesus Christ. This book teaches you how to labor effectively to get results.

> *Therefore, my agape/beloved brethren, be ye stedfast, unmoveable, always abounding in the work of the Lord, forasmuch as ye know that your labour is not in vain in the Lord.*   1 Corinthians 15:58

OK, God, Now What?

Activating His Ancient Secrets To Success

BY

Donald C. Mann

www.CovenantPeaceMinistries.com

OK, GOD, NOW WHAT?
Copyright © 2011, 2012, 2013, 2017, 2018 by Donald C. Mann
ALL RIGHTS RESERVED, AMERICAN, PAN-AMERICAN AND INTERNATIONAL.

This book is protected under the copyright laws of the United States of America and may not be copied or reprinted for commercial gain or profit. The use of short quotations or occasional page copying for personal or group study is permitted and encouraged. Permission will be granted upon request. No part of this publication may be stored in a retrieval system, transmitted, or reproduced in any way, including but not limited to photocopy, photograph, magnetic or other record, without prior agreement and written permission from the author.

Unless otherwise noted, all Scripture references are from *The Holy Bible, Authorized King James Version*. References marked "AMP" are from *The Holy Bible, Amplified Version*, copyright © 1954, 1958, 1962, 1964, 1965, 1987 by The Lockman Foundation, La Habra, California. All rights reserved. Used by permission.

Non-Medical Advice: The information presented in this book is in no way intended as advice or instruction concerning the use of medicine, medical treatment, or the avoidance thereof. Each person is responsible to investigate all methods of remedy they are contemplating. No one has a right or responsibility to make your decision except you. Any reference to medicine or medical treatment is solely for historical or informational purposes.

The author is in no way responsible or liable for the successful application of the material or for the manner of the reader's application or future re-presentation of the material in this book or their results. Nor is the author in any way a trained medical or psychological professional. By using this material for any purpose, the reader holds the author harmless of any liability.
Please see additional disclaimers in the section: "About the Use of the Author's Study Helps"

Excerpts taken from other books by the author include:
The Mind Renewing Battle Prayer, The Prayer Cards,
and *Battle Prayer for Divine Healing, Field Manual 2.*

Published by:

McDougal & Associates
18896 Greenwell Springs Road
Greenwell Springs, Louisiana   70739
www.thepublishedword.com

McDougal & Associates is an organization dedicated to the spreading the Gospel of the Lord Jesus Christ to as many people as possible in the shortest time possible.

ISBN 978-1-934769-34-8

Printed on demand in the USA, the UK and Australia
For worldwide distribution

Acknowledgments

I thank the ever-faithful Lord Jesus Christ of Nazareth, who purchased me with His blood and now intercedes for me by the will of Father God and Holy Spirit who dwells within me.

I also thank my wife, Cindy, and our children, Christina and Jonathan, who have been used of the Lord to show me His goodness and love.

I also thank Margie and Carroll Harlow for being such good friends and for Margie's invaluable help in the final proofing of this work.

THE 2018 REVISED AND UPDATED EDITION

This revision adds some new material and fixes some typos. The original content is still accurate but is now enhanced. These revisions do make the truth of the Bible more powerful and accurate in the English language.

We added the word *actions* to *faith, hope* and *agape/love* as these get closer to the original language meanings. For *trust, believe,* and *take courage* we added *by* or *in continual right faith actions*, or the shorter, *by* or *in faith actions*, as this, again, fits a more accurate understanding of the original language words. We also add a Glossary entry on *Faith Actions* to explain this better. As we did not want to change the current pagination and overall book size, we added these terms (actions) where we had room. So not every use of the words *faith, belief, believe, believing, believer, courage, courageous, trust, hope* or *agape/love* has these amplifying additions. The reader is invited to add these amplifying additions wherever we did not explicitly add them, to be more accurate in their understanding and speaking of the Bible text.

We also added an *Agape Love Warrior's Confession* on page 186 in the printed and PDF versions.

We also added "Yahoo!" at the end of many of the Affirmation Magnets to help the reader to remember to do joy actions as they work with the Affirmations. Doing gladness and joy behaviors throughout the Affirmations, within and at the end, increase the benefits of the heart-writing, mind-renewing process.

This book is designed to help you understand how to walk in the awesome Gospel of Jesus Christ, which Paul preached. Col 1:25 "Whereof I am made a minister, according to the dispensation of God which is given to me for you, to fulfil the word of God; 26 even the mystery which hath been hid from ages and from generations, but now is made manifest to his saints: 27 to whom God would make known what is the riches of the glory of this mystery among the Gentiles; **which is Christ in you, the hope of glory**: 28 whom we preach, warning every man, and teaching every man in all wisdom; that we may present every man perfect in Christ Jesus: 29 whereunto I also labour, striving according to his working, which worketh in me mightily."

One of the great tools of God is understanding that faith is action, what those actions are, and then doing them. We hope you find these revisions and updates helpful in enhancing your walk in Christ.

CONTENTS

Bible Book Abbreviations Used 8
About the Use of the Author's Study Helps 9
Introduction 12
Getting Started 19

Part I: Gaining an Understanding 23
1. Understanding the Need for New Attitudes 25
2. Understanding the Salvation God Offers 44
3. Understanding Christian Biology 47
4. Understanding How to Avoid Missing God 64
5. Understanding How to Renew the Heart 76
6. Understanding the Biology and Spirituality of Affirmations 80
7. Understanding Resistance to Change 85
8. Understanding the Power of Fear 89
9. Understanding the Power of Faith 96
10. Understanding the Need for Persistence 101
11. Understanding the Power of Right Attitudes 106
12. Understanding How to Avoid Schemes and Maintain Peace 119
13. Understanding How to Move Beyond What Is Seen 128
14. Understanding How to Avoid Hypocrisy 132
15. Understanding How to Go to the Next Level 148
16. Understanding How to Approach Healing 152
17. Understanding How to Use the Affirmations 164

Part II: The Affirmations 187
18. Affirmations in Christ 189
19. Now What? 275

Appendices 279
   A Glossary of Terms 281
   Bibliography and Recommended Reading 340
   Ministry Page 341

Bible Book Abbreviations Used

For Old Testament Books

Gen	Genesis
Ex	Exodus
Lev	Leviticus
Num	Numbers
Deut	Deuteronomy
Josh	Joshua
Judg	Judges
Ruth	Ruth
1 Sam	1 Samuel
2 Sam	2 Samuel
1 Kings	1 Kings
2 Kings	2 Kings
1 Chron	1 Chronicles
2 Chron	2 Chronicles
Ezra	Ezra
Neh	Nehemiah
Esther	Esther
Job	Job
Ps	Psalms
Prov	Proverbs
Eccl	Ecclesiastes
Song	Song of Solomon
Isa	Isaiah
Jer	Jeremiah
Lam	Lamentations
Ezek	Ezekiel
Dan	Daniel
Hos	Hosea
Joel	Joel
Am	Amos
Ob	Obadiah
Jon	Jonah
Mic	Micah
Nah	Nahum
Hab	Habakkuk
Zeph	Zephaniah
Hag	Haggai
Zech	Zechariah
Mal	Malachi

For New Testament Books

Matt	Matthew
Mark	Mark
Luke	Luke
John	John
Acts	Acts
Rom	Romans
1 Cor	1 Corinthians
2 Cor	2 Corinthians
Gal	Galatians
Eph	Ephesians
Phil	Philippians
Col	Colossians
1 Thes	1 Thessalonians
2 Thes	2 Thessalonians
1 Tim	1 Timothy
2 Tim	2 Timothy
Titus	Titus
Philem	Philemon
Heb	Hebrews
James	James
1 Pet	1 Peter
2 Pet	2 Peter
1 John	1 John
2 John	2 John
3 John	3 John
Jude	Jude
Rev	Revelation

EXAMPLE: 2 Cor 5:17 refers to the book, 2 Corinthians and the scripture found in chapter 5, verse 17. 2 Cor 5:17-6:2 refers to the book 2 Corinthians with the passage starting at chapter 5, verse 17 and going through to chapter 6, verse 2 of that book.

About the Use of the Author's Study Helps

For the following reasons, we have included study helps within the various Scriptures used in this book:

1. To seek to expand the depth of meaning from the original Bible documents and languages.
2. To connect the current verse to other relevant verses or biblical concepts.
3. To apply the Scriptures as prayers and affirmations, to help renew the mind.

In these pages there are five basic types of study, or application, helps:

a) We include some key original language words right with the translated word, such as *aiteo*/ask.
b) We include expanded definitions of the translated word to better describe the original language word, for example: *aiteo*/ask (*require, demand and expect as due by covenant promise*).
c) We add words that fit the concept but are not found in that exact Scripture, for example: Rom 8:11 "But if the Spirit of him that raised up Jesus from the dead dwell in you, he that raised up Christ from the dead shall also quicken your [*current*] mortal bodies by his Spirit that dwelleth in you."
d) For prayers and affirmations we may modify existing words to the appropriate person or tense, and/or add relevant connecting words to fit the flow of our English language, while trying to let the Scripture translation shine through. For example, please see below where Heb 3:12-13 is used as the basis for a prayer.
e) At the back of the book we added a glossary of oft-misunderstood biblical words with definition and pronunciation guides for the original language words.

Our primary sources for these study helps include *Strong's Exhaustive Concordance, Vine's Expository Dictionary of Old and New Testament Word, PC Study Bible* software, Wuest's *The New Testament, An Expanded Translation* and other Bible translations. Here are the rules we followed to include these study helps:

ITALICS: Wherever a scripture reference is underlined, any adjustments in tense, person, count or additions are italicized. This identifies what has been modified or added to the text of the original translation. The original language Old or New Testament (i.e., Hebrew or Greek) words are added occasionally for emphasis in the format of *aiteo* or *aiteo*/ask.

CAPITALIZATION: Multiple scriptures after the same reference have the capitalization adjusted where there is no capitalization across verses, after commas, colons and semicolons except when the new word is either someone speaking, or a quote from another part of the Bible.

QUOTATION MARKS AROUND SCRIPTURE: These are not used at the discretion of the author when in a prayer, affirmation, confession or a list of scriptures such as in the Affirmations section. See prayer example below. When no quotation marks are used, any added words between or after the scriptures are in italics to the end of the paragraph, as in the example below.

THE USE OF PARENTHESES AND SQUARE BRACKETS: Additional meanings and expansions within scripture are placed in parentheses and italicized. Also inserted implications are placed in square brackets and italicized. Occasionally the punctuation is changed to fit the content.

AN EXAMPLE: Heb 3:12-13, as a personal prayer, becomes: **Father, in the name of Jesus,** work in us so that I and those I pray for: Heb 3:12 Take heed, *among the* brethren, lest there be in any of *us* an evil heart of unbelief (*unpersuadableness, offense or lack of confidence and lack of right faith actions*), in departing from *You,* Father, the *zao*/living God. 13 But *by Your grace in us we* exhort one another daily, while it is called To day; lest any *of us* be hardened through the deceitfulness of sin [*in corrupt thoughts, words and actions in believing that, You, Father God, are not my friend, helper, near or that Your Word can fail, and thus living in the mind of the carnal flesh and not the Spirit by the Word of God*]. *Thank You, Father, in the name of Jesus. Thank You!*

AFFIRMATION AND PRAYER IRREGULARITIES: We have worked with these Affirmations and prayers for about 20 years now, trying to find the best way to let the Scriptures shine through, while adding explanations and applications to other scripture and events in life. So far, we have found no way that could be considered remotely perfect. Nor do we claim that what we have done in this book is perfect. The only solid rule we have followed is that any change to the original translation of the Scriptures is in italics. What we felt we could *not* do was to make the structure as complex as that found in the Amplified Bible, which we highly respect, but which is hard for many to read out loud, and these Affirmations and prayers are for daily use to be read out loud. For many people, a large amount of symbols—such as parentheses, brackets, etc.—make the resultant text very cumbersome to navigate. Therefore, at our option, sometimes these symbols and markings have been left out for ease of reading. The effect is that the prayers and affirmations become application paraphrases by the author. We highly regard the Word of God and in no way do we want to diminish the accuracy of the Scriptures. If you find any place/s where you think we have gone beyond reasonable bounds, please let us know, and we will endeavor to correct it.

HOLY SPIRIT: You will notice that there is no "the" in addressing or describing Holy Spirit where His name is written by the author. Holy Spirit is the third person of the Godhead, and Holy Spirit is His revealed name. He is not an "it" but a person. The article "the" is not in the original Greek and, unless used within the particular translation used, it is not used by the author to address Him. The King James often translates the Greek word *pneuma* as "ghost" or "spirit." Holy Spirit is used by the author rather than Holy Ghost, recognizing that *ghost* and *spirit* mean exactly the same.

Introduction

Jamie knew he needed more of God, but how? He had gone back to church and heard the preaching, but where was God? Jamie was tired of quick fixes that kept him busy but did not satisfy the empty spot in his gut. He knew the answer was God, but again how? He had made a decision to get closer to the Lord, but now what was he to do?

Sarah had been born again two years before, and she was excited. She had seen God give some wonderful answers to prayer, but it seemed almost like her heart was now slowing down. She was busy, but stayed empty. She had been to the altar and cried for days at a time about this, but there was no relief. She was really starting to get mad at God about why things did not seem to be working for her.

Marcia knew she needed God. It has been years since she had been in church, but no matter what she did—from parties to sex to mediation—within her heart that pull to the God of the Bible would not stop. If she got still for even a moment, she felt its tug. But where was God and how did she, as lost as she was, get back to Him? She had started out so great. It had been wonderful, but now all Marcia felt was "wrong" on the inside.

Rev. Bob had taught the Gospel for twenty years and had run out of steam. Yes, he had seen God move, but all the pat answers he was preaching every week were not working, and he knew it. They were not working for the people of his congregation, and they were not working for him either. He had led revivals and seen excitement, but in three to five years, all was back to what it had been before. And now most discussions started with the phrase, "Remember when God … ." He had "held on" and "let go" so many times he felt like a yo-yo. He'd had glimpses of glory, but nothing that built a bridge or a walkway. Instead he had glimpsed spread-out islands of glory, but as much as he wanted more, he did not know how to get it.

Pastor Harry was excited. He and his people had been working with the local youth league, and now fifty boys and young men were coming regularly. But he was worried. He had seen this many times before, and after about a year, only a few remained. He could lead men in the sinner's prayer, but how do you pray to become an airline pilot or own a restaurant? The ones who wanted to "get ahead" would get busy in school and would soon stop coming to the youth meetings. That is ... unless he could find some girls who could keep their interest. Why was God not sufficient for them and why did he need games, rock bands, movies and girls to keep boys involved?

What did all these people have in common?

- They had experienced, seen or felt obstacles to their success in whatever good they desired.
- They were coming to God looking for answers and sincerely wanted His answers.
- All thought, at least at one time, they had done the right thing/s.
- They knew there had to be more from God, but they didn't know how to get it because what they were doing had not been good enough.

The interesting thing is that these are all the same issues businesspeople, government leaders, scientists and anyone who wants to improve their future needs answers to. I once sat in an auditorium and listened to an Olympic Gold Medal winner tell her story. She was a national champion in swimming, but swimming is won in fractions of a second, so victory is in the details. All of the competitors knew how to swim, but how to get their bodies to maximize their potential was a different matter. Her coach said, "We barely have enough time, six months. If you are going to win, then you must scrap everything you know and relearn swimming, but this time perfectly. You are good, but if you want to maximize what you can do and fulfill your destiny as an Olympic winner, you have to start again. And we barely have enough time." He knew what it took, and he knew that it would not be instantaneous.

The champion swimmer went on to tell how every day she not only continued her physical training in excruciating detail, in order to develop strength and exact precision in each and every movement, but also she had to learn to excel at the "head" game. She spent hours each day, not in the water, but in her mind, visualizing exactly correct motions, actions and decisions for each event she would be competing in. She studied how the exactly correct motions felt and then relived them in her imagination over and over and over, and she did this every single day.

Three fourths of the way through her training, her time started to improve. Soon she was routinely excelling over her previous times and over her other known competitors. But that was still not good enough. She knew she could do more, and she knew she had to do more. So she kept at it.

Gradually her times got better and better and more consistent, and in the end, she won. It was, she told us, not because of the physical or body part of the equation, but through the training of her brain. She won the "head" game and, as a result, she won her gold medals.

So let's start with a few basic concepts now, and then we'll go into much more detail later in the book. Modern man thinks of humans as two-part beings, having a soul and a body. He calls the spirit and heart the *attitude* or *emotions* or *will*. God, however, calls man a three-part being. 1 Thes 5:23 "And the very God of peace sanctify you wholly; and I pray

God your whole spirit and soul and body be preserved blameless unto the coming of our Lord Jesus Christ."

The Bible describes man as a spirit who inhabits a body and has a soul. When we are born again, receive the righteousness of God in Christ Jesus and eternal *zoe*/life, we are born again in spirit. We call this *salvation*. John 1:12 "But as many as received him, to them gave he power to become the sons of God, even to them that believe on his name: 13 which were born, not of blood, nor of the will of the flesh, nor of the will of man, but of God." John 3:5 "Jesus answered, Verily, verily, I say unto thee, Except a man be born of water and of the Spirit, he cannot enter into the kingdom of God. 6 That which is born of the flesh is flesh; and that which is born of the Spirit is spirit. 7 Marvel not that I said unto thee, Ye must be born again. 8 The wind bloweth where it listeth, and thou hearest the sound thereof, but canst not tell whence it cometh, and whither it goeth: so is every one that is born of the Spirit." Notice the spirit is reborn, not the soul.

Much of our modern Christian language is not helpful. For the newly born-again, we say, "___ souls got saved last night." Technically, that is not correct. Souls did not get saved; spirits did. Notice what God says: 1 Cor 6:20 "For ye are bought with a price (*redeemed, ransomed*): therefore glorify God in your body, and in your spirit, which are God's." You are born again in spirit and are guaranteed a new resurrection body, but in this life, for now, the salvation of your soul is up to you, not God. He must be involved, but it is our responsibility.

God has sent a Helper and Teacher, Holy Spirit, the Spirit of Truth, but Holy Spirit does not do the work of *sozo*/saving our souls in this life. Instead, He helps you as you do it. John 14:16 "And I (*Jesus*) will ask the Father, and He will give you another Comforter (*Counselor, Helper, Intercessor, Advocate, Strengthener, and Standby*), that He may remain with you forever." AMP Holy Spirit goes alongside of you and helps you as you do the work.

Although being born again brings us access to the total salvation of God in spirit, soul and body, when we go to be with Him, we will get a brand-new resurrection body; we do not have that body now. What does get changed, or "saved," here is our spirit. Our body will be "saved" at the resurrection or the "rapture," but not before. Our soul is in the process of being saved, and this is not up to God right now; it is our job.

The New Covenant promise is that God will change our hearts and our minds. Heb 10:16 "This is the covenant that I will make with them after those days, saith the Lord, I will put my laws into their hearts, and in their minds will I write them; 17 and their sins and iniquities will I remember no more." This sounds just like the work of a computer programmer. A new program will be written in our hearts and our minds so that the way we live will look like Jesus. This is full soul salvation.

The job description for every Christian alive on the Earth today is this: James 1:21 "Wherefore lay apart all filthiness and superfluity of naughtiness, and *lambano*/receive with meekness the engrafted word, which is able to *sozo*/save your souls. 22 But be ye doers of the word, and not hearers only, deceiving your own selves."

So the soul-saving process is twofold: (1) Receiving and holding on to the Word of God in Christ, no matter what, and (2) Doing what that Word says. You need both, not just either or. So God will write His laws on your hearts and your minds so that you will also, like Jesus, become living words of God, but you are required to participate in the process. It is more a matter of, "Do it now, or I will do it for you later; but what you don't get done now will cost you later."

This is what our Olympic champion did. She learned what was required, and then she did it physically and, even more perfectly in her mind, using her imagination of what could be and not focusing on what now was. What she did was to train her soul along with her body. In Bible terms, she "saved" her soul in the area of swimming.

For the purposes of this book, we will consider the soul to consist of your heart, mind, will and emotions. Many consider the heart and the spirit to be the same thing. We will go into that in more detail later. This debate over the heart and spirit and soul has been going on for a very long time. The process of training, or "saving," the soul does not depend on the answer to this debate, but in order for the soul to be "saved," the heart must be absolutely involved. And the heart is trainable or reprogrammable. That is the key.

The Bible calls this the "renewing of the mind," and the result is transformation. It is a process, so the steps along the way can be seen. It is not like the new birth, in which God virtually instantaneously recreates the spirit in the new creation. You were *this*, and *poof*, now you are *that*. Renewing the mind, however, is the process of "saving" your soul over time and then keeping it that way against the pull of the world system. Rom 12:2 "And be not conformed to this world: but be ye transformed by the renewing of your mind, that ye may prove what is that good, and acceptable, and perfect, will of God."

Rom 12:2 describes this mind-renewing process as one in which you are constantly fighting the pressure of the world system to conform, mold or shape you in your soul to its manner of life and not God's. We live our life out of our soul. That is why the Greek word *psuche* is translated as "soul" or "life," depending on the context. What you exhibit in the thoughts you allow, the words you speak and what you do, are all controlled by the soul and, thus, produce your manner of living, played out and seen in your physical body.

The human spirit is the deep inner you and is limited to accessing the body and the world around us, except as it moves through or around the soul. A soul in agreement with your born-again spirit looks like Jesus in you and can be seen by others. How much of Jesus or the mind of Christ is actually displayed in your body and in your manner of life is dependent upon the amount of renewing in the Word of God your soul experiences.

So what do Jamie, Sarah, Marcia, Rev. Bob, Pastor Harry and our Olympic champion have in common? Their primary battles are or were in renewing the mind or soul, and our Olympic champion won her battle for her time.

The title of this book, *OK, God, Now What?*, answers the question "Now what?" What do we do to move into the powerful destiny God has called each of us to as Christians, so we, too, can become His champions in our time?

The understanding for this book came about as I saw that the principles that business people and top professional athletes were using to produce extraordinary results were the same ones I was seeing in the Scriptures. I was in a sales training class, and as the instructor described the key principles for peak performance in the face of everyday sales resistance, I started "hearing" scripture after scripture race though my mind. These were coming in multiples, at almost every word the instructor uttered. He was not a godly man, but every word he said triggered the Word of God in me. Why? He was speaking the truth of God, and I was privileged to "hear" some of it.

If you read my business resume, many call me a "turn-around guy," or a "new business" guy. What I have done most of my life is to enter impossible business and people situations and, with the same people (not a special team, but those same people who have not performed well in the past), lead those involved to extraordinary technical, financial and people results. Before, even though I had done it, I did not know *how* I had done it. My most important secret is that I strive to pray two hours every day in tongues (see Acts 2 and 1 Corinthians 12 and 14) and read the Scriptures and/or biblically-sound books for an hour a day, and the result is that I end up doing the right things.

I started asking God to explain to me how I did it, and what I learned is in this book. It answers the question, "What do you do to bring the Kingdom of God to Earth in a consistent manner?" That question becomes "*OK, God, Now What?*"

This is not a book based on a few scriptures. The breadth of scripture on this topic is large, so I have included many scriptures so you can see much of what God has to say about this without the need to keep your Bible open before you. But please go back to your Bible and read each reference in the context of one or two chapters before and after each reference and, thus, become personally persuaded about what God is saying to each of us by His unchangeable written Word. That persuasion process is part of renewing the mind.

I discovered the secrets to health, wealth, prosperity and a long life in the middle of a crisis. I barely made it through that crisis, but finally, by the grace of God, did triumph. I wrote *OK, God, Now What?* so you could triumph even better than I did, and build a life better than you could ever have dreamed of.

We live in a world where advertising and daily life shout that there is no help in God. If you don't fight back, these ideas will overwhelm and ultimately kill you, and this journey is designed to make you miserable. The effects are seen in our bodies and our minds. 2/3 of all bankruptcies are for medical reasons. 20% of Americans have clinical mental illness today, and 50% will have clinical depression in their lifetime. 84% of all Americans will visit a doctor at least 4 times in one year, and the most common diagnosis is hypertension or stress, or the results of hypertension or stress (which are controlled by how you think). And 30% will have a diagnosis of cancer. Interestingly enough, some doctors believe cancer is caused by evil fear, which is a form of toxic thinking.

Toxic thoughts lead to leaky neurons that stress your body every time you think such ungodly, fear-based thoughts. It is even worse if you let yourself get into the evil emotions attached to the ungodly thoughts. Fear and envy kills, worry makes you sick, and a corrupt mouth, the fruit of a corrupt subconscious mind or heart, shortens your life. The average family of four spends $20,000 a year in health care; 40% of that is out of pocket. That is $8,000 a year, every year, and that figure is growing. Medical science says there is no reason why anyone could not live a healthy 120 years, or even ever have to die. After all, a healthy body replaces itself every 7 to 10 years.

Each family could easily save $1,800 or more per year with a) a godly thinking program that heals and restores what is lost or damaged, including health, b) regular life maintenance to keep your mind and mouth clean, and c) a life-building program to make Heaven on your part of the Earth. There are three situations we have to manage in a godly manner for success in life: 1) urgent events, 2) ongoing maintenance, and 3) life-building for a godly future. All of this is to be found in *OK, God, Now What?* This is how you not only avoid being a bankruptcy statistic, but how you walk in health, wealth, prosperity and long life, and how you make Heaven on your part of the Earth, just as Adam was supposed to do, and just as Jesus actually did.

As Christians, we have been told to bring every thought captive to the obedience of Christ, so what is your batting average? Before you answer, consider how you act when someone cuts you off on the highway, gets the last sale item in a store, says an unkind remark about you or treats you or yours unfairly. Every day you delay in doing a program like is found in *OK, God, Now What?* you are building and exercising leaky neurons with toxic thoughts by letting evil fear run your life, limiting your creativity and love, and building such things as poverty, murmuring, complaining, fault finding, depression, cheap Band-Aid thinking, Alzheimer's and no supernatural power of God, as the daily habits of your life.

The secrets for the promises of God to become active in your life are found in the Bible, and are now explained by the modern science of neurology and the subconscious mind. If I had found such a program, I would not have written *OK, God, Now What?* and frankly without *OK, God, Now What?*, I would still be a fear-bound Christian trapped in nearly ritual prayer, Bible study, worship and token good deeds, with few acts of supernatural power or evangelism. Where do you stack up? Is your trust in your health plan, Medicare or God? Your pension or savings, or your account in Heaven?

Now you know why I am so passionate about this book and the potential for you and your family. God's best can be had if you will work at it in the right way. I did the hard work, spending years in Bible and scientific study and practice, and now, with the keys I have put in this book, you can launch into a program that will transform your life to something beyond your best dreams and free your brain of leaky neurons and toxic thoughts.

OK, God, Now What? came about as I had to explain how I took a failing company and helped it to make $500 million in sales in six years with the very same people. I had gone into my boss's office one day feeling good and came out numb. Just then, in the hallway, another vice president met me and said, "Better men than you have tried to turn that plant around. So long; it's been nice knowing you." So much for a confidence boost!

Not only was the job impossible, but an entire town and thousands of lives depended on solving the problems. The issues were not managerial but technical, and the only scientists and engineers who knew this technology were the same ones locked in fear, with its anger, denial and faultfinding. And the only way out was to get them out of fear and get them to face the facts and own the problem in order to fix it.

My challenge was not to drive them into any more mind-limiting fear, but to give them vision and hope to get them moving again. Fear is contagious, so my first job was to keep myself from overt and subtle forms of fear. For that, I started a program in the Scriptures to keep me focused on God and His goodness. Then, with eyes scanning the horizon like a radar beam, I moved forward, expecting God's help to show up.

And we did it! In six years we went from losing money to $500 million in sales, and we did it with the very same people who had failed before. In the annals of business success, this is a rare event. It was fifteen years later that I learned both the biblical truth and the science that explained what I had done for myself and the people in that plant.

This very same program which I developed years ago was the genesis of *OK, God, Now What?* The same principles apply for getting any good from God, so now anyone of you can have the best life possible, no matter where you are starting from.

When I first started writing, I thought the focus was right attitudes, but as I labored, I discovered the great secret of God in the New Testament. His answer for everything is learning how to walk in our new-creation identity in Christ. With that right self-identity, then you will seek after right attitudes and get rid of, or reject, wrong attitudes. What I did in this book was to make the program more effective for faster results.

The New Testament boldly proclaims we are now adopted, redeemed and accepted in the Beloved. This change in legal reality and personal perspective is what Jesus came to accomplish for us. My goal is for you to learn these awesome truths and then, as many others have done, to learn to apply them to your daily life so you can walk in more of what Jesus obtained for you.

So now sit back, start reading, and let the Word of God wash you. If you want to accelerate progress, go to Part II: The Affirmations, and say them for at least one half hour a day while you read the book. It would be better to do all of them every day, but a half hour will get you started experiencing God's Word at a deeper level.

Donald C. Mann
Landenberg, Pennsylvania

Getting Started

Modern society is addicted to easy answers. Sound bites rule the day, and success is sought in slogans. After all (or so goes the modern wisdom), every problem in the world can be solved in a half-hour- or hour-long television show, and if really big, it might take a two-to-four-hour special. "Take this pill," "eat this for a week," "do this for six weeks," etc., and if that doesn't work, just wait; there will be another instant solution in a week or so, and you can try that. Unfortunately, human life is like a baby: under most conditions, it takes nine months to produce a new life. If born in less than nine months, the baby may not survive without serious intervention. And if born too early, it will only survive with major effort. Depending on the society, that baby will not be ready for adult life until after twelve to twenty-five more years of development. Is growing in Christ so different?

In order to grow in Christ, we Christians are commanded in the New Testament to renew our minds, the way we think about ourselves and our behavior. Eph 4:22 "That ye put off concerning the former conversation the old man, which is corrupt according to the deceitful lusts; 23 and be renewed in the spirit of your mind." To make our faith walk effective, actually seeing the results of God in our daily Christian life, we are to obey Philem 6: "That the communication (*outworking*) of thy faith may become effectual (*bringing Heaven to Earth in power*) by the acknowledging of every good thing which is in you in Christ Jesus." The question is, "How do we stand on the shoulders of the original apostles so that God can move in us more today?"

The incarnation of Jesus as God in the flesh is the great work, or the mighty Arm, of God. Isa 53:1 "Who hath believed our report? and to whom is **the arm of the Lord** revealed?" This book is designed to help us Christians in the process of "acknowledging of every good thing which is in *us* in Christ Jesus," and thus achieving the calling or mission assigned us in this wonder of wonders, "Christ in you, the hope of glory" (Col 1:27). *This means you are the hope of Heaven for the glory of the Lord to fill the Earth.* This "Christ in you the hope of glory" is one of the main fruits of the mighty Arm of God, Jesus, the Christ of God.

Following this introduction, there is a section on salvation so that you can accurately understand how to receive this wonderful gift of God on His terms. Next comes a description of the various aspects of God's wisdom hidden in plain sight for thousands of years in the Bible, integrated with modern science's recent findings on how the human mind works. After this groundwork is laid, then we have a series of Affirmation Magnets of who and what we are in Christ. The last half of these Affirmations, or confessions, deals with how to meet our financial and life needs, to confirm God's covenant of abundance. The final section of the book is a short glossary, as many of the key words and concepts used here may be unfamiliar to the reader. In the Glossary, these words and concepts are explained in detail, and you may actually want to read that material first, to help you better understand what the Scriptures are saying.

The primary purpose of this book is to identify the Bible principles for renewing the mind in proclamation, prayer and affirmations. To that end, we provide scriptural ideas and God's Word as prayer, in the assurance that these are His will, so the one who prays and makes affirmations (a form of prayer) may have confidence that God will hear them and will respond, as they remain in faith. This is promised in: 1 John 5:14 "And this is the confidence that we have in him, that, if we *aiteo*/ask (*keep on asking, by demanding, or requiring as due by covenant promise*) any thing according to his will, he heareth us: 15 and if we know that he hear us, whatsoever we *aiteo*/ask (*demand, require and expect as due by covenant promise, knowing Jesus has met all the requirements*), we know that we have the *aiteo*/petitions that we *aiteo*/desired (*demanded, required, and expected as due by covenant promise*) of him (Father God)."

[NOTE: the original Old and New Testament words, such as *aiteo*, are added for emphasis. (For more detail, please see the Glossary for an explanation of each word.)]

Before we proceed, we must ask the question: **What is an affirmation**? According to dictionary.com, an affirmation is "an assertion that something exists or is true; a statement or proposition that is declared to be true; a confirmation or ratification of the truth or validity of a prior judgment or decision." Today champion athletes, entrepreneurs and other high-performing people are using affirmations to direct their subconscious mind to help them achieve their goals. And it works!

The Bible contains many promises for correct affirmations. For instance: Job 22:26 "For then shalt thou have thy delight in the Almighty, and shalt lift up thy face unto God. 27 Thou shalt make thy prayer unto him, and he shall hear thee, and thou shalt pay thy vows. 28 Thou shalt also decree a thing, and it shall be established unto thee: and the light (*of God's ways and truth*) shall shine upon thy ways." When you decree a thing which is God's will for the Earth, you are declaring it to be true and expecting, as did Job, for God to bring it to pass.

Christian affirmation can be defined in the words of Philem 6 "... acknowledging of every good thing which is in you in Jesus Christ." You may not walk in it yet, but you mature by faith, meaning that you proclaim you have it before you actually see it done. As we make affirmations about what God says in the Scriptures that we are or can have, those affirmations become your saying of faith in God, for Him to perform. Mark 11:22 "And Jesus answering saith unto them, Have faith *(actions)* in God *(or the faith actions of God)*. 23 For verily I say unto you, That whosoever shall say unto this mountain, Be thou removed, and be thou cast into the sea; and shall not doubt in his heart, but shall believe *(by faith actions)* that those things which he saith shall come to pass; he shall have whatsoever he saith. 24 Therefore I say unto you, What things soever ye *aiteo*/desire *(demand as due by His Bible promises)*, when ye pray, believe *(by faith actions)* that ye receive them, and ye shall have them."

Learning what the word *aiteo* means and its implications is a mind-renewing event all by itself. The word is so powerful and so opposite to what many teach about prayer that it is a major revelation of what Jesus was talking about. (Please see the Glossary for more details on this subject.)

All of God's promises are fulfilled in Jesus. 2 Cor 1:20 "For all the promises of God in him *(Jesus)* are yea, and in him Amen, unto the glory of God by us." So as you speak to yourself or your life (or someone else's) anything that needs to be like Jesus (or Heaven on Earth) and see yourself with that thing or characteristic, you are obeying 2 Cor 3:18: "But we all, with open face beholding as in a glass *(mirror, in the imagination or vision of your mind)* the glory of the Lord *(Jesus operating in our lives)* are changed into the same image from glory to glory, even as by the Spirit of the Lord."

As you speak and visualize what possession of God's promise of Jesus will be like in you, unto thanksgiving and joy, you are operating in faith actions, and Holy Spirit will transform you into that vision and speaking. So Jesus and Heaven are the blueprint, and Holy Spirit and you are the construction crew.

Thus, affirmations of what we have and are in Christ can become one of the prayer tools by which Holy Spirit matures us into Jesus and brings Heaven to Earth. In the process, you build a new mental image of who and what you are, and your attitudes and heart are changed, and, thus, your mind is renewed or restored into God's truth in the work of His mighty Arm, Jesus of Nazareth.

As an example, here is one of the great biblical affirmations penned some three thousand years ago, for God to perform in our time, as we put it on our lips: **Ps 23:1** "The Lord is my shepherd; I shall not want. 2 He maketh me to lie down in green pastures: he leadeth me beside the still waters. 3 He restoreth my soul: he leadeth me in the paths of righteousness for his name's sake. 4 Yea, though I walk through the valley of the shadow of death, I will fear no evil: for thou art with me; thy rod and thy staff they comfort me. 5 Thou preparest a table before me in the presence of mine enemies: thou anointest my head with oil; my cup runneth over. 6 Surely goodness and *chesed*/mercy shall follow *(pursue and overtake)* me all the days of my life: and I will dwell in the house of the Lord for ever." Hallelujah! Thank You, Father!

As we make such affirmations of God's truth to us, we are overcoming the enemy of our souls and our bodies. Rev 12:10 "And I heard a loud voice saying in heaven, Now is come *soteria*/salvation, and strength, and the kingdom of our God, and the power of his Christ: for the accuser of our brethren is cast down, which accused them before our God day and night. 11 And they overcame him by the blood of the Lamb, and by the word of their testimony; and they loved not their lives unto the death." The effect of righteous scripture and scriptural affirmations is that you attack the lies of the devil and ultimately bring healing and Heaven to Earth in every part of your life. Thus, increased answers to right prayer and the love of God displayed in His power become a larger and larger part of your daily reality.

Ancient Technology: One of my startling recent conclusions is that in the ancient world known by the writers of the Bible, people understood how to renew or reprogram the human mind to serve God more fully. Therefore the command to renew the mind was not hidden technology to them, as it has been to us until now. The knowledge they possessed was lost to our modern world, and it is only recently that a variety of writers began a serious discussion of various aspects of this wonderful skill. (For a key understanding on this please see the definition of the Greek word *zoe* and *faith actions* in the Glossary.)

One of the key tools in this ancient technology is regular affirmations of God's truth in Jesus. Titus 3:8 "This is a faithful saying, and these things I will that **thou affirm constantly**, that they which have believed in God might be careful to maintain good works. These things are good and profitable unto men." And Philem 6 "That the communication of thy faith may become effectual by the (*continual*) acknowledging of every good thing which is in you in Christ Jesus [*by the new birth*]." To this end we have a whole section called Affirmation Magnets to help you in this process.

Let us begin by first laying that proper foundation of understanding, and then we can move on to the Affirmation Magnets in Christ. As you do the Affirmations, they will draw you to God like a strong magnet. The issue has never been God's love for us, but our lack of love back to Him. With these Affirmations you can actually magnetize yourself so you seek and stay close to God continually. With the proper effort, these Affirmations can be written on your heart, with each Affirmation acting like a super-magnet, drawing and keeping you close to God, no matter what evils attack you. That is the place of blessing.

PART I
GAINING AN UNDERSTANDING

CHAPTER 1

UNDERSTANDING THE NEED FOR NEW ATTITUDES

If your problem is a devil, then the cure can be rather fast, as Jesus demonstrated in all His miracles. Acts 10:38 "How God anointed Jesus of Nazareth with the Holy Ghost and with power: who went about doing good, and healing all that were oppressed (*under the active dominion, reign or lordship*) of the devil; for God was with him." But if it is a matter of the heart—as when the disciples could not believe when Jesus came back from the dead—then the cure may take much longer. This cure is described as a renewed mind or a pure, Christ-like heart. 1 Tim 1:5 "Now the end of the commandment (*instruction, doctrine*) is *agape*/charity out of a pure heart, and of a good conscience, and of faith unfeigned."

An amazing discovery, at least for me, is that modern athletes and their coaches are using these same mind-renewing concepts described in the ancient pages of the Bible to turn themselves into world-class athletes and to become champions in their desired sport. They are demonstrating around the world that these techniques work in any culture of excellence. While these concepts and practices have been hidden in the plain pages of the Bible, we are now discovering their power for athletics and even in the biological and psychiatric sciences for all people everywhere.

OK, God, Now What?

We have always understood that power is in a changed or controlled attitude, yet we are only recently discovering how critical to human success a right attitude is. Most have known that life goes better if you fake good emotions, even when you do not feel like it. You do the behavior, even if you don't want to. You can even stir yourself up into right emotions when desired. We dress our bodies to fit the occasion, with the proper clothes, and we dress our souls with the proper behaviors (in our bodies) until we get the right feelings. Many call this "putting on your game face." Now, however, science has proven that this has not only the same effects as "real" good emotions, but that these effects are very beneficial in many ways. For success in God and becoming a champion in Christ, it is no different.

Let us start with a fundamental work Jesus accomplished through the cross. God summarized the born-again, new creation obtained by Jesus this way: 2 Cor 5:16 "Wherefore henceforth know we no man after the flesh: yea, though we have known Christ after the flesh, yet now henceforth know we him no more. 17 Therefore if any man be in Christ, he is a new creature (*a new kind of being*): old things are passed away; behold, all things are become new. 18 And all things are of God [*God is spirit, so He deals in spirit first*], who hath reconciled us to himself by Jesus Christ, and hath given to us the ministry of reconciliation; 19 to wit, that God was in Christ, reconciling the world unto himself, not imputing their trespasses unto them; and hath committed unto us the word of reconciliation. 20 Now then we are ambassadors for Christ, as though God did beseech you by us: we pray you in Christ's stead, be ye reconciled to God. 21 For he hath made him to be sin for us, who knew no sin; that we might be made the righteousness of God in him. 6:1 We then, as workers together with him, beseech you also that ye receive not the grace of God in vain. 2 (For he saith, I have heard thee in a time accepted, and in the day of *soteria*/salvation have I succoured thee: behold, now is the accepted time; behold, now is the day of *soteria*/salvation)." And in: Gal 3:13 "Christ hath redeemed us from the curse of the law, being made a curse for us: for it is written, Cursed is every one that hangeth on a tree: 14 that the blessing of Abraham might come on the Gentiles through Jesus Christ; that we might receive the promise of the Spirit through faith."

Attitudes, self-images and prejudices are the filters, positions, dispositions, orientations and feelings by which you view every aspect of life, those which you actually experience and those that merely occur in your thoughts, intents and imaginations. Wrong attitudes prevent you from hearing, seeing, understanding and doing right. Even if Jesus were to talk directly to you, if you had the wrong attitudes, you could not "hear" Him. This happened to the leaders of His day, and even to His own disciples. So when you have the wrong attitudes and expectations you cannot hear God, even when He speaks directly to you.

The overriding attitude of every part of your life, once you are born again and in Christ, is to develop right attitudes in God, such as:

Understanding the Need for New Attitudes

a) You are forever changed in the new creation. Rom 11:29 "For the gifts and calling of God are without repentance." Gal 6:15 "For in Christ Jesus neither circumcision availeth anything, nor uncircumcision, but a new creature."

b) Sin is no longer an issue with God because He paid for all sin with the body, blood and life of Jesus for you. 1 Tim 2:5 "For there is one God, and one mediator between God and men, the man Christ Jesus; 6 who gave himself a ransom for all, to be testified in due time." Heb 10:10 "By the which will we are sanctified through the offering of the body of Jesus Christ **once for all**." Heb 9:28 "So Christ was once offered to bear the sins of many…" (1 Peter 3:18, Heb 7:27, 9:12, 26, 28, 10:14-18, 1:3, Rev 1:5, Acts 20:28, 1 Cor 6:11 and Rom 4:24-5:10).

c) God is not at war with you, but aggressively looking for ways, not only to answer your prayers, but to bless you with "Heaven on Earth," abundance in every part of life (the meaning of the word *reconciled*): 2 Cor 5:16-6:2.

d) Based on the work of Jesus, and not yours, God has made you His righteousness in Jesus; and now you are as right with God as He is with Himself in Jesus. As you are made the righteousness of God in Jesus, all the covenant promises of God are yours by faith actions, because of the holiness of Jesus, and not your works: Rom 3, 4 and 5.

e) In every situation of life, God begs you to know you are reconciled to Him, and He is there for you in Jesus: 2 Cor 5:20-6:2.

f) You are sent to overcome all the works of the devil by the salvation of God in Jesus: Rom 16:20 "And the God of peace shall bruise Satan under your feet shortly (*as shattered glass*). The grace of our Lord Jesus Christ is with you (*to know, be, will and do this*). Amen."

g) You now have death-destroying *zoe*/life in you: Gal 2:20 "I am (*have been*) crucified with Christ: nevertheless I *zao*/live; yet not I, but Christ *zao*/liveth in me: and the life which I now *zao*/live in the flesh I *zao*/live by the faith (*actions*) *in* the Son of God, who *agape*/loved me, and gave himself for me. 21 I do not frustrate the grace of God: for if righteousness come by the law, then Christ is dead in vain."

h) You are to know you have the *zoe*/life of God in you and are to use the name of Jesus to do good. 1 John 5:13 "These things have I written unto you that believe on the name of the Son of God; that ye may know that ye have eternal *zoe*/life, and that ye may believe on the name of the Son of God. 14 And this is the confidence that we have in him, that, if we *aiteo*/ask (*keep on asking*) any thing according to his will, he heareth us: 15 and if we know that he hear us, whatsoever we *aiteo*/ask (*demand as due by His covenant promises*), we know that we have the *aiteo*/petitions that we *aiteo*/desired (*demanded, required, and expected as due by covenant promise*) of him."

John 14:13 "And whatsoever ye shall *aiteo*/ask (*demand, require, and expect as due by covenant promise*) in my name, that will I do, that the Father may be glorified in the Son. 14 If ye shall *aiteo*/ask (*demand as due by Bible promise*) any thing in my name, I will do it."

i) When you think your behavior (or feelings) determines your relationship with God, you have fallen from grace. Gal 5:4 "Christ is become of no effect unto you, whosoever of you are justified by the law; ye are fallen from grace."

j) You are to obey Jesus' words: Matt 22:37 "Jesus said unto him, Thou shalt *agape*/love the Lord thy God with all thy heart, and with all thy soul, and with all thy mind. 38 This is the first and great commandment. 39 And the second is like unto it, Thou shalt *agape*/love thy neighbour as thyself. 40 On these two commandments hang all the law and the prophets."

k) You *agape*/love God by *agape*/loving your neighbor just as Jesus did. Rom 13:10 "*Agape*/love worketh no ill to his neighbour: therefore *agape*/love is the fulfilling of the law. 11 And that, knowing the time, that now it is high time to awake out of sleep: for now is our *soteria*/salvation nearer than when we believed. 12 The night is far spent, the day is at hand: let us therefore cast off the works of darkness, and let us put on the armour of light. 13 Let us walk honestly, as in the day; not in rioting and drunkenness, not in chambering and wantonness, not in strife and envying. 14 But put ye on the Lord Jesus Christ, and make not provision for the flesh, to fulfil the lusts thereof."

l) You are to obey gladly Paul's admonition: 2 Cor 13:5 "Examine yourselves (*continually*), whether ye be in the faith; prove your own selves. Know ye not your own selves, how that Jesus Christ is in you, except ye be reprobates (*useless, like garbage*)?"

m) You have to keep yourself stirred up in God to freely operate and cooperate with Holy Spirit. 2 Tim 1:6 "Wherefore I put thee in remembrance that thou stir up the gift of God [*by continual right faith actions*].... 7 For God hath not given us the spirit of fear; but of *dunamis*/power (*supernatural ability*), and of *agape*/love, and of a sound mind (*to think, speak and act like Jesus would*)."

n) You rest in confidence that you already have access to all the power of God to operate as Jesus did as God has given you the same, exact Holy Spirit that God gave Jesus and for the same purpose. John 20:21 "Then said Jesus to them again, Peace be unto you: as my Father hath sent me, even so send I you." John 17:18 "As thou (*Father God*) hast sent me (*Jesus*) into the world, even so have I also sent them into the world." Acts 1:8 "But ye shall receive *dunamis*/power, after that the Holy Ghost is come upon you: and ye shall be witnesses unto me both in Jerusalem, and in all Judaea, and in Samaria, and unto the uttermost part of the earth." Acts 10:38 "How God anointed Jesus of Nazareth with the Holy Ghost and with power: who went about doing good, and healing all that

Understanding the Need for New Attitudes

were oppressed (*under the active dominion, reign or lordship*) of the devil; for God was with him." Rom 8:11 "But if the Spirit of him that raised up Jesus from the dead dwell in you, he that raised up Christ from the dead shall also quicken your [*current*] mortal bodies by his Spirit that dwelleth in you." Gal 4:6 "And because ye are sons, God hath sent forth the Spirit of his Son into your hearts, crying, Abba (*Daddy*), Father." Same spirit, same job!

o) You are sent by God to do the works of Jesus, as a believer. Therefore the promises of God become personal for you and your confession becomes: Mark 16:17 "And these signs shall follow them that believe; In *Jesus'* name *I, as a believer,* cast out devils; *I, as a believer,* speak with new tongues; 18. *I, as a believer,* take up serpents; and if *I, as a believer,* drink any deadly thing, it shall not hurt *me; I, as a believer,* lay hands on the sick, and they shall recover *totally right then.*" For I constantly walk in the absolute certainty, and: Luke 10:19 "Behold *that I* have power to tread on serpents and scorpions, and over all the power of the enemy: and nothing shall by any means hurt *me*. 20 Notwithstanding in this *I* rejoice not, that the spirits are subject unto *me*; but rather *I* rejoice, because *my name is* written in heaven." You are equipped and commanded to walk as Jesus walked. God said: 1 John 2:5 "But whoso keepeth his word, in him verily is the *agape*/love of God perfected: hereby know we that we are in him. 6 He that saith he abideth in him ought himself also so to walk, even as he walked." You are to follow/imitate God as Jesus did. Eph 5:1 "Be ye therefore followers (*imitators*) of God, as *agapetos*/dear (*loved*) children; 2 and walk in *agape*/love, as Christ also hath *agape*/loved us, and hath given himself for us an offering and a sacrifice to God for a sweetsmelling savour." Therefore you can affirm: 1 Cor 2:4 "And my speech and my preaching *are* not with enticing words of man's wisdom, but in demonstration of the Spirit and of power: 5 that o*ur* faith should not stand in the wisdom of men, but in the power of God … . 12 Now *I* have received, not the spirit of the world, but the spirit which is of God; that *I* might know the things that are freely given to us of God." You are made for and get *zoe*/life for anyone in any sin or any effect of sin, including sickness or disease, for: 1 John 5:16 "If any man see his brother sin a sin which is not unto death, he shall *aiteo*/ask (*by requiring, demanding, expecting as due by covenant promise*), and he (*Father God*) shall give him *zoe*/life for them … ." By the grace of God, by believing in and using the power of the Word of God and the Name of Jesus, you are not to let sin, sickness or disease rule in you or others. Rom 6:14 "For sin shall not have dominion over you: for ye are not under the law, but under grace." You are to *zao*/live for God to serve others for and with God. 2 Cor 5:15 "And that he died for all, that they which *zao*/live should not henceforth *zao*/live unto themselves, but unto him which died for them, and rose again."

p) You, yourself, now that you are born again in Jesus, are *sozo*/saved, but your works in this life will be judged, and that which God does not approve will be thoroughly destroyed. 1 Cor 3:11 "For other foundation can no man lay than that is laid, which is Jesus Christ. 12 Now if any man build upon this foundation gold, silver, precious stones, wood, hay, stubble; 13 every man's work shall be made manifest: for the day shall declare it, because it shall be revealed by fire; and the fire shall try every man's work of what sort it is. 14 If any man's work abide which he hath built thereupon, he shall receive a reward. 15 If any man's work shall be burned, he shall suffer loss: but he himself shall be *sozo*/saved; yet so as by fire. 16 Know ye not that ye are the temple of God, and that the Spirit of God dwelleth in you?"

q) This is the Day of Salvation and not Judgment from God upon men, but rather the judgment of God against the devil and his works, so you can trust Him in all things for healing, restoration and wholeness against the works of the devil, into the glorious abundance of "Heaven on Earth." John 16:11 "About judgment, because the ruler (evil genius, prince) of this world [Satan] is judged and condemned and sentence already is passed upon him." AMP Rom 8:2 "For the law of the Spirit of *zoe*/life in Christ Jesus hath made me free from the law of sin and death." Titus 2:13 "Looking for that blessed hope, and the glorious appearing of the great God and our Saviour Jesus Christ; 14 who gave himself for us, that he might redeem us from all iniquity (*wrong thinking and desires*), and purify unto himself a peculiar people, zealous of (*doing*) good works." Titus 3:1 "(*Keep continually*) in mind to be subject to principalities and powers, to obey magistrates, to be ready to every good work, 2 to speak evil of no man, to be no brawlers, but gentle, shewing all meekness unto all men. 3 For we ourselves also were sometimes foolish, disobedient, deceived, serving divers lusts and pleasures, living in malice and envy, hateful, and hating one another. 4 But after that the kindness and *agape*/love of God our Saviour toward man appeared, 5 not by works of righteousness which we have done, but according to his mercy he *sozo*/saved us, by the washing of regeneration, and renewing of the Holy Ghost; 6 which he shed on us abundantly through Jesus Christ our Saviour; 7 that being justified by his grace, we should be made heirs according to the hope of eternal *zoe*/life. 8 This is a faithful saying, and these things I will that **thou affirm constantly**, that they which have believed in God might be careful to maintain good works. These things are good and profitable unto men. 9 But avoid foolish questions, and genealogies, and contentions, and strivings about the law; for they are unprofitable and vain."

r) Knowing your new creation identity in Christ, you gladly obey: Jude 20 "But ye, *agape*/beloved, building up yourselves on your most holy faith, praying in

UNDERSTANDING THE NEED FOR NEW ATTITUDES

the Holy Ghost, 21 keep yourselves in the *agape*/love of God, looking for the mercy of our Lord Jesus Christ unto eternal *zoe*/life. 22 And of some have compassion, making a difference: 23 and others *sozo*/save with fear, pulling them out of the fire; hating even the garment spotted by the flesh. 24 Now unto him that is able to keep you from falling, and to present you faultless before the presence of his glory with exceeding joy, 25 to the only wise God our Saviour, be glory and majesty, dominion and power, both now and ever. Amen."

s) You are to change and continually re-affirm your self identity from the old, natural man to the new-creation man, the born-again man in Christ. This is the "word of Christ." 1 John 4:17 "… because as *He* is, so are we in this world." Rom 13:10 "*Agape*/love worketh no ill to his neighbour: therefore *agape*/love is the fulfilling of the law. 11 And that, knowing the time, that now it is high time to awake out of sleep: for now is our *soteria*/salvation nearer than when we believed. 12 The night is far spent, the day is at hand: let us therefore cast off the works of darkness, and let us put on the armour of light. 13 Let us walk honestly, as in the day; not in rioting and drunkenness, not in chambering and wantonness, not in strife and envying. 14 But put ye on the Lord Jesus Christ (*in your self-image and behaviors*), and make not provision for the flesh, to fulfil the lusts thereof." Rom 6:8 "Now if we be dead with Christ, we believe that we shall also *zao*/live with him: 9 knowing that Christ being raised from the dead dieth no more; death hath no more dominion over him. 10 For in that he died, he died unto sin once: but in that he *zao*/liveth, he *zao*/liveth unto God. 11 Likewise reckon ye also yourselves to be dead indeed unto sin, but (*instead, reckon yourself*) *zao*/alive unto God through Jesus Christ our Lord." Eph 4:20 "But ye have not so learned Christ; 21 if so be that ye have heard him, and have been taught by him, as the truth is in Jesus: 22 that ye put off concerning the former conversation the old man, which is corrupt according to the deceitful lusts; 23 and be renewed in the spirit of your mind (*in your self-image*); 24 and that ye put on the new man, which after God is created in righteousness and true holiness." Col 3:9 "Lie not one to another, seeing that ye have put off the old man with his deeds; 10 and have put on the new man, which is renewed (*made real in this life*) in *epignosis*/knowledge after the image of him that created him: 11 where there is neither Greek nor Jew, circumcision nor uncircumcision, Barbarian, Scythian, bond nor free: but Christ is all, and in all. 12 Put on therefore, as the elect of God, holy and *agape*/beloved, bowels of mercies, kindness, humbleness of mind, meekness, longsuffering; 13 forbearing one another, and forgiving one another, if any man have a quarrel against any: even as Christ forgave you, so also do ye. 14 And above all these things put on *agape*/charity, which is the bond of perfectness. 15 And let the peace of God rule in your hearts, to the which also ye are called in one body; and be ye thankful. 16 Let the word of Christ dwell in you richly in all wisdom; teaching and admonishing one another in psalms and hymns and spiritual songs, singing with grace in your hearts to the Lord. 17 And whatsoever ye do in word or deed, do all in the name of the Lord Jesus, giving thanks to God and the Father by him."

t) You take the Lord's Supper, knowing your healing is in His broken body, by the bread ("by His stripes you were healed," 1 Pet 2:24), and by the cup, your sins purged by His blood, and you are made one with Him in the New Covenant of His blood. You judge all your sickness, failures, and sins to be upon Jesus and are healed by His resurrection, according to Isa 53, 1 Cor 11:24-32, Rom 4:25 and 1 Pet 2:24.

These make up a basic "starter set" of new-creation attitudes for beginning a walk in Christian maturity. There are many more, and if we were doing a basic Christianity program we would also follow next with: Heb 6:1 "... the principles of the doctrine of Christ [*which includes Christ in you the hope of glory*], let us go on unto perfection (*completeness or Christian maturity*); ... laying ... the foundation of repentance from dead works, and of faith toward God, 2 of the doctrine of baptisms, and of laying on of hands, and of resurrection of the dead, and of eternal judgment."

These are not studied just to answer test questions in Sunday School, a Bible study or a seminary program. These are to become your deep inner understandings and attitudes by which you approach, filter and judge every issue of life, knowing that you must constantly renew your mind throughout the day, to keep this attitude successfully, to the glory of God, with right thoughts, words, and actions. 2 Pet 3:14 "Wherefore, *agape*/beloved, seeing that ye look for such things, **be diligent** that ye may be found of him in peace, without spot, and blameless."

Remember, while it is the Father's good pleasure and delight to give you His kingdom, it is not without a fight, and part of the battleground is your heart. Luke 12:28 "If then God so clothe the grass, which is to day in the field, and to morrow is cast into the oven; how much more will he clothe you, O ye of little faith? 29 And seek not ye what ye shall eat, or what ye shall drink, neither be ye of doubtful mind. 30 For all these things do the nations of the world seek after: and your Father knoweth that ye have need of these things. 31 But rather seek ye the kingdom of God; and all these things shall be added unto you. 32 Fear not, little flock; for it is your Father's good pleasure to give you the kingdom. 33 Sell that ye have, and give alms; provide yourselves bags which wax not old, a treasure in the heavens that faileth not, where no thief approacheth, neither moth corrupteth. 34 **For where your treasure is, there will your heart be also.**" Matt 11:12 "And from the days of John the Baptist until now the kingdom of heaven suffereth violence, and the violent take it by force." Luke 16:15 "And he said unto them, Ye are they which justify yourselves before men; **but God knoweth your hearts**: for that which is highly esteemed among men is abomination in the sight of God. 16 The law and

Understanding the Need for New Attitudes

the prophets were until John: since that time the kingdom of God is preached, and every man presseth into it." It takes much effort to "win" and preserve your heart for God against the pull of the world.

In the new creation, your spirit is recreated, made new. John 3:6 "That which is born of the flesh is flesh; and that which is born of the Spirit is spirit." 1 Cor 6:17 "But he that is joined unto the Lord is one spirit." Heb 12:9 "Furthermore we have had fathers of our flesh which corrected us, and we gave them reverence: shall we not much rather be in subjection unto the Father of spirits, and *zao*/live?" Rom 8:9 "But ye are not in the flesh, but in the Spirit, if so be that the Spirit of God dwell in you. Now if any man have not the Spirit of Christ, he is none of his. 10 And if Christ be in you, the body is dead because of sin; but the Spirit is *zoe*/life because of righteousness." John 1:13 "Which were born, not of blood, nor of the will of the flesh, nor of the will of man, but of God." Your body may or may not get healed when you are recreated in God. You may have a partial change of attitude, but in general, you still have all your old memories. So your mind (and therefore your soul) did not get made new or recreated. It is your spirit that is recreated (born again) in God in the new creation. Walking in this new creation is the challenge of our day, and this requires a deep change in the attitude of your heart. We can start by ridding ourselves of fundamentally wrong attitudes that limit our ability to hear God and obey Him in gladness.

A major attitude of our times is that those who are close to God are special called-out ones. There is an element of truth and an element of lie in that statement. Here is a contrary declaration from God for all men: James 4:8 "Draw nigh to God, and he will draw nigh to you … ." This statement says if you want more of God you draw nigh to Him, and He will come to you. He has already made His move, so if you want more of Him, the next move is yours. If someone you see has more of God in them than you, then they have spent more effective time "drawing nigh" to Him than you have. Gal 6:7 "Be not deceived; God is not mocked: for whatsoever a man soweth, that shall he also reap. 8 For he that soweth to his flesh shall of the flesh reap corruption; but he that soweth to the Spirit shall of the Spirit reap *zoe*/life everlasting. 9 And let us not be weary in well doing: for in due season we shall reap, if we faint not."

There are very few people of "natural" talents. Most of those whom we consider to have natural talents have put so many years into their art and craft that they make it look easy. That kid who can throw a ball or draw a picture has spent years not doing other things, but rather spending countless hours perfecting what you see done with such seeming ease. With growth in God it is the same. Heb 11:6 "But without faith it is impossible to please him: for he that cometh to God must believe that he is, and that he is a rewarder of them that diligently seek him." Diligence means hard work, when it is easier to give up. If you want God, get His Word into you and get to know Him through His Word, and this will take hard work. To that end, pray Ps 119 and Eph 1:16-23 often.

OK, God, Now What?

Another seemingly standard belief or attitude of our modern times is this: "No one can be like God or Jesus Christ." This modern deception totally ignores the clear call of Jesus and the New Testament. Jesus commanded: Matt 5:48 "Be ye therefore perfect, even as your Father which is in heaven is perfect." Paul made clear what is the goal of the Christian life: Eph 4:11 "And he gave some, apostles; and some, prophets; and some, evangelists; and some, pastors and teachers; 12 for the perfecting of the saints, for the work of the ministry, for the edifying of the body of Christ: 13 till we all come in the unity of the faith, and of the knowledge of the Son of God, **unto a perfect man, unto the measure of the stature of the fulness of Christ**: 14 that we henceforth be no more children, tossed to and fro, and carried about with every wind of doctrine, by the sleight of men, and cunning craftiness, whereby they lie in wait to deceive; 15 but speaking the truth in *agape*/love, **may grow up into him in all things**, which is the head, even Christ." When the work of the gifts of God ("some apostles; and some, prophets; and some, evangelists; and some, pastors and teachers") is done, then we will know, as a group, that we have met His goal for each person Jesus died to save, and for whom God raised Jesus from the dead. If that goal in this life is to "grow up into Him in all things," then that must be possible.

Sin is missing the mark of expected thinking and behavior. Sin, to God, is missing the mark or target set by Him. The definition of sin is given this way, with God's answer for those with any sin: Rom 3:23 "For all have sinned, and come short of the glory of God; 24 being justified (*made in perfect right standing just like Jesus*) freely by his grace through the redemption that is in Christ Jesus." Notice the all-encompassing definition of sin as anything that is not like God's best and greatest (the definition of glory), and the solution for failure to meet this awesome standard is in His Son, Jesus Christ, who was once a carpenter from Nazareth and now carries the title of King of Kings and Lord of Lords.

We can debate how well one meets the target, but if you do not even aim at the right target, you surely cannot expect to hit it. And not hitting the target is sin. Paul summarized the journey to the target this way: Phil 3:13 "Brethren, I count not myself to have apprehended: but this one thing I do, forgetting those things which are behind, and reaching forth unto those things which are before, 14 I press toward the mark for the prize of the high calling of God in Christ Jesus." This calling is worthy of the price Jesus paid to earn it. What other calling required the death of God's own Son so that you could have purpose in life? Only a calling worthy of the God of all creation. Gal 3:26 "For ye are all the children (*sons*) of God by faith in Christ Jesus. 27 For as many of you as have been baptized into Christ have put on Christ."

So if this is the calling, how do we walk in it? To that end, Holy Spirit prayed through Paul: Eph 3:16 "That he would grant you, according to the riches of his

Understanding the Need for New Attitudes

glory, to be strengthened with might by his Spirit in the inner man; 17 that Christ may dwell in your hearts by (*continual right*) faith (*actions*); that ye, being rooted and grounded in *agape*/love, 18 may be able to comprehend with all saints what is the breadth, and length, and depth, and height; 19 and to know the *agape*/love of Christ, which passeth knowledge, that ye might be filled **with all the fulness of God**. 20 Now unto him that is able to do exceeding abundantly above all that we *aiteo*/ask or think, according to the power that worketh in us, 21 unto him be glory in the church by Christ Jesus throughout all ages, world without end. Amen." Notice that the new creation is instant, but it takes prayer and continued faith action effort to mature the heart to all the fullness of God.

The mind-renewing process necessary to enter into this calling requires you to do the work. Rom 13:14 "But put ye on the Lord Jesus Christ (*in the attitude of your mind and heart, as your new nature is just like His*), and make not provision for the flesh, to fulfil the lusts thereof (*measure and reject any thoughts that Jesus would not think or do*)." Eph 4:20 "But ye have not so learned Christ; 21 if so be that ye have heard him, and have been taught by him, as the truth is in Jesus: 22 that ye put off (*no longer identify with in your self-image*) concerning the former conversation (*lifestyle reflected in thought, words and deeds*) the old man (*in the mind of the flesh, carnality, devil, a mere human*), which is corrupt according to the deceitful lusts; 23 and be renewed in the spirit of your mind; 24 and that ye put on the new man (*in your self-image of who and what you now are in Christ Jesus*), which after God is created in righteousness and true holiness." Col 3:8 "But now ye also put off all these; anger, wrath, malice, blasphemy, filthy communication out of your mouth. 9 Lie not one to another, seeing that ye have put off the old man with his deeds; 10 and have put on the new man (*in your self-image*), which is renewed (*transformed/made effective*) in knowledge (*deep understanding with experientially superior results*) after the image [*blueprint*] of him that created him: 11 where there is neither Greek nor Jew, circumcision nor uncircumcision, Barbarian, Scythian, bond nor free: but Christ is all, and in all." Rom 6:8 "Now if we be dead with Christ, we believe that we shall also *zao*/live with him: 9 knowing that Christ being raised from the dead dieth no more; death hath no more dominion over him. 10 For in that he died, he died unto sin once: but in that he *zao*/liveth, he *zao*/liveth unto God. 11 Likewise reckon (*count in spite of the evidence of your sin and failures and inadequacies*) ye also yourselves to be dead indeed unto sin, but *zao*/alive unto God through Jesus Christ our Lord." 1 John 4:17 "… because as he (*Jesus*) is, so are we in this world."

God gives a stern warning and a command to Christians: Rom 12:2 "And be not conformed (*continually shaped and molded*) to this world: but be ye transformed (*into what He has called you to be*) by the renewing of your mind … ." This is not instantaneous, but a gradual molding or refining process, from faith to faith and glory to glory. To the Bible writers, this was a well understood technology.

OK, God, Now What?

This is related to another message of transformation for the Christian: 2 Cor 3:17 "Now the Lord is that Spirit: and where the Spirit of the Lord is, there is liberty. 18 But we all, with open face beholding as in a glass (*mirror*) the glory of the Lord, are changed into the same image from glory to glory, even as by the Spirit of the Lord." Combined, these scriptures show that your job is to renew your mind and grow into Jesus in your thoughts, imaginations, words and actions, by seeing the glory of Jesus in every part of your life, in faith. As you see and call those things that appear not as if they were, visualizing yourself as doing or having them anyway, Holy Spirit will change you into the image you have of yourself in Jesus.

In order to become a human champion, make your self-image the best that mere mortals are capable of, but in order to grow in God, make your self-image what Champion God says you have been made into, so you can now walk in it—Jesus, the fullness of God in the flesh. Being born again is instant; maturity takes time, from glory to glory or faith to faith. And, thus, it is a process or a journey. Spirit is instant, but the soul is a process.

So how do attitudes get developed? They are in your heart, and we write into our heart in three basic ways:

1. You do the same thing again and again, either on purpose or because of your environment,
2. You relive a thing in your imagination and memory again and again, or
3. Others recall or remind you of something again and again.

Each method works, whether by one path or in combination. Whether it is the minister at church, the news on radio, the music in the background, nightmares, the boys on the basketball team, reading a book, remembering things said and done in the past, daydreams or visualizations of today, military boot camp or some other means, the effect is the same. Memories and attitudes are written in your heart. Then, as you experience a great variety of life, these memories are integrated with other memories and become "attitudes," or automatic responses and dispositions to the situations of life. This is a moment-by-moment activity, whether you are aware of it or not. So the key issue is to control, to the maximum extent possible, what is being written in your heart and make it what you want it to be.

This is why God says to the Christian who does not yet walk like Jesus: Rom 13:11 "And that, knowing the time, that now it is high time to awake out of sleep (*living in the lower standard of mere humans and the vain traditions inherited from the "normal" world*): for now is our *soteria*/salvation nearer than when we believed. 12 The night is far spent, the day is at hand: let us therefore cast off the works of darkness (*cast out with violence anything not just like Jesus*), and let us put on the armour of light. 13 Let us walk honestly, as in the day; not in rioting and drunkenness,

UNDERSTANDING THE NEED FOR NEW ATTITUDES

not in chambering and wantonness, not in strife and envying. 14 But put ye on the Lord Jesus Christ (*in your mental image of who and what you are, what you think, speak and do*), and make not provision for the flesh, to fulfil the lusts thereof." (See the Glossary for an explanation of the phrase The Wrath of God and the ten-step process shown there for renewing your mind when you have sinned.)

Instead of making provision for the flesh, we are to make provision to obey: Col 3:3 "For ye are dead, and your *zoe*/life is hid with Christ in God." John 15:4 "Abide in me (*because of the promises of the Word of God, you know you are now in Christ Jesus, even when you sin*), and I in you (*and because of the promises of the Word of God, you know Jesus now dwells in you by His Spirit, so now agree this is true, even if you fail and still sin*). As the branch cannot bear fruit of itself, except it abide in the vine; no more can ye, except ye abide in me (*so make your confession the truth of Rom 6:11, 13:14, Eph 4:24 and Col 3:10*). 5 I am the vine, ye are the branches: he that abideth in me, and I in him, the same bringeth forth much fruit: for without me ye can do nothing. 6 If a man abide not in me, he is cast forth as a branch, and is withered; and men gather them, and cast them into the fire, and they are burned. 7 If ye abide in me, and my words abide in you, ye shall *aiteo*/ask (*demanding, requesting or expecting as due by covenant promise*) what ye will, and it shall be done unto you. 8 Herein is my Father glorified, that ye bear much fruit; so shall ye be my disciples. 9 As the Father hath *agape*/loved me, so have I *agape*/loved you: continue ye in my *agape*/love." 1 John 2:6 "He that saith he abideth in Jesus ought himself also so to walk, even as he (*Jesus*) walked." 1 John 4:17 "… because as he (*Jesus*) is, so are we in this world." 1 John 4:4 "Ye are of God, little children, and have overcome them: because greater is he that is in you, than he that is in the world."

This abiding is not the process of "Christ consciousness" as practiced by some, independently of the reality of Jesus Christ dwelling in you by Holy Spirit because of the goodness of God through Jesus Christ. This kind of practice focuses on the standard of Jesus as the best way to live. While valid, this is much lower than the reality of the new creation in Christ Jesus, with indwelling Holy Spirit. This is not "moral Christ consciousness," but Christ's presence and relationship as an essential element of effective Christian life. 2 Cor 13:5 "Examine yourselves, whether ye be in the faith; prove your own selves. Know ye not your own selves, how that Jesus Christ is in you, except ye be reprobates (*useless, like garbage, ineffective, impotent, worthy to be thrown away*)?"

God's answer is always through a Person; the Gospel is never independent of the person of Jesus Himself. Col 1:25 "Whereof I am made a minister, according to the dispensation of God which is given to me for you, to fulfil the word of God; 26 even the mystery which hath been hid from ages and from generations, but now is made manifest to his saints: 27 to whom God would make known what is the riches of the glory of this mystery among the Gentiles; **which is Christ in you, the**

hope of glory: 28 whom we preach, warning every man, and teaching every man in all wisdom; that we may present every man perfect in Christ Jesus: 29 whereunto I also labour, striving according to his working, which worketh in me mightily." 1 John 4:4 "Ye are of God, little children, and have overcome them: because greater is **he that is in you**, than he that is in the world." 2 Cor 13:5 "Examine yourselves, whether ye be in the faith; prove your own selves. Know ye not your own selves, how that **Jesus Christ is in you**, except ye be reprobates?" *Reprobate* means "useless, ineffective, counted only as garbage." You can have any opinion you want, but only some opinions are useful in God, and only the ones He approves will survive the Day of Judgment.

I invite you to join with me in going for the target assigned by God to us all. Acts 17:30 "And the times of this ignorance God winked at; but now commandeth all men every where to repent: 31 because he hath appointed a day, in the which he will judge the world in righteousness by that man whom he hath ordained; whereof he hath given assurance unto all men, in that he hath raised him from the dead."

Included in this word *repent* is the meaning "to change the way you think, so you change the way you live." You are to start by acknowledging the Jesus of the Bible as the absolute Lord of All, and one day He will decide what is right and what is wrong by the words of the Bible, and your opinion on that Day will not matter one bit. Matt 12:36 "But I say unto you, That every idle (*useless, will-not-survive-the-Day-of-Judgment*) word that men shall speak, they shall give account thereof in the day of judgment. 37 For by thy words thou shalt be justified, and by thy words thou shalt be condemned." John 12:47 "And if any man hear my words, and believe not, I judge him not: for I came not to judge the world, but to *sozo*/save the world. 48 He that rejecteth me, and receiveth not my words, hath one that judgeth him: the word that I have spoken, the same shall judge him in the last day. 49 For I have not spoken of myself; but the Father which sent me, he gave me a commandment, what I should say, and what I should speak. 50 And I know that his commandment is *zoe*/life everlasting: whatsoever I speak therefore, even as the Father said unto me, so I speak."

The Jews understood the process of repentance. It was to obey Proverbs chapters 1-9 and pray Psalm 119 and many other things a righteous Jewish believer would do. No one expected it to be an instantaneous process, but rather a work of focused faith actions that translated to long-term right behaviors, a process counted in months and not days. This is why Jesus answered Peter: Matt 18:21 "Then came Peter to him, and said, Lord, how oft shall my brother sin against me, and I forgive him? till seven times? 22 Jesus saith unto him, I say not unto thee, Until seven times: but, Until seventy times seven [*because this could take a long time*]."

Part of the repentance process, for a Jew, was to go back and, not only emphasize religious observances, but also rehearse the entire Old Testament, judge their

Understanding the Need for New Attitudes

life by its requirements, start to agree with what needed changing and then work to bring about that change, all the while maintaining a time of constant prayer to the Lord. Ps 119:10 "With my whole heart have I sought thee: O let me not wander from thy commandments. 11 Thy word have I hid in mine heart, that I might not sin against thee. 12 Blessed art thou, O Lord: teach me thy statutes."

This process was also known as working with the Lord to unite your heart to His ways. Notice that the process includes prayer, thanksgiving and praise to God. Ps 86:10 "For thou art great, and doest wondrous things: thou art God alone. 11 Teach me thy way, O Lord; I will walk in thy truth: unite my heart to fear thy name. 12 I will praise thee, O Lord my God, with all my heart: and I will glorify thy name for evermore. 13 For great is thy *chesed*/mercy toward me: and thou hast delivered my soul from the lowest hell."

One of the meanings of the word *Torah* is "the path." Another meaning is "the way to reach a goal or objective." These are the ways of thinking and acting that release God into the Earth, so you can have all of Him in your life to maximize His goodness in the Earth. Man is the chosen vessel, through right thought and action, to bring God to the Earth. Your thoughts and actions control how much of God is in your life and how much of His blessing is manifested in the Earth.

No process with the Scriptures was ever expected to be purely academic, but men and women were to translate the academic instruction of the Scriptures into right behaviors in every part of their lives, so that God could inhabit or dwell in those right thoughts and actions. Where God is, there is blessing.

A typical Jew had memorized the Torah, the first five books of the Bible, by the age of fourteen and by the age of thirty, most of the rest of the Old Testament. This included a heart exam with God for any sin or wrong desire. Ps 139:23 "Search me, O God, and know my heart: try me, and know my thoughts: 24 and see if there be any wicked way in me, and lead me in the way everlasting." Jer 17:9 "The heart is deceitful above all things, and desperately wicked: who can know it? 10 I the Lord search the heart, I try the reins, even to give every man according to his ways, and according to the fruit of his doings." Ps 26:2 "Examine me, O Lord, and prove me; try my reins and my heart." Jer 4:1 "If thou wilt return, O Israel, saith the Lord, return unto me: and if thou wilt put away thine abominations out of my sight, then shalt thou not remove. 2 And thou shalt swear, The Lord liveth, in truth, in judgment, and in righteousness; and the nations shall bless themselves in him, and in him shall they glory. 3 For thus saith the Lord to the men of Judah and Jerusalem, Break up your fallow ground, and sow not among thorns. 4 Circumcise yourselves to the Lord, and take away the foreskins of your heart, ye men of Judah and inhabitants of Jerusalem: lest my fury come forth like fire, and burn that none can quench it, because of the evil of your doings." Hos 10:12 "Sow to yourselves in righteousness, reap in mercy; break up your fallow ground: for it is time to seek the Lord, till he come and rain righteousness upon you. 13 Ye have plowed wickedness, ye have reaped iniquity; ye have eaten the fruit of lies: because thou didst trust in thy way, in the multitude of thy mighty men." Hos 8:6 "For from Israel was it also: the workman made it; therefore it is not God: but the calf of Samaria shall be broken in pieces. 7 For they have sown the wind, and they shall reap the whirlwind: it hath no stalk: the bud shall yield no meal: if so be it yield, the strangers shall swallow it up." Ps 105:4 "Seek the LORD, and his strength: seek his face evermore. 5 Remember his marvellous works that he hath done; his wonders, and the judgments of his mouth; 6 O ye seed of Abraham his servant, ye children of Jacob his chosen. 7 He is the LORD our God: his judgments are in all the earth. 8 He hath remembered his covenant for ever, the word which he commanded to a thousand generations."

The Gentile converts or proselytes to the Jewish faith (like Cornelius of Acts 10) basically did the same for repentance, going back and renewing their initial conversion experience in which their first actions were to memorize the Torah and then the rest of the Old Testament in a three-to-seven-year process and re-emphasize a daily prayer life (see Matt 5-7). 2 Tim 2:19 "Nevertheless the foundation of God standeth sure, having this seal, The Lord knoweth them that are his. And, Let every one that nameth the name of Christ depart from iniquity (*wicked thoughts that lead to wicked words and actions*). 20 But in a great house there are not only vessels of gold and of silver, but also of wood and of earth; and some to honour, and some to dishonour. 21 If a man therefore purge himself from these, he shall be a vessel unto honour, sanctified, and meet for the master's use, and prepared unto every good work." We are to do the purging.

For Christians (since the New Testament was not written until later), repentance also meant continually staying in right Christian teaching. 2 Tim 2:21 "If a man therefore purge himself from these, he shall be a vessel unto honour, sanctified, and meet for the master's use, and prepared unto every good work. 22 Flee also youthful lusts: but follow righteousness, faith, *agape*/charity, peace, with them that call on the Lord out of a pure heart. 23 But foolish and unlearned questions avoid, knowing that they do gender strifes. 24 And the servant of the Lord must not strive; but be gentle unto all men, apt to teach, patient, 25 in meekness instructing those that oppose themselves; if God peradventure will give them repentance to the acknowledging of the truth; 26 and that they may recover themselves out of the snare of the devil, who are taken captive by him at his will." So the Christian minister works on his or her own purity and patiently teaches Christ to others, as long as they keep coming back. The job of the one seeking revelation toward repentance was to keep coming back to right teachers in a mind-renewing process that gives freedom from the devil's control and, thus, to walk more like Christ.

This basic requirement to cleanse ourselves by actively working with Holy Spirit and the Scriptures is repeated again as part of the righteous attitude for ex-

Understanding the Need for New Attitudes

pecting the Lord's great return. 1 John 3:1 "Behold, what manner of *agape*/love the Father hath bestowed upon us, that we should be called the sons of God: therefore the world knoweth us not, because it knew him not. 2 *Agape*/beloved, now are we the sons of God, and it doth not yet appear what we shall be: but we know that, when he shall appear, we shall be like him; for we shall see him as he is. 3 And every man that hath this hope in him purifieth himself, even as he is pure. 4 Whosoever committeth sin transgresseth also the law: for sin is the transgression of the law." Your real acceptance of the Gospel of "Christ in you the hope of glory" is demonstrated by how well you work with Holy Spirit to obey: 1 John 3:3 "And every man that hath this hope in him purifieth himself, even as he is pure." This is the main message of Psalm 119. Ps 119:5 "O that my ways were directed to keep thy statutes! 6 Then shall I not be ashamed, when I have respect unto all thy commandments. 7 I will praise thee with uprightness of heart, when I shall have learned thy righteous judgments." A Christian life without the Scriptures unto right thoughts and action is not *zao*/life and does not release this *zoe* into the Earth. It may be in you, but it does not get out to accomplish good.

For New Testament Christians, the basic process above is to be followed when we find ourselves in sin (see the ten-step process for recovery from sin in the Glossary under the heading The Wrath of God), and to focus on the revelation of the new creation revealed only in the New Testament, specifically as given to Paul and repeated by Peter. Col 1:25 "Whereof I am made a minister, according to the dispensation of God which is given to me for you, to fulfil the word of God; 26 **even the mystery which hath been hid from ages and from generations**, but now is made manifest to his saints: 27 to whom God would make known what is the riches of the glory of **this mystery among the Gentiles; which is Christ in you, the hope of glory**: 28 whom we preach, warning every man, and teaching every man in all wisdom; that we may present every man perfect (*mature*) in Christ Jesus." Eph 3:1 "For this cause I Paul, the prisoner of Jesus Christ for you Gentiles, 2 if ye have heard of the dispensation of the grace of God which is given me to you-ward: 3 **how that by revelation he made known unto me the mystery**; (as I wrote afore in few words, 4 whereby, when ye read, ye may understand my knowledge in the mystery of Christ) 5 **which in other ages was not made known unto the sons of men, as it is now revealed unto his holy apostles and prophets by the Spirit**; 6 **that the Gentiles should be fellowheirs, and of the same body, and partakers of his promise in Christ by the gospel**: 7 whereof I was made a minister, according to the gift of the grace of God given unto me by the effectual working of his power. 8 Unto me, who am less than the least of all saints, is this grace given, that I should preach among the **Gentiles the unsearchable riches of Christ**; 9 **and to make all men see what is the fellowship of the mystery**, which from the beginning of the world hath been hid in God, who created all things by Jesus Christ." 1 Pet 1:9

OK, GOD, NOW WHAT?

"Receiving the end of your faith, even the *soteria*/salvation of your souls. 10 Of which *soteria*/salvation the prophets have inquired and searched diligently, who prophesied of the grace that should come unto you: 11 searching what, or what manner of time the Spirit of Christ which was in them did signify, when it testified beforehand the sufferings of Christ, and the glory that should follow. 12 **Unto whom it was revealed, that not unto themselves, but unto us they did minister the things, which are now reported unto you by them that have preached the gospel unto you** with the Holy Ghost sent down from heaven; which things the angels desire to look into." 2 Pet 1:1 "Simon Peter, a servant and an apostle of Jesus Christ, to them that have obtained like precious faith with us through the righteousness of God and our Saviour Jesus Christ: 2 grace and peace be multiplied unto you through the knowledge of God, and of Jesus our Lord, 3 **according as his divine power hath given unto us all things that pertain unto *zoe*/life and godliness,** through the knowledge of him that hath called us to glory and virtue: 4 whereby are given unto us exceeding great and precious promises: **that by these ye might be partakers of the divine nature**, having escaped the corruption that is in the world through lust." Gal 5:24 "**And they that are Christ's have crucified the flesh with the affections and lusts**. 25 **If we *zao*/live in the Spirit**, let us also walk in the Spirit. 26 Let us not be desirous of vain glory, provoking one another *to evil*, envying one another." 2 Pet 3:14 "Wherefore, *agape*/beloved, seeing that ye look for such things, be diligent that ye may be found of him in peace, without spot, and blameless. 15 And account that the longsuffering of our Lord is *soteria*/salvation; even as our *agape*/beloved brother Paul also **according to the wisdom given unto him hath written unto you**; 16 as also in all his epistles, speaking in them of these things; in which are some things hard to be understood, which they that are unlearned and unstable wrest, as they do also the other scriptures, unto their own destruction. 17 Ye therefore, *agape*/beloved, seeing ye know these things before, beware lest ye also, being led away with the error of the wicked, fall from your own stedfastness. 18 **But grow in grace, and in the knowledge of our Lord and Saviour Jesus Christ**. To him be glory both now and for ever. Amen."

If you want rules to live by, or law, the New Testament has some one thousand and fifty commands versus the six hundred and thirteen of the Torah. Christ in you the hope of glory is one way to state the core Gospel of Jesus Christ. This is the unique message of the New Testament and Christianity. It is not found in the Old Testament and must become a foundational part of the successful Christian's life. 2 Cor 13:5 "Examine yourselves, whether ye be in the faith; prove your own selves. Know ye not your own selves, how that Jesus Christ is in you, except ye be reprobates (*useless, worthy of garbage, impotent and ineffective*)?" 1 Cor 3:16 "Know ye not that ye are the temple of God, and that the Spirit of God dwelleth in you?" 1 John 3:1 "Behold, what manner of *agape*/love the Father hath bestowed upon us, that we

Understanding the Need for New Attitudes

should be called the sons of God: therefore the world knoweth us not, because it knew him not. 2 *Agape*/beloved, now are we the sons of God, and it doth not yet appear what we shall be: but we know that, when he shall appear, we shall be like him; for we shall see him as he is. 3 And every man that hath this hope in him purifieth himself, even as he is pure." Philem 6 "That the communication of thy faith may become effectual by the acknowledging of every good thing which is in you in Christ Jesus." Eph 4:23 "And be renewed in the spirit of your mind; 24 and that ye put on the new man, which after God is created in righteousness and true holiness." Col 3:9 "Lie not one to another, seeing that ye have put off the old man with his deeds; 10 and have put on the new man, which is renewed in knowledge after the image of him that created him: 11 where there is neither Greek nor Jew, circumcision nor uncircumcision, Barbarian, Scythian, bond nor free: but Christ is all, and in all." Rom 13:14 "… put ye on the Lord Jesus Christ, and make not provision for the flesh, to fulfil the lusts thereof." 2 Pet 3:18 "But grow in grace, and in the (*deep experiential*) knowledge of our Lord and Saviour Jesus Christ (*by walking just like Jesus*). To him be glory both now and for ever. Amen."

How important is it to learn to walk in this new attitude God requires? Consider the amazing history of Israel, the history of miracles beyond imagination among a small sect in the ancient desert. Here God revealed His ways for success and the consequences of ignorance and disobedience. Ezek 18:30 "Therefore I will judge you, O house of Israel, every one according to his ways, saith the Lord God. Repent, and turn yourselves from all your transgressions; so iniquity shall not be your ruin. 31 Cast away from you all your transgressions, whereby ye have transgressed; and make you a new heart and a new spirit: for why will ye die, O house of Israel? 32 For I have no pleasure in the death of him that dieth, saith the Lord God: wherefore turn yourselves, and live ye."

If in this passage is heard the agony of a loving God, trying to stop people from killing themselves, then the message is clear: change, not just your behavior, but also your attitudes that drive that behavior. This is not a vengeful cry; it is the cry that says, "If you don't stop, I cannot stop the consequences." In Christ, God gives us a new spirit, and next we need a new or refreshed-into-the-truth-of-God heart.

To fulfill the purpose God has for you in this life and to survive and thrive in that final Day, He invites us to enter into His wonderful, beyond-imagination salvation through His Son, Jesus of Nazareth, and the Christ of God. Rom 1:6 "Among whom are ye also the called of Jesus Christ." 1 Cor 1:9 "God is faithful, by whom ye were called unto the (*total and permanent covenantal*) fellowship of his Son Jesus Christ our Lord." Gal 1:6 "… him (*Father God*) that called you into the grace of Christ … ."

> Destiny

Chapter 2

Understanding The Salvation God Offers

Here is the basic Gospel: You can only be right with the God of all creation and enter His great love plan for you through Jesus Christ. John 14:6 "Jesus saith unto him, I am the way, the truth, and the *zoe*/life: no man cometh unto the Father, but by me. 7 If ye had known me, ye should have known my Father also: and from henceforth ye know him, and have seen him."

If you want to know what Father God is really like, just look at Jesus. Col 1:13 "… his *agape*/dear Son: 14 in whom we have redemption through his blood, even the forgiveness of sins: 15 who is the image (*exact likeness*) of the invisible God, the firstborn of every creature." To know God, study Jesus in all He said, did and still does.

Rom 4:24 "But for us also, to whom it (*righteousness*) shall be imputed (*counted as valid in spite of conflicting facts*), if we believe on him that raised up Jesus our Lord from the dead; 25 who was delivered for our offences, and was raised again for our justification (*being made just as if you had never sinned or will sin again, to right standing, as a joint heir with Jesus, as a son of God, connected to God forever by Holy Spirit*)."

1 Cor 15:1 "Moreover, brethren, I declare unto you the gospel which I preached unto you, which also ye have received, and wherein ye stand; 2 by which also ye are *sozo*/saved, if ye keep in memory what I preached unto you, unless ye have be-

Understanding the Salvation God Offers

lieved in vain. 3 For I delivered unto you first of all that which I also received, how that Christ died for our sins according to the scriptures; 4 and that he was buried, and that he rose again the third day according to the scriptures."

Jesus is now seated at the right hand of the Father, never to die for sins again. Heb 10:12 "But this man, after he had offered one sacrifice for sins for ever, sat down on the right hand of God."

So how are we made the righteousness of God in Jesus? Rom 10:8 "But what saith it? The word is nigh thee, even in thy mouth, and in thy heart: that is, the word of faith, which we preach; 9 that if thou shalt confess with thy mouth the Lord Jesus, and shalt believe in thine heart that God hath raised him from the dead, thou shalt be *sozo*/saved. 10 For with the heart man believeth unto righteousness; and with the mouth confession is made unto *soteria*/salvation. 11 For the scripture saith, Whosoever believeth on him shall not be ashamed." So you are made righteous by believing God raised Jesus from the dead, and you receive salvation by confessing or agreeing as true, with your mouth, that Jesus is Lord, Owner and Judge of all.

The first step is the new birth or the new creation. John 1:12 "But as many as received him, to them gave he power to become the sons of God, even to them that believe on his name: 13 which were born, not of blood, nor of the will of the flesh, nor of the will of man, but of God." This is where your spirit is recreated and made the righteousness of God in Christ Jesus, and your task is to now renew your mind/soul and to do good works, with God working in and through you.

A salvation prayer: "Lord Jesus, I believe You died for my sins, were buried and were raised by Father God on the third day for my justification, according to the Scriptures. I make you Lord of my life. Come rule and reign in and through me, my King. Baptize me with Your Holy Spirit and fire. Heal every part of my life. Teach me Your truth in love, that I may walk to Your glory. Amen and thank You."

A simpler prayer: "Jesus, God raised You from the dead. You are Lord. Fill me with Your Spirit to walk in *agape*/love. Thank You!"

Now that you are born again by the action of God in your spirit, the next step is for you to be water baptized. Matt 28:19 "Go ye therefore, and teach all nations, baptizing them in the name of the Father, and of the Son, and of the Holy Ghost." So find a local church to join and get baptized there.

If you want to know what God is really like, the Bible makes it very plain: Look to Jesus. Heb 1:1 "God, who at sundry times and in divers manners spake in time past unto the fathers by the prophets, 2 hath in these last days spoken unto us by his Son, whom he hath appointed heir of all things, by whom also he made the worlds; 3 who being the brightness of his glory, and the express image of his person, and upholding all things by the word of his power, when he had by himself purged our sins, sat down on the right hand of the Majesty on high." So whatever your view of God, He declares that the right view has to include all that Jesus was and now is, not His people (who obviously still fail), but Jesus Himself.

In and through Jesus, God set things the way He wants them: Col 1:12 "Giving thanks (*continually*) unto the Father, which hath made us meet to be partakers of the inheritance of the saints in light: 13 who hath delivered us from the power of darkness, and hath translated us into the kingdom of his *agape*/dear Son: 14 in whom we have redemption through his blood, even the forgiveness of sins: 15 who is the image of the invisible God, the firstborn of every creature."

Salvation has two parts: an eternal one with God and another with our life here on Earth in the here and now. The earthly process of salvation is how God finishes the job of making Heaven on Earth, and this is a key to the Lord's Prayer. Matt 6:9 "After this manner therefore pray ye: Our Father which art in heaven, Hallowed be thy name. 10 Thy kingdom come. Thy will be done in earth, as it is in heaven. 11 Give us this day our daily bread. 12 And forgive us our debts, as we forgive our debtors. 13 And lead us not into temptation, but deliver us from evil: for thine is the kingdom, and the power, and the glory, for ever. Amen. 14 For if ye forgive men their trespasses, your heavenly Father will also forgive you: 15 but if ye forgive not men their trespasses, neither will your Father forgive your trespasses."

This includes you forgiving God, as well as anyone else who has offended you in any way. Many have opinions about how the world is, and ultimately they blame God. Forgiving Him for our ignorance and pride is a key part of success. Then, include forgiving others who have hurt you in any way. Ask God for His grace to do this work in you.

Here is a summary of the Gospel Jesus preached. Jesus, the Christ/Messiah, came to demonstrate that now is the Day of Salvation from the evil rule of Satan in the present world system. This was seen in Jesus' preaching of truth, and in the miracles of healing, dead raising, food multiplication, stopping storms and walking on water. This means God solved the problem of how God, by Jesus, through Holy Spirit, can reign on the Earth through men to bring Heaven to Earth and destroy the kingdom of darkness. This restores man to his original position as the vehicle by which God will fill the Universe with the glory of God. Man is the hope of Heaven, and Jesus did the work to make this a past completed potential. When you get born again, with indwelling Holy Spirit, you step into this awesome potential.

Men must pray and act for God to get the job done. Titus 2:13 "Looking for that blessed hope, and the glorious appearing of the great God and our Saviour Jesus Christ; 14 who gave himself for us, that he might redeem us from all iniquity (*wrong thinking, acts and desires*), and purify unto himself a peculiar people, zealous of [*doing*] good works."

Stirring yourself in God, in His *agape*/love and compassion, to renew your mind into His way of thinking is one such good work and gets you operating more in God's great love plan for you.

CHAPTER 3

UNDERSTANDING CHRISTIAN BIOLOGY

We start with the spirit first, as the new creation is the definition of Christian biology, when we are made the righteousness of God in Christ Jesus, with indwelling Holy Spirit. Good works do not make you righteous, or as right as God is with Jesus; faith in the blood of Jesus does that. But the righteous do good works. Praying often does not make you righteous; believing that God raised Jesus from the dead does. But the righteous pray often. Going to church does not make you righteous; believing that Jesus is the Son of God does. But the righteous go to church. Phil 3:8 "Yea doubtless, and I count all things but loss for the excellency of the knowledge of Christ Jesus my Lord: for whom I have suffered the loss of all things, and do count them but dung, that I may win Christ, 9 and be found in him, not having mine own righteousness, which is of the law (*doing what God requires*), but that which is through the faith of Christ, the righteousness (*perfect right standing, just like Jesus, and knowing all your faults were paid for and healed in Jesus, so your failures cannot limit God in you, and thus, you can never fail God, nor can He count your failures against you, as He sees them and their consequences paid for and healed in Jesus*) which is of God by faith." The spiritual biology is that a Christian is now made the righteousness of God in Christ Jesus by indwelling Holy Spirit and, thus, is vastly different from non-Christians who, by this definition, do not have Holy Spirit dwelling within them.

OK, God, Now What?

This understanding of our righteousness in Jesus is the source of knowing we are right with God because of Jesus, and not ourselves, so God can bless us in all ways. He has set us free from the law of sin and death. Rom 8:2 "For the law of the Spirit of *zoe*/life in Christ Jesus hath made me free from the law of sin and death."

God has reconciled all mankind to Himself by Christ Jesus. This is the essence of the New Covenant. 2 Cor 5:18 "And all things are of God, who hath reconciled us to himself by Jesus Christ, and hath given to us the ministry of reconciliation; 19 to wit, that God was in Christ, reconciling the world unto himself, not imputing their trespasses unto them; and hath committed unto us the word of reconciliation. 20 Now then we are ambassadors for Christ, as though God did beseech you by us: we pray you in Christ's stead, be ye reconciled to God. 21 For he hath made him to be sin for us, who knew no sin; that we might be made the righteousness of God in him." Heb 8:10 "For this is the covenant that I will make with the house of Israel after those days, saith the Lord; I will put my laws into their mind, and write them in their hearts: and I will be to them a God, and they shall be to me a people: 11 and they shall not teach every man his neighbour, and every man his brother, saying, Know the Lord: for all shall know me, from the least to the greatest. 12 For I will be merciful to their unrighteousness, and their sins and their iniquities will I remember no more. 13 In that he saith, A new covenant, he hath made the first old. Now that which decayeth and waxeth old is ready to vanish away."

This legally removes the evil fear of God, that He is out to get you. Yet modern science is now proving what God has always said: evil fear is the source of all death in our lives. This applies to minor aches and pains, sickness or disease, and to an early grave. Thus, physical or biological life and death are related to spiritual truth.

This death by evil- or devil-induced fear is a fundamental problem in our earthly life and one of the main reasons Jesus came. Heb 2:14 "Forasmuch then as the children are partakers of flesh and blood, he (*Jesus*) also himself likewise took part of the same; that through death he might destroy him that had the power of death, that is, the devil; 15 and deliver them who **through fear of death were all their lifetime subject to bondage**. 16 For verily he took not on him the nature of angels; but he took on him the seed of Abraham." Rom 8:14 "For as many as are led by the Spirit of God, they are the sons of God. 15 For ye have not received the spirit of bondage again to fear; but ye have received the Spirit of adoption, whereby we cry, Abba (*Daddy*), Father. 16 The Spirit itself beareth witness with our spirit, that we are the children of God." Gal 3:26 "For ye are all the children of God by faith in Christ Jesus. 27 For as many of you as have been baptized into Christ have put on Christ." Gal 3:13 "Christ hath redeemed us from the curse of the law, being made a curse for us: for it is written, Cursed is every one that hangeth on a tree: 14 that the blessing of Abraham might come on the Gentiles through Jesus Christ; that we might receive the promise of the Spirit through faith." 2 Tim 1:6 "Wherefore I put thee in remembrance that thou stir up the gift of God, which is in thee by the putting on of my hands. 7 For God hath not given us the spirit of fear; but of power, and of *agape*/love, and of a sound mind." The main promise of the gift of God is Holy Spirit dwelling in a man/woman/boy/girl, just as He does in Jesus.

So the first part of the biology of a Christian is that you have been changed into a new kind of creature, one in whose spirit Holy Spirit now dwells, and He now speaks directly to your heart. 1 Cor 6:17 "But he that is joined unto the Lord is one spirit." Rom 5:5 "And hope maketh not ashamed; because the *agape*/love of God is shed abroad in our hearts by the Holy Ghost which is given unto us. 6 For when we were yet without strength, in due time Christ died for the ungodly." 2 Cor 5:17 "Therefore if any man be in Christ, he is a new creature: old things are passed away; behold, all things are become new." John 3:6 "That which is born of the flesh is flesh; and that which is born of the Spirit is spirit."

Many people believe man is only a two-part being, a soul and a body. God, the one who made us, gives a different description, that man is made of three major parts: spirit, soul and body. When the spirit of man was placed into his body, man became a living soul. Gen 2:7 "And the LORD God formed man of the dust of the ground, and breathed into his nostrils the breath (*spirit*) of life; and man became a living soul (*original language:* nepesh/*soul*)." Zech 12:1 "The burden of the word of the LORD for Israel, saith the LORD, which stretcheth forth the heavens, and layeth the foundation of the earth, and formeth the spirit (*original language:* ruwach/*spirit*) of man within him." While closely related, the spirit and the soul are maintained throughout both the Old and New Testaments as two different things. Job 7:11 "Therefore I will not refrain my mouth; I will speak in the anguish of my *ruwchiy*/spirit; I will complain in the bitterness of my *napshiy*/soul."

Our understanding is that when God placed the spirit into the human body, our soul was formed. Our spirits are a link to the spiritual world and our souls. Our souls are the link between our inner spirit-self and the outer, physical world through our bodies. Our outer life is an immediate reflection of our soul. So the link between the Christian, born-again spirit and how our body interacts with the world is our soul. (See Spirit/Soul/Body in the Glossary for more details on this subject.)

Many modern Bible scholars believe the heart and the spirit are the same thing, and this has been the subject of much debate. This certainly does not appear true in the Old Testament. The Bible tells us that King David had a heart after God (see 1 Kings 15:3), yet men could not be born again in spirit until after Jesus sent Holy Spirit on the Day of Pentecost. So here *heart* and *spirit* are different. Again: Ps 51:17 "The sacrifices of God are a broken (*shattered, all pride removed*) spirit: a broken and a contrite (*sorrowful, ashamed to have sinned*) heart, O God, thou wilt not despise." While closely related, the words for spirit and heart are different, and the words for broken and contrite are different. Thus, we can conclude, spirit and heart are different. So we have several alternatives. The heart and spirit are different, the heart and soul are different, the heart is a combination of the spirit and soul, i.e., the combined inner man, or a part of the spirit or a part of the soul. One can find scriptures to support any of these options.

In all cases, the heart is changeable, and the spirit, in general, is not. Jesus said: John 3:6 "That which is born of the flesh is flesh; and that which is born of the Spirit is spirit." Spirit is the same "stuff" as God and other spirit beings. John 4:24 "God is a Spirit: and they that worship him must worship him in spirit and in truth." Heart, soul and spirit seem to share many attributes and are, thus, closely related. In practical usage, heart is more about the will or purpose of a being in daily life. Ezek 36:26 "A new heart also will I give you, and a new spirit will I put within you: and I will take away the stony heart out of your flesh, and I will give you an heart of flesh." We are born again in spirit and then renewed in our mind.

The heart is changeable or programmable. According to the New Covenant, God will write or reprogram our hearts and our minds. Heb 8:10 "For this is the covenant that I will make with the house of Israel after those days, saith the Lord; I will put my laws into their mind, and write them in their hearts: and I will be to them a God, and they shall be to me a people."

The heart seems to be closely related to both the spirit and soul, but as it is the changeable part, it appears to be more soul-like in its nature. Heb 4:12 "For the word of God is quick, and powerful, and sharper than any twoedged sword, piercing even to the dividing asunder of soul and spirit, and of the joints and marrow, and is a discerner of the thoughts and intents of the heart." Thoughts and intents sound like the will and determination of the inner man and, thus, more like the heart, which may actually be a combination of the spirit and soul. Mark 12:30 "And thou shalt *agape*/love the Lord thy God with all thy heart, and with all thy soul, and with all thy mind, and with all thy strength: this is the first commandment."

God, in the Old and New Testaments, demands man to walk in *agape*/love with all his heart. Since the spirit was dead from sin, then that leaves the soul to drive appropriate behavior that pleases God. Remember, all action of the body is the result of the soul, which is the connection between the spirit and the body. The heart is an inner part, along with the spirit and soul. We are commanded to manage or control our hearts as a way of life. Your spirit is born again, with a new nature or substance. That is a work God does, and man cannot make himself a new creation. But your heart, like the soul and the mind, requires maintenance on our part. Prov 4:20 "My son, attend to my words; incline thine ear unto my sayings. 21 Let them not depart from thine eyes; keep them in the midst of thine heart. 22 For they are life unto those that find them, and health to all their flesh. 23 Keep thy heart with all diligence; for out of it are the issues of life. 24 Put away from thee a froward mouth, and perverse lips put far from thee."

Understanding Christian Biology

    This is described in scripture as a heart that is renewed, renovated, trained or reprogrammed to trust God, no matter what. Ps 112:6 "Surely he shall not be moved for ever: the righteous shall be in everlasting remembrance. 7 He shall not be afraid of evil tidings: his heart is fixed, trusting in the Lord. 8 His heart is established, he shall not be afraid, until he see his desire upon his enemies (*adversaries*)."

    This man is unshaken by the evil and difficult events of life. His trust is in God and not in his own ability. He has become expert at speaking out loud his trust in God. Ps 27:1 "The Lord is my light and my salvation; whom shall I fear? the Lord is the strength of my life; of whom shall I be afraid? 2 When the wicked, even mine enemies and my foes, came upon me to eat up my flesh, they stumbled and fell. 3 Though an host should encamp against me, my heart shall not fear: though war should rise against me, in this will I be confident. 4 One thing have I desired of the Lord, that will I seek after; that I may dwell in the house of the Lord all the days of my life, to behold the beauty of the Lord, and to inquire in his temple. 5 For in the time of trouble he shall hide me in his pavilion: in the secret of his tabernacle shall he hide me; he shall set me up upon a rock. 6 And now shall mine head be lifted up above mine enemies round about me: therefore will I offer in his tabernacle sacrifices of joy; I will sing, yea, I will sing praises unto the Lord."

    Notice that part of the process is to make vocal praise to God. This man's constant confession is this: Ps 57:7 "My heart is fixed, O God, my heart is fixed: I will sing and give praise. 8 Awake up, my glory; awake, psaltery and harp: I myself will awake early. 9 I will praise thee, O Lord, among the people: I will sing unto thee among the nations. 10 For thy *chesed*/mercy is great unto the heavens, and thy truth unto the clouds. 11 Be thou exalted, O God, above the heavens: let thy glory be above all the earth."

    The Psalms are the prayer and songbook of the Bible, so they are meant to be spoken and sung out loud. Ps 118:6 "The Lord is on my side; I will not fear: what can man do unto me? 7 The Lord taketh my part with them that help me: therefore shall I see my desire upon them that hate me. 8 It is better to trust in the Lord than to put confidence in man. 9 It is better to trust in the Lord than to put confidence in princes."

    This unshakable, fixed-on-God-hearted man has become expert at writing trust in God on his heart. Prov 3:3 "Let not *chesed*/mercy (*lovingkindness, grace*) and truth forsake thee: bind them about thy neck; **write them upon the table of thine heart**: 4 So shalt thou find favour and good understanding in the sight of God and man. 5 Trust in the Lord with all thine heart; and lean not unto thine own understanding. 6 In all thy ways acknowledge him, and he shall direct thy paths." You acknowledge with your mind by what thoughts you allow and by your words and your actions. It is something you do continually in the face of the events of life.

    Here is a description of what a right soul looks like to God. Remember, the punctuation, chapter and verse designations are not in the original language, so the subject here is a soul that operates just like Jesus did under difficult circumstances: 1 Pet 2:25 "For you were going astray like [so many] sheep, but now you have come back to the Shepherd and Guardian (the Bishop) **of your souls**. [Isa 53:5-6] 3:1 In like manner, you married women, be submissive to your own husbands [subordinate yourselves as being secondary to and dependent on them, and adapt yourselves to them], so that even if any do not obey the Word [of God], they may be won over not by discussion but by the [godly] lives of their wives, 2 when they observe the pure and modest way in which you conduct yourselves, together with your reverence [for your husband; you are to feel for him all that reverence includes: to respect, defer to, revere him—to honor, esteem, appreciate, prize, and, in the human sense, to adore him, that is, to admire, praise, be devoted to, deeply love, and enjoy your husband]. 3 Let not yours be the [merely] external adorning with [elaborate] interweaving and knotting of the hair, the wearing of jewelry, or changes of clothes; 4 but let it be the inward adorning and beauty of the hidden person of the heart, with the incorruptible and unfading charm of a gentle and peaceful spirit, which [is not anxious or wrought up, but] is very precious in the sight of God. 5 For it was thus that the pious women of old who hoped in God were [accustomed] to beautify themselves and were submissive to their husbands [adapting themselves to them as themselves secondary and dependent upon them]. 6 It was thus that Sarah obeyed Abraham [following his guidance and acknowledging his headship over her by] calling him lord (master, leader, authority). And you are now her true daughters if you do right and let nothing terrify you [not giving way to hysterical fears or letting anxieties unnerve you]." AMP

Many use 1 Peter 3:4 to say the heart and the spirit are the same. Here is a different interpretation based on all the above scriptures. A heart that trusts in the Lord, no matter what, is one who, like Sarah, could calmly hear her husband say, "God told us to pack up and travel to a strange land. I know He has given no more details, but we will trust in His goodness and just go anyway, and He will show us where we are to live." Gen 11:31 "And Terah took Abram his son, and Lot the son of Haran his son's son, and Sarai his daughter in law, his son Abram's wife; and they went forth with them from Ur of the Chaldees, to go into the land of Canaan; and they came unto Haran, and dwelt there. 32 And the days of Terah were two hundred and five years: and Terah died in Haran. 12:1 Now the Lord had said unto Abram, Get thee out of thy country, and from thy kindred, and from thy father's house, unto a land that I will shew thee." Sarah was to go from being a city-dweller to a wilderness tent-dweller without having any further details of what would happen.

Here is a description of Sarah, using this scripture, but replacing the *he* with *she*: Ps 112:6 "Surely *she* shall not be moved for ever: the righteous shall be in everlasting remembrance. 7 *She* shall not be afraid of evil tidings: *her* heart is fixed, trusting in the Lord *(with continual faith actions)*. 8 *Her* heart is established, *she* shall not be afraid, until *she* see *her* desire upon *her* enemies *(adversaries)*."

Now look at: 1 Pet 3:3 "Whose adorning *(that of wives)* let it not be that outward adorning of plaiting the hair, and of wearing of gold, or of putting on of apparel; 4 but let it be the hidden man of the heart, in that which is not corruptible *(easily frightened or troubled)*, even the ornament of a meek and quiet spirit *(in the face of the unknown and adversity)*, which is in the sight of God of great price." A wife such as these is adorning her heart with a gentle and meek spirit, based on the scriptures to trust in God. She is not adorning her heart with her heart, but she is adorning her heart with something different. She is making beautiful her heart by renewing it to let her born-again spirit, created in true righteousness and holiness after the image of God, shine through in a lifestyle of continual New Testament faith actions.

As a Christian, with the mind of Christ and a born-again spirit, just like Jesus has, a godly woman is to train, renew, renovate or cleanse her heart and mind to operate just as Jesus did when He went to the cross with His trust in God by the promises in the Scriptures. She is to let a mind renewed in the Word of God allow her born-again spirit to shine freely through her soul, to reflect the glory of the Lord in the face of adversity. This trust in God is of great value to Him and comes at the price of a flesh-driven mind that operates in worldly fear, like a "mere" man. Rom 8:5 "For they that are after the flesh do mind the things of the flesh; but they that are after the Spirit *(by the Word of Christ in the Scriptures in a lifestyle of continual New Testament faith actions)* the things of the Spirit. 6 For to be carnally minded *(with no hope and no confidence in God in the circumstances of life)* is death; but to be spiritually minded *(by the Word of Christ in the Scriptures)* is *zoe*/life and peace. 7 Because the carnal mind is enmity against God: for it is not subject to the law of God, neither indeed can be. 8 So then they that are in the flesh cannot please God."

This is how we are to exercise *agape*/love for God. James 1:2 "My brethren, count it all joy when ye fall into divers temptations; 3 knowing this, that the trying of your faith worketh patience *(faithfulness, consistency, reliability and calm trust in God)*. 4 But let patience have her perfect work *(in purifying your heart)*, that ye may be perfect *(mature)* and entire, wanting nothing … .12 Blessed is the man that endureth temptation: for when he is tried, he shall receive the crown of *zoe*/life, which the Lord hath promised to them that *agape*/love him."

We *agape*/love God by holding on to His promises to endure in gladness and joy and not letting our hearts and minds be troubled. John 14:1 "Let not your heart be troubled: ye believe in God, believe also in me *(Jesus)* … . 27 Peace I leave with you, my peace I give unto you: not as the world giveth, give I unto you. Let not your heart be troubled, neither let it be afraid." John 16:33 "These things I have spoken unto you, that in me ye might have peace. In the world ye shall have tribulation: but be of good cheer; I have overcome the world."

OK, God, Now What?

We are guaranteed troubles, and the shape of our heart will determine how well we *agape*/love the Lord in the midst of them. So in the midst of life's troubles or imperfections that we encounter in our walk in the Lord, we are still commanded to renew or renovate our minds and hearts by: Rom 13:10 "*Agape*/love worketh no ill to his neighbour: therefore love is the fulfilling of the law. 11 And that, knowing the time, that now it is high time to awake out of sleep: for now is our *soteria*/salvation nearer than when we believed. 12 The night is far spent, the day is at hand: let us therefore cast off the works of darkness, and let us put on the armour of light. 13 Let us walk honestly, as in the day; not in rioting and drunkenness, not in chambering and wantonness, not in strife and envying. 14 But put ye on the Lord Jesus Christ (*in your self-identity to walking like Him*), and make not provision for the flesh, to fulfil the lusts thereof."

The practical action it takes to purify our hearts does not really depend on resolution of this debate, as to whether the heart is part of the spirit or of the soul. For the purposes of this book, the heart and spirit are considered different, or at least not the exact same things, and the heart is considered part of the soul, or governed by the soul, and not the spirit. The spirit is instantly recreated by the pathway provided by a softened or pure heart. This is how one "hears" the Gospel and believes it unto a new creation. The rest of the heart (and soul) must be properly purified, trained and maintained, else they become corrupted. James 4:8 "Draw nigh to God, and he will draw nigh to you. Cleanse your hands, ye sinners; and purify your hearts, ye double minded." Acts 15:8 "And God, which knoweth the hearts, bare them witness, giving them the Holy Ghost, even as he did unto us; 9 and put no difference between us and them, purifying their hearts by faith (*so they were not hardened, as the Jewish leaders were, and could 'hear' the Gospel to obedience*)." Ezek 18:31 "Cast away from you all your transgressions, whereby ye have transgressed; and make you a new heart and a new spirit: for why will ye die, O house of Israel?"

The soul of the born-again Christian is the path by which God works in our spirit to get us to act like Jesus in the world. The quality or programming of the soul by continual faith actions is what allows the new-creation spirit and God to manifest into the world through our body. Thus, our purpose now is to purify our souls for a habitation of God, as revealed by the prayer of Eph 3:17. A soul (heart, mind, will and emotions) that is in unity with God results in thoughts, words and actions like Jesus. But a hardened Christian heart (just like a hardened non-Christian heart) cannot receive that which Holy Spirit is continually communicating within and without. Therefore Holy Spirit has warned Christians in the Scriptures, when faced with difficult times, just as He did ancient Israel: Heb 3:15 "While it is said, To day if ye will hear his voice, harden not your hearts, as in the provocation."

God is spirit and deals with spirit. It takes flesh to deal directly in this Earth. The link for your spirit into this world is your soul and, specifically, your heart.

UNDERSTANDING CHRISTIAN BIOLOGY

With the regeneration of our spirit in the new creation, we now have a very different spirit than those not so born again, but as history has shown, it is entirely possible for Christians to act just like those who are not new creations in Christ Jesus. Eph 4:17 "This I say therefore, and testify in the Lord, that ye henceforth walk not as other Gentiles walk, in the vanity of their mind, 18 having the understanding darkened, being alienated from the *zoe*/life of God through the ignorance that is in them, because of the blindness of their heart: 19 who being past feeling have given themselves over unto lasciviousness, to work all uncleanness with greediness. 20 But ye have not so learned Christ." You do not tell people to stop acting like someone else, unless they have been acting that way. Notice the issue is in the soul, in a vain and ignorant mind and a hardened heart.

So, as a Christian, you are made a new kind of being, a "Christ-like one" or a "little Christ." Col 2:8 "Beware lest any man spoil you through philosophy and vain deceit, after the tradition of men, after the rudiments of the world, and not after Christ. 9 For in him dwelleth all the fulness of the Godhead bodily. 10 **And ye are complete in him**, which is the head of all principality and power: 11 in whom also ye are circumcised with the circumcision made without hands, in putting off the body of the sins of the flesh by the circumcision of Christ: 12 buried with him in baptism, wherein also ye are risen with him through the faith of the operation of God, who hath raised him from the dead." Philosophy is a way of thinking or viewing the world, and it sets the attitudes by which we operate in life. Wrong philosophies lead to deception and not living up to your potential in Christ.

So this new creation has all it needs (is complete with all the parts it needs) to mature by a process of learning and doing: 2 Pet 1:2 "Grace and peace be multiplied unto you through the (*deep and experiential*) knowledge of God, and of Jesus our Lord, 3 according as his divine power hath given unto us all things that pertain unto *zoe*/life and godliness, through the (*deep and experiential*) knowledge of him that hath called us to glory and virtue: 4 whereby are given unto us exceeding great and precious promises: that by these ye might be partakers of the divine nature, having escaped the corruption that is in the world through lust." Eph 4:13 "Till we all come in the unity of the faith, and of the knowledge of the Son of God, unto a perfect man, unto the measure of the stature of the fulness of Christ: 14 that we henceforth be no more children, tossed to and fro, and carried about with every wind of doctrine, by the sleight of men, and cunning craftiness, whereby they lie in wait to deceive; 15 but speaking the truth in *agape*/love, may grow up into him in all things, which is the head, even Christ." Hence the warning in Col 2:8 above to be very careful what information you allow to enter your mind and, thus, control how you live, i.e., learning unto doing or true knowing.

Part of this learning is to not let the life in the physical world control your ability to relate properly to Holy Spirit, who now dwells within the new-creation

Christian. 2 Tim 1:6 "Wherefore I put thee in remembrance that thou stir up (*get in tune with, in excitement with and in the power of God, and not as the world gives*) the gift of God, which is in thee by the putting on of my hands. 7 For God hath not given us [*as a gift by Jesus*] the spirit of fear; but the Spirit of power, and of *agape*/love, and of a sound mind." Notice that while Jesus came to set us free from fear, we must continuously "stir" ourselves up by continual right faith actions to focus on the reality that we actually have Holy Spirit in us, if you are born again into a new creature in Christ Jesus. 2 Cor 5:17 "Therefore if any man be in Christ, he is a new creature: old things are passed away; behold, all things are become new." Eph 4:23 "And be renewed in the spirit of your mind; 24 and that ye put on the new man, which after God is created in righteousness and true holiness." The message is clear: without the diligent effort of continual faith actions you will succumb to living by your corrupt soul (the old man) and not Holy Spirit (the new man).

The Bible has always talked about man as three parts: spirit, soul and body. 1 Thes 5:23 "And the very God of peace sanctify you wholly; and I pray God your whole spirit and soul and body be preserved blameless unto the coming of our Lord Jesus Christ." There is a fourth part of man talked about in the Bible: the heart. From modern science, we understand this to be the heart with thoughts (versus the one that pumps blood), as located in or with the ganglia around the blood-pumping heart and with other ganglia dispersed throughout the body, and, as such, what the Bible calls the heart is (or is part of or connected to) the subconscious mind.

The spirit of man is often thought of as physically connected to or near the heart or solar plexus region. The spirit also experiences emotions, so feelings in the spirit or the unconscious mind within the ganglia around the heart region are felt in the same parts of the body and are easily confused as to their source, spirit or heart/soul. Body and soul or body and spirit are easily separated, but with so many common attributes, soul and spirit are not; it requires a spiritual tool to separate them. Heb 4:12 "For the word of God is quick, and powerful, and sharper than any twoedged sword, piercing even to the dividing asunder of soul and spirit, and of the joints and marrow, and is a discerner of the thoughts and intents of the heart."

Modern science calls the conscious mind the cerebral cortex, the seat of the "self," or your cognitive mind. In the Bible, the conscious man is considered the "self," and is independent of the soul. Ps 116:7 "Return unto thy rest, O my soul; for the Lord hath dealt bountifully with thee." Luke 21:19 "In your patience possess (*win to true life*) ye your souls." In both of these scriptures, the soul is different from the "self" or person and supposedly inferior to or to be controlled by the self. Modern science does not recognize the spirit, so it includes self in the soul.

The exact definitions for soul, mind, self, spirit, heart and conscious have been the subject of debate for centuries, and, for practical purposes, in this book they

UNDERSTANDING CHRISTIAN BIOLOGY

are simplified into working definitions. Taking 1 Thes 5:23 as the lead, man is three major parts, spirit, soul and body, and various sub-parts may also be emphasized.

The heart and the spirit are different. The original language words for heart and spirit are very different, as seen in these scriptures: Ps 34:18 "The LORD is nigh unto them that are of a broken *leeb*/heart; and saveth such as be of a contrite *ruwach*/spirit." Ps 77:5 "I have considered the days of old, the years of ancient times. 6 I call to remembrance my song in the night: I commune with mine own *leeb*/heart: and my *ruwach*/spirit made diligent search." And from the New Testament Greek: 2 Cor 1:22 "Who hath also sealed us, and given the earnest of the *pneumatos*/Spirit in our *kardiais*/hearts." The point is that they are different words and, thus, had different meanings to the biblical writers.

Jesus used three different Greek words and included the heart, soul and mind as all required to *agape*/love God properly. Matt 22:37 "Jesus said unto him, Thou shalt *agape*/love the Lord thy God with all thy *kardia*/heart, and with all thy *psuche*/soul, and with all thy *dianioa*/mind (*inner thoughts, imagination*)."

As a working definition, the heart can be understood as the non-cognitive part of the mind. The body, as directed by the soul, does the sinning or the righteous works in the thoughts, words and actions we allow. The human spirit is either entirely or partially where Holy Spirit initially dwells in the Christian. In this book, we assume the spirit is entirely made new—"all things." 2 Cor 5:17 "Therefore if any man be in Christ, he is a new creature: old things are passed away; behold, **all things** are become new. 18 And **all things** are of God, who hath reconciled us to himself by Jesus Christ, and hath given to us the ministry of reconciliation." The spirit is recreated by new birth, the heart trained and maintained, just like the rest of the soul is. So the issue is: how does our soul get reprogrammed to allow Holy Spirit to fully posses or operate in it at will?

As the born-again Christian's spirit is one with God (1 Cor 6:17 "But he that is joined unto the Lord is one spirit"), Holy Spirit cannot be corrupted by sin, yet the Christian heart can be corrupted. In the New Testament, Christians are warned not to let their hearts be corrupted by sin. Heb 3:12 "Take heed, brethren, lest there be in any of you an evil heart of unbelief, in departing from the *zao*/living God. 13 But exhort one another daily, while it is called To day; lest any of you be hardened through the deceitfulness of sin." James 3:14 "But if ye have bitter envying and strife in your hearts, glory not, and lie not against the truth." James 4:8 "Draw nigh to God, and he will draw nigh to you. Cleanse your hands, ye sinners; and purify your hearts, ye double minded." 1 John 3:20 "For if our heart condemn us, God is greater than our heart, and knoweth all things." Thus, the Christian heart is in need of constant maintenance and/or major remedial work so that it can stay in cooperation with Holy Spirit.

The heart and Holy Spirit are linked, as seen in 2 Cor 1:22, where Holy Spirit is described as the "earnest (*payment of ownership or security deposit for full possession later*) of the *pneumatos*/Spirit in our *kardiais*/hearts." Holy Spirit is perfect, for He is God. Our heart is not perfect and is not God. But all education is a process of instilling new facts and ideas into the soul. And for true change to occur, this must take place in the heart. God's intent is that your heart will become the full possession of Holy Spirit, as you grow in Christian maturity into Jesus. Thus, a new born-again Christian also has a changed heart, for God has put a deposit into the heart that will one day lead to full possession by Him, just as Jesus is fully possessed by God. Eph 4:15 "But speaking the truth in *agape*/love, may grow up into him in all things, which is the head, even Christ."

We are told we have the mind of Christ, Holy Spirit. 1 Cor 2:12 "Now we have received, not the spirit of the world, but the spirit which is of God; that we might know the things that are freely given to us of God … . 16 For who hath known the mind of the Lord, that he may instruct him? But we have the mind of Christ." Just as with conflicting computer programs or two people trying to converse in languages neither of the other understands, if our soul does not match or accept the mind of Christ, we cannot understand or link to that Christ mind.

God's goal is for our soul to be so aligned by the Word of God that Holy Spirit can actually dwell comfortably in our hearts (soul). By the new creation, Holy Spirit is already one with our spirit. 1 Cor 6:17 "But he that is joined unto the Lord is one spirit." This desire/goal for our hearts is found in the prayer in Ephesians 3: Eph 3:16 "That he (*Father God*) would grant you, according to the riches of his glory, to be strengthened with might by his Spirit in the inner man; 17 that Christ may dwell (*fully, gladly and freely*) in your hearts by faith (*actions*); that ye, being rooted and grounded in *agape*/love …"

This means He who will dwell in or occupy in authority all of the Earth will also dwell in or occupy with authority our spirit, soul and body. If Holy Spirit is outside of your soul, then He must first talk into it, but the goal of God is for Holy Spirit to freely and gladly dwell in your soul forever. That is the promise of the New Covenant found in Hebrews 8 and 10. The initial stage of this process starts with Holy Spirit talking to us from outside our soul, and as we agree, He can actually move into that area, and then we act "full of Holy Spirit" for a time. The plan of God for those born-again in Jesus is for that condition to be as full as it was in Jesus when He walked the Earth, and as much as it is now in Jesus in Heaven.

This is part of the implications of "Christ in us the hope of glory." 1 John 4:17 "Herein is our *agape*/love made perfect, that we may have boldness in the day of judgment: because as he is, so are we in this world." Jesus is the Word of God made flesh, the *agape* love of God made flesh, the *zoe* life of God made flesh, the righteousness of God made flesh, the glory of God made flesh and the light of God made flesh. That is what we are made now in the new birth/new creation. How much of this we walk in depends on how well we renew our mind (soul/heart) so it is a happy dwelling place for Holy Spirit where He can occupy in authority to get the will of God done through us as He does through Jesus now.

A soul in which Holy Spirit can freely talk, and we will obey in our thoughts, words and deeds is described as being "full of the spirit." This can be momentary, on a particular subject or event, or it can become a lifestyle. Luke 4:1 "And Jesus being full of the Holy Ghost returned from Jordan, and was led by the Spirit into the wilderness." Acts 7:55 "But he (*Stephen*), being full of the Holy Ghost, looked up stedfastly into heaven, and saw the glory of God, and Jesus standing on the right hand of God." Acts 11:24 "For he (*Barnabas*) was a good man, and full of the Holy Ghost and of faith: and much people was added unto the Lord." Acts 2:4 "And they were all filled with the Holy Ghost, and began to speak with other tongues, as the Spirit gave them utterance." 1 Cor 12:31 "But covet earnestly the best gifts [*of Holy Spirit*]: and yet shew I unto you a more excellent way." 1 Cor 14:1 "Follow after *agape*/charity, and desire spiritual gifts [*of Holy Spirit*], but rather that ye may prophesy." Eph 5:18 "And be not drunk with wine, wherein is excess; but be (*Greek: continually be being*) filled with the Spirit; 19 speaking to yourselves in psalms and hymns and spiritual songs, singing and making melody in your heart to the Lord; 20 giving thanks always for all things unto God and the Father in the name of our Lord Jesus Christ; 21 submitting yourselves one to another in the fear of God."

These last three scriptures describe how being full of the Spirit can become a lifestyle, i.e. our becoming single-mind with God. Ps 32:8 "I will instruct thee and teach thee in the way which thou shalt go: I will guide thee with mine eye. 9 Be ye not as the horse, or as the mule, which have no understanding: whose mouth must be held in with bit and bridle, lest they come near unto thee." A bridle speaks of control by force. Being guided by the eye is attitude change and willing cooperation to always do what pleases the Master. As Jesus said: John 8:29 "And he that sent me is with me: the Father hath not left me alone; for I do always those things that please him."

The Bible does talk about double minds and double or split hearts, as refers to believing, trusting and obeying God. Ps 86:11 "Teach me thy way, O Lord; I will walk in thy truth: unite my heart to fear thy name." James 1:8 "A double minded man is unstable in all his ways."

This scripture indicates the main problem is in the heart: James 4:8 "Draw nigh to God, and he will draw nigh to you. Cleanse your hands, ye sinners; and purify your hearts, ye double minded." So to be of two minds you have conflicting deep inner, long-lasting, decision-confusing concepts within your heart, and this is demonstrated by vacillation between two or more points in your cognitive mind. The result is that you cannot make a quality, long-lasting decision or full-hearted commitment, as demonstrated by what you actually now say and do for the long term. A heart not set single-mindedly on God is a heart full of wrong programming, and that leads to wrong attitudes in how you approach every aspect of life, thus producing or allowing wrong thoughts, words and deeds.

OK, God, Now What?

The situation in a "double-minded" person is that you may have two or more sets of "facts" or "beliefs," and you are not persuaded in your heart, or subconscious mind, what is the right choice. You may agree with your conscious mind on one path, but if your subconscious is not in agreement or there are multiple thoughts deep in your subconscious, you are internally "conflicted" and outwardly confused in your behavior. This is often described as a lack of commitment or loyalty, or as "playing both sides against the middle."

For modern athletes, this is described as having wrong attitudes about their sport and wrong training in how they react in competitive situations. Thus, an Olympic hopeful will review tapes of previous performances with the coach and study what movement can be improved. They then start a rigorous athletic and mental program to "cook in" the right movements and get rid of the wrong actions.

People who make decisions in this double-minded state may agree one day but not carry through the next. Or they may make the right movement one time and the wrong the next. The purpose of this book is to help you become single-minded and heart-united to godly fear and glad to obey God in all parts of your life continually, so that you can receive the abundance of His prosperity in every aspect of that life. Job 28:28 "… the fear of the Lord, that is wisdom; and to depart from evil is understanding."

God, through the Scriptures (the only valid physical link between the true God and man), has always talked about the heart of man as being where the real issues of life are found. The heart can be understood as the inner you or the part of you that is below your conscious mind. Prov 4:20 "My son, attend to my words; incline thine ear unto my sayings. 21 Let them not depart from thine eyes; keep them in the midst of thine heart. 22 For they are life unto those that find them, and health to all their flesh. 23 **Keep thy heart with all diligence; for out of it are the issues of life.** 24 Put away from thee a froward mouth, and perverse lips put far from thee. 25 Let thine eyes look right on, and let thine eyelids look straight before thee. 26 Ponder the path of thy feet, and let all thy ways be established. 27 Turn not to the right hand nor to the left: remove thy foot from evil." Our modern world stresses the conscious mind and not the inner man or the heart. God's wisdom, however, has told us for thousands of years that the issue is in the inner man, not just the outer or cognitive mind. Science is now confirming this, and champion athletes are demonstrating it through extraordinary new levels of performance.

Again the Bible reaffirms that while the heart and mind exist, rightly dividing the Word of truth is an inner-man matter. Our soul is the earth-related part of our inner man and is made up of at least two major parts: 1) the conscious or cogitative mind, and 2) the inner man consisting of the heart or the subconscious mind. It is not what you are taught in the cognitive mind that makes the difference for the long term, but how you receive it in your subconscious or heart. And this inner matter, combined with the Word of God, is what releases us into the best God has for us as a way of life. But achieving that best will require you to labor. Heb 4:9 "There remaineth therefore a rest to the people of God. 10 For he that is entered into his rest, he also hath ceased from his own works, as God did from his, 11 **let us labour therefore** to enter into that rest, lest any man fall after the same example of unbelief. 12 For the word of God is quick, and powerful, and sharper than any twoedged sword, piercing even to the **dividing asunder of soul and spirit**, and of the joints and marrow, and is **a discerner of the thoughts and intents of the heart**."

Here the primary tool to find out what is soul and spirit and what is Holy Spirit or devil-induced thoughts and intentions of the heart is the Word of God. For this reason, the affirmations we have written contain much scripture, and the person using them must put forth diligent effort or "labor." One way to look at this is that it takes right labor, along with the Word of God, to see the division between your soul and your spirit and the validity of the thoughts and intents of your heart. Otherwise, just because you think and desire it, you may decide a thing is good or even claim it is from God, when, in reality, it is not. Prov 18:2 "A fool hath no delight in understanding, but that his heart may discover itself." Prov 15:7 "The lips of the wise disperse knowledge: but the heart of the foolish doeth not so." Prov 1:7 "The fear of the LORD is the beginning of knowledge: but fools despise wisdom and instruction." Prov 19:3 "The foolishness of man perverteth his way: and his heart fretteth against the LORD." Prov 12:15 "The way of a fool is right in his own eyes: but he that hearkeneth unto counsel is wise." Prov 12:23 "A prudent man concealeth knowledge: but the heart of fools proclaimeth foolishness." Prov 19:21 "There are many devices in a man's heart; nevertheless the counsel of the LORD, that shall stand." Prov 20:9 "Who can say, I have made my heart clean, I am pure from my sin?" Prov 24:1 "Be not thou envious against evil men, neither desire to be with them. 2 For their heart studieth destruction, and their lips talk of mischief." Prov 28:26 "He that trusteth in his own heart is a fool: but whoso walketh wisely, he shall be delivered." Isa 5:21 "Woe unto them that are wise in their own eyes, and prudent in their own sight!" Jer 17:9 "The heart is deceitful above all things, and desperately wicked: who can know it? 10 I the LORD search the heart, I try the reins, even to give every man according to his ways, and according to the fruit of his doings." John 3:19 "And this is the condemnation, that light is come into the world, and men *agape*/loved darkness rather than light, because their deeds were evil. 20 For every one that doeth evil hateth the light, neither cometh to the light, lest his deeds should be reproved. 21 But he that doeth truth cometh to the light, that his deeds may be made manifest, that they are wrought in God." Eph 5:13 "But all things that are reproved are made manifest by the light: for whatsoever doth make manifest is light. 14 Wherefore he saith, Awake thou that sleepest, and arise from the dead, and Christ shall give thee light."

OK, God, Now What?

Our soul and our spirit are different, yet closely tied together. The Scriptures describe both the spirit and the soul as having emotions, so it is very hard to tell them apart. It takes labor with the Word of God, with Holy Spirit's guidance, to be able to tell the difference. And the fruit of that labor includes rightly determining if the thoughts of your heart are worthy of God and will release God into the Earth. For the purposes of this book, the fact that the heart has thoughts makes it part of our soul, which includes our mind.

To help discern who or what is speaking to our heart, we are commanded: 1 John 4:1 "*Agape*/beloved, believe not every spirit, but try the spirits whether they are of God: because many false prophets are gone out into the world. 2 Hereby know ye the Spirit of God: Every spirit that confesseth that Jesus Christ is come in the flesh is of God: 3 and every spirit that confesseth not that Jesus Christ is come in the flesh is not of God: and this is that spirit of antichrist, whereof ye have heard that it should come; and even now already is it in the world."

Notice that in this passage the difference is the messenger, not the sound or character of the "voice" you are hearing. Apparently all spirit "voices" sound the same to us. The first way to spot whether a particular voice is from God, you or the devil is the message it brings. If your heart is corrupt in the area of the message, you cannot tell the difference, as a corrupt heart will accept a corrupt message, while a heart steeped in truth in that particular area will not. This scriptural testing process separates the message from the source of the message. A messenger of God will gladly confess: "Jesus Christ has come in the flesh"; a false, deceiving messenger will not. Once you know the source, then you can accept that which is of God and reject that which is of the devil/antichrist.

Notice again that the issues for this life are three-fold, as revealed in this Holy Spirit-directed prayer or blessing: 1 Thes 5:23 "And the very God of peace sanctify (*allow you to see what is of God and not of God, so you always choose God*) you wholly; and I pray God your whole spirit and soul and body be preserved blameless unto the coming of our Lord Jesus Christ." Also notice that the blameless part is related to the judgment that will take place when Jesus comes again.

Also notice that our dealing with the Word of God opens the potential for us to deal with the real and living God at the same time. Heb 4:13 "Neither is there any creature that is not manifest in his sight: but all things are naked and opened unto the eyes of him with whom we have to do." John 12:48 "He that rejecteth me (*Jesus*), and *lambano*/receiveth not my words, hath one that judgeth him: the word that I have spoken, the same shall judge him in the last day."

The people who put Jesus on the cross had the entire Old Testament memorized, as part of the standard life of a good Jew, and still they missed God entirely. So the issue is more than just memorizing scriptures. But memorizing scripture is

UNDERSTANDING CHRISTIAN BIOLOGY

a first key step in renewing the mind. We can consider memorizing scripture as the frame of a house. Without walls and roof, it is still not ready for safe living. It is like a skeleton, providing a firm backbone for the flexibility of life to be constructed upon.

The biology of man includes the three parts: spirit, soul and body. The biology of the human body is designed to handle what God has decreed for both the spirit and soul. The biology of a Christian is that their spirit has been reborn and is no longer like a natural, unregenerate or earthly man, but is made a new creation in Christ Jesus, made the righteousness of God in Christ Jesus unto *zoe*/life, made one with Holy Spirit, sealed with Holy Spirit and made a new man in the image and likeness of God in "righteousness and true holiness."

By majoring on these spiritual and physical realities, we can then start to obey: Philem 6 "That the communication (*outworked walk of Christ in you, the hope of glory*) of thy faith (*in what Jesus accomplished by the cross and God did in you by the new birth, and your destiny in Him*) may become effectual (*producing the results of you walking like Jesus, in grace, truth, righteousness, peace, joy,* dunamis/*power,* agape/*love and a mind like Christ, to the present life glory of* God) by the (*continual and diligent*) epignosis/acknowledging of every good thing which is in you in Christ Jesus."

While the Christian is "complete" in Jesus, in the new birth, walking in this requires faith action labor on our part. You have this wondrous new biology by the new birth, along with the baptism of Holy Spirit. You are transformed to manifest the life of Jesus by the continual renewing of your mind into the facts of redemption, the nature and character of God and the promises of God by continual faith actions. Equipping, enabling, releasing or strengthening you to manifest this "Christ in you the hope of heaven to fill the earth with the glory of God like Jesus through you," in this New Creation biology, is the purpose of the Affirmation Magnets and the mind-renewing program in this book.

Chapter 4

Understanding How To Avoid Missing God

Jesus said the reason the leaders of His day missed God and, instead, became His enemy was a matter of the heart or, as we understand it from current science, the subconscious mind. Matt 15:15 "Then answered Peter and said unto him, Declare unto us this parable. 16 And Jesus said, Are ye also yet without understanding? 17 Do not ye yet understand, that whatsoever entereth in at the mouth goeth into the belly, and is cast out into the draught? 18 But those things **which proceed out of the mouth come forth from the heart**; and they defile the man. 19 For out of the **heart proceed evil thoughts**, murders, adulteries, fornications, thefts, false witness, blasphemies: 20 these are the things which defile a man: but to eat with unwashen hands defileth not a man." Mark 7:18 "And he saith unto them, Are ye so without understanding also? Do ye not perceive, that whatsoever thing from without entereth into the man, it cannot defile him; 19 because it entereth not into his heart, but into the belly, and goeth out into the draught, purging all meats? 20 And he said, That which cometh out of the man, that defileth the man. 21 For from within, **out of the heart of men**, proceed evil thoughts, adulteries, fornications, murders, 22 thefts, covetousness, wickedness, deceit, lasciviousness, an evil eye (*stingy, greedy*), blasphemy, pride, foolishness: 23 all these evil things come from within, and defile the man." Matt 12:34 "O generation of vipers, how can ye, being evil, speak good things? for **out of the abundance of the heart the mouth speaketh**. 35 A good man out of the good treasure of the heart bringeth forth good things: and an evil man out of the evil treasure bringeth forth evil things. 36 But I say unto you, That every idle (*useless for God*) word that men shall speak, they shall give account thereof in the day of judgment. 37 For by thy words thou shalt be justified, and by thy words thou shalt be condemned."

By definition, a Christian is born-again, with Holy Spirit dwelling within. Still, through sad messages in the New Testament letters and two thousand years of Christian history, we know that Christians, even born-again, Spirit-filled ones, can sin and talk, just as Jesus described the Jews of His day, with defiled hearts. Since none of these are actions of Holy Spirit, but of the heart, the heart must be different from the Christian spirit that is united to the Lord.

Jesus made it clear: the issue of success in life and with God is determined by what comes out of your mouth, and what comes out of your mouth is a direct measure of what is in your heart. To clean up your life, you start with controlling your mouth and reprogramming your heart, as an intentional action or process.

What the Jews of that day had forgotten was that this is not just about truth, but about full truth that allows you to love yourself and others with the *agape*/love of God. Matt 22:36 "Master, which is the great commandment in the law? 37 Jesus said unto him, Thou shalt *agape*/love the Lord thy God with all thy heart, and with all thy soul, and with all thy mind. 38 This is the first and great commandment. 39 And the second is like unto it, Thou shalt *agape*/love thy neighbour as thyself. 40 On these two commandments hang all the law and the prophets."

And again: 1 John 4:20 "If a man say, I *agape*/love God, and hateth his brother, he is a liar: for he that *agape*/loveth not his brother whom he hath seen, how can he *agape*/love God whom he hath not seen? 21 And this commandment have we from him, That he who *agape*/loveth God *agape*/love his brother also." Here the measure of how well you *agape*/love God is shown to be how well you *agape*/love others. To show the depth of this, Jesus gave the story of the Good Samaritan in Luke 10:30-37 as the way the Kingdom of God is to operate in *agape* love.

The message is clear: perfection for its own end is an inward death spiral, but perfection, allowing the *agape*/love of God to flow to all the world through you, is one of the secrets of staying in God. The perfection God is concerned about is not in the Christian spirit, because that is what is "saved" when you get born again and Holy Spirit comes to dwell within you. Col 2:10 "And ye are complete in him, which is the head of all principality and power." Gal 3:26 "For ye are all the children (*sons*) of God by faith in Christ Jesus." This means you have the tools or basic structure to mature into Christ in the new creation, which is not the "new evolution."

The new creation of our spirit is virtually instantaneous and irreversible; the transformation of our soul is a process and reversible, taking time and effort. Just like a house that has been dusted, once the soul (and heart) are cleaned, they must be maintained, or they can become corrupted again. 2 Cor 11:3 "But I fear, lest by any means, as the serpent beguiled Eve through his subtilty, so your minds should be corrupted from the simplicity that is in Christ." Col 2:8 "Beware lest any man spoil you through philosophy and vain deceit, after the tradition of men, after the rudiments of the world, and not after Christ. 9 For in him dwelleth all the fulness of the Godhead bodily. 10 And ye are complete in him, which is the head of all principality and power."

The issue is the perfection, maturing or transformation of your soul, as you learn to walk in the new creation, as measured by the amount of *agape*/love you demonstrate. Heb 6:1 "Therefore leaving the principles of the doctrine of Christ, let us go on unto perfection; not laying again the foundation of repentance from dead works, and of faith toward God." 2 Cor 13:9 "For we are glad, when we are weak, and ye are strong: and this also we wish, even your perfection." 1 John 3:14 "We know that we have passed from death unto *zoe*/life, because we *agape*/love the brethren. He that *agape*/loveth not his brother abideth in death." 1 John 2:3 "And hereby we do know that we know him, if we keep his commandments. 4 He that saith, I know him, and keepeth not his commandments, is a liar, and the truth is not in him. 5 But whoso keepeth his word, in him verily is the *agape*/love of God perfected: hereby know we that we are in him. 6 He that saith he abideth in him ought himself also so to walk, even as he walked." True Bible knowledge is not that you can quote even the entire Bible but that you walk like Jesus, i.e., as a partaker of Christ.

One of the purposes of this life is the development or right completion of your soul for rewards on the Day of Judgment. Matt 16:24 "Then said Jesus unto his disciples, If any man will come after me, let him deny himself, and take up his cross, and follow me. 25 For whosoever will save his *psuche*/life (*soul*) shall lose it: and whosoever will lose his *psuche*/life (*soul*) for my sake shall find it. 26 For what is a man profited, if he shall gain the whole world, and lose his own *psuche*/soul (*life*)? or what shall a man give in exchange for his *psuche*/soul (*life*)? 27 For the Son of man shall come in the glory of his Father with his angels; and then he shall reward every man according to his works." Here Jesus makes it plain that while the issue is to walk in *agape*/love toward God and man, the evidence of your walk is what you actually ponder on, say and do, and your actions are a direct reflection of the true godliness (manifested Christ-likeness) in your soul.

Your soul (*psuche*) is distinct from your spirit, but very closely related. Your soul consists of your mind, your heart, your will and your emotions. In general, recent medical research shows, your soul is physically housed in two parallel regions: your conscious mind (two to four percent of your body's neural mass: in brain, spinal chord, etc.) and the unconscious mind (ninety-six to ninety-eight percent your body's neural mass). Truth, in just the conscious mind, is mental as-

Understanding How to Avoid Missing God

sent and, by itself, of little power in the Earth or with God. You may agree with something as truth in your mind, but as all those New Year's resolutions show, such agreement does not result in a changed manner of living.

Let's look at a New Year's resolution for a moment. You notice that your clothes are tight, and so you decide, in your cognitive mind, you need to lose weight. You may actually even take some action if you have reached or exceeded the tipping point. So you go to the gym a few times. Physical fitness experts tell us, however, that within just a few months after New Year's Day seventy-five percent of the people stop going to the gym. What happened to those seventy-five percent? The answer, for most of them, is simple: they had other needs in their heart, other thoughts and memories, and were double-minded, heart-divided, on working out to lose weight.

What about the other twenty-five percent, those who stuck it out? Their hearts were united in the matter, and so they lasted longer in the gym. Unless you do the necessary things to unite your heart on a matter, you will be the same as those who failed to lose the unwanted weight. You will not last for the long haul. You may start, in the cognitive mind, but you may not finish.

One way to unite your heart is by the company you keep. In the example with the gym, joining with others who can encourage you will make you last much longer. The more you do the things that unite your heart, the longer you will last—even when others fall away. 1 Cor 15:33 "Be not deceived: evil communications (*conversations in or outside the mind*) corrupt good manners (*the way you live*)."

This book is about a long-lasting heart uniting that will allow us to hit the target God has set for us: Eph 4:13 "Till we all come in the unity of the faith, and of the knowledge of the Son of God, unto a perfect man, unto the measure of the stature of the fulness of Christ: 14 that we henceforth be no more children, tossed to and fro, and carried about with every wind of doctrine, by the sleight of men, and cunning craftiness, whereby they lie in wait to deceive; 15 but speaking the truth in *agape*/love, may grow up into him in all things, which is the head, even Christ."

When something is in your heart, it controls the way you live. Prov 23:7 "For as he thinketh in his heart, so is he ... ." So the solution for a successful life is to put the Word of God in our hearts in a way that makes us successful with God. Ps 119:11 "Thy word have I hid in mine heart, that I might not sin against thee." The alternative, for the source of wicked thoughts, words and behaviors is: Ps 10:3 "For the wicked boasteth of his **heart's** desire, and blesseth the covetous, whom the Lord abhorreth. 4 The wicked, through the pride of his countenance, will not seek after God: God is not in all his thoughts. 5 His ways are always grievous; thy judgments are far above out of his sight: as for all his enemies, he puffeth at them. 6 He hath said in his **heart**, I shall not be moved: for I shall never be in adversity. 7 His mouth is full of cursing and deceit and fraud: under his tongue is mischief and vanity. 8 He sitteth in the lurking places of the villages: in the secret places doth he murder the innocent: his eyes are privily set against the poor. 9 He lieth in wait secretly as a lion in his den: he lieth in wait to catch the poor: he doth catch the poor, when he draweth him into his net. 10 He croucheth, and humbleth himself, that the poor may fall by his strong ones. 11 He hath said in his **heart**, God hath forgotten: he hideth his face; he will never see it. ... 13 Wherefore doth the wicked contemn God? he hath said in his **heart**, Thou wilt not require it."

Our modern world seems to glorify the idea of following your own heart, but here is what Holy Spirit had to say about that: Ps 40:7 "Then said I, Lo, I come: in the volume of the book it is written of me, 8 I delight to do thy will, O my God: yea, thy law is within my heart." John 4:34 "Jesus saith unto them, My meat is to do the will of him that sent me, and to finish his work." John 5:30 "I can of mine own self do nothing: as I hear, I judge: and my judgment is just; because I seek not mine own will, but the will of the Father which hath sent me." John 6:38 "For I came down from heaven, not to do mine own will, but the will of him that sent me." Matt 20:28 "Even as the Son of man came not to be ministered unto, but to minister, and to give his *psuche*/life a ransom for many." Rom 15:3 "For even Christ pleased not himself; but, as it is written, The reproaches of them that reproached thee fell on me" (Ps 69:9, 69:20, 89:50-51). John 10:10 "The thief cometh not, but for to steal, and to kill, and to destroy: I am come that they might have *zoe*/life, and that they might have it more abundantly." Jesus has a right heart.

While the born-again process may change your heart in some way, it does not make it like Jesus' heart. Christians do not start with a right heart; their heart must be developed, reprogrammed and retrained. As for getting a right heart, Christians are commanded: Phil 2:5 "Let (*make*) this mind (*regard, opinion, set-affections-on, delight-in, attitude*) be in you, which was also in Christ Jesus: 6 who, being in the form of God, thought it not robbery to be equal with God: 7 but made himself of no reputation, and took upon him the form of a servant, and was made in the likeness of men." Ps 37:3 "Trust (*by continual faith actions*) in the Lord, and do good; so shalt thou dwell in the land, and verily thou shalt be fed. 4 Delight thyself also in the Lord; and he shall give thee the desires of thine heart. 5 Commit thy way unto the Lord; trust (*by continual faith actions*) also in him; and he shall bring it to pass." Heb 10:7 "Then said I, Lo, I come (in the volume of the book it is written of me,) to do thy will, O God." Ps 40:8 "I delight to do thy will, O my God: yea, thy law is within my heart." Ps 119:70 "Their heart is as fat as grease; but I delight in thy law." Prov 18:2 "A fool hath no delight [*in understanding in the ways of God to think and do them*], but that his heart may discover itself." 2 Chron 12:14 "And he did evil, because he prepared not his heart to seek the Lord." Ps 119:1 "Blessed are the undefiled in the way, who walk in the law of the Lord. 2 Blessed are they that keep his testimonies, and that seek him with the whole heart. 3 They also do no iniquity:

they walk in his ways. 4 Thou hast commanded us to keep thy precepts diligently. 5 O that my ways were directed to keep thy statutes!" 1 Tim 1:5 "Now the end of the commandment (*strong teaching and direct training you are to obey*) is *agape*/charity out of a pure heart, and of a good conscience, and of faith unfeigned." 1 Pet 1:18 "Forasmuch as ye know that ye were not redeemed with corruptible things, as silver and gold, from your vain conversation received by tradition from your fathers; 19 but with the precious blood of Christ, as of a lamb without blemish and without spot: 20 who verily was foreordained before the foundation of the world, but was manifest in these last times for you, 21 who by him do believe in God, that raised him up from the dead, and gave him glory; that your faith and hope might be in God. 22 Seeing ye have purified your souls in obeying the truth through the Spirit unto unfeigned *phileo*/love of the brethren, see that ye *agape*/love one another with a pure heart fervently."

You may add new information to your soul/heart in a short "cramming" session, even enough to start taking some right action. Short periods of a few hours or days of intense immersion will have effects that last for three to five days, as these only deal with the cognitive mind. While short-lived, they can still allow you to be more effective in prayer or, for athletes, on the playing field. But if you do not clean out the old, corrupt ideas, you will remain double-minded for the long term. How long will this "tipping" or confused state last? It will last until you reprogram your mind with the Word and attitudes of God and until you subdue the networks of evil thoughts and evil habits of interpretations, prejudices, and attitudes that are in your cognitive and subconscious mind and heart. That will take some time. Motivation may keep you going for the short term, but the cleaning-out process is not instant.

For any given thought or attitude, science shows us it will take twenty-one days to build a new thought pattern neural network, forty days to build a new mindset or attitude, and at least ninety days before the old one is subdued. Can God work miracles? Sure, He does, and often it is the specific things you may need at the moment, but it is not the fullness of a life that has been commanded to renew and keep renewed your own mind. Gal 6:7 "Be not deceived; God is not mocked: for whatsoever a man soweth, that shall he also reap. 8 For he that soweth to his flesh shall of the flesh reap corruption; but he that soweth to the Spirit shall of the Spirit reap *zoe*/life everlasting. 9 And let us not be weary in well doing: for in due season we shall reap, if we faint not. 10 As we have therefore opportunity, let us do good unto all men, especially unto them who are of the household of faith." It takes continual right sowing in continual faith actions to have continual right reaping.

If you strive to only get by and not to excel in Jesus, you will reap the fruit of those who still love the world, because you reap what you sow, and you will be in constant conflict with your new nature, that only wants to do those things that fully please God. God, as your Father, will pace you properly through the trials of life that we all have. He is not a cruel Master, and He knows exactly what you can handle. Phil 4:13 "I can do all things through Christ which strengtheneth me." Your success will depend on how well you work with God in the trials and how well you subdue the devil, who is the source of all your troubles.

The devil knows or seeks to find out what you can handle without God and is constantly looking for ways to attack you, and when he does attack you, he does it without mercy. For this, God gives His great promise that has stood the test of millennia. Job understood it, and Holy Spirit had Paul write it: 1 Cor 10:13 "There hath no temptation taken you but such as is common to man: but God is faithful, who will not suffer you to be tempted above that ye are able; but will with the temptation also make a way to escape, that ye may be able to bear it. 14 Wherefore, my dearly *agape*/beloved, flee from idolatry." Some of the tools that will enable you to endure the trials ahead are found in Psalms 23 and 91, among many other scriptures.

The major intent of this proper programming of the heart or subconscious mind should be this: Matt 23:23 "Woe unto you, scribes and Pharisees, hypocrites! for ye pay tithe of mint and anise and cummin, and have omitted the weightier matters of the law, judgment, mercy, and faith: these ought ye to have done, and not to leave the other undone." Luke 11:42 "But woe unto you, Pharisees! for ye tithe mint and rue and all manner of herbs, and pass over judgment and the *agape*/love of God: these ought ye to have done, and not to leave the other undone." Gal 5:6 "For in Jesus Christ neither circumcision availeth anything, nor uncircumcision; but faith which worketh by *agape*/love." Rom 13:10 "*Agape*/love worketh no ill to his neighbour: therefore *agape*/love is the fulfilling of the law." In summary, the righteous requirements of the Law, including judgment, mercy, faith (*in God*) and *agape*/love, are to be built into your heart, soul and mind for success in God by Christ Jesus.

This message, to walk in actual *agape*/love, is part of the warning Jesus gave to the early Ephesian believers. Rev 2:1 "Unto the angel of the church of Ephesus write; These things saith he that holdeth the seven stars in his right hand, who walketh in the midst of the seven golden candlesticks; 2 I know thy works, and thy labour, and thy patience, and how thou canst not bear them which are evil: and thou hast tried them which say they are apostles, and are not, and hast found them liars: 3 and hast borne, and hast patience, and for my name's sake hast laboured, and hast not fainted. 4 Nevertheless I have somewhat against thee, because **thou hast left thy first *agape*/love. 5 Remember therefore from whence thou art fallen, and repent, and do the first works**; or else I will come unto thee quickly, and will remove thy candlestick out of his place, except thou repent. 6 But this thou hast, that thou hatest the deeds of the Nicolaitans, which I also hate. 7 He that hath an ear, let him hear what the Spirit saith unto the churches; To him that overcometh will I give to eat of the tree of *zoe*/life, which is in the midst of the paradise of God." Notice that true repentance in God results in different works or lifestyle wrought in God.

Understanding How to Avoid Missing God

Jesus commended these Ephesian believers for rightly dividing truth. They could spot false apostles (vs. 2), and they hated the deeds of the Nicolaitans, which He also hated (vs. 6). They had a good understanding of truth in theology, yet, because they lost *agape*/love, they would also lose their ability to see, i.e., their candlestick was to be taken away.

Theology and *agape*/love are two major legs of Christian life, and we need both. Look at the reproof Jesus offered to those who claimed they saw, and yet, because of a lack of *agape*/love, did not. Matt 15:13 "But he answered and said, Every plant, which my heavenly Father hath not planted, shall be rooted up. 14 Let them alone: they be blind leaders of the blind. And if the blind lead the blind, both shall fall into the ditch." And the great warning to religious pride in the Scriptures: John 9:41 "Jesus said unto them, If ye were blind, ye should have no sin: but now ye say, We see; therefore your sin remaineth." Such is the price of ignoring the Christ, the Mighty Arm of God.

Also notice the great reproof because the religious leaders did not know the *agape*/love of God. John 5:39 "Search the scriptures; for in them ye think ye have eternal *zoe*/life: and they are they which testify of me. 40 And ye will not come to me, that ye might have *zoe*/life. 41 I receive not honour from men. 42 But I know you, that ye have not the *agape*/love of God in you. 43 I am come in my Father's name, and ye receive me not: if another shall come in his own name, him ye will receive. 44 How can ye believe, which receive honour one of another, and seek not the honour that cometh from God only?" [NOTE: Excessive concern over what others think will cause you to walk in unbelief. Fear of man has always been one of the devil's weapons. Prov 29:25 "The fear of man bringeth a snare: but whoso putteth his trust *(by continual faith actions)* in the Lord shall be safe."]

Again: 1 John 2:15 "*Agape*/love not the world, neither the things that are in the world. If any man *agape*/love the world, the *agape*/love of the Father is not in him. 16 For all that is in the world, the lust of the flesh, and the lust of the eyes, and the pride of *bios*/life, is not of the Father, but is of the world. 17 And the world passeth away, and the lust thereof: but he that doeth the will of God abideth for ever." 1 John 3:17 "But whoso hath this world's good, and seeth his brother have need, and shutteth up his bowels of compassion from him, how dwelleth the *agape*/love of God in him? 18 My little children, let us not *agape*/love *(just)* in word, neither *(just)* in tongue *(the way you talk)*; but in deed and in truth." How awesome! The more you walk in the *agape*/love of God by the Scriptures, the more you will recognize God when He shows up (see John 5:39-44).

A hardened heart comes about as you fill or defend your subconscious mind with beliefs, attitudes and prejudices that do not match the mind of Christ. God's rules are that if you will not think and do right, you reap what you sow. He takes credit for this process of heart hardening. Matt 13:14 "And in them is fulfilled the prophecy of Esaias, which saith, By hearing ye shall hear, and shall not understand; and seeing ye shall see, and shall not perceive: 15 for this people's heart is waxed gross, and their ears are dull of hearing, and their eyes they have closed; lest at any time they should see with their eyes, and hear with their ears, and should understand with their heart, and should be converted, and I should heal them. 16 But blessed are your eyes, for they see: and your ears, for they hear."

Here we see Jesus' answer to shake the disciples out of this process in which they were headed in a negative or devilish direction. Mark 16:14 "Afterward he (*Jesus*) appeared unto the eleven as they sat at meat, and upbraided them with their unbelief and hardness of heart, because they believed not them which had seen him after he was risen."

The process by which the heart keeps us on track was designed by God. The devil uses this to keep us in bondage, so death works on us, in a fast or slow manner, and we, thus, miss or ignore God. 2 Cor 4:3 "But if our gospel be hid, it is hid to them that are lost (*living in fast or slow death*): 4 in whom the god of this world hath blinded the minds of them which believe not, lest the light of the glorious gospel of Christ, who is the image of God, should shine unto them. 5 For we preach not ourselves, but Christ Jesus the Lord; and ourselves your servants for Jesus' sake. 6 For God, who commanded the light to shine out of darkness, hath shined in our hearts, to give the light of the knowledge of the glory of God in the face of Jesus Christ."

The "believe not" of verse 4 means to fail to rejoice at a coming good from God unto thanksgiving, praise and worship and, instead, place priority on only what your eyes see right now or any offenses in your heart. This was part of the process that Satan used to tempt Adam. He challenged God's truth and stated that God was withholding good. Gen 3:5 "For God doth know that in the day ye eat thereof, then your eyes shall be opened, and ye shall be as gods, knowing good and evil. 6 And when the woman saw that the tree was good for food, and that it was pleasant to the eyes, and a tree to be desired to make one wise, she took of the fruit thereof, and did eat, and gave also unto her husband with her; and he did eat."

Over time, the devil built a mental or heart stronghold, so that when Eve sinned, Adam, instead of going to God, his Helper and his Friend, went his own way away from God, to join Eve. We know this because, as the devil lied, Adam did not correct him or banish him. Instead, Adam let him talk on. After Adam and Eve sinned, God even came looking for them, to help them, and they ran from Him. Their running was an example of being blinded to the Good News, the Gospel that God was there to help them. Gen 3:8 "And they heard the voice of the Lord God walking in the garden in the cool of the day: and Adam and his wife hid themselves from the presence of the Lord God amongst the trees of the garden. 9 And the Lord God called unto Adam, and said unto him, Where art thou? 10 And he said, I heard thy voice in the garden, and I was afraid, because I was naked; and I hid myself."

Understanding How to Avoid Missing God

Pilate understood why the religious leaders of Jesus' day wanted Him killed. Matt 27:18 "For he knew that for envy they had delivered him." These men feared Jesus' miracle power and the fact that the people listened to Him. It is amazing that Jesus freely gave the authority to work miracles to the twelve and then the seventy. At any time, the religious leaders could have had the same, but because they honored man and not God, they were envious of what they could freely have been given.

Jesus' attitude was that if the religious leaders would not get the people healed, He would appoint others who would. Matt 9:36 "But when he saw the multitudes, he was moved with compassion on them, because they fainted, and were scattered abroad, as sheep having no shepherd. 37 Then saith he unto his disciples, The harvest truly is plenteous, but the labourers are few; 38 pray ye therefore the Lord of the harvest, that he will send forth labourers into his harvest. 10:1 And when he had called unto him his twelve disciples, he gave them power (*authority, pre-permission*) against unclean spirits, to cast them out, and to heal all manner of sickness and all manner of disease." Mark 6:34 "And Jesus, when he came out, saw much people, and was moved with compassion toward them, because they were as sheep not having a shepherd: and he began to teach them many things." Luke 10:1 "After these things the Lord appointed other seventy also, and sent them two and two before his face into every city and place, whither he himself would come. 2 Therefore said he unto them, The harvest truly is great, but the labourers are few: pray ye therefore the Lord of the harvest, that he would send forth labourers into his harvest. 3 Go your ways: behold, I send you forth as lambs among wolves (*the unbelieving religious leaders*). ... 8 And into whatsoever city ye enter, and they receive you, eat such things as are set before you: 9 and heal the sick that are therein, and say unto them, The kingdom of God is come nigh unto you."

Today many say that if Jesus was to come again and work miracles they would believe. But that did not happen in the day when He was here, so why should it be any different today? John 12:37 "But though he had done so many miracles before them, yet they believed not on him: 38 that the saying of Esaias the prophet might be fulfilled, which he spake, Lord, who hath believed our report? and to whom hath the arm of the Lord been revealed? 39 Therefore they could not believe, because that Esaias said again, 40 He hath blinded their eyes, and hardened their heart; that they should not see with their eyes, nor understand with their heart, and be converted, and I should heal them. 41 These things said Esaias, when he saw his glory, and spake of him. 42 Nevertheless among the chief rulers also many believed on him; but because of the Pharisees they did not confess him, lest they should be put out of the synagogue: 43 for they *agape*/loved the praise of men more than the praise of God. 44 Jesus cried and said, He that believeth on me, believeth not on me, but on him that sent me. 45 And he that seeth me seeth him that sent me. 46 I am come a light into the world, that whosoever believeth on me should not abide in darkness." Mark 3:1 "And he (*Jesus*) entered again into the synagogue; and there was a man there which had a withered hand. 2 And they watched him, whether he would heal him on the sabbath day; that they might accuse him. 3 And he saith unto the man which had the withered hand, Stand forth. 4 And he saith unto them, Is it lawful to do good on the sabbath days, or to do evil? to *sozo*/save *psuche*/life, or to kill? But they held their peace. 5 And when he had looked round about on them with anger, being grieved for the hardness of their hearts, he saith unto the man, Stretch forth thine hand. And he stretched it out: and his hand was restored whole as the other. 6 And the Pharisees went forth, and straightway took counsel with the Herodians against him, how they might destroy him." Here's what Jesus said to them: John 5:39 "Search the scriptures; for in them ye think ye have eternal *zoe*/life: and they are they which testify of me. 40 And ye will not come to me, that ye might have *zoe*/life. 41 I receive not honour from men. 42 But I know you, that ye have not the *agape*/love of God in you. 43 I am come in my Father's name, and ye receive me not: if another shall come in his own name, him ye will receive. 44 How can ye believe, which receive honour one of another, and seek not the honour that cometh from God only?" These men were so hardened that Jesus' physical presence and the miracles He did failed to move them.

Notice that the terms "hard heart" and "hard mind" can be used interchangeably. Dan 5:20 "But when his heart was lifted up, and his mind hardened in pride, he was deposed from his kingly throne, and they took his glory from him." James 4:8 "Draw nigh to God, and he will draw nigh to you. Cleanse your hands, ye sinners; and purify your hearts, ye double minded." Or the mind of the spirit versus the mind of the flesh or the carnal mind: Rom 8:5 "For they that are after the flesh do mind the things of the flesh; but they that are after the Spirit the things of the Spirit. 6 For to be carnally minded is death; but to be spiritually minded is *zoe*/life and peace. 7 Because the carnal mind is enmity against God: for it is not subject to the law of God, neither indeed can be. 8 So then they that are in the flesh cannot please God."

It appears that a simple equation can be derived from these truths: love of the world = a carnal mind = a hard mind = a hard heart = a double-minded person = a person at war/enmity/alienated in attitude, belief, and preconception against God = blindness of heart = not able to see God = not able to hear God = unbelief = not able to understand = death working in you = abiding in darkness = not like Jesus = cut off from the *zoe*/life of God. So God commands us: Eph 4:17 "This I say therefore, and testify in the Lord, that ye henceforth walk not as other Gentiles walk, in the vanity of their mind, 18 having the understanding darkened, being alienated from the *zoe*/life of God through the ignorance that is in them, because of the blindness of their heart: 19 who being past feeling have given themselves over unto lasciviousness, to work all uncleanness with greediness."

UNDERSTANDING HOW TO AVOID MISSING GOD

Short-term efforts (hours or days) may let the cognitive mind produce good results, but unless the heart is improved, purged and maintained in a focused long-term effort, there are no long-lasting results in behavior change.

Just as Jesus lamented over Jerusalem: Luke 19:44 "… because thou knewest not the time of thy visitation (*inspection*)," we may profess our theological pontifications and yet, with a hard heart, miss God, as He ever speaks to us. Or, as Jesus warned the Ephesians: Rev 2:5 "Remember therefore from whence thou art fallen, and repent, and do the first works (*of* agape/*love*); or else I will come unto thee quickly, and will remove thy candlestick out of his place, except thou repent." Then you will be left claiming you see, yet be blind.

As we have learned, repentance is a process which, at a minimum, takes months to purge or renew a hardened heart. When we get it right, 1 John 2:5 "But whoso keepeth his (*Jesus'*) word, in him verily is the *agape*/love of God perfected: hereby know we that we are in him. 6 He that saith he abideth in him ought himself also so to walk, even as he (*Jesus*) walked."

And what does this walk look like? Here is one definition given by God: Acts 10:38 "How God anointed Jesus of Nazareth with the Holy Ghost and with power: who went about doing good, and healing all that were oppressed (*under the active rule and lordship*) of the devil; for God was with him." Those who obey the Gospel we are to preach will do similarly: Mark 16:17 "And these signs shall follow them that believe; In my (*Jesus'*) name shall they cast out devils; they shall speak with new tongues; 18 they shall take up serpents; and if they drink any deadly thing, it shall not hurt them; they shall lay hands on the sick, and they shall recover."

So if you are abiding in the Gospel, your prayer life will be dynamic and effective. John 15:7 "If ye abide in me, and my words abide in you, ye shall *aiteo*/ask (*require, demand and expect as due by covenant promise*) what ye will, and it shall be done unto you. 8 Herein is my Father glorified, that ye bear much fruit; so shall ye be my disciples."

This is rather blunt. If this is not your testimony, then it is time to aggressively purify your heart in continual right faith actions to become single-minded in God. James 4:8 "Draw nigh to God, and he will draw nigh to you. Cleanse your hands, ye sinners; and purify your hearts, ye double minded." The Affirmations in this book are a great way to start a godly mind-renewing-and-maintenance program, to make your heart ever more tender and obedient to God. For greater effectiveness, add in at least two hours a day in loud, hard and fast tongues, per 1 Cor 12 and 14.

Chapter 5
Understanding How to Renew the Heart

How does our heart get into the shape it is in? Your heart is a reflection of what you allow to enter into your thoughts, past your cognitive or judging mind. You are exposed to vast amounts of information all day and night. That which you actively seek or do not reject can enter and become the foundation of your heart. If not protected and continuously cleansed, your heart will become corrupted in the normal process of living. Prov 4:20 "My son, attend to my words; incline thine ear unto my sayings. 21 Let them not depart from thine eyes; keep them in the midst of thine heart. 22 For they are life unto those that find them, and health to all their flesh. 23 Keep thy heart with all diligence; for out of it are the issues of life. 24 Put away from thee a froward mouth, and perverse lips put far from thee." Again: Ps 53:1 "The fool hath said in his heart, There is no God. Corrupt are they, and have done abominable iniquity: there is none that doeth good. 2 God looked down from heaven upon the children of men, to see if there were any that did understand, that did seek God. 3 Every one of them is gone back: they are altogether become filthy; there is none that doeth good, no, not one." 1 Cor 15:33 "Be not deceived: evil communications (*words and lifestyles*) corrupt good manners."

How do your reprogram your heart? You do it with understanding of the process, as you imprint information into your heart with repetition and controlled emotional intensity, not feeling. Modern science and biblical commands tell us your subconscious mind cannot tell if you are faking joy or really feeling it. Joy, thanksgiving and praise are highly emotional and active words in their true, original-language meaning. They are not gentle or passive, like polite manners. So, with intensity and emotion, you can overwrite or subdue fear and lies in your heart, with love and truth. Phil 4:6 "Be careful for nothing; but in every thing by prayer and supplication with thanksgiving let your requests be made known unto God. 7 And the peace of God, which passeth all understanding, shall keep your hearts and minds through Christ Jesus." As you apply strong, excited (*faking-it-if-need-be*) thanksgiving, you write over fear and unbelief with trust in God and His goodness. Healing is mostly about agreeing with God in truth in your mind and heart.

Praise, thanksgiving and joy are not simple emotions, but actions that can lead to emotions. Obey with gladness and intensity, as a focused decision, with your cognitive mind, and you write those praises, thanks and joys into your subconscious (heart, inner man), to release the love of God. As you read a truth such as Phil 4:13 "I can do all things through Christ which strengtheneth me," don't read fast. Instead, stop and dwell on what you are saying. Repeat it with joy, praise and thanksgiving, to drive or write it onto your heart and overwrite the fears that keep you in bondage. Encourage yourself daily in this way. Resistance is an indication that there are probably more thoughts in your heart that need subduing.

Phil 4:6-7 is telling us to identify our fears, pray to God about them, fix whatever the concern and the people involved, and then give Him deep, strong and loud thanks (which is all in the meaning of thanksgiving), and do this every time evil fear attacks. Then the Peacemaker, the One who makes peace by destroying the works of the devil, will rule in your heart (subconscious mind) and your conscious mind, to think like Jesus. The more you think like Jesus on any aspect of salvation (which is all of life), the more you will see of God's healing and saving power. Faint not!

To retrain your subconscious, a great starting place is to say the Our Father and Psalm 23 and 91 three or four times a day, like a medicine. Doing it with enthusiasm and thanksgiving it is even better. This gets a lot easier when you decide that the Bible is what it advertises itself to be, the inerrant Word of God, and any errors are man's and not God's. The only physical link between God and man is the Bible. Of the supposed errors I know about, 99% are resolved in better original word definitions. For me, Jesus solved the problem of the entire Old Testament this way: Matt 5:18 "For verily I say unto you, Till heaven and earth pass, one jot or one tittle shall in no wise pass from the law (*Old Testament*), till all be fulfilled." You can debate the New Testament all you want, but there is enough in the Old to keep you busy for ten thousand years.

I am not a theorist; I am a workman, so I need tools to accomplish what God has sent me to do, and it starts with His Word. (All New Testament references to the Scriptures could only have meant the Old Testament, because the New Testament was not codified until around 400 A.D.)

The latest scientific research is that the human mind is made up of at least two parts, the conscious mind and the unconscious mind. The unconscious mind also seems to be housed in two parts: the deep inner brain and the entire nervous system of the body, outside the brain, including the ganglia masses around the heart. So to properly program or correctively reprogram the mind you must consider all aspects of the entire neural system.

What is the heart? In the Bible, unless the context is different, the heart is the unconscious mind, and the "mind" is the conscious or cognitive mind. Simple head knowledge is in the cognitive mind, but life happens in the heart. Jesus said: Matt 12:34 "O generation of vipers, how can ye, being evil, speak good things? for out of the abundance of the heart the mouth speaketh. 35 A good man out of the good treasure of the heart bringeth forth good things: and an evil man out of the evil treasure (*of his heart*) bringeth forth evil things. 36 But I say unto you, That every idle word that men shall speak, they shall give account thereof in the day of judgment."

Part of the process also includes who you count as friends and what you watch on television and the Internet. **Ps 1:1** "Blessed is the man that walketh not in the counsel of the ungodly, nor standeth in the way of sinners, nor sitteth in the seat of the scornful. 2 But his delight is in the law of the LORD; and in his law doth he meditate day and night. 3 And he shall be like a tree planted by the rivers of water, that bringeth forth his fruit in his season; his leaf also shall not wither; and whatsoever he doeth shall prosper. 4 The ungodly are not so: but are like the chaff which the wind driveth away. 5 Therefore the ungodly shall not stand in the judgment, nor sinners in the congregation of the righteous. 6 For the LORD knoweth the way of the righteous: but the way of the ungodly shall perish." 1 Cor 15:33 "Be not deceived: evil communications corrupt good manners. 34 Awake to righteousness, and sin not; for some (*of you*) have not the knowledge of God: I speak this to your shame."

What gets written on your heart is what you are exposed to twenty-four hours a day—awake or asleep. If you do not control what is being written on your heart, others will. This is either an active or a passive process. God calls us to an active process of continual heart maintenance of continual right faith actions against the equally continual pull of the world. So this must be a lifestyle. It may start as an event, but it needs to become a continual-right-faith-actions lifestyle to be effective.

Heart writing is by repetition with emotional content over a period of at least ninety days. To change your heart you need to change what is repetitive in your life, and to make that new information more effective, add supporting emotional content. Faking-it emotion works fine for the subconscious mind, as it cannot tell the difference. But what has high emotional content is recalled first by the subconscious/heart to the cognitive mind in the situations of life. Emotions are the result of your thoughts, words and actions. Once stirred, these emotions help you maintain your thoughts, words and actions that initially stirred or released those emotions. This is easily confused, as often the igniting force is thoughts, but the resulting emotions are manifested, or seen, in the outward behavior. This applies to all emotions.

Your emotions follow your thoughts, words and deeds. Once active, your emotions then help keep you in those thoughts, words and deeds. Change your thoughts, words and/or deeds, and you can change your current emotions and direct new ones. If you do not control your emotions, they will control you. This is part of: 2 Cor 10:5 "Casting down imaginations, and every high thing that exalteth itself against the knowledge of God, and bringing into captivity every thought to the obedience of Christ."

Since emotions reside primarily in the subconscious mind, once released, you are usually not aware that you are in control of these emotions, or what started them. But as you become aware of them, you can manage your emotions at will.

The measure of what is in your heart is found in the words that come out of your mouth and your subsequent actions. As Jesus said: Luke 6:43 "For a good tree bringeth not forth corrupt fruit; neither doth a corrupt tree bring forth good fruit. 44 For every tree is known by his own fruit. For of thorns men do not gather figs, nor of a bramble bush gather they grapes. 45 A good man out of the good treasure of his heart bringeth forth that which is good; and an evil man out of the evil treasure of his heart bringeth forth that which is evil: for of the abundance of the heart his mouth speaketh." Matt 12:36 "But I (*Jesus*) say unto you, That every idle (*useless, does not release Heaven into the Earth*) word that men shall speak, they shall give account thereof in the day of judgment. 37 For by thy words thou shalt be justified, and by thy words thou shalt be condemned."

If you want to know the shape of your heart, get a tape recorder or ask a child (or your spouse) to help you. Do it now or face the cleansing fire of Jesus on that last day. It's your choice.

CHAPTER 6

UNDERSTANDING THE BIOLOGY AND SPIRITUALITY OF AFFIRMATIONS

Modern science is shedding light on how to get a clean, unconscious mind or heart so we can produce results that will survive the last day of God's judgment. What is even more amazing is that many of the bad or negative thoughts that God calls sin can be seen in actual tests twisting or damaging the human mind, to keep it from operating properly. For more detail, I suggest you start with any of the works of Daniel G. Amen, MD or Dr. Caroline Leaf (see Bibliography).

All thoughts in the brain are electrical impulses. New thoughts ride on top of the conscious mind and, if agreed to and thought on repetitively, cause the body to make neural networks to keep them and allow them to flow more efficiently. These networks are masses of nerve cells that adapt, grow and rebuild to transmit the new thoughts. There appear to be no real limits to how much the brain can grow this way. Driven deep enough by repetition and intensity, these thoughts or thinking habits enter your heart, and this is how you now live and handle life. As your words are the fruit of your heart, the life you live is a reflection of your heart and what has been truly embedded in it (past tense). Also, your outward life is a reflection of what you really think on as self affirmations, i.e. self-talk, not what you say you think on.

Understanding the Biology and Spirituality of Affirmations

We humans operate on self-affirmations, thoughts or voice of the conscious with their attached emotions, such as: "I like … ," "I always … ," "I love to … ," "Those people … ," "I must … ," "That makes me feel … ,"etc. These then guide or drive our attitudes, words and behaviors. Most come from the subconscious and are called self affirmations. As we obey these, we then use our brains in thought processes and actions, which work specific parts of the brain and, thus, establish our current brain structure and outward behaviors. If you change these self affirmations, you then change the brain processes and structure and, thus, your attitudes and behavior. This feature is called brain plasticity.

Your future is determined by what you think on now and either write anew, strengthen or subdue in your heart. If you do not control what your heart, or subconscious, accepts as affirmations and their emotions, then you are doomed to live by your past and what you now allow to be written into your heart. And, if you are not controlling it, others are doing it for you.

What is even more amazing is that science is discovering that a healthy mind can repair itself, and the way to get healthy is essentially to obey Phil 4:6-9. As people get rid of bitterness, unforgiveness, anger, rage, etc., their physical brains get healthier, and even major damage can be reversed or healed. Just a short few months is needed before significant results can be seen. Using the technology of men and women like Dr. Amen, experts can actually see the brain healing itself, as people forgive others and make reconciliations. Part of the key seems to be that the patient knows what they are doing and actually has faith that, as they think right thoughts and attitudes, their brains will heal, and they do.

This lends even more understanding to why Jesus said: <u>Mark 11:25</u> "And when ye stand praying, forgive, if ye have ought against any: that your Father also which is in heaven may forgive you your trespasses. 26 But if ye do not forgive, neither will your Father which is in heaven forgive your trespasses." As seen by modern science, this is not an active judgment by God. Rather, evil thoughts produce neural connections that poison your body. Again, as Holy Spirit said: <u>Isa 6:9</u> "And he said, Go, and tell this people, Hear ye indeed, but understand not; and see ye indeed, but perceive not. 10 Make the heart of this people fat, and make their ears heavy, and shut their eyes; lest they see with their eyes, and hear with their ears, and understand with their heart, and convert, and be healed." [NOTE: healing is released as you think and then act properly. Or, as shown by modern science, less toxins are released as you think more good thoughts and subdue the evil, unforgiving and anti-God thoughts.]

A wise person makes it their goal to allow their heart to be the source of God's life through them into the Earth. <u>Prov 10:8</u> "The wise in heart will receive commandments: but a prating fool shall fall. 9 He that walketh uprightly walketh surely: but he that perverteth his ways shall be known. 10 He that winketh with the eye causeth sorrow: but a prating fool shall fall. 11 The mouth of a righteous man is a well of life: but violence covereth the mouth of the wicked. 12 Hatred stirreth up strifes: but love covereth all sins. 13 In the lips of him that hath understanding wisdom is found: but a rod is for the back of him that is void of understanding. 14 Wise men lay up knowledge: but the mouth of the foolish is near destruction." Prov 13:1 "A wise son heareth his father's instruction (*to walk in the right ways of the true and living God*): but a scorner heareth not rebuke. 2 A man shall eat good by the fruit of his mouth: but the soul of the transgressors shall eat violence. 3 He that keepeth his mouth keepeth his life: but he that openeth wide his lips shall have destruction."

All long-lasting thoughts and habit patterns are cellular, neural networks. The latest information is that it takes about four days of repeated thought and action to start building a new neural network in the subconscious. Once received, thoughts and their emotions can never be removed, but they can be subordinated, by assigning new emotions and providing new thoughts. It takes about twenty-one days of a constant thought to form these new neural networks so your subconscious and conscious can handle the new thought, and about forty days to integrate them into your thought process to develop a new mindset or attitude. It takes ninety days to subordinate an old thought pattern when you attack it every day. When done, the new neural network becomes the prime thought, memory or attitude, and the old one becomes buried. If you do not attack the old, negative thought, it stays strong and is always ready to rise again and make sure you remain double-minded.

So if you go to church once a week, how effective is that in reprogramming your mind? Once a week is not very effective, as you have not built neural pathways for the teaching to remain. At best, the information stays in your cognitive mind for three to five days, and then it is lost. Occasional refreshing only keeps these thoughts in your cognitive mind in the realm of mental assent (the same as a typical New Year's resolution). You have the information, but it is not a long-lasting part of the way you live. You may quote the Scriptures but not live them.

If you listen to a sermon every day, say three to six times a day, you begin to build neural pathways after four days. But you need to repeat out loud for twenty-one continuous days the same message to "get it in you," and it also requires that you add some joy and thanksgiving. Then you need to work for the full ninety days to make it a priority attitude in your heart over other conflicting thoughts. Turn the message into a song, and sing or chant it for ninety days, and it will start to take a priority position. No matter how you cut it, this is not an overnight process, and it takes three months of solid, repeated and emotional work to get solid results and see new behaviors that remain. All this from one sermon! No wonder God had John the Baptist go before Jesus to prepare His way.

Effectiveness is in a lifestyle, not sporadic events. Now you can see why God says: Eph 5:18 "And be not drunk with wine, wherein is excess; but be (*continuously*

UNDERSTANDING THE BIOLOGY AND SPIRITUALITY OF AFFIRMATIONS

being) filled with the Spirit; 19 speaking to yourselves in psalms and hymns and spiritual songs, singing and making melody in your heart to the Lord; 20 giving thanks always for all things unto God and the Father in the name of our Lord Jesus Christ."

Songs of truth, sung for months, can make a critical difference. This is why I recommend only listening to and singing scripture songs (much of the so-called ancient, old or new Christian music cannot stand a strong scriptural review, and as such, actually hinders your growth in God or your ability to stand in a faith battle).

This right reprogramming is then made more solid by continual repetition and actual practice. Practice without the understanding of scripture does not build new attitudes very fast or completely, and attitudes without action are not right attitudes. Matt 3:5 "Then went out to him (*John*) Jerusalem, and all Judaea, and all the region round about Jordan, 6 and were baptized of him in Jordan, confessing their sins. 7 But when he (*John*) saw many of the Pharisees and Sadducees come to his baptism, he said unto them, O generation of vipers, who hath warned you to flee from the wrath to come? 8 Bring forth therefore fruits meet for repentance."

Reprogramming must translate into new and right behaviors. Continued reprogramming while doing right actions is best. The purpose is threefold:

1. To change the way you react to events with new attitudes, understandings, prejudices and interpretations,
2. To develop new or continued right behaviors governed by these new attitudes, understandings, prejudices and interpretations, and, finally,
3. To rid yourself of unrighteous thoughts, words and deeds.

All of this limits the devil in his ability to keep us deceived and driven by lust, evil fear and pride. As James put this so well: James 2:17 "Even so faith, if it hath not works, is dead, being alone. 18 Yea, a man may say, Thou hast faith, and I have works: shew me thy faith without thy works, and I will shew thee my faith by my works. 19 Thou believest that there is one God; thou doest well: the devils also believe, and tremble. 20 But wilt thou know, O vain man, that faith without works is dead?" James 1:22 "But be ye doers of the word, and not hearers only, deceiving your own selves. 23 For if any be a hearer of the word, and not a doer, he is like unto a man beholding his natural face in a glass: 24 for he beholdeth himself, and goeth his way, and straightway forgetteth what manner of man he was. 25 But whoso looketh into the perfect law of liberty, and continueth therein, he being not a forgetful hearer, but a doer of the work, this man shall be blessed in his deed. 26 If any man among you seem to be religious, and bridleth not his tongue, but deceiveth his own heart, this man's religion is vain. 27 Pure religion and undefiled before God and the Father is this, To visit the fatherless and widows in their affliction, and to keep himself unspotted from the world."

OK, God, Now What?

Self-deception in this means that just because you can quote a few scriptures or even the entire Bible but you do not walk like Jesus walked more and more, then you are not making progress in God. You may be growing in esteem with man, but not in faith, working by *agape*/love. In this deception, we substitute outworked maturity with intellectual familiarity and ritual. So you know about healing the sick or raising the dead, but you cannot do it at will, as dictated by need or desire. Or you may know the Law inside and out, yet walk in unforgiveness toward God or man.

There is strong evidence that what thoughts you allow (and, therefore, what behaviors you find acceptable) can have dramatic reactions in your actual brain structure, i.e., your current brain biology. Dr. Daniel Amen, in his book, *Change Your Brain Change Your Life* (New York: Three River Press: 1998) and Dr. Carolyn Leaf, in her book, *Who Switched Off My Brain* (Switch On Your Brain USA: 2008), relate that biblically negative thoughts, such as unforgiveness, bitterness, rage, etc., actually produce different types of neural connections. So when we think bad or destructive thoughts with these neurons, we release toxins into the blood stream, which, over time, can make the body sick, weak and even cause it to die early. The more you think these evil thoughts, the more you poison yourself. This is the biology of sin, as it is virtually impossible to do any action without supporting thoughts and, for most people, supporting words.

Neural connections supporting positive and good thoughts do not have these toxic features. This is the biology of righteousness. The way you talk is a reflection of what is in your heart and, thus, the physical features of your brain. God has long ago said: Ps 34:12 "What man is he that desireth life, and loveth many days, that he may see good? 13 Keep thy tongue from evil, and thy lips from speaking guile. 14 Depart from evil, and do good; seek peace, and pursue it." 1 Pet 3:10 "For he that will *agape*/love life, and see good days, let him refrain his tongue from evil, and his lips that they speak no guile: 11 let him eschew evil, and do good; let him seek peace, and ensue (*aggressively seek*) it." Prov 10:20 "The tongue of the just is as choice silver: the heart of the wicked is little worth. 21 The lips of the righteous feed many: but fools die for want of wisdom." Prov 17:4 "A wicked doer giveth heed to false lips; and a liar giveth ear to a naughty tongue."

The brain is much like a muscle, and the parts that you use most often will show a different level of development and blood supply than those parts used less often. This can actually be seen with technology. Again, unacceptable or non-biblical and non-blessed behaviors can actually cause the brain to adapt to those kinds of thoughts and, thus, show a different kind of functioning than biblically-blessed behaviors or a brain more practiced in blessed behaviors. The implications are that long life may have less to do with what you eat or physical exercise and more with how well you match the Bible standard of a righteous life and, most importantly, a righteous tongue and righteous affirmations.

CHAPTER 7

UNDERSTANDING RESISTANCE TO CHANGE

As you are building new thoughts, and while you ignore or attack old thoughts and their neural pathways, they actually call out to you not to do the new ideas and, thus, they give you unease. This is because the subconscious thinks that whatever is programmed into it is "normal," and the self-correcting mechanism fights to get back to "normal." So the sum total of your past is your "normal," but we are designed by God to go into corrupt places and clean them up. (In Genesis 1, God told Adam to subdue and establish dominion for and with God.) If you think like God, then your natural mechanism keeps you thinking that way while you go into places of confusion and bring about God's right order. Thus, if you start off with a right heart and keep it clean daily, you, like Jesus, can go into "the valley of the shadow of death" and still "fear no evil."

We may call this inner-defense mechanism our conscience. The trouble is that our conscience also must be retrained or reprogrammed. 1 Cor 8:12 "But when ye sin so against the brethren, and wound their weak conscience, ye sin against Christ. 13 Wherefore, if meat make my brother to offend, I will eat no flesh while the world standeth, lest I make my brother to offend." 1 Tim 4:2 "Speaking lies in hypocrisy; having their conscience seared with a hot iron." Titus 1:15 "Unto the pure all things are pure: but unto them that are defiled and unbelieving is nothing pure; but even their mind and conscience is defiled. 16 They profess that they know God; but in works they deny him, being abominable, and disobedient, and unto every good work reprobate." 1 Tim 1:5 "Now the end of the commandment is *agape*/charity out of a pure heart, and of a good conscience, and of faith unfeigned."

Thus, the quite common statement, "follow your conscience," is only valid if your conscience thinks like Jesus. This "self-correcting," or "past-reaffirming" part called the conscience needs purifying and continual maintenance with continual right faith actions to stay aligned with the Holy Spirit mind of Christ.

If you think like the devil, then that same "self-normalizing" mechanism of the subconscious keeps you thinking like the devil, even if you do not want those thoughts. On top of that, this is how the devil keeps us in bondage. He blasts those same thoughts at us incessantly. As long as you do not replace them and then attack them, you think them, and you drive and reinforce them into your heart and therefore remain in bondage.

Your logical, cogitative mind may want to go one way, but your subconscious, that self-normalizing powerhouse, keeps serving you your own emotion-laden thoughts to keep you where you have been. So to reprogram or establish right thinking with authority in your mind and heart, you do not ignore evil thoughts; you attack them and replace them with *agape*/love and truth. You must continue this for some ninety days before they are subdued, and you must do this one by one as they are discovered.

Top athletes use this same technology. The subconscious cannot tell real life from your imagination or what you read in a book. So if you visualize the right action and walk through the right actions repeatedly in your mind, your "natural" instincts will start to match your visualizations. Positive emotions make it even stronger.

My son is an airline pilot and a former combat pilot. Good pilots visualize often what to do in all possible conditions, so when critical situations arise, they can do the right things without thinking or "second guessing." It is the same for top athletes. Positive proper visualization trains the subconscious, and the more you do it, the more you will act as you trained your subconscious when you need it most. The result is that bad-performance thought patterns are extinguished or lessened, and good patterns and thoughts are strengthened. A star athlete or a ballerina "in the zone" has complete congruency between their conscious mind, their unconscious mind and their body, to operate at peak performance, according to the strong emotion-linked images and affirmations in their subconscious. Again, this is a process in which it takes at least several months to see improved results.

Let's look at a case needing divine healing. You decide to believe God for a healing, and you proclaim healing scriptures such as: Isa 53:5 "But he was wounded for our transgressions, he was bruised for our iniquities: the chastisement of our

Understanding Resistance to Change

peace was upon him; and with his stripes we are healed." But every time you do it, your mind is filled with thoughts, such as, "This is not real," "What are you, a saint?" "The doctor said ... ," and on and on it goes. If you are double-minded, not united in your heart, you will give up before seeing the victory. If you are more single-minded, you will not ever stop. Thus, success depends on persistence and diligence in the face of much resistance and confusion. You are in the world of the Parable of the Sower and the Seed, according to Matt 13, Mark 4 and Luke 8.

Your worldly, trained protective system will tell you (and, according to the Parable of the Sower, the devil will also tell you) prayer for healing will not work. Still, as you persevere through the chaos in your mind, you will see results. Part of what you are doing, as you pray night and day according to Luke 18:1-4, is reprogramming your mind and heart. As long as you are single-minded in what you are doing, even if you are plagued with negative thoughts and the words of negative people, you will finally reap good results. [NOTE: If this is your situation, please get our book, *Battle Prayer for Divine Healing, Field Manual 2*, for more details on getting healing results.]

Even professional athletes describe having to battle through these self-normalizing thoughts, or the old, evil conscience, to improve their performance. They, just like the person striving for healing, have to keep at it against a constant bombardment of past thoughts, habits, attitudes and ways of doing things. The more the athlete does to reaffirm the right behaviors and attitudes and attack the counterproductive ones, the less the old normalizing thoughts come, and the more the new thoughts take priority. It is still a ninety-day process, at best, and can take much longer if you exercise little diligence. Of course, athletes typically do not recognize the devil as part of the process in keeping them bound in failure, but truth will set you free. So, along with their coach, they keep focused on right actions, and they do see results. This is just as Jesus said: John 8:31 "Then said Jesus to those Jews which believed on him, If ye continue in my word, then are ye my disciples indeed; 32 and ye shall know the truth, and the truth shall make you free." High-intensity mind and body work is included in the words *"continue in my words"* and *"know the truth."*

An athlete will achieve human results, if he follows this as a medical or scientific process. If he calls on God to help him in the process, then he can get supernatural results also. Rom 2:11 "For there is no respect of persons with God." 2 Chron 19:7 "Wherefore now let the fear of the LORD be upon you; take heed and do it: for there is no iniquity with the LORD our God, nor respect of persons, nor taking of gifts." A good man and a bad man can plant the same seed in the same soil. If they both do the same things, they will both get the same harvest. If a man activates the blessing of God in the process, he will receive blessed results or abundance.

OK, God, Now What?

A key in this process is to know that as you work to manifest God's Word in your life with continual godly faith actions you will experience resistance (a combination of your past, corrupted subconscious mind of godless strongholds and the devil defending his work of lies and deception in you and those around you). Jesus promised this resistance for anyone attempting to turn to more of God's ways in repentance or godly growth. The devil will attack you to make you stop believing the Word of God you are exercising faith for. This is one of the main messages of the Parable of the Sower and the Word of God as Seed in Matthew 13, Mark 4 and Luke 8. Knowing this parable is to know one of the major secrets of the Kingdom of God. Whether you sow the Word of God into yourself or others sow it for you, the effect is the same; you are now in a fight with the devil over that Word of God.

Such attacks or resistance from the devil are described in these ways:

1. Taking the Word of God out of your heart right away, as you are already hardened in that area of truth.
2. Making you offended at God and others over that Word through times of temptation, trial and offense.
3. Distracting you with the cares and pleasures of this world so you no longer *lambano* or do the faith works to allow God to manifest that Word.

Only those who weather/*lambano* God in His Word by continual right faith actions against this intense confusion and storms of life by the expert liar, tempter and deceiver will bring forth the promised fruit, or manifestation, of that Word in abundance.

Failure to understand this battle process means you will spend much time in bewilderment and offense, while the devil keeps you distracted. Daily use of the Affirmations and the Psalms will help you to move from offended victim to a valiant overcomer, by a vigorous, diligent and long-term mind-renewing program.

As a start, try reading Galatians, Ephesians, Philippians and Colossians every day. For most, this takes about an hour, or roughly 15 minutes per letter. The Affirmation Magnets are a more efficient tool, but reading these letters every day, for say 1 year, will get you started. Remember, repetition of the same material over and over is how you write things on your heart. Then gradually add in the full set of Affirmation Magnets as you can. This can be the start of your life-transforming, mind-renewing program.

Chapter 8

Understanding The Power of Fear

The Scriptures indicate that the root of bondage to anything in your life that is not like Jesus is fear. Heb 2:14 "Forasmuch then as the children are partakers of flesh and blood, he also himself likewise took part of the same; that through death he might destroy him that had the power of death, that is, the devil; 15 and deliver them who through fear of death were all their lifetime subject to bondage." The only fear you are to have is the fear of God, and that causes you to seek, hear and obey Him. That puts you in the Old Testament. Understanding comes in the New Testament.

A simple way to understand this is that evil or standard fear is an anointing to believe that what the devil says can happen, will happen. Bible faith is an anointing to believe that what God says can happen, will happen. The issue is whose report will you believe and advertise? Isa 53:1 "Who hath believed (*advertised, done faith actions over*) our report? and to whom is the arm of the Lord revealed?"

Throughout the Bible we are told, some three hundred and sixty-five times, not to fear or be afraid, and many more times by inference. For example, look at this New Testament command: Phil 4:6 "Be careful (*anxious, fearful*) for nothing; but in every thing by prayer and supplication with thanksgiving let your requests be made known unto God. 7 And the peace of God, which passeth all understanding, shall keep your hearts and minds through Christ Jesus."

OK, God, Now What?

Notice the first part of verse 6, "Be careful/*anxious* for nothing." What is left out of "nothing?" For most of us, the reality is that we do not obey this command, but, rather, we color our lives with hidden meaning, to allow us to remain in evil fear, while God has commanded us not to tolerate it. Rebellion is not doing things God's way, and rebellion against God and His commands is sin. When we tolerate fear, then where are we? Rom 14:23 "… for whatsoever is not of faith is sin." 1 John 5:17 "All unrighteousness is sin … ." 1 John 3:8 "He that committeth sin is of the devil; for the devil sinneth from the beginning. For this purpose the Son of God was manifested, that he might destroy the works of the devil."

Who but the devil would want you to disobey God and not get rid of the very things that keep you from the abundance of *zoe*/life that Jesus came to give us? John 10:10 "The thief cometh not, but for to steal, and to kill, and to destroy: I am come that they might have *zoe*/life, and that they might have it more abundantly."

So how do you attack fear to obey Phil 4:6? Here it the answer addressed directly to Christians who do not have a Jewish heritage. Phil 4:4 "Rejoice in the Lord alway: and again I say, Rejoice. 5 Let your moderation (*right living in God*) be known unto all men. The Lord is at hand. 6 Be careful (*anxious, even of mild fear*) for nothing; but in every thing by prayer and supplication with thanksgiving let your *aiteo*/requests be made known unto God. 7 And the peace of God, which passeth all understanding, shall keep your hearts and minds through Christ Jesus. 8 Finally, brethren, whatsoever things are true, whatsoever things are honest, whatsoever things are just, whatsoever things are pure, whatsoever things are lovely, whatsoever things are of good report; if there be any virtue, and if there be any praise, think on these things. 9 Those things, which ye have both learned, and received, and heard, and seen in me, do: and the God of peace shall be with you." Notice, in verse 6, that you are to detect and attack every fear, even mild anxieties, whenever you discover them. Large or small fear of anything but God is your enemy.

The only fear you are allowed is the fear of God, knowing that His ways are best and, on the Day of Judgment, that which you built in your life without Him is called wood, hay and stubble and will be destroyed. That which you and He built together is called gold, silver and jewels, and these are of value to you forever. Notice that for the Christian this is not about you; it is about your works.

For the Christian: 1 Cor 3:11 "For other foundation can no man lay than that is laid, which is Jesus Christ. 12 Now if any man build upon this foundation gold, silver, precious stones, wood, hay, stubble; 13 every man's work shall be made manifest: for the day shall declare it, because it shall be revealed by fire; and the fire shall try every man's work of what sort it is. 14 If any man's work abide which he hath built thereupon, he shall receive a reward. 15 If any man's work shall be burned, he shall suffer loss: but he himself shall be *sozo*/saved; yet so as by fire. 16 Know ye not that ye are the temple of God, and that the Spirit of God dwelleth in you?" Notice that, for the Christian, it is your life's works that are tested, not you, the born-again one. As a Christian, you are a new kind of creature, and Holy Spirit is one with your spirit. 1 Cor 6:17 "But he that is joined unto the Lord is one spirit." You will survive that Day, but your un-Jesus-like works and thoughts will not.

Let us go back to Phil 4:6. This is like a daily scrubbing after you finally get clean; you still have to get rid of the dirt of the day every day. Just as you bathe physically, you need to bathe spiritually. God's answer was given in: Josh 1:8 "This book of the law shall not depart out of thy mouth; but thou shalt meditate therein day and night, that thou mayest observe to do according to all that is written therein: for then thou shalt make thy way prosperous, and then thou shalt have good success. 9 Have not I commanded thee? Be strong and of a good courage; be not afraid, neither be thou dismayed: for the LORD thy God is with thee whithersoever thou goest." This command is included in a lifestyle of continual right faith actions.

This is an everyday and all-day chewing of the cud of God's Word, the meaning of the Hebrew word translated as *meditation*. It is not emptying your mind; rather it is keeping it filled with the right stuff—God's Word—with an attitude of doing it in muttering, speaking, chanting or singing. So the promise to Joshua was: here is how you fight fear daily because you will face lots of it in the days to come. Notice, the promise was that you would be attacked with fear often and continuously. Fear God or fear the devil. Whatever you do you are fearing someone. Choose to fear God, and thus, obey Him and live.

Now we can understand what is happening. When we ask God to bless us, He starts with cleaning up our mouth and attitudes and by getting truth into us, so that we can make our own way successful, with right words and deeds emanating from good thoughts in our hearts. Then He can magnify or make those right thoughts and deeds more abundant or blessed. He then gets us to do right works that He can bless. John 8:31 "Then said Jesus to those Jews which believed on him, If ye continue in my word, then are ye my disciples indeed; 32 and ye shall know the truth, and the truth shall make you free." 2 Tim 2:24 "And the servant of the Lord must not strive; but be gentle unto all men, apt to teach, patient, 25 in meekness instructing those that oppose themselves; if God peradventure will give them repentance to the acknowledging of the truth; 26 and that they may recover themselves out of the snare of the devil, who are taken captive by him at his will."

We attack fear by obeying: Phil 4:6 "Be careful (*anxious*) for nothing; but in every thing by prayer and supplication with thanksgiving let your *aiteo*/requests be made known unto God." Here we are commanded, not asked, to fight fear, and we are to do it through *aiteo* prayer. This means quoting a scripture promise over the problem, demanding that God do what He said He would do and fulfill that scripture, and supplicating Him to heal the hearts of all the people involved (yours included). You are to do this every time you feel any fear or evil anger, no matter how tiny. After you have thus *aiteo*/prayed, you then enter into thanksgiving. Then you can go about doing what you can to resolve the things you were careful about or in great fear of.

This *thanksgiving* is not quiet or polite. Imagine a football game in which your team has just made a touchdown. The crowd goes wild with rejoicing, and you also go wild, and in the process, thank the players and the coaches for doing such a great job. That is thanksgiving. So to obey Phil 4:6, you give thanks until you are thankful. It may take one second, one hour, one day, one week, one month, one year, or one decade. Whatever it takes, you repeat it until you *are* thankful, because you know it is taken care of, and you *will* see God's answer. Thank God that your mighty weapons of rejoicing include laughing, dancing, proclaiming Scripture, arm waving, shouting and singing in joy, praise and thanksgiving!

Also included in this process is dealing with unforgiveness. Jesus warned that unforgiveness could be a major hindrance to your faith in God in prayer. Since fear is the opposite, or the enemy, of faith, unforgiveness opens you to evil fear. Matt 6:12 "And forgive us our debts, as we forgive our debtors. 13 And lead us not into temptation, but deliver us from evil: for thine is the kingdom, and the power, and the glory, for ever. Amen. 14 For if ye forgive men their trespasses, your heavenly Father will also forgive you: 15 but if ye forgive not men their trespasses, neither will your Father forgive your trespasses." Mark 11:22 "And Jesus answering saith unto them, Have faith in God. 23 For verily I say unto you, That whosoever shall say unto this mountain, Be thou removed, and be thou cast into the sea; and shall not doubt in his heart, but shall believe that those things which he saith shall come to pass; he shall have whatsoever he saith. 24 Therefore I say unto you, What things soever ye *aiteo*/desire (*demand, require and expect as due by covenant promise*), when ye pray, believe (*by faith actions*) that ye receive them, and ye shall have them. 25 And when ye stand praying, forgive, if ye have ought against any: that your Father also which is in heaven may forgive you your trespasses. 26 But if ye do not forgive, neither will your Father which is in heaven forgive your trespasses."

In both of these major passages on prayer, Jesus tells us that unforgiveness is a major prayer hindrance, so ask the Lord to show you where you have any unforgiveness toward anyone, including God Himself. You can even harbor unforgiveness against Him for allowing you to experience the trouble that causes you to fear, or you might be thinking, "Lord, if You loved me so much, how did You let this happen?" "Why has it taken so long to be resolved?" "Why are these people so stupid and/or mean?" The answer is the same in all cases: Luke 6:27 "But I say unto you which hear, *Agape*/love your enemies, do good to them which hate you, 28 bless them that curse you, and pray for them which despitefully use you." Matt 5:44 "But I say unto you, *Agape*/love your enemies, bless them that curse you, do good to them that hate you, and pray for them which despitefully use you, and

Understanding the Power of Fear

persecute you; 45 that ye may be the children of your Father which is in heaven: for he maketh his sun to rise on the evil and on the good, and sendeth rain on the just and on the unjust." This is also the reason we are to bless and praise the Lord at all times, so that we can keep our heart right when things go wrong. A good place to start is to repeat all one hundred and fifty of the psalms for a heart-check (this takes four to six hours for most people).

There is a dark side of fear that science is now recognizing: Fear kills. The more fear you walk in, the more you walk in the anointing of what the devil says is true and will happen and, therefore, the more you walk in death. Through brain scans, science can now spot a brain trained in fear. Like a muscle, the brain gets more blood to those parts of the brain that are used most often. If you focus on fear, then those parts of the brain become open for more blood, and this can be seen in the scan. The more you think in evil fear, the more the blood flows to those areas, and the more easily those parts of the brain are used. They become the first or easiest choice.

At the microscopic level, the neurons that form to support the fear-based thoughts are different from those formed by positive, overcoming thoughts. These evil fear neurons actually leak poisons into the body, as they are exercised by the fear-based thoughts. Thus, each evil fear thought is like a tiny pump that releases toxic neurochemicals into the blood stream. It is not just the situations of life that are the problem; it is how we react to those situations that controls the quality of our life and the type of neurons we develop and maintain. Continued negative and ungodly responses to the guaranteed problems of life actually kill or shorten your life. Of course, the more you tolerate and exercise evil fear, the more vocal you will be in anger, rage and negativism, contaminating those around you.

Our bodies have many natural chemicals in them, which, in their place, are beneficial, but if released into your system, can be deadly. For example, stomach acids are critical to digestion, but if released by either acid reflux or when there is damage to the stomach lining, these same acids form painful and even deadly ulcers. Negative, fear-based neurons leak neurochemicals that act as toxins to the rest of the body. Due to the increased blood flow in these well-exercised evil or normal fear neurons, the toxins then get quickly into the blood, to poison or stress the rest of your body. Of course, the more you focus on fear and worry, stress and all the myriad of ways we as a culture disguise them—such as irritation, shortness of temper, sadness, selfishness, "reality," depression, and pessimism, etc.—the more you pump these damaging toxins into your systems.

Do you need to respond to the things that cause worry? Absolutely, starting with Phil 4:6-9, and then going and doing what you can, but refuse to operate in fear. First obey Phil 4:6, until you can go on in glad confidence that God has heard you and will answer. Remember, faith prays the end from the beginning and calls those things that be not as if they were, and does it all in the name of Jesus. 2 Cor 5:7 "For

OK, GOD, NOW WHAT?

we walk by faith (*actions in advance of the answer*), not by sight (*what you now see*)." So keep confessing scripture over the situation, commanding the problem to go, and commanding the situation to get right, as you want it to be in the end, according to God's covenant promises. Do all this with glad thanksgiving—faking it if necessary. According to Luke 18:1, we are to keep at it until we see the answer.

It is when you improperly handle these things that incite worry that you make a way for worry and fear to continue and, thus, keep poisoning yourself. Heb 2:14 "Forasmuch then as the children are partakers of flesh and blood, he also himself likewise took part of the same; that through death he might destroy him that had the power of death, that is, the devil; 15 and deliver them who through fear of death were all their lifetime subject to bondage. 16 For verily he took not on him the nature of angels; but he took on him the seed of Abraham. 17 Wherefore in all things it behoved him to be made like unto his brethren, that he might be a merciful and faithful high priest in things pertaining to God, to make reconciliation for the sins of the people. 18 For in that he himself hath suffered being tempted, he is able to succour them that are tempted."

One secret from the Scriptures is that the only kind of fear that does not release deadly toxins is right fear, fear of the Lord, the fear Jesus walked in. This kind of godly fear causes you to seek, hear and gladly obey God, even when you do not fully understand Him. Had we done this all our lives, then we would have obeyed Phil 4:6-9 and: Eph 5:14 "Wherefore he saith, Awake thou that sleepest, and arise from the dead, and Christ shall give thee light. 15 See then that ye walk circumspectly, not as fools, but as wise, 16 redeeming the time, because the days are evil. 17 Wherefore be ye not unwise, but understanding what the will of the Lord is. 18 And be not drunk with wine, wherein is excess; but be filled with the Spirit; 19 speaking to yourselves in psalms and hymns and spiritual songs, singing and making melody in your heart to the Lord; 20 giving thanks always for all things unto God and the Father in the name of our Lord Jesus Christ; 21 submitting yourselves one to another in the fear of God."

Had we obeyed these New Testament scriptures faithfully, this would have put us on the path of obeying and walking in: Josh 1:5 "There shall not any man be able to stand before thee all the days of thy life: as I was with Moses, so I will be with thee: I will not fail thee, nor forsake thee. 6 Be strong and of a good courage: for unto this people shalt thou divide for an inheritance the land, which I sware unto their fathers to give them. 7 Only be thou strong and very courageous, that thou mayest observe to do according to all the law, which Moses my servant commanded thee: turn not from it to the right hand or to the left, that thou mayest prosper whithersoever thou goest. 8 This book of the law shall not depart out of thy mouth; but thou shalt meditate therein day and night, that thou mayest observe to do according to all that is written therein: for then thou shalt make thy way prosperous, and then thou shalt have good success. 9 Have not I commanded thee? Be strong and of a good courage; be not afraid, neither be thou dismayed: for the LORD thy God is with thee whithersoever thou goest."

We are promised many troubles in this life, first, just because we are here and the devil is still loose and, second, because we are to go and destroy the works of the devil and make the world a better place for God, according to His command to Adam and Eve. Gen 1:28 "And God blessed them, and God said unto them, Be fruitful, and multiply, and replenish the earth, and subdue it: and have dominion over the fish of the sea, and over the fowl of the air, and over every living thing that moveth upon the earth." Just as Jesus did, go and find where the devil is operating and subdue him and establish God's right dominion. This is the proper response of God for any evil fear or condition we encounter. Doing this will keep you in the righteous fear of God and out of the evil (or normal) fear of the devil. But as we operate in evil fear to the issues of life, we are really saying that the devil's ways are lord, and we are not attacking them to effectively establish and re-affirm the Lordship of Jesus Christ.

God says it takes these fear-inducing paths to refine or grow your soul: Ps 23:3 "He restoreth my soul: he leadeth me in the paths of righteousness for his name's sake. 4 Yea, though I walk through the valley of the shadow of death, I will fear no evil: for thou art with me; thy rod and thy staff they comfort me." It is in the valley (either because of our sin, other's sin, the devil attacking us, or our attacking the enemy) that we get to face the devil eye-to-eye. Satan wants you to operate in evil fear so that he can get you to kill yourself and be ineffective in your awesome power in Jesus. God wants you to stand so that you can receive His life. Ps 23:5 "Thou preparest a table before me **in the presence of mine enemies**: thou anointest my head with oil; my cup runneth over. 6 Surely goodness and *chesed*/mercy shall follow me all the days of my life: and I will dwell in the house of the LORD for ever."

God is for you in the evil day, so that you can stand against the devil and win. Eph 6:10 "Finally, my brethren, be strong in the Lord, and in the power of his might. 11 Put on the whole armour of God, that ye may be able to stand against the wiles of the devil. 12 For we wrestle not against flesh and blood, but against principalities, against powers, against the rulers of the darkness of this world, against spiritual wickedness in high places. 13 Wherefore take unto you the whole armour of God, that ye may be able to withstand in the evil day, and having done all, to stand. 14 Stand (*by faith actions*) therefore, having your loins girt about with truth, and having on the breastplate of righteousness; 15 and your feet shod with the preparation of the gospel of peace; 16 above all, taking the shield of faith (*actions*), wherewith ye shall be able to quench all the fiery darts of the wicked. 17 And take the helmet of salvation, and the sword of the Spirit, which is the word of God: 18 praying always with all prayer and supplication in the Spirit, and watching thereunto with all perseverance and supplication for all saints; 19 and for me, that utterance may be given unto me, that I may open my mouth boldly [*in the face of evil fear*], to make known the mystery of the gospel." Notice that our job is to be strong in the strength of the Lord, standing, girding, putting on, taking and praying in the evil day. He will strengthen you in your standing. Ps 27:14 "Wait (*entwine by faith actions*) on the LORD: be of good courage (*by faith actions*), and he shall strengthen thine heart: wait (*entwine by faith actions*), I say, on the LORD."

CHAPTER 9

UNDERSTANDING THE POWER OF FAITH

Sheer persistence, grit and determination do count! They are actually part of the process, part of real faith. Unbelief fears that God will not do it, but faith believes that God will fulfill His Word with thanksgiving. God requires that we keep proclaiming His Word, expecting Him to do it over any situation, until it is done. We know, at even the natural-law level, that speaking life and right working produces abundant results in plants and animals. So, rather than complaining at what is not working, keep telling the non-working part to work well until it does.

Moving to the Christian level, doing the same in the name of Jesus actives the unlimited and all-powerful *zoe* life of God. Again, faith is a matter of persistence, grit and determination. Like tiny grains of sand in a bucket, if your faith is small, keep adding grains of sand one at a time, and eventually the bucket will be full. Like a small seed, keep it alive, and it will grow into a mighty tree.

Jesus summed it up this way: Luke 18:1 "And he spake a parable unto them to this end, that men ought always to pray, and not to faint." This word *pray* does not mean to beg, but to command that things go the way God wants. There is no sickness or disease or infirmity in Heaven, so God does not have any of that to dish out. Keep commanding for your health to become what God intended and do it in the name of Jesus, and it will.

Understanding the Power of Faith

Look at the "Our Father" for the number of command words underlined: <u>Matt 6:9</u> "After this manner therefore pray ye: Our Father which art in heaven, <u>hallowed be</u> thy name. 10 <u>Thy kingdom come</u>. <u>Thy will be done in earth</u>, as it is in heaven. 11 <u>Give us</u> this day our daily bread. 12 And <u>forgive us</u> our debts, as we forgive our debtors. 13 And <u>lead us</u> not into temptation, but <u>deliver us</u> from evil: For thine is the kingdom, and the power, and the glory, for ever. Amen." Now count the number of begging words in that prayer. That is right, THERE ARE NONE! If this is the sample, then this is the path of persistence, grit and determination. Faith is counting the unseen as done. Faith in God is expecting Him to produce as we follow His processes. So get with His process, and start counting a few of those blessings in thanksgiving!

Again, recognize all evil fear—large or small—quote a greater promise of God, and then demand that He perform that word in you as He has promised (see the Greek definition in the Glossary of the word *aiteo*, often translated as "ask" {see John 14-16 for its repeated use}), and then thank Him for what you do not yet see. Thank Him with loud and strong actions, joy and praise, and keep at it until you are walking in gratitude. If this sounds extreme, consider which definition of life you want: a happy four-year-old or a semi-drugged forty-year-old.

We now understand some of the mechanics of God's ancient ways, available to all who will perform them in obedience. The heart, often mentioned in the Bible, can be considered your subconscious mind. <u>Prov 4:23</u> "Keep thy heart with all diligence; for out of it are the issues of life." *Diligence* implies regular, consistent and hard work, no matter what tries to get in the way. Like the U.S. Postman, nothing stops you; every single day you deliver, no matter what. That is diligence.

From science we learn that the subconscious mind does not know right from wrong, the real from imagination, but operates on whatever it is told. The two primary mechanisms are:

a) What you experience every day—from outside your body and inside your soul,
b) What you control by thoughts and dreams, visualizations or imagination – from inside your body by or through your soul.

Thoughts, combined with right faith actions such as giving thanks for something you do not yet see, are just as real to the subconscious as if you already had what you are thinking. This is the realm of faith. You are in true faith when you act in joy for what you hope for, as hope is not a wish, but a rejoicing that you have what is yet unseen, based on God's promise. This is true biblical hope, not the hope we see in modern usage.

God honors His Word and faith in His Word, not our wishes or our needs. According to Phil 4:6, as you quote a scripture containing a good promise and demand that God perform it, you release Him to start to work. With high-intensity thanksgiving, you drive the goal into your subconscious, and the more you drive it in, or write it on your heart, the more neural pathways are created, and the deeper the pathway or the higher the priority the thought has for recall. Do this often enough, and you will walk around in joy, praise and thanksgiving, knowing that God is at work for you, and you will see His goodness in the land of the living. Just as you are assured that a catalog order is on the way, so is your needed answer, as you remain in thanksgiving over it. The more you attack every anxiety this way, the more joy you will walk in, and the more answers to prayer you will receive. This is what is meant by 2 Cor 5:7 "For we walk by faith (*continual faith actions*), not by sight." Consider the situation, consider God, and then give Him the glory in right faith actions.

Here is a biblical description of faith: Heb 11:1 "Now faith is the substance of things hoped for (*the joyful praises of coming expected good, and this joyful expectation to loud praises and thanksgiving is*) the evidence of things not seen. 2 For by it the elders obtained a good report. 3 Through faith we understand that the worlds were framed by the word of God, so that things which are seen were not made of things which do appear." This is powerful stuff. You take a promise of God, convince yourself in your heart that He cannot lie and then demonstrate faith or believing by loud and joyful praise and thanksgiving. By this, you counter the world-view that what is will be, and you cannot change it in any way. Instead, watch Father God perform His Word at the direction of your faith actions in Him, by Jesus.

The functional definition of faith is the same, for the evidence of faith is the thanksgiving and joy you display (included in the meaning of the biblical word *hope*). Can you get answered prayer without active joy, thanksgiving and praise? Yes, but you will not walk in a victorious life, because, by definition, a victorious life knows it has everything needed at any time and will overcome no matter what, knows that God is there to get it done through thanksgiving, praise and joy, in faith actions, working by *agape*/love.

Remember, in the Bible a simple definition is that your mind is your conscious mind, and your heart is your unconscious mind. Both are to be trained into the true ways of God. 2 Cor 10:4 "(For the weapons of our warfare are not carnal, but mighty through God to the pulling down of strong holds;) 5 casting down imaginations, and every high thing that exalteth itself against the knowledge of God, and bringing into captivity every thought to the obedience of Christ." So the battle is thought by thought, not day by day.

With the goals of attacking every anxiety and bringing every thought into submission to Jesus, you can see why Paul said: 1 Cor 15:10 "But by the grace of God I am what I am: and his grace which was bestowed upon me was not in vain; but I laboured more abundantly than they all: yet not I, but the grace of God which was

Understanding the Power of Faith

with me." God will help us do the work, but we have to make the required effort. Ps 27:14 "Wait (*entwine by faith actions*) on the Lord: be of good courage (*by faith actions*), and he shall strengthen thine heart: wait (*entwine by faith actions*), I say, on the Lord." Ps 31:24 "Be of good courage (*by faith actions*), and he shall strengthen your heart, all ye that hope in the Lord." He is there to help us, as we do the work of being courageous with continual right faith actions, but ultimate success is up to us.

Here is a great prayer: "Lord, get and keep me moving in Your paths." Ps 25:4 "Shew me thy ways, O Lord; teach me thy paths. 5 Lead me in thy truth, and teach me: for thou art the God of my salvation; on thee do I wait (*by continual right faith actions*) all the day. 6 Remember, O Lord, thy *racham*/tender mercies and thy *chesed*/lovingkindnesses; for they have been ever of old." Ps 27:11 "Teach me thy way, O Lord, and lead me in a plain path, because of mine enemies." Ps 119:33 "Teach me, O Lord, the way of thy statutes; and I shall keep it unto the end. 34 Give me understanding, and I shall keep thy law; yea, I shall observe it with my whole heart. 35 Make me to go in the path of thy commandments; for therein do I delight. 36 Incline my heart unto thy testimonies, and not to covetousness. 37 Turn away mine eyes from beholding vanity; and quicken thou me in thy way. 38 Stablish thy word unto thy servant, who is devoted to thy fear."

Then start thanking God, because He says: Phil 2:13 "For it is God which worketh in you both to will and to do of his good pleasure. 14 Do all things without murmurings and disputings: 15 that ye may be blameless and harmless, the sons of God, without rebuke, in the midst of a crooked and perverse nation, among whom ye shine as lights in the world; 16 holding forth the word of *zoe*/life; that I may rejoice in the day of Christ, that I have not run in vain, neither laboured in vain."

How amazing! The God of the Universe is working in us, and often we do not even acknowledge that He is there, much less that He is interested in what we do day by day and moment by moment. Yet Jesus taught us to call God our Father, and the Spirit within us calls Him Daddy.

Since by definition faith is the joyful expectation of a coming good, as you do the works of faith (in the actions of thanksgiving, praise, rejoicing and supporting acts), you are continually processing strong, positive, godly thoughts and emotion-actions. And with diligent and glad repetition you build good neurons and replace or heal existing toxic neurons. This builds godly attitudes and strengthens your health, lifespan and quality of life.

One summation of this faith action process is found in Phil 4:4-9. As you counter every evil fear, worry, concern or major threat rightly:

a. You build and maintain good neural connections.
b. You build godly faith attitudes in your heart/subconscious mind and cognitive mind.

OK, God, Now What?

c. You heal/replace/diminish old toxic neural connections.
d. You build the paths that allows God to manifest Heaven on Earth for and through you.
e. With new godly attitudes, you prevent new evil fear, toxic neural connections from forming.
f. Your joy, love, peace, physical prosperity, health and longevity increase.
g. Your confidence in God, by His covenant promises, increases, so your prayer life becomes powerful, for yourself and others.
h. You start to complete the mission given to Adam and re-initiated by Jesus to subdue and establish the dominion of God, as you crush and bruise Satan in destroying his works of darkness and his lordship in the Earth. Rom 16:20 "And the God of peace shall bruise (*crush, destroy, remove from power*) Satan under your feet shortly (*as shattered glass*). The grace of our Lord Jesus Christ be with you [*to know, be, do and desire this*]. Amen."
i. You go from being a victim to an *agape* love warrior of God who enjoys bringing Heaven to Earth.

The understanding of biblical faith is to know that the power of faith actions releases the pressure of righteousness unto *zoe* life to release the Kingdom of God wherever you continually apply it in continual right faith actions. Thus, persistence and grit in continual-right-faith actions is how God has sovereignly decreed what man is to do to make the Kingdom of God a reality on the Earth.

Jesus said: Matt 18:18 "Verily I say unto you, Whatsoever ye shall bind on earth shall be bound in heaven: and whatsoever ye shall loose on earth shall be loosed in heaven." Heaven is waiting on you to make a faith-action stand. When a child of God speaks like Jesus, Heaven agrees, and Hell obeys. You are connected to the greatest God in the Universe. He is waiting to enforce your faith-action stand. 1 Tim 6:12 "Fight the good fight of faith (*continual right faith actions*), *lambano*/lay hold on eternal *zoe*/life, whereunto thou art also called, and hast professed a good profession before many witnesses." And 1 Cor 15:58 "Therefore, my *agape*/beloved brethren, be steadfast, unmovable, always abounding in the (*faith action*) work of the Lord, since you know that your (*faith action*) labor is not in vain in the Lord."

If it were easy, God would not be giving us these strong messages. This is where grit and determination pay off, in spite of present conditions that say the promises of God cannot be. This is the labor, the work, of faith actions: 2 Thess 1:11 "Therefore also we pray always for you, that our God would count you worthy of this calling, and fulfill all the good pleasure of his goodness, and the work of faith (*actions*) with *dunamis*/(*miracle*) power."

CHAPTER 10

UNDERSTANDING THE NEED FOR PERSISTENCE

Just as often as we brush our teeth, comb our hair, check for the correct time or take a breath, we should be filling our heart with God's truth and not the devil's lies. According to Joshua 1 and Ephesians 4 and 5, this need is every day, all day and all night. This is the proper response to the real human condition. To that end, we have included a set of Affirmations that you can make daily. Mix them with the Psalms. If you have a time conflict, turn off the TV, cut out those things that add no real value to your life and get up earlier and serve God by hiding His Word in your heart. Success in this will mean that you must establish God as a priority for your life every single day. Tithing time every day is 2.4 hours in God every day.

Make the Affirmations two to four times a day. I typically do them in the morning and then fifteen to thirty minutes again before I go to bed at night. Then, as I sleep, I listen to scripture and command my mind to receive the Word. During the day I tend to "chew" on one or more scriptures throughout the day. Also I try to daily read at least one chapter from John G. Lake or Curry Blake, among other great Christian writers, along with my Bible reading.

Somehow we are under the impression that this is a new concept. In reality, every day, all day, by what we see, think about, talk about, hear, smell, feel, fear and celebrate, we are building new neural pathways, subduing old ones and reinforcing others. Choose life, and start building that which will last forever by continual right faith-actions, rather than what will one day be destroyed. Isa 55:2 "Wherefore do ye spend money for that which is not bread? and your labour for that which satisfieth not? hearken diligently unto me, and eat ye that which is good, and let your soul delight itself in fatness. 3 Incline your ear, and come unto me: hear, and your soul shall live; and I will make an everlasting covenant with you, even the sure *chesed*/mercies of David." John 6:27 "Labour not for the meat which perisheth, but for that meat which endureth unto everlasting *zoe*/life, which the Son of man shall give unto you: for him hath God the Father sealed."

Now you know the source of the power of positive thinking. It is a natural law of the Universe we live in, because this Universe was created as the ultimate home of God, according to Revelation chapters 21 and 22. God is the ultimate positive thinker, and we are to be like Him. The biblical word *children* is not only about your parents; it is also about the source of the way you live your life.

At the natural-law level, the laws of positive thinking, even without faith in God by Jesus Christ (just as good and bad people can fly airplanes), will work. You can even work miracles without knowing Jesus, as He Himself said. Matt 7:22 "Many will say to me in that day, Lord, Lord, have we not prophesied in thy name? and in thy name have cast out devils? and in thy name done many wonderful works? 23 And then will I profess unto them, I never knew you: depart from me, ye that work iniquity." So the laws work, with or without one knowing the Lord, but the Day of Judgment will sort out that which truly lasts.

If you don't want the results bad enough, then you won't do the necessary right faith-action labor to see it come to pass. This is like paddling up a swift river in a canoe. If you slow down or stop laboring, you will go backward. If you want the results, like Jesus, do the faith action work—affirmations and thanksgiving till your sides hurt! If you want what the devil dishes out to the world, remain an average person, but be forewarned: Gal 6:7 "Be not deceived; God is not mocked: for whatsoever a man soweth, that shall he also reap. 8 For he that soweth to his flesh shall of the flesh reap corruption; but he that soweth to the Spirit shall of the Spirit reap *zoe*/life everlasting. 9 And let us not be weary in well doing: for in due season we shall reap, if we faint not." These principles produce, no matter what. Rom 2:11 "For there is no respect of persons with God." God's laws operate for whoever operates them. A bullet, operating by natural law, does not care if a policeman or a criminal fires it. It does what is does, regardless.

Remember, whether awake or asleep, this process goes on. You are always, never not putting new memories and re-prioritizing and strengthening others in your mind and your heart. So to be in control of your life and your results with God, it is up to you to choose with your cogitative mind and then write God's laws on your heart and your mind, else you are writing the devil's. So this is not about

Understanding the Need for Persistence

a new thing that is going on, but to explain how it goes on, and has always gone on, and how you can choose, not only success in this life, but how you can enjoy the Day of Judgment. Rom 6:20 "For when ye were the servants of sin, ye were free from righteousness. 21 What fruit had ye then in those things whereof ye are now ashamed? for the end of those things is death." Rom 12:2 "And be not conformed (*continually molded*) to this world: but be ye transformed by the renewing of your mind, that ye may prove what is that good, and acceptable, and perfect, will of God." 1 John 2:28 "And now, little children, abide in him (*Jesus*); that, when he shall appear, we may have confidence, and not be ashamed before him at his coming."

It is the way we think that controls how much of the *zoe*/life of God we operate in. Eph 4:17 "This I say therefore, and testify in the Lord, that ye henceforth walk not as other Gentiles walk, in the vanity of their mind, 18 having the understanding darkened, being alienated from the *zoe*/life of God through the ignorance that is in them, because of the blindness of their heart: 19 who being past feeling have given themselves over unto lasciviousness, to work all uncleanness with greediness."

Notice again that this is like paddling up a swift river in a canoe. If you slow down or stop laboring, you will go backward. If you do not keep your mind on Jesus in continual right faith actions, you will produce the sad fruit of verse 19. Become alarmed that you are wasting time, and get busy renewing your mind. 2 Cor 5:10 "For we must all appear before the judgment seat of Christ; that every one may receive the things done in his body, according to that he hath done, whether it be good or bad. 11 Knowing therefore the terror of the Lord ..."

Eph 4:17-19 is the fruit of an unrenewed mind that, by the way it thinks, is at war with the *zoe*/life of God. Gal 5:16 "This I say then, Walk in the Spirit, and ye shall not fulfil the lust of the flesh. 17 For the flesh lusteth against the Spirit, and the Spirit against the flesh: and these are contrary the one to the other: so that ye cannot do the things that ye would (*because your born-again spirit allows Holy Spirit to always shed the* agape/*love of God into your heart*). 18 But if ye be led of the Spirit, ye are not under the law." Rom 8:5 "For they that are after the flesh do mind the things of the flesh; but they that are after the Spirit the things of the Spirit. 6 For to be carnally minded is death; but to be spiritually minded is *zoe*/life and peace (*confidence and assurance that you will overcome, to everything working well in all ways, to God's abundance, health and prosperity by continual right faith actions*). 7 Because the carnal mind is enmity against God: for it is not subject to the law of God, neither indeed can be. 8 So then they that are in the flesh cannot please God."

The command of God is the exact opposite of the lusts of the mind of flesh. The command is to not go with the way of the world or flesh, but to renew your mind correctly. Eph 4:20 "But ye have not so learned Christ; 21 if so be that ye have heard him (*to glad obedience*), and have been taught by him, as the truth is in Jesus: 22 that ye put off concerning the former conversation the old man, which is corrupt according to the deceitful lusts; 23 and be renewed in the spirit of your mind; 24 and that ye put on the new man, which after God is created in righteousness and true holiness." Rom 13:14 "But put ye on the Lord Jesus Christ, and make not provision for the flesh, to fulfil the lusts thereof." This is the core of these Affirmations, so that you can obey: Philem 6 "That the communication of thy faith may become effectual by the acknowledging of every good thing which is in you in Christ Jesus."

Christianity is a learn-by-doing-until-you-do-it-just-like-Jesus-would process. First, you obey to get you to start doing. Then study is the next part you do, so that you can understand, as you obey in the doing. I know people who could not even read one page of these Affirmations, so great was their resistance to this truth. They were filled with visions and voices that said, "Stop! This cannot be true! You are not good enough!" etc., but they worked at it until they could get through the Affirmations page by page, and now they see more of God's power in their lives.

In the process, they set a new normal for their unconscious mind, one that more closely matches what the New Testament says and, thus, is closer to how God wants us to think, to produce His goodness in the Earth. Do it diligently with two to six hours a day, night and day, for nine months, accompanied by behaviors of thanksgiving, gladness, joy and delight (faking it emotionally, if necessary), and then give me your opinion.

Here is one way Holy Spirit has summed this up (notice that you have to gird up, strengthen and prepare your mind for work in this process): 1 Pet 1:13 "Wherefore gird up the loins of your mind, be sober, and hope to the end for the grace that is to be brought unto you at the revelation of Jesus Christ; 14 as obedient children, not fashioning yourselves according to the former lusts in your ignorance: 15 but as he which hath called you is holy, so be ye holy in all manner of conversation; 16 because it is written, Be ye holy; for I am holy. 17 And if ye call on the Father, who without respect of persons judgeth according to every man's work, pass the time of your sojourning here in fear: 18 forasmuch as ye know that ye were not redeemed with corruptible things, as silver and gold, from your vain conversation received by tradition from your fathers (*that mind of the flesh that keeps you in darkness and mockery of God*); 19 but with the precious blood of Christ, as of a lamb without blemish and without spot: 20 who verily was foreordained before the foundation of the world, but was manifest in these last times for you, 21 who by him do believe in God, that raised him up from the dead, and gave him glory; that your faith and hope might be in God. 22 Seeing ye have purified your souls in obeying the truth through the Spirit unto unfeigned love of the brethren, see that ye *agape*/love one another with a pure heart fervently: 23 being born again, not of corruptible seed, but of incorruptible, by the word of God, which *zao*/liveth and abideth for ever. 24 For all flesh is as grass, and all the glory of man as the flower of grass. The grass withereth, and the flower thereof falleth away: 25 but the word of the Lord en-

Understanding the Need for Persistence

dureth for ever. And this is the word which by the gospel is preached unto you." Also this is the Word by which we are born again.

Can shorter periods of making affirmations work? Yes, but anything less than twenty-one days leaves the ideas in the cognitive mind, and they are lost after three to five days without any active development. This is how short-term "pep" talks and motivational speakers produce some results. Even a short period of effort can improve prayer results. Thus, books like *Battle Prayer for Divine Healing, Field Manual 2* can get results for an immediate need.

As for the old thoughts: if you keep your mind active in the new thoughts, such as in an immersion process, then you can "cram" enough to get some results in a few days, but as soon as you slack off, the old thoughts rise up in your past-maintaining, self-normalizing system or conscience. They will distract you from your commitment, unless:

1. You have a series of "fortuitous" supporting events, or
2. You plan a continuous program to keep yourself focused and diligent.

One of the key tools in this ancient technology program is regular affirmations of God's truth in Jesus. Titus 3:8 "This is a faithful saying, and these things I will that **thou affirm constantly**, that they which have believed in God might be careful to maintain good works. These things are good and profitable unto men." And Philem 6 "That the communication of thy faith may become effectual by the (*continual*) acknowledging of every good thing which is in you in Christ Jesus [*by the new birth*]." To this end we have a whole section called Affirmation Magnets to help you in this process.

CHAPTER 11

UNDERSTANDING THE POWER OF RIGHT ATTITUDES

Attitudes are automatic response to situations and approaches to life. We are learning that all sensory information we receive (normal and so-called paranormal) is stored somewhere in our memory. All thoughts (or thinking), hearing, smelling, touching (or feeling), seeing, daydreaming or imaginations (imagining)—even soul awareness—are stored in our memory system. It seems there is no limit to this memory system, but accessing this system requires skill levels many of us have not strengthened or "gotten good at." Part of the memory process includes, not just the facts of the memory, but also emotions associated with them and the interpretation you assigned to them when the information came in.

Typically, as we receive information, we first assign an interpretation, attitude or judgment to that information, and then an emotion can be attached to the information. This is an emotion from either an existing event/information or similar one or a repeated event, such as your mother yelling at you or the comfort of a candy bar. For brand-new information, when you do not yet know what emotion to assign to it, no emotion is assigned. The right affirmations adjust the interpretation, judgment or attitude you use as a filter to perceiving, assigning emotions to and/or acting on the information.

Understanding the Power of Right Attitudes

One way to describe a culture is a group of shared attitudes or judgment of concepts, thoughts and actions. So when two strangers meet, they typically look for common, shared attitudes or interpretations of events. Before conversation can really occur, we first typically determine if we are sufficiently "like minded" to share a common understanding or interpretation of various events. Even when two old friends meet, they talk about shared perceptions and attitudes in the process of "catching up." Usually they recall certain events and assigning the same attitudes and judgments to them, and then they start talking about what is currently going on in their lives. This re-affirmation process is critical to their relationship as old friends. This was summed up thousands of years ago with these words: Amos 3:3 "Can two walk together, except they be agreed?"

No one can walk with another person if they do not agree, but for full agreement between them to occur, to a sense of unity and deep cooperation in action, they must have good levels of shared attitudes, interpretations, judgments and understandings. When this is true, they are "agreed." Walking with someone we do not agree with may last for a time, for a specific purpose, like at work or on a project, but when given the chance, the person who senses that they are not in agreement will not seek additional relationship. The two may tolerate each other for a specific purpose, but they cannot "walk" together in unity of life.

Thus, God, because of Jesus, can walk with us, but if we do not share a good level of shared attitudes, understandings, interpretations and judgments with Him, then we will be the one to leave Him in our daily "walk." We may reserve one hour at church once a week for Him (or once a year or only in times of trouble), but otherwise we may be very fine with our own "walk," which may be very much out of agreement with God. In spite of this, because of Jesus: Heb 13:5 "... for he (*God*) hath said, I will never leave thee, nor forsake thee." But that does not guarantee you will hear and relate to Him in the process.

The Affirmations in this book are mostly New Testament scriptures adjusted to fit the reader, as affirmations and, occasionally, as prayers. The intent is to re-program or renew your subconscious mind and your cogitative mind with truth so that you start to, more often, interpret, understand, judge and have the same attitude as God in the events of your daily life, and to do the same for all of your memories, so that you produce Jesus-like thoughts and actions. The result will be that you will agree with God more often and, thus, hear and obey Him more often. And as you mature in Christ, you will become more like Jesus.

Every day, all day long, we are processing events and information at various levels. It is how we interpret these events or our attitudes about them that governs our next actions. Babies are born without such judgments. They operate without fear. They will play happily with a hungry lion, a poisonous snake, a knife or a soft teddy bear. Babies do this until they "learn" to fear or respect certain things and avoid them. This is called "learning." Over time our learning experiences build in us a set of attitudes, instant responses to information, interpretations, prejudices (pre-judging without thought), opinions or understandings of events that are designed to get us to operate quickly and safely in a world of potential and very real dangers, and to find only those things that give us pleasure, safety and joy.

With proper upbringing, as described in the Scriptures, learning will also allow us to be as effective as Jesus was in doing the will of God in all situations. For example, the purpose of the Sabbath Day, for believers of old, was to speak only God's words and do no other work, but to exercise joy in God's truth in every part of life, as a demonstration to their children of how to walk effectively with and in God. It was to be a day of joy, gladness and celebration. That, unfortunately, does not sound even close to the lives of many people today, even "good Christians."

Notice the sad warning or prediction of what would happen for failure to serve the Lord in joy and gladness: Deut 28:47 "Because thou servedst not the LORD thy God with joyfulness, and with gladness of heart, for the abundance of all things; 48 therefore shalt thou serve thine enemies which the LORD shall send against thee (*because you violated God's laws and would not confess your sin or ask Him for help and be thankful and, thus, reaped the fruit of the flesh*), in hunger, and in thirst, and in nakedness, and in want of all things: and he shall put a yoke of iron upon thy neck, until he have destroyed thee." All the tragedies Israel suffered in ancient times were linked to failure to obey these commands. Historically this also seems to have applied to Christianity and, thus, we can accept it as a general principle from God.

Notice in verse 47 the promise of abundance in all things. Failure to credit the Lord for those things will also bring the penalty, unless you acknowledge your sin as fully healed in Jesus, and the healing for your heart as already obtained by Jesus, so thanksgiving and joy in the Lord must become main elements of your life. Ps 92:1 "It is a good thing to give thanks unto the LORD, and to sing praises unto thy name, O most High: 2 to shew forth thy *chesed*/lovingkindness in the morning, and thy faithfulness **every night**, 3 upon an instrument of ten strings, and upon the psaltery; upon the harp with a solemn sound." 1 Thes 5:18 "In **every thing** give thanks: for this is the will of God in Christ Jesus concerning you." Notice the use of the word *every* in these scriptures. Complaining about the rules or failure to follow them does not change them. Asking God to help you obey them gets the results you really want through your new-creation-nature, joyful agreement.

The Affirmations in this book are designed to change your cogitative and unconscious mental filters that interpret or judge events as they occur. These filters or attitudes control our immediate reactions to the information we are constantly receiving. That same hungry lion that the baby plays with will evoke a very different set of interpretations of that event in the child's mother, as she screams and rushes to save her baby, even at the risk of her own life. As your subconscious gets reprogrammed, your unrighteous attitudes will be reprogrammed, to evaluate thoughts and events as Jesus would, and to respond with godly thoughts, words and actions in *agape*/love.

On the other side of awareness, as a graduate student I learned to "tune out" all distractions so that I could study. Many is the wife who has said, "Didn't you hear the baby crying?" to the oblivious male engrossed in a television show or a book. Men can change. When I decided that raising the children was my God-given responsibility according to the Scriptures, I could then beat my wife to the baby, if some unhappy signal was given. My fundamental attitudes had been changed.

The Affirmations do not remove memories; they change the emotions attached to them and the filters by which we interpret them. For example, God says that one of the major hindrances to success with Him and other men is unforgiveness. Modern science is demonstrating this reality in hard biology. A brain exercised in unforgiveness actually looks different than a brain that knows much less unforgiveness. Not only does it look different, but the neural connections for unforgiveness are different, and they release toxins into the blood stream and stress or damage the physical body, as they operate in the habit of unforgiveness. With unforgiveness in your heart, it is impossible to obey fully: Rom 13:10 "*Agape*/love worketh no ill to his neighbour: therefore *agape*/love is the fulfilling of the law."

If you find yourself dealing with unforgiveness, confess it as sin and not of God, put on the new man in Christ, confess that your new nature does not sin in unforgiveness, and pray for those who offended you. Rom 12:14 "Bless them which persecute you: bless, and curse not. ... 19 Dearly *agape*/beloved, avenge not yourselves, but rather give place unto wrath: for it is written, Vengeance is mine; I will repay, saith the Lord. 20 Therefore if thine enemy hunger, feed him; if he thirst, give him drink: for in so doing thou shalt heap coals of fire on his head. 21 Be not overcome of evil, but overcome evil with good." Luke 6:27 "But I (*Jesus*) say unto you which hear, *Agape*/love your enemies, do good to them which hate you, 28 bless them that curse you, and pray for them which despitefully use you." Notice that *agape*/love does good, blesses and prays for those to whom it is directed.

With the constant affirmation that your purpose is to set others free, then: 1 John 5:16 "If any man see his brother sin a sin which is not unto death, he shall *aiteo*/ask, and he (*God*) shall give him *zoe*/life for them ... ." Instead of judging behavior as sin and shunning the person, because you have built truth into your heart/subconscious mind, and can now "hear" the *agape*/love of God by Holy Spirit, you will go into prayer to help them and will not stop until you have gotten them free of that and even other sins. This is part of what Jesus meant when He washed the disciples' feet. John 13:14 "If I then, your Lord and Master, have washed your feet; ye also ought to wash one another's feet. 15 For I have given you an example, that ye should do as I have done to you. 16 Verily, verily, I say unto you, The servant is not greater than his lord; neither he that is sent greater than he that sent him. 17 If ye know these things, happy are ye if ye do them." Doing just this would radically change the conversations most people engage in and definitely change the flavor of the nightly news. And, according to modern science, it would also remove toxins from your blood.

Another attitudinal shift will occur when you realize that the unhappy trials and tribulations of your life are schemes of the devil and not from God. Then you can see how to handle trials. You count them (act as if they are joy and not miseries) so God can empower your words to blessing. James 1:2 "My brethren, count it all joy when ye fall into divers temptations; 3 knowing this, that the trying of your faith worketh patience. 4 But let patience have her perfect work, that ye may be perfect and entire, wanting nothing. ... 12 Blessed is the man that endureth temptation: for when he is tried, he shall receive the crown of *zoe*/life, which the Lord hath promised to them that *agape*/love him. 13 Let no man say when he is tempted, I am tempted of God: for God cannot be tempted with evil, neither tempteth he any man: 14 but every man is tempted, when he is drawn away of his own lust, and enticed. 15 Then when lust hath conceived, it bringeth forth sin: and sin, when it is finished, bringeth forth death. 16 Do not err, my *agape*/beloved brethren. 17 Every good gift and every perfect gift is from above, and cometh down from the Father of lights, with whom is no variableness, neither shadow of turning. 18 Of his own will begat he us with the word of truth, that we should be a kind of firstfruits of his creatures." That thing in you that finds fault with your trials and tribulations is called lust (the carnal mind) and is an enemy of you and God. It is usually based on a corrupt heart in need of renewing. You must know that it is not God trying to teach you through evil circumstances and unhappy events, but the devil trying to get you to fear his power and make you let go of God's promises. God's response to you, in these evil events, may be teaching you, but God is not causing the events.

Notice God's cultural answer to standing firm in trials. Phil 1:27 "Only let your conversation (*common attitudes about life and what you actually do*) be as it becometh the gospel of Christ: that whether I come and see you, or else be absent, I may hear of your affairs, that ye stand fast in one spirit, with one mind striving together for the faith (*actions*) of the gospel; 28 and in nothing terrified by your adversaries: which is to them an evident token of perdition, but to you of *soteria*/salvation, and that of God." Your lack of evil fear in trials is a constant reminder to the devil that Christ is in you, and you are operating in Holy Spirit glory and not worldly lusts.

These schemes of the devil—such as sickness, disease, poverty, famine, storms, imprisonment, slavery, war, etc.—are what occupy most of human activity, and actual work to resolve them is critical, but not without dealing with the root cause, else they will be repeated. We are told: Mark 4:13 "And he said unto them,

UNDERSTANDING THE POWER OF RIGHT ATTITUDES

Know ye not this parable? and how then will ye know all parables? 14 The sower soweth the word. 15 And these are they by the way side, where the word is sown; but when they have heard, Satan cometh immediately, and taketh away the word that was sown in their hearts. 16 And these are they likewise which are sown on stony ground; who, when they have heard the word, immediately *lambano*/receive it with gladness; 17 and have no root in themselves, and so endure but for a time: afterward, when affliction or persecution ariseth for the word's sake, immediately they are offended. 18 And these are they which are sown among thorns; such as hear the word, 19 and the cares of this world, and the deceitfulness of riches, and the lusts of other things entering in, choke the word, and it becometh unfruitful. 20 And these are they which are sown on good ground; such as hear the word, and receive it [*with joy*], and bring forth fruit, some thirtyfold, some sixty, and some an hundred."

Notice that when the Word of God is preached and heard, the devil comes immediately to take it out of your subconscious, your heart. He does that with negative thoughts and/or distractions. If that does not work, then he attacks with trials and tribulations. These can range from famine to opportunities to be mistreated and then the temptation to fall into unforgiveness or become offended. Notice in verse 17 above that the person becomes offended. This is unforgiveness toward other people and/or God because, as they start to believe the Word of God, it does not appear to be working (the underground work of a seed before it spouts in a stem is not usually visible). Then the devil attacks with evil situations, and things look worse than when the person started to believe God's promises could be true. Offended, they accuse God and others.

Notice in verse 18 that if the trials don't get you, then prosperity, lusts and riches will distract you. You still have the Word growing in you. It has sprouted, but no God-fruit is coming forth yet. You may get natural-law results, but you do not get supernatural results. This is where many get lost, whether Christians or those who espouse positive thinking and concepts such as the Laws of Abundance. They get results, but not God-results. Those with well-prepared hearts/subconscious minds will not become distracted with natural-law results, but will hold on by continual right faith actions and receive supernatural, God-results. The only results that will stand the test on the Day of Judgment for you are God-results, those that you and He did together. According to Mark 4:17, this is described as God's Word having "root" in good ground in your heart or the Word having been "engrafted" into and growing well in you. James 1:21 "Wherefore lay apart all filthiness and superfluity of naughtiness, and *lambano*/receive with meekness the engrafted word, which is able to *sozo*/save your souls. 22 But be ye doers of the word, and not hearers only, deceiving your own selves."

OK, God, Now What?

This attitude of holding on for supernatural results is seen when Jesus cursed, spoke negatively to, the fig tree that did not produce supernatural results. Mark 11:13 "And seeing a fig tree afar off having leaves, he came, if haply he might find any thing thereon: and when he came to it, he found nothing but leaves; for the time of figs was not yet. 14 And Jesus answered and said unto it, No man eat fruit of thee hereafter for ever. And his disciples heard it. ... 20 And in the morning, as they passed by, they saw the fig tree dried up from the roots. 21 And Peter calling to remembrance saith unto him, Master, behold, the fig tree which thou cursedst is withered away. 22 And Jesus answering saith unto them, Have faith (*actions*) in God (*or the faith of God*). 23 For verily I say unto you, That whosoever shall say unto this mountain, Be thou removed, and be thou cast into the sea; and shall not doubt in his heart, but shall believe that those things which he saith shall come to pass; he shall have whatsoever he saith. 24 Therefore I say unto you, What things soever ye *aiteo*/desire, when ye pray, believe that ye receive them, and ye shall have them. 25 And when ye stand praying, forgive, if ye have ought against any: that your Father also which is in heaven may forgive you your trespasses. 26 But if ye do not forgive, neither will your Father which is in heaven forgive your trespasses."

Jesus is the ultimate message of God. He did not allow any man to force Him into unforgiveness. Even as He was dying on the cross, He forgave. Luke 23:34 "Then said Jesus, Father, forgive them; for they know not what they do. And they parted his raiment, and cast lots." We can *agape*/love or forgive, as we know we are forgiven. Luke 7:47 "Wherefore I say unto thee, Her sins, which are many, are forgiven; for she *agape*/loved much: but to whom little is forgiven, the same *agape*/loveth little. 48 And he said unto her, Thy sins are forgiven." Eph 4:32 "And be ye kind one to another, tenderhearted, forgiving one another, even as God for Christ's sake hath forgiven you."

If you struggle with thinking that you have no sin, remember the standard of God, to be just like Him or deserve death. Rom 3:23 "For all have sinned, and come short of the glory of God; 24 being justified freely by his grace through the redemption that is in Christ Jesus ..." Eph 4:13 "Till we all come in the unity of the faith, and of the knowledge of the Son of God, unto a perfect man, unto the measure of the stature of the fulness of Christ." Rom 6:23 "For the wages of sin is death; but the gift of God is eternal *zoe*/life through Jesus Christ our Lord." Rom 8:2 "For the law of the Spirit of *zoe*/life in Christ Jesus hath made me free from the law of sin and death."

Notice the relationship between ungodly fruit and unforgiveness, as described concerning the supernatural fruit of God. Unforgiveness leads to or is part of almost all these evil fruit, while walking in *agape*/love produces the opposite good fruit of God: Gal 5:19 "Now the works (*fruit*) of the flesh are manifest, which are these; Adultery, fornication, uncleanness, lasciviousness, 20 idolatry, witchcraft, hatred, variance, emulations, wrath, strife, seditions, heresies, 21 envyings, murders, drunkenness, revellings, and such like: of the which I tell you before, as I have also told you in time past, that they which do such things shall not inherit (*produce*) the kingdom of God. 22 But the fruit of the Spirit (*that brings the Kingdom*) is *agape*/love, joy, peace, longsuffering, gentleness, goodness, faith, 23 meekness, temperance: against such there is no law." Rom 14:17 "For the kingdom of God is not meat and drink; but righteousness, and peace, and joy in the Holy Ghost."

As others have described, these Holy Spirit fruit are the fruit of *agape*/love that you and Holy Spirit together grow in your life. It is possible to have *agape*/love toward your brother or sister and unforgiveness at the same time. This is doing right, even though your insides are in turmoil. Do not ignore the turmoil. Ask God to help you *agape*/love. Just because the devil uses people to offend you does not mean you are to walk in offense, else you will descend into and walk in bitterness. Heb 12:15 "Looking diligently lest any man fail of the grace of God; lest any root of bitterness springing up trouble you, and thereby many be defiled."

A major offense can go right to the heart. We call this a "hurt." So while you deal with the hurt (usually unforgiveness and fear) you will struggle with mixed thoughts until you renew your mind to think like Jesus. Eph 4:22 "That ye put off concerning the former conversation the old man, which is corrupt according to the deceitful lusts; 23 and be renewed in the spirit of your mind; 24 and that ye put on the new man, which after God is created in righteousness and true holiness." You do that by looking at your sinful thoughts and behaviors and confessing this is not your real new nature. Instead, you confess to yourself that you are born again after the image of God, and your new nature is just like Jesus in all ways. Then go do acts of *agape*/love for the one who offended you, just as Jesus would, in *agape*/love and power. As a start, bless and pray for them, and then look for a way to do good for them. Notice how this whole process overwrites the hurt (fear/unforgiveness) in your subconscious.

Remember, your unconscious mind does not know past or future; it only knows now. So confess what you want to be in Jesus, and you will start to be what is not yet seen. 2 Cor 3:18 "But we all, with open face beholding as in a glass (*mirror*) the glory of the Lord, are changed into the same image (*that you see in your mind's eye*) from glory to glory, even as by the Spirit of the Lord." Gal 3:26 "For ye are all the (*mature*) children of God by faith (*actions*) in Christ Jesus." Rom 13:14 "But put ye on the Lord Jesus Christ, and make not provision for the flesh, to fulfil the lusts thereof." As you "see" what part of Jesus you want in your life and believe God to make you into that image, you are transformed into that image or portion of Jesus by Holy Spirit, who works in you. This is growth/transformation by faith actions according to Gal 3:26. That transformation includes your heart.

In this case, where you are "hurt," what you do not see in yourself (acting just like Jesus) is not what you really are now. You really are now born again in true righteousness and true holiness before God, with the mind of Christ in your spirit. Your memory may fight you, your old-man unconscious mind may fight you, the mind of the flesh may fight you, and the devil will, for sure, fight you, but put your trust in what God says about you in His Word and call those things that appear to be not as if they were. See yourself acting like Jesus would toward that person, as demonstrated in the gospels. This is how the Affirmations are built and using them correctly, your heart will be rightly renewed or reprogrammed and maintained.

Let us go back to some basic understandings. Attitudes are first-level responses to information that enters our brain. They are efficient shortcuts, so we react without much thought. Our brains store information that has emotion attached to it with much higher priority than to information that has no emotion. Thus, the vast amount of data we receive that has no direct, perceived emotion may be in our memory system, but with no attached emotion, it is not readily available.

Of even higher priority is the strength of the emotion. As a rule, because we are controlled by fear in the natural man, those emotions based on fear are stronger than those of pleasure. One can call this a survival efficiency. Running from the lion is more important than picking the sweetest berries. If all the strongest emotions are negative, then those are the thoughts recalled first, to fit any situation by our heart or subconscious. Thus, your prime controlling core attitude is evil fear in all its many forms.

The process of obeying Phil 4:6 has us identify a fear, go to God for help and then spend time creating a positive and strong emotion of intense thanksgiving to overwrite the evil fear we are attacking. Thus, it does take extreme effort to create a stronger emotion than the fear (ninety days worth as a minimum). As we do this for every fear, our subconscious will go from reaction to assessment and then to planning a proactive response. Instead of dwelling on evil fear, the subconscious will immediately prompt your cognitive mind to go to God, quote a scripture, *aiteo*/ask Him to perform it, *aiteo*/ask Him to help with any people involved and then enter into joyful thanksgiving, as you speak to the situation the change you want, knowing with confidence that He has heard you, and you *lambano*/receive the answer, knowing that you will have it.

The promise of God is that as we attack evil fear, by faith actions in Him to perform His promises, we then release Him to do what we are believing Him for. Ps 34:3 "O magnify the LORD with me, and let us exalt his name together. 4 I sought the LORD, and he heard me, and delivered me from all my fears. 5 They looked unto him, and were lightened: and their faces were not ashamed. 6 This poor man cried, and the LORD heard him, and saved him out of all his troubles. 7 The angel of the LORD encampeth round about them that fear him, and delivereth them. 8 O taste and see that the LORD is good: blessed is the man that trusteth (*by faith actions*) in him. 9 O (*rightly*) fear the LORD (*just like Jesus*), ye his saints: for there is no want to them that (*rightly*) fear him. 10 The young lions do lack, and suffer hunger: but they that seek the LORD (*by continual right faith actions*) shall not want any good thing."

Understanding the Power of Right Attitudes

Now, by your continuous, diligent and obedient labors to obey Phil 4:6-9, you have a new attitude toward any evil fear, anxiety or care. Unforgiveness and offense will evoke a blessing and not a curse. You will look for ways to bless your friends and also those who consider themselves your enemies. But you will have no evil fear. Instead, your attitude will be one of *agape*/love. 1 Cor 13:1 "Though I speak with the tongues of men and of angels, and have not *agape*/charity, I am become as sounding brass, or a tinkling cymbal. 2 And though I have the gift of prophecy, and understand all mysteries, and all knowledge; and though I have all faith, so that I could remove mountains, and have not *agape*/charity, I am nothing. 3 And though I bestow all my goods to feed the poor, and though I give my body to be burned, and have not *agape*/charity, it profiteth me nothing. 4 *Agape*/charity suffereth long, and is kind; *agape*/charity envieth not; *agape*/charity vaunteth not itself, is not puffed up, 5 doth not behave itself unseemly, seeketh not her own, is not easily provoked, thinketh no evil; 6 rejoiceth not in iniquity, but rejoiceth in the truth; 7 beareth all things, believeth all things, hopeth all things, endureth all things. 8 *Agape*/charity never faileth ... ."

While you are speaking the Affirmations, you can add strong, positive emotions. As you meditate-chew on a few scriptures each day, add positive emotions of joy, acceptance, curiosity and interest on how God will do it, or plan for how surprised you will be when you remember this was an answer that you prayed about, and, of course, gratitude to God for the so many different ways He shows you that He loves you. Ps 97:12 "Rejoice in the Lord, ye righteous; and give thanks at the remembrance of his holiness."

For those things you want to avoid, you may want to add negative emotions—such as anger, fear, sadness, disgust or revulsion. Thus, as you are tempted to follow negative thoughts and behaviors, the negative emotions you attach to them will help you stand against them. Along with these negative thoughts and emotions, add the positive, opposite thoughts and the positive emotions. Heb 1:9 "Thou hast *agape*/loved righteousness, and hated iniquity; therefore God, even thy God, hath anointed thee with the oil of gladness above thy fellows." For example, you may have fear of deception and disgust at any other source of power other than Holy Spirit, such as witchcraft. You can respond by making intercession for those entrapped in any of the various forms of witchcraft, and then expressing gratitude that the Lord keeps you close to Him. In this way, even when enticed to witchcraft, you can count on His strength. Visualize yourself turning to God rather than to other answers when things look bad or difficult.

As you go through the Psalms, you will notice the range of emotions expressed and recognize them in yourself, and know that it is okay, no matter how you feel. No matter what, you will fear no evil, nor be dismayed at evil reports. Instead, you will trust by continual faith actions that God will give you the answers you need, for "He maketh you to lie down in green pastures." Ps 112:7 "He shall not be afraid of evil tidings: his heart is fixed, trusting (*by continual faith actions*) in the Lord." Or go back and obey Phil 4:6-9.

OK, God, Now What?

As you obey: Eph 4:22 "That ye **put off** concerning the former conversation the old man, which is corrupt according to the deceitful lusts; 23 and be renewed in the spirit of your mind; 24 and that ye **put on** the new man, which after God is created in righteousness and true holiness," you are developing the attitude that any thought, attitude, habit or emotion that is not like Jesus is your enemy and not worthy of you. You are assigning negative emotions to these carnal, fleshly, devilish thoughts and attitudes, and you are assigning positive emotions and attitudes by faith actions to how Jesus would respond in that same situation. James 3:15 "This wisdom descendeth not from above, but is earthly, sensual, devilish. 16 For where envying and strife is, there is confusion and every evil work. 17 But the wisdom that is from above is first pure, then peaceable, gentle, and easy to be intreated, full of mercy and good fruits, without partiality, and without hypocrisy. 18 And the fruit of righteousness is sown in peace of them that make peace."

As you become aware of the awesome and terrible greatness of Christ in you (the hope of the manifestation of the glory of God in every part of your life, by faith actions), as you put off the old, carnal man-mind and put on the new-creation Christ-mind, you expect, by faith, with glad thanksgiving and joy, Holy Spirit to manifest that part of Jesus in you. 2 Cor 3:17 "Now the Lord is that Spirit: and where the Spirit of the Lord is, there is liberty (*to be all God has made of you in Jesus, and He is no longer limited in you*). 18 But we all, with open face beholding as in a glass (*mirror*) the glory of the Lord (*in our own life and not identifying with our flesh*), are changed into the same image from glory to glory, even as by the Spirit of the Lord."

It is commonly believed that you can only think one thought at a time, but that is not quite true. When you are under the control of a strong, high emotion thought, which could be described as a full *zoe* (life) or anti-*zoe* (death, as seen in all the forms of evil fear, lust and destruction), then the thought is in strong control. If it were not possible for us to think other thoughts, then you could not bring yourself out to "put off" and "put on." Except in a state of high control, in which case another may need to shout or yell at you, hit you or even have a policeman restrain you, in most cases you are able to slightly step aside in your mind and evaluate if you will accept the intervention or stay in the same mental state. Other times, especially for evil events, it may require more intervention or longer time, depending on how deep the corrupt thoughts are and how well the devil has convinced you, at some point or another, to assign strong emotions to them, so he can readily control you with the slightest reminders.

At some point, you can "come back to your senses." If this is hard, or you cannot, then that is a sign that the devil is in strong control, and you also will need to include in your "put off" casting out the devil of the sin. (Again, refer to the ten-step process found in the Glossary under the heading The Wrath of God.) Notice, as you do this that you are now assigning a strong emotion and developing a strong attitude unacceptable to that thought pattern. God does not use gentle words or small rewards for success in this process. Heb 1:8 "But unto the Son he saith, Thy throne, O God, is for ever and ever: a sceptre

Understanding the Power of Right Attitudes

of righteousness is the sceptre of thy kingdom. 9 Thou hast *agape*/loved righteousness, and hated iniquity; therefore God, even thy God, hath anointed thee with the oil of gladness above thy fellows." Or, as John described why he wrote the letter known as First John: 1 John 1:4 "And these things write we unto you, that your joy may be full. 5 This then is the message which we have heard of him, and declare unto you, that God is light, and in him is **no darkness at all**."

As you diligently labor to renew and then keep renewed your mind by continual right faith actions, you develop an attitude (automatic response to situations and approaches to life) that puts you above circumstances and into the grace, truth, a*gape*/love and strength of the Gospel. This attitude-development process is described this way: Col 3:1 "If ye then be risen with Christ, **seek** those things which are above, where Christ sitteth on the right hand of God. 2 **Set** your affection (*things that bring you thankfulness and joy*) on things above, not on things on the earth. 3 For ye are dead, and your *zoe*/life is hid with Christ in God. 4 When Christ, who is our *zoe*/life, shall appear, then shall ye also appear with him in glory. 5 **Mortify** (*call dead, put off*) therefore your members (*in any sin*) which are upon the earth; fornication, uncleanness, inordinate affection, evil concupiscence, and covetousness, which is idolatry: 6 for which things' sake the wrath of God cometh on the children of disobedience: 7 in the which ye also walked some time, when ye *zao*/lived in them. 8 But now ye also **put off all** these; anger, wrath, malice, blasphemy, filthy communication out of your mouth. 9 **Lie not** one to another, **seeing that ye have put off** (*in your present state as a new creation in Christ Jesus*) the old man with his deeds; 10 and have **put on the new man** (*in your present state as a new creation in Christ Jesus*), which is renewed in knowledge after the image of him that created him: 11 where there is neither Greek nor Jew, circumcision nor uncircumcision, Barbarian, Scythian, bond nor free: but Christ is all, and in all. 12 **Put on** therefore, as the elect of God, holy and *agape*/beloved, bowels of mercies, kindness, humbleness of mind, meekness, longsuffering; 13 **forbearing** one another, and **forgiving** one another, if any man have a quarrel against any: even as Christ forgave you, **so also do ye**. 14 And above all these things **put on** *agape*/charity, which is the bond of perfectness. 15 And (*make*) **let** the peace of God rule in your hearts, to the which also ye are called in one body; and **be ye thankful.** 16 (*Make*) **let** the word of Christ dwell in you richly in all wisdom; **teaching** and **admonishing** one another in psalms and hymns and spiritual songs, **singing** with grace in your hearts to the Lord. 17 And whatsoever ye do in word or deed, **do all** in the name of the Lord Jesus, **giving thanks** to God and the Father by him."

So the real solution is to always put on Jesus and *agape*/love, as commanded, and then operate in the thankful, glad, joyous and enthusiastic *zoe* of God by faith actions, hating and putting off any anti-*zoe* or evil fear, sin or death from the devil. The more you obey to rightly "put off" and "put on," the more you develop the attitude that if you are operating in evil fear-death-devilish thoughts, you learn to not just resist them, but also hate them and love only righteousness by faith actions, just like Jesus, our example, did.

OK, GOD, NOW WHAT?

Heb 1:9 "Thou hast *agape*/loved righteousness, and hated iniquity; therefore God, even thy God, hath anointed thee with the oil of gladness above thy fellows."

Because our attitudes, thoughts and habits are really highly complex neural structures/networks with physical and spiritual connections, then the subjection of wrong thoughts and assigning of negative emotions to them can take quite a while, which is why God says: Heb 3:12 "Take heed, brethren, lest there be in any of you an evil heart of unbelief, in departing from the *zao*/living God. 13 But exhort one another daily, while it is called To day; lest any of you be hardened through the deceitfulness of sin. 14 For we are made partakers of Christ, if we hold the beginning of our confidence stedfast unto the end."

If no one will exhort you daily, then you must exhort yourself daily, and whether you are exhorted effectively by others or not, you must go and exhort others effectively, so they will walk more like Jesus every day. Eph 4:29 "Let no corrupt communication proceed out of your mouth, but that which is good to the use of edifying, that it may minister grace unto the hearers. 30 And grieve not the holy Spirit of God, whereby ye are sealed unto the day of redemption. 31 Let all bitterness, and wrath, and anger, and clamour, and evil speaking, be put away from you, with all malice: 32 and be ye kind one to another, tenderhearted, forgiving one another, even as God for Christ's sake hath forgiven you." Heb 12:12 "Wherefore lift up the hands which hang down, and the feeble knees; 13 and make straight paths for your feet, lest that which is lame be turned out of the way; but let it rather be healed. 14 Follow peace with all men, and holiness, without which no man shall see the Lord: 15 looking diligently lest any man fail of the grace of God; lest any root of bitterness springing up trouble you, and thereby many be defiled."

The solution is not just the praying and commanding part, and not just the right confession part, but the actual walking-in-and-doing-good-to-others-not-just-for-yourself part. Gal 6:7 "Be not deceived; God is not mocked: for whatsoever a man soweth, that shall he also reap. 8 For he that soweth to his flesh shall of the flesh reap corruption; but he that soweth to the Spirit shall of the Spirit reap *zoe*/life everlasting. 9 And let us not be weary in well doing: for in due season we shall reap, if we faint not. 10 As we have therefore opportunity, let us do good unto all men, especially unto them who are of the household of faith." As your attitudes, the automatic filters of life, are renewed in Jesus, your thoughts, words and actions will change to be more like Jesus, and others will see it. The evidence of a changed life is a changed life that others can see. And if you are not doing those things to change and keep your life changed, you are not doing them, and there is little evidence of that changed life. The tape recording of your life will tell where you really are in all of this.

CHAPTER 12

UNDERSTANDING HOW TO AVOID SCHEMES AND MAINTAIN PEACE

God describes our present situation in this way: Ps 34:19 "Many are the afflictions of the righteous: but the LORD delivereth him out of them all." Eph 6:10 "Finally, my brethren, be strong in the Lord, and in the power of his might. 11 Put on the whole armour of God, that ye **may be able to stand against the wiles of the devil**. 12 For we wrestle not against flesh and blood, but against principalities, against powers, against the rulers of the darkness of this world, against spiritual wickedness in high places. 13 Wherefore take unto you the whole armour of God, that ye may be able to withstand in the evil day, and having done all, to stand. 14 Stand (*by faith actions*) therefore … ."

We are forewarned that evil days will come, things will look terrible, life threatening and wealth threatening, but we are to make a stand with continual right faith actions, not against people, flesh and blood, but against the true source of the evil. This term *flesh and blood* includes not only people, but all living flesh—snakes, spiders and horses—anything that moves—including diseases and viruses. If you are fighting just flesh and blood, you're only engaged in half the war! Matt 3:10 "And now also the axe is laid unto the root of the trees: therefore every tree which bringeth not forth good fruit is hewn down, and cast into the fire."

Jesus described the source of evil: Luke 10:19 "Behold, I give unto you power to tread on serpents and scorpions, and over all the power of the enemy: and nothing shall by any means hurt you. 20 Notwithstanding in this rejoice not, that the spirits are subject unto you; but rather rejoice, because your names are written in heaven." Jesus identified all the evil biology in the Earth as being caused by evil spirits, the devil. When the seventy had demonstrated success with healing, Jesus then gave them power over every form of devil oppression on Earth. And, according to Jesus, you have authority to defeat the devil in every case too, and legally he cannot counterattack you. The devil may try, but none of his efforts will stand. Men may kill you, but poisons and disease will not—if you fight by right faith actions.

This word *tread* is also a military term. It means "stomp and stomp or crush and crush again under your feet." In other words, you will fight until the enemy has no power left and is totally subdued under you. Ps 91:13 "Thou shalt tread upon the lion and adder: the young lion and the dragon shalt thou trample under feet." So the devil, as the source of all evil, would rather have you attack the wiles, the schemes, the devices, and the symptoms, and not him, the cause. His best defense is to keep you occupied with symptoms and not him as, according to Luke 10:19, you have more than enough power to overcome him—if you so choose.

Notice that the starting point is to gird up your mind so that you have available to you all the power of God. Eph 6:10 "Finally, my brethren, be strong in the Lord, and in the power of his might. 11 Put on the whole armour of God, that ye may be able to stand against the wiles of the devil. 12 For we wrestle not against flesh and blood, but against principalities, against powers, against the rulers of the darkness of this world, against spiritual wickedness in high places." The Christian has all the power of God, "the strength of the Lord," available to him, but if you are occupied with symptoms and not the devil, you will attack the branches or the tree itself, but not the roots. Of course, if you are fighting people who do not like you and offend and mistreat you or germs and broken limbs, you will be busy and have lots of repeat business. This becomes so much harder if you are still one of those Christians who does not even believe that there is a devil. If that is the case, he is relatively safe with you.

This word *stand* is also a military term. It means "to quit running, turn around and attack those who are chasing or pressuring you." You pick your ground, and you decide to retreat no farther. Instead, you turn and face the enemy and you either wait for him to attack or go out and attack him. But you are through with running or following his orders. So the command in Eph 6:12 is for you to put on the armor and make a stand against him who has you on the run with his wiles and schemes. For some, this could be a doctor's report of cancer or imminent death, for others, a bank default, and for others, a divorce notice. Whatever it is, decide to make your stand. If you die, at least you will die facing the enemy, and all the arrows will be in your chest and not your back.

When we stand, we are promised that the devil will flee from us. James 4:7 "Submit yourselves therefore to God. Resist the devil, and he will flee from you. 8 Draw nigh to God, and he will draw nigh to you. Cleanse your hands, ye sinners; and purify your hearts, ye double minded." But success in this battle is a matter of determined heart and mind, since you already have the necessary weapons.

As a Christian, you are God's local agent on the scene, and you are to walk in His *agape*/love and not in evil fear. 1 John 4:16 "And we have known and believed the *agape*/love that God hath to us. God is *agape*/love; and he that dwelleth in *agape*/love dwelleth in God, and God in him. 17 Herein is our *agape*/love made perfect, that we may have boldness in the day of judgment: because as he is, so are we in this world. 18 There is no fear in *agape*/love; but perfect *agape*/love casteth out fear: because fear hath torment. He that feareth is not made perfect in *agape*/love. 19 We *agape*/love him, because he first *agape*/loved us."

With these faith action affirmations of truth in your heart and mind, you will be able to obey the rest of this powerful scripture. Eph 6:13 "Wherefore take unto you the whole armour of God, that ye may be able to withstand in the evil day, and having done all, to stand. 14 Stand (*by faith actions*) therefore, having your loins girt about with truth, and having on the breastplate of righteousness; 15 and your feet shod with the preparation of the gospel of peace."

To simplify: to be effective, you need the whole armor, not just part of it, and you must do the putting on. Do not forget that you start with the knowledge that you have all of God's power available to you. Next, you put on truth, and Jesus came to give us grace and truth. The truth is that God, who is *agape*/love, can inhabit a man, just as He does Jesus, and that includes you (remember the Gospel is Christ in you the hope of glory). This includes the fact that Father God is your Helper.

As is noted in the Parable of the Sower and the Seed (Matt 13, Mark 4 and Luke 8), the devil will attack as you start to proclaim the promises of God against a situation. That is the evil day, when things will look like God is a liar, and you must trust Him anyway. But to trust does not mean that you are passive. No, get ready for war, and then go out to do battle. Trust is a warring process. You put on the righteousness of God, knowing that He has made you the righteousness of God in Christ Jesus. This can be a real act of faith, as you may be living a life that looks very unChristlike, and you must put this on, by faith in the Word of forgiveness and righteousness in Christ, and not in your behavior or works. This is part of what Jesus meant: Mark 1:15 "And (*Jesus*) saying, The time is fulfilled, and the kingdom of God is at hand: repent ye, and believe the gospel."

OK, God, Now What?

Your affirmation might sound like this: "Yahoo, Jesus, you died for my sins two thousand years ago, 2 Cor 5:21 "for *Father God* hath made *You, Lord Jesus* to be sin for *me*, who knew no sin; that I might be made the righteousness of *Father* God in You, *Lord Jesus*." So, as I confess this over my memory of sins and failures, I say: Rom 8:31 "What shall I then say to these things? If God be for *me*, who can be against *me*? 32 He that spared not his own Son, but delivered him up for us all, how shall he not with him also freely give *me* all things? 33 Who shall lay any thing to the charge of *me, one of* God's elect? It is God that justifieth me." Thank you, Lord Jesus, and thank You, Father, in the name of Jesus. Keep me standing in Your grace. Thank You!

Next is the Gospel of Peace from the God of Peace. The peace He offers is not a drugged state in which you feel no pain. Look at these descriptions of what the God of Peace does: Rom 16:20 "And the God of peace shall bruise Satan under your feet shortly. The grace of our Lord Jesus Christ be with you (*to know, be and do this*). Amen." 1 Thes 5:23 "And the very God of peace sanctify you wholly; and I pray God your whole spirit and soul and body be preserved blameless unto the coming of our Lord Jesus Christ. 24 Faithful is he that calleth you, who also will do it." Heb 13:20 "Now the God of peace, that brought again from the dead our Lord Jesus, that great shepherd of the sheep, through the blood of the everlasting covenant ..."

In every verse, this God of Peace looks like a warrior conquering the works of the devil so that Heaven on Earth can become a reality. Whether in your heart, in your body, or even in Jesus in the pit of Hell after the crucifixion, the work of peace is to set people free from the corruptions and oppressions of the devil unto Heaven on Earth. Isa 32:17 "And the work of righteousness (*acting just like Jesus*) shall be peace (*everything working in right order, with nothing missing, nothing broken to the abundance of Heaven on Earth*); and the effect of righteousness quietness and assurance (*in God, knowing God will defeat all the oppressions of the devil through me, as I fight by faith actions in the name of Jesus against the devil, and not flesh and blood*) for ever."

So a better meaning for peace than mind-numbing tranquility is that no matter what, you will destroy all the enemies that rise up against you, so that the Heaven of God can operate freely and reliably on Earth all the time. This is included as part of God's definition of what it means to be "blessed." Deut 28:7 "The LORD shall cause thine enemies that rise up against thee to be smitten before thy face: they shall come out against thee one way, and flee before thee seven ways." Think peace-maker or officer, as lawmen are called. Yes, this is radically different from what is often offered as the meaning of peace in our day.

Almost all cultures have some dreams of utopia, but few have dreams that they are part of the clean-up team to bring it about. Gen 1:28 "And God blessed them (*Adam and Eve*), and God said unto them, Be fruitful, and multiply, and replenish the earth, and **subdue it: and have dominion** over the fish of the sea, and over the fowl of the air, and

UNDERSTANDING HOW TO AVOID SCHEMES AND MAINTAIN PEACE

over every living thing that moveth upon the earth." *Subdue* is definitely a fighting, or warring word, and *dominion* means to keep the peace or maintain it once the job is done.

Notice the perfect Messenger of Peace and how He preached peace: Acts 10:36 "The word which God sent unto the children of Israel, preaching peace by Jesus Christ: (he is Lord of all:) 37 that word, I say, ye know, which was published throughout all Judaea, and began from Galilee, after the baptism which John preached; 38 how God anointed Jesus of Nazareth with the Holy Ghost and with power: who went about doing good, and healing all that were oppressed of the devil; for God was with him." Jesus preached peace by blasting the works of the devil off of people, wherever and whenever He found them. Thus, the peace process includes blasting the devil off of people, in any oppression of any kind, by exercising the judgment of God against the devil and the blessing of God for people.

The work of peace, by God's definition, is not free time to go to the beach or some other distraction (remember the Parable of the Sower and how the devil attacks, according to Mark 4:19), but to go "about doing good, and healing all that were oppressed of the devil; for God" is with you. You can do this in obedience to Luke 10:19, knowing that you are anointed by God with Holy Spirit and power, just as Jesus is. 2 Cor 1:21 "Now he which stablisheth us with you in Christ, and hath anointed us, is God." Gal 4:6 "And because ye are sons, God hath sent forth the Spirit of his Son into your hearts, crying, Abba (*Daddy*), Father. 7 Wherefore thou art no more a servant, but a son; and if a son, then an heir of God through Christ." Sons bring the peace of God to Earth and maintain it.

Consider that a Christian today has the same anointing, the same Spirit, the same calling as Jesus and the same command to destroy the works of the devil. We must have the same job: Acts 10:38 "How God anointed Jesus of Nazareth with the Holy Ghost and with power: who went about doing good, and healing all that were oppressed (*under the active dominion, reign or lordship*) of the devil; for God was with him." Matt 28:18 "And Jesus came and spake unto them, saying, All power is given unto me in heaven and in earth. 19 Go ye therefore, and teach all nations, baptizing them in the name of the Father, and of the Son, and of the Holy Ghost: 20 teaching them to observe all things whatsoever I have commanded you: and, lo, I am with you alway, even unto the end of the world. Amen." John 17:18 "As thou hast sent me (*Jesus*) into the world, even so have I also sent them into the world." John 20:21 "Then said Jesus to them again, Peace (*success in setting men free from the lies and the fruit of the lies of the devil and in bringing Heaven to Earth*) be unto you: as my Father hath sent me, even so send I you."

No wonder the devil strives to keep us in the bondage of fear, lust and pride, because his very life, his very ability to function, depends on it. When we wake up to our victory in Jesus, that we are made champions of God in Jesus, and get about our jobs, we will then fulfill: Eph 6:16 "Above all, taking the shield of faith (*actions*), wherewith ye shall be able to quench all the fiery darts of the wicked. 17 And take the helmet of *soteria*/salvation, and the sword of the Spirit, which is the word of God." Notice that the fiery darts are not the devil but what the devil uses to attack us. So whether it is people who curse and abuse us or sickness or famine, these darts are real and need to be dealt with by faith actions. All these schemes or symptoms can be destroyed or healed or made a blessing by faith actions in God.

You will be effective, as long as you keep your head filled with the salvation of God. 2 Cor 1:19 "For the Son of God, Jesus Christ, who was preached among you by us, even by me and Silvanus and Timotheus, was not yea and nay, but in him was yea. 20 For all the promises of God in him are yea, and in him Amen, unto the glory of God by us. 21 Now he which stablisheth us with you in Christ, and hath anointed us, is God; 22 who hath also sealed us, and given the earnest of the Spirit in our hearts." 2 Cor 6:1 "We then, as workers together with him, beseech you also that ye receive not the grace of God in vain. 2 (For he saith, I have heard thee in a time accepted, and in the day of *soteria*/salvation have I succoured thee: behold, now is the accepted time; behold, now is the day of *soteria*/salvation.)"

The Day of Salvation means God has decreed that people, nations and the planet are to be freed from the works of Satan. It means that the judgment of God against the devil is for now. You have Holy Spirit, and today is the Day of Salvation, so let us go about giving deliverance to those who need some good and those who need freedom from the oppressions of the devil.

What are you to do with all this armor and your weapon of the Word of God on your lips? Eph 6:18 "Praying always with all prayer and supplication in the Spirit, and watching thereunto with all perseverance and supplication for all saints; 19 and for me, that utterance may be given unto me, that I may open my mouth boldly, to make known the mystery of the gospel, 20 for which I am an ambassador in bonds: that therein I may speak boldly, as I ought to speak." You have the armor and the Sword of Holy Spirit in the Word of God, so set others free! Build others in Christ! And enable other warriors to fight even more!

We are to pray to set others free and for those who preach the Gospel in the power of God and not the wisdom of men, or to pray for those who preach by the wisdom of men to move into the power of God. And how do we pray? Here is what Jesus said: Mark 11:24 "Therefore I say unto you, What things soever ye *aiteo*/desire (*by requiring, demanding and expecting as due by covenant promise of God*) when ye pray, believe that ye receive them, and ye shall have them." Wow! What a message! But this will not happen if your mind has filters that will not let you operate in this truth.

Do not be too hard on yourself. Look at the disciples. Jesus told them several times that He would be killed and then rise from the dead. Still, after the crucifixion, they did not believe and were in total despondency. Mark 16:14 "Afterward he (*Jesus*) appeared unto the eleven as they sat at meat, and upbraided them with their

Understanding How to Avoid Schemes and Maintain Peace

unbelief and hardness of heart, because they believed not them which had seen him after he was risen." Notice that unbelief and hardness of heart are linked. Put the Word of God in your heart, with positive emotions, quit pointing your finger at or accusing God and His servants, and belief will come by continual faith actions.

A hard heart toward God will keep you from seeing God, even if He shows up in physical form and in power. The people who were looking for the help of God, the Jewish nation, killed the very One who was sent to set them free. They missed their time of visitation, or the inspection of God, by God's Man. Luke 19:43 "For the days shall come upon thee, that thine enemies shall cast a trench about thee, and compass thee round, and keep thee in on every side, 44 and shall lay thee even with the ground, and thy children within thee; and they shall not leave in thee one stone upon another; because thou knewest not the time of thy visitation (*inspection*)." That is the penalty for a hard heart lost in idolatry, lust, pride and evil fear and that looks to men for prosperity rather than to God.

Considering the history of Christianity, we are no better. This is the power of the filters of our expectations, prejudices, interpretations, understanding, attitudes and judgments to cause us to miss God in any or every part of life. The Affirmation Magnets in this book directly attack these, so that you can begin to truly see what is hidden in plain sight.

The main control the devil has on us is to keep thoughts, interpretations and attitudes in our minds and hearts that limit our ability to hear and obey what God says in the Bible, much less through one of His messengers. This is called hardness of heart. Mark 3:5 "And when he had looked round about on them with anger, being grieved for the **hardness of their hearts**, he saith unto the man, Stretch forth thine hand. And he stretched it out: and his hand was restored whole as the other." Therefore Jesus said: John 8:31 "Then said Jesus to those Jews which believed on him, If ye continue in my word, then are ye my disciples indeed; 32 and ye shall know the truth, and the truth shall make you free."

Again, a similar message: 2 Tim 2:24 "And the servant of the Lord must not strive; but be gentle unto all men, apt to teach, patient, 25 in meekness instructing those that oppose themselves; if God peradventure will give them repentance to the acknowledging of the truth; 26 and that they may recover themselves out of the snare of the devil, who are taken captive by him at his will." 2 Thes 2:8 "And then shall that Wicked be revealed, whom the Lord shall consume with the spirit of his mouth, and shall destroy with the brightness of his coming: 9 even him, whose coming is after the working of Satan with all power and signs and lying wonders, 10 and with all deceivableness of unrighteousness in them that perish; because they received not the *agape*/love of the truth, that they might be *sozo*/saved." The greatest freedom is found in knowing how truly loved we are by God and that He is ever there to love us and others through us. As 2 Tim 2:24-26 reveals, this takes constant repetition.

OK, God, Now What?

John said it this way: 1 John 2:1 "My little children, these things write I unto you, that ye sin not. And if any man sin, we have an advocate with the Father, Jesus Christ the righteous: 2 and he is the propitiation for our sins: and not for ours only, but also for the sins of the whole world. 3 And hereby we do know that we know him, if we keep his commandments. 4 He that saith, I know him, and keepeth not his commandments, is a liar, and the truth is not in him. 5 But whoso keepeth his word, in him verily is the *agape*/love of God perfected: hereby know we that we are in him. 6 He that saith he abideth in him ought himself also so to walk, even as he walked." 1 John 4:16 "And we have known and believed the *agape*/love that God hath to us. God is *agape*/love; and he that dwelleth in *agape*/love dwelleth in God, and God in him. 17 Herein is our *agape*/love made perfect, that we may have boldness in the day of judgment: because as he is, so are we in this world. 18 There is no fear in *agape*/love; but perfect *agape*/love casteth out fear: because fear hath torment. He that feareth is not made perfect in *agape*/love. 19 We *agape*/love him, because he first *agape*/loved us."

The message of this book is that until you renew your mind you can read and read and read, but the information will not make it past the evil filters built by a mind that has not been kept in the obedience of Christ. Isa 26:3 "Thou wilt keep him in perfect peace, whose mind is stayed on thee: because he trusteth (*by continual faith actions*) in thee. 4 Trust (*by continual faith actions*) ye in the Lord for ever: for in the Lord Jehovah is everlasting strength." This is not talking about the kind of tranquility you might get from drugs or even physical exertion. Instead, it is about the ability to be about the Father's business of setting others free, with the strength of God, knowing that no matter how great the obstacles, you will overcome, to the glory of God, through Jesus Christ.

Is it invalid to use that scripture for tranquility? Of course not, but to leave it at that is to miss the message of God, through the filters of a society that is trying to avoid God at all costs, in a world ruled by the one who does not want you to know who and what you are in Jesus, the devil's absolute Master. 1 John 5:19 "And we know that we are of God, and the whole world lieth in wickedness." 2 Cor 4:3 "But if our gospel be hid, it is hid to them that are lost (*have death working in them, either fast or slow*): 4 in whom the god of this world hath blinded the minds of them which believe not, lest the light of the glorious gospel of Christ, who is the image of God, should shine unto them. 5 For we preach not ourselves, but Christ Jesus the Lord; and ourselves your servants for Jesus' sake." Luke 10:19 "Behold, I give unto you power (*authority*) to tread on serpents and scorpions, and over all the *dunamis*/power (*ability*) of the enemy: and nothing shall by any means hurt you. 20 Notwithstanding in this rejoice not, that the spirits are subject unto you; but rather rejoice, because your names are written in heaven." So labor with right faith actions to get past the schemes and symptoms, and attack the devil in the process.

Understanding How to Avoid Schemes and Maintain Peace

Just as it took an army powered by God's strength to conquer the Promised Land, Jesus said: Luke 12:31 "But rather seek ye the kingdom of God; and all these things (*of normal life*) shall be added unto you. 32 Fear not, little flock; for it is your Father's good pleasure to give you the kingdom." We are now to use the name of Jesus to make God's peace on the Earth, just as Jesus did. John 20:21 "Then said Jesus to them again, Peace be unto you: as my Father hath sent me, even so send I you."

CHAPTER 13

UNDERSTANDING HOW TO MOVE BEYOND WHAT IS SEEN

It takes faith action to move past terrible defeat, dismay, lack, loss and despair. The main message of the physical world around is that what is (what now exists) cannot be changed into what is not (what does not now exist in that situation or place). In other words, what is now is what will be. The systems and choices are all fixed, and the best you can do is discover a few variations. You cannot make things change. A sick child can only be healed, if at all, by a science that attacks the symptoms and not the root cause. Heaven on Earth is a pipe dream at best, or "the opiate of the masses" at worst. This is a core message of the world system.

A mind set on what is now, without the faith actions in God to change what is seen into the Kingdom of God, according to His covenant promises, is a mind set on the flesh. Rom 8:5 "For they that are after the flesh (*what is independent of God*) do mind the things of the flesh; but they that are after the Spirit the things of the Spirit. 6 For to be carnally minded is death; but to be spiritually minded (*set on believing in the goodness of God and His promises to overcome any evil and keep Heaven on Earth by agape/love working by faith actions*) is zoe/life and peace. 7 Because the carnal mind is enmity against God: for it is not subject to the law of God, neither indeed can be. 8 So then they that are in the flesh cannot please God."

This mind set on the flesh cannot please God because: Heb 11:6 "... without faith (*actions*) it is impossible to please him: for he that cometh to God must believe (*by faith actions*) that he is, and that he is a rewarder of them that diligently seek him (*by faith actions*)." A mind set on faith is just the opposite; it diligently seeks God, knowing it will get the good thing it wants from God, according to His Word. Notice that this takes diligent work, not haphazard effort. So you are to focus on the goodness of God, by His promises, and you will see the goodness of the Lord in the land of the living. Ps 107:8 "Oh that men would praise the LORD for his *chesed*/goodness, and for his wonderful works to the children of men! 9 For he satisfieth the longing soul, and filleth the hungry soul with goodness." Extending little praise to God means that you perceive little good and, therefore, find fault with Him and/or see very little of His hand at work. Much praise means that you perceive much good and see much of God's hand.

What is the principal characteristic of faith in God? Anyone can praise and give thanks after they have the answer; faith gives thanks, praise and joy BEFORE the answer comes from God. Faith looks at the failure and impossibility of the situation, looks at the Word of God, sees the answer from God's promise in the imagination, proclaims what will be by a promise from God and in the name of Jesus, tells the problem or unhappy situation to leave in the name of Jesus, and praises God, again, in the name of Jesus, before seeing the answer that He will bring. Great faith is giving great thanks; small faith is giving small thanks; and weak faith gives weak thanks, if any.

To renew your mind in a given situation, face the fear, the lack and the need, with faith actions in God through His Word, visualize His promise made real, and start by thanking Him in advance. The longer and the greater the thanksgiving and persistence, the greater the faith and the more your mind is renewed.

Faith is demonstrated by joy and thanksgiving actions on your part in advance of receiving a promise from God, before you see it. This is how Abraham, the father of faith, did it. Rom 4:17 "(As it is written [*concerning Abraham*], I have made thee a father of many nations,) before him whom he believed, even God, who quickeneth the dead, and calleth those things which be not as though they were. 18 Who against hope believed in hope, that he might become the father of many nations; according to that which was spoken, So shall thy seed be. 19 And being not weak in faith (*actions*), he considered not his own body now dead, when he was about an hundred years old, neither yet the deadness of Sara's womb: 20 he staggered not at the promise of God through unbelief; but was strong in faith (*actions*), giving glory (*loud praise and thanksgiving in advance of seeing the answer*) to God; 21 and being fully persuaded that, what he had promised, he was able also to perform."

Renewing the mind is the persuasion process. This starts at the first sign of the need or the promise and ends when you walk in gratefulness for His faithfulness and His love for you. 1 John 4:17 "Herein is our *agape*/love made perfect, that we may have boldness in the day of judgment: because as he is, so are we in this world. 18 There is no fear in *agape*/love; but perfect *agape*/love casteth out fear: because fear hath torment. He that feareth is not made perfect in *agape*/love. 19 We *agape*/love him, because he first *agape*/loved us."

Believing God, in His goodness and through His Word, has always been the key to seeing the fruits He offers. Even Jesus had to do this when He went to the cross. Rom 4:22 "And therefore it was imputed to him (*Abraham*) for righteousness. 23 Now it was not written for his sake alone, that it was imputed to him; 24 but for us also, to whom it shall be imputed, if we believe on him that raised up Jesus our Lord from the dead; 25 who was delivered for our offences, and was raised again for our justification (*being made as right as Jesus is with and in God*)." Luke 9:22 "(*Jesus*) saying, The Son of man must suffer many things, and be rejected of the elders and chief priests and scribes, and be slain, and be raised the third day." This was Jesus talking in faith, by making an affirmation of what would be, based on God's Word.

As the Scriptures say: Col 3:1 "If ye then be risen with Christ, seek those things which are above, where Christ sitteth on the right hand of God. 2 Set your affection on things above, not on things on the earth. 3 For ye are dead, and your *zoe*/life is hid with Christ in God." Titus 2:11 "For the grace of God that bringeth *soteria*/salvation hath appeared to all men, 12 teaching us that, (*continually*) denying ungodliness and worldly lusts (*by renewing our minds in continual faith actions*), we should *zao*/live soberly, righteously, and godly, in this present world; 13 looking for that blessed hope, and the glorious appearing of the great God and our Saviour Jesus Christ; 14 who gave himself for us, that he might redeem us from all iniquity, and purify unto himself a peculiar people, zealous of good works. 15 These things speak, and exhort, and rebuke with all authority. Let no man despise thee."

Ps 37:3 "Trust in the LORD, and do good; so shalt thou dwell in the land, and verily thou shalt be fed. 4 Delight thyself also in the LORD; and he shall give thee the desires of thine heart. 5 Commit thy way unto the LORD; trust also in him; and he shall bring it to pass. 6 And he shall bring forth thy righteousness as the light, and thy judgment as the noonday." One way to delight yourself in the Lord is to speak twenty to fifty of the psalms each day, and, of course, the Affirmations in this book, at least once a day. Three times a day would be much better.

Yes, this takes real effort and lots of time. Matt 16:26 "For what is a man profited, if he shall gain the whole world, and lose his own *psuche*/soul (*life*)? or what

UNDERSTANDING HOW TO MOVE BEYOND WHAT IS SEEN

shall a man give in exchange for his *psuche*/soul (*life*)?" The key is to learn how to live this way every minute and not in just a few bursts of activity. At first, it may take focused sessions, say six to twelve half-hour sessions throughout each day. That would match the expected prayer life of the New Testament. This should be interspersed with obedience to scriptures such as: Col 3:14 "And above all these things put on *agape*/charity, which is the bond of perfectness. 15 And let the peace of God rule in your hearts, to the which also ye are called in one body; and be ye thankful. 16 Let (*make*) the word of Christ dwell in you richly in all wisdom; teaching and admonishing one another in psalms and hymns and spiritual songs, singing with grace in your hearts to the Lord. 17 And whatsoever ye do in word or deed, do all in the name of the Lord Jesus, giving thanks to God and the Father by him." Ps 119:62 "At midnight I will rise to give thanks unto thee because of thy righteous judgments." What will be the price of your soul on the Day of Judgment?

Faith in God performing His Word starts with: Heb 11:1 "Now faith is the substance of things hoped for (*the joyful expectation of coming good*), the evidence of things not seen. 2 For by it the elders obtained a good report. 3 Through faith we understand that the worlds were framed by the word of God, so that things which are seen were not made of things which do appear. ... 6 But without faith (*actions*) it is impossible to please him: for he that cometh to God must believe (*by faith actions*) that he is, and that he is a rewarder of them that diligently seek him (*by continual faith actions*)."

Rom 10:17 "So then faith cometh by hearing, and hearing by the word of God." This *hearing* of the Word of God starts with believing, as evidenced by thanksgiving, praise and joy, and ends with doing what that Word says, so that you can gain the reward promised through the Parable of the Sower and the Seed. Renewing the mind is the process by which we are able to *lambano*/receive the Word, throughout the planting and growing process, to produce the fruit of God. Mark 4:20 "And these are they which are sown on good ground; such as hear the word, and *lambano*/receive it, and bring forth fruit, some thirtyfold, some sixty, and some an hundred." So, according to Luke 18:1, whether this process takes one minute or a thousand years, *lambano* in affirmations, prayer, *aiteo*, thanksgiving and praise, along with acts of *agape* love of divine (healing, casting out demons, etc.) and natural good works, until you get the desired answer.

CHAPTER 14

UNDERSTANDING HOW TO AVOID HYPOCRISY

The word *hypocrite* is often used without understanding. The word translated *hypocrite* in the Old Testament means "soiled with sin, impious, or wicked and not in the normal state, as defined by God's expectations." In the New Testament, it means "actor." A hypocrite is not behaving as he really is or does not speak truth. He is acting, to fit a mask and not his real self. This fits with what Jesus taught: Matt 7:4 "Or how wilt thou say to thy brother, Let me pull out the mote out of thine eye; and, behold, a beam is in thine own eye? 5 Thou **hypocrite**, first cast out the beam out of thine own eye; and then shalt thou see clearly to cast out the mote out of thy brother's eye." Here the word means that you are applying a standard to others that you do not apply to yourself, and therefore, you are acting out of character to what you are called to be, a living example of God's truth, power, love and wisdom.

But let's look at God's principle. We are to judge, and we do judge all the time things that we consider right and good or bad and evil. It is what we are made for. Our basic responsibility, according to Genesis 2, is to "subdue and establish dominion" for God in the Earth. We must judge what needs subduing and what needs more dominion. Our subconscious, if trained properly, is designed to keep a mental image of what it should be, so that we can judge what is right or wrong, good or bad. Then we judge, so we can overcome or subdue whatever is necessary

Understanding How to Avoid Hypocrisy

to make that internal image a reality in the Earth. This brings Heaven on Earth. So all men judge all the time, to determine what needs to be subdued and what needs to be kept in dominion, to match that inner vision. The issue is not that we judge, but that we judge rightly, by the right vision, and in the right way. Jesus was not saying that we should not exercise judgment, because for that to be true, we would have to be dead.

To judge can also mean to make a decision for or against. In this scripture, the word *judge* does not mean to make a decision; it means to make a decision against or to punish. Listen to what Jesus said: Matt 7:1 "Judge not (*against or to punish*), that ye be not judged (*against or to be punished*). 2 For with what judgment (*against others*) ye judge (*for punishment*), ye shall be judged (*against or for punishment*): and with what measure ye mete, it shall be measured to you again." You are to exercise enlightened self-interest as you judge against others, knowing how you judge to punish others is exactly the same way you will be judged, for your own punishment. So, instead of judging against others, find a way to judge for them.

This was the same concept spoken by a devil, as Jesus judged against him by casting him out. Mark 5:7 "And cried with a loud voice, and said, What have I to do with thee, Jesus, thou Son of the most high God? I adjure thee by God, that thou torment me not (*do not judge against me*). 8 For he said unto him, Come out of the man, thou unclean spirit." Here the devil equates judging against or punishment as torment, when Jesus commanded him to go.

Here is a similar scripture, in context, in which Jesus said the same thing: Luke 6:31 "And as ye would that men should do to you, do ye also to them likewise. 32 For if ye *agape*/love them which *agape*/love you, what thank have ye? for sinners also *agape*/love those that *agape*/love them. 33 And if ye do good to them which do good to you, what thank have ye? for sinners also do even the same. 34 And if ye lend to them of whom ye hope to receive, what thank have ye? for sinners also lend to sinners, to receive as much again. 35 But *agape*/love ye your enemies, and do good, and lend, hoping for nothing again; and your reward shall be great, and ye shall be the children (*imitators*) of the Highest: for he is kind unto the unthankful and to the evil. 36 Be ye therefore merciful, as your Father also is merciful. [Matt 5:45 "That ye may be the children of your Father which is in heaven: for he maketh his sun to rise on the evil and on the good, and sendeth rain on the just and on the unjust."] 37 Judge not (*against or for punishment*), and ye shall not be judged (*against or for punishment*): condemn not, and ye shall not be condemned: forgive, and ye shall be forgiven: 38 give, and it shall be given unto you; good measure, pressed down, and shaken together, and running over, shall men give into your bosom. For with the same measure that ye mete withal it shall be measured to you again."

Notice that the secret to being blessed by others is to give to others the blessing of living judgment. The enlightened self-interest part is knowing that how you judge is how you will be judged. The principle is without variation, as described in verse 38: "... For with the same measure that ye mete withal it shall be measured to you again." If you want help, give help; if you want people to work well with you, work well with them. According to verse 31, the principle of enlightened self-interest: "And as ye would that men should do to you, do ye also to them likewise." Why? Because the way you treat others—men, women and children—is how you will be treated. The laws of the Universe, as designed by God, make it so. Gal 6:7 "Be not deceived; God is not mocked: for whatsoever a man soweth, that shall he also reap. 8 For he that soweth to his flesh shall of the flesh reap corruption; but he that soweth to the Spirit shall of the Spirit reap *zoe*/life everlasting."

In Luke 6:37, we see that forgiveness is related to the process of judging negatively or against or to punish others. God does not judge against the wicked people in this, the Day of Salvation. He is merciful to people but relentless against devils. But if you do not hear His Word, you will reap what you sow. Prov 12:13 "The wicked is snared by the transgression of his lips: but the just shall come out of trouble." Prov 1:31 "Therefore shall they eat of the fruit of their own way, and be filled with their own devices. 32 For the turning away of the simple shall slay them, and the prosperity of fools shall destroy them. 33 But whoso hearkeneth unto me shall dwell safely, and shall be quiet from fear of evil." Prov 5:21 "For the ways of man are before the eyes of the LORD, and he pondereth all his goings. 22 His own iniquities shall take the wicked himself, and he shall be holden with the cords of his sins. 23 He shall die without instruction; and in the greatness of his folly he shall go astray." Matt 22:39 "And the second is like unto it, Thou shalt *agape*/love thy neighbour as thyself. 40 On these two commandments hang all the law and the prophets." Matt 6:14 "For if ye forgive men their trespasses, your heavenly Father will also forgive you: 15 but if ye forgive not men their trespasses, neither will your Father forgive your trespasses." Matt 7:2 "For with what judgment ye judge, ye shall be judged: and with what measure ye mete, it shall be measured to you again." Matt 7:12 "Therefore all things whatsoever ye would that men should do to you, do ye even so to them: for this is the law and the prophets." Mark 11:25 "And when ye stand praying, forgive, if ye have ought against any: that your Father also which is in heaven may forgive you your trespasses. 26 But if ye do not forgive, neither will your Father which is in heaven forgive your trespasses." Matt 6:12 "And forgive us our debts, as we forgive our debtors. 13 And lead us not into temptation, but deliver us from evil: for thine is the kingdom, and the power, and the glory, for ever. Amen. 14 For if ye forgive men their trespasses, your heavenly Father will also forgive you: 15 but if ye forgive not men their trespasses, neither will your Father forgive your trespasses." Ps 115:3 "But our God is in the heavens: he hath done whatsoever he hath pleased. 4 Their idols are silver and gold, the work of men's hands. 5 They have mouths, but they speak not: eyes have they, but they

Understanding How to Avoid Hypocrisy

see not: 6 they have ears, but they hear not: noses have they, but they smell not: 7 they have hands, but they handle not: feet have they, but they walk not: neither speak they through their throat. 8 They that make them are like unto them; so is every one that trusteth in them." Ps 1:5 "Therefore the ungodly shall not stand in the judgment, nor sinners in the congregation of the righteous. 6 For the LORD knoweth the way of the righteous: but the way of the ungodly shall perish." Ps 5:9 "For there is no faithfulness in their mouth; their inward part is very wickedness; their throat is an open sepulchre; they flatter with their tongue. 10 Destroy thou them, O God; let them fall by their own counsels; cast them out in the multitude of their transgressions; for they have rebelled against thee." Ps 7:11 "God judgeth [*to bless*] the righteous, and God is angry with the wicked every day. 12 If he turn not, he will whet his sword; he hath bent his bow, and made it ready. 13 He hath also prepared for him the instruments of death; he ordaineth his arrows against the persecutors. 14 Behold, he travaileth with iniquity, and hath conceived mischief, and brought forth falsehood. 15 He made a pit, and digged it, and is fallen into the ditch which he made. 16 His mischief shall return upon his own head, and his violent dealing shall come down upon his own pate. 17 I will praise the LORD according to his righteousness: and will sing praise to the name of the LORD most high." Ps 34:14 "The wicked have drawn out the sword, and have bent their bow, to cast down the poor and needy, and to slay such as be of upright conversation. 15 Their sword shall enter into their own heart, and their bows shall be broken."

You get what you give is the fundamental law of sowing and reaping, and God does not have to intervene in order for this law to take effect. Still, almost every recorded miracle of Jesus was, in some way, freeing people from what sin, evil or godlessness they or someone else had sown. This was God intervening in the affairs of men through One who was and is the exact image of how Father God really is, One whose thinking was so like God that they walked in total agreement. John 8:29 "And he that sent me is with me: the Father hath not left me alone; for I do always those things that please him." So every act and word of Jesus was pleasing to the Father. Ps 103:3 "Who forgiveth all thine iniquities; who healeth all thy diseases; 4 who redeemeth thy life from destruction; who crowneth thee with *chesed*/lovingkindness and *racham*/tender mercies; 5 who satisfieth thy mouth with good things; so that thy youth is renewed like the eagle's. 6 The LORD executeth righteousness and judgment for all that are oppressed."

Just like us, Jesus did this by operating in faith. Heb 11:5 "By faith Enoch was translated that he should not see death; and was not found, because God had translated him: for before his translation he had this testimony, that he pleased God. 6 But without faith it is impossible to please him: for he that cometh to God must believe that he is, and that he is a rewarder of them that diligently seek him."

OK, God, Now What?

So, like Jesus, we sow to the spirit of God, and we reap of the Spirit of God, to salvation and judgment against the devil. Acts 10:36 "The word which God sent unto the children of Israel, preaching peace by Jesus Christ: (he is Lord of all:) 37 that word, I say, ye know, which was published throughout all Judaea, and began from Galilee, after the baptism which John preached; 38 how God anointed Jesus of Nazareth with the Holy Ghost and with power: who went about doing good, and healing all that were oppressed of the devil; for God was with him." This was God actively judging against the devil, to deliver the benefits of salvation through a Man with a renewed mind, THE Christ Mind. Today, Holy Spirit begs us: Phil 2:5 "Let (*make*) this mind be in you, which was also in Christ Jesus."

Reaping what you sow is part of the law of sin and death. You sin, you die. Whether the death is fast or slow (the ground swallows you whole, or sickness or poverty eat away at you), you still die or have death working in you, and have not the *zoe*/life of God. This is called the law of sin and death. But learn to walk in the knowledge of what Father God has done for us in Jesus, and you can use the greater law of the Spirit of *zoe*/life in Christ Jesus to break or mitigate the normal consequences due. Rom 8:2 "For the law of the Spirit of *zoe*/life in Christ Jesus hath made me free from the law of sin and death." Rom 5:17 "For if by one man's offence death reigned (*as king, by Satan, to enforce the law of sin and death*) by one; much more they which (*continually*) *lambano*/receive [*by faith actions*] abundance of grace and of the [*permanent*] gift of righteousness [Rom 11:29 "For the gifts and calling of God are without repentance."] shall reign (*as kings, for Jesus, just like Jesus operated*) in *zoe*/life by one, Jesus Christ.) 18 Therefore as by the offence of one judgment came upon all men to condemnation; even so by the righteousness of one the free gift came upon all men unto justification of *zoe*/life. 19 For as by one man's disobedience many were made sinners, so by the obedience of one shall many be made righteous. 20 Moreover the law entered, that the offence might abound. But where sin abounded, grace did much more abound: 21 that as sin hath reigned (*as king, enforcing the law of sin and death*) unto death, even so might grace reign (*as king*) through righteousness unto eternal *zoe*/life by Jesus Christ our Lord."

To reign for and with Jesus you must continually *lambano*/hold to, no matter what, and receive the abundance of grace and the permanent gift of righteousness, according to Rom 5:17. This takes a renewed mind and a right heart, with no double-mindedness toward or with God.

The life of Jesus is the message that God is not against you; He is for you, with you and ever ready to help you. Matt 1:23 "Behold, a virgin shall be with child, and shall bring forth a son, and they shall call his name Emmanuel, which being interpreted is, God with us." Not once did Jesus say that He would not heal someone because of their sin. Often He didn't even ask their permission to heal them;

Understanding How to Avoid Hypocrisy

He just did it. He did warn those who were healed to not sin again, but sin never stopped Him from healing them, and it never stopped Him from going to the cross for them.

His own people proved, without a doubt, that they were not worthy of His love, and yet He said concerning all mankind: Luke 23:34 "Then said Jesus, Father, forgive them; for they know not what they do. And they parted his raiment, and cast lots." They were so caught up in their own deceptions that they went about their own business, even as the Lord of Glory forgave them and died for them. If He had not done that, who could stand the judgment due them, for such bold hatred of God?

Here is the principle again: Gal 6:1 "Brethren, if a man be overtaken in a fault, ye which are spiritual, restore such an one in the spirit of meekness; considering thyself, lest thou also be tempted. 2 Bear ye one another's burdens, and so fulfil the law of Christ. 3 For if a man think himself to be something, when he is nothing, he deceiveth himself. 4 But let every man prove his own work, and then shall he have rejoicing in himself alone, and not in another. 5 For every man shall bear his own burden. 6 Let him that is taught in the word communicate unto him that teacheth in all good things. 7 Be not deceived; God is not mocked: for whatsoever a man soweth, that shall he also reap. 8 For he that soweth to his flesh shall of the flesh reap corruption; but he that soweth to the Spirit shall of the Spirit reap *zoe/* life everlasting. 9 And let us not be weary in well doing: for in due season we shall reap, if we faint not." Obviously this "well doing" will take time.

Here in Gal 6:1, the judgment is made that a brother or sister is, in some way, doing wrong. If you were to correct him in a wrong manner, not *agapeing*/loving him as yourself, then you would be judged by God to go through the same thing: "tempted in like manner." In Gal 6:7-9, Holy Spirit gives the principle. If you want corruption in your life, do Gal 6:1 in the wrong way.

This is what Jesus commanded: John 15:12 "This is my commandment, That ye *agape*/love one another, as I have *agape*/loved you. 13 Greater *agape*/love hath no man than this, that a man lay down his *psuche*/life *(soul)* for his friends." So you are to lay down your wrong judgments, made in your soul, and instead, make a decision in your soul to get *zoe*/life for the one who sins, and Holy Spirit will release life from your born-again spirit. 1 John 5:16 "If any man see his brother sin a sin which is not unto death, he shall *aiteo*/ask *(require, demand and expect as due by covenant promise)*, and he *(Father God)* shall give him *zoe*/life for them ... ." James 5:19 "Brethren, if any of you do err from the truth, and one convert him; 20 let him know, that he which converteth the sinner from the error of his way shall *sozo*/save a soul from death *(the effects of the law of sowing and reaping to the flesh)*, and shall hide a multitude of sins."

Look at the same principle in this prayer of Jesus, known as the "Our Father": Matt 6:9 "After this manner therefore pray ye: Our Father which art in heaven, hallowed be thy name. 10 Thy kingdom come. Thy will be done in earth, as it is in heaven. 11 Give us this day our daily bread. 12 And forgive us our debts, as we forgive our debtors. 13 And lead us not into temptation, but deliver us from evil: for thine is the kingdom, and the power, and the glory, for ever. Amen. 14 For if ye forgive men their trespasses, your heavenly Father will also forgive you: 15 but if ye forgive not men their trespasses, neither will your Father forgive your trespasses."

Verse 13 has at least two meanings: First, because you forgive, you are asking God to remove evil from your own land. Another meaning is this: because you do not forgive, you are asking God not to judge you as you deserve, subjecting you to the same temptation, but rather, to set you free of the evil of unforgiveness, for unforgiveness is not *agape*/loving your brother or sister.

[NOTE: According to Romans 13:1-10, God gives government the sword for those who do evil. The commandment "Thou shalt not kill," has, as the original word meaning, "Thou shalt not murder." Murder is illegal killing or killing not authorized by the government. For this reason, we are commanded, in 1 Tim 2 and many other scriptures, to pray for our governments. Those who will not forgive or are evil predators and try to rob, kill and destroy, must face God's sword of justice, exercised by government. If you will not repent, like the people of Nineveh did at the preaching of Jonah, then you will reap what you sow. The ultimate case of this terrible reaping is seen in the judgments released in book of the Revelation of John.]

Notice that if you will not forgive others, then you prohibit God from forgiving you. In that case, you will not receive grace, and, instead, you will get law, because you have shut out or limited God. This means that you will not reap Heaven on Earth, but, rather, Hell on Earth, because unforgiveness (and its evil twins, gossip and cursing) is sowing to the flesh, and of the flesh we reap corruption—death in some form. Jesus put this principle very directly, as He attempted to get men to see the error of their ways: John 8:42 "Jesus said unto them, If God were your Father (*source of the thoughts and intentions of your heart*), ye would *agape*/love me: for I proceeded forth and came from God; neither came I of myself, but he sent me. 43 Why do ye not understand my speech? even because ye cannot hear my word. 44 Ye are of your father the devil (*as your source of thoughts and intentions of the heart*), and the lusts of your father ye will do. He was a murderer from the beginning, and abode not in the truth, because there is no truth in him. When he speaketh a lie, he speaketh of his own: for he is a liar, and the father of it."

When you, as a Christian, ignore God's laws, His answer is to let you be judged in this life by the world, without His help. 1 Cor 11:31 "For if we would judge ourselves, we should not be judged. 32 But when we are judged, we are chastened of the Lord, that we should not be condemned with the world." What is this judgment? If you ignore the work of Christ, that you are redeemed by His blood, that by His stripes you were healed and that He took all the chastisement due you for ignoring God in any way, then you get what those who ignore the Mighty Arm of God get, no blessing from God, but, rather, the fruit of their wicked ways. In this case, you live as a "mere" human, with all the sad accompanying reaping of corruption from the law of sin and death. This is the law that says: If you sin, you die. Rom 6:23 "For the wages of sin is death; but the gift of God is eternal zoe/life through Jesus Christ our Lord."

Ignore God and you die, become single-minded on God through Jesus in continual right faith actions and you operate in the zoe/life of God, for every aspect of life now, and build, for yourself, gold, silver and jewels for that coming Day. Yes, you can put treasures in Heaven that will be there waiting for you when you arrive. Matt 6:19 "Lay not up for yourselves treasures upon earth, where moth and rust doth corrupt, and where thieves break through and steal: 20 but lay up for yourselves treasures in heaven, where neither moth nor rust doth corrupt, and where thieves do not break through nor steal: 21 for where your treasure is, there will your heart be also." Matt 19:21 "Jesus said unto him, If thou wilt be perfect, go and sell that thou hast, and give to the poor, and thou shalt have treasure in heaven: and come and follow me." Luke 12:32 "Fear not, little flock; for it is your Father's good pleasure to give you the kingdom. 33 Sell that ye have, and give alms; provide yourselves bags which wax not old, a treasure in the heavens that faileth not, where no thief approacheth, neither moth corrupteth. 34 For where your treasure is, there will your heart be also." 1 Pet 1:3 "Blessed be the God and Father of our Lord Jesus Christ, which according to his abundant mercy hath begotten us again unto a lively hope by the resurrection of Jesus Christ from the dead, 4 to an inheritance incorruptible, and undefiled, and that fadeth not away, reserved in heaven for you, 5 who are kept by the power of God through faith unto soteria/salvation ready to be revealed in the last time." 1 Cor 3:12 "Now if any man build upon this foundation gold, silver, precious stones, wood, hay, stubble; 13 every man's work shall be made manifest: for the day shall declare it, because it shall be revealed by fire; and the fire shall try every man's work of what sort it is. 14 If any man's work abide which he hath built thereupon, he shall receive a reward. 15 If any man's work shall be burned, he shall suffer loss: but he himself shall be sozo/saved; yet so as by fire. 16 Know ye not that ye are the temple of God, and that the Spirit of God dwelleth in you?" According to Matt 6:19 and Luke 12:34, what survives the Day of Judgment, what you can take with you when you die, is a matter of the heart. Yet, in spite of any rottenness in your heart, you, the Christian, are sozo/saved, according to 1 Cor 3:15.

Now, let us look at this truth from a Christian perspective. Rom 3:23 "For all have sinned, and come short of the glory of God; 24 being justified freely by his grace through the redemption that is in Christ Jesus: 25 whom God hath set forth to be a propitiation through faith in his blood, to declare his righteousness for the remission of sins that are past, through the forbearance of God; 26 to declare, I say, at this time his righteousness: that he might be just, and the justifier of him which believeth in Jesus. 27 Where is boasting then? It is excluded. By what law? of works? Nay: but by the law of faith (*actions*). 28 Therefore we conclude that a man is justified (*just as if you had never sinned or will sin again*) without the deeds of the law." Rom 5:17 "For if by one man's offence death reigned by one; much more they which (*continually*) *lambano*/receive [*by faith actions*] abundance of grace and of the gift of righteousness shall reign in *zoe*/life by one, Jesus Christ.) 18 Therefore as by the offence of one judgment came upon all men to condemnation; even so by the righteousness of one the free gift came upon all men unto justification of *zoe*/life."

All fall short of the glory of God, so God sent Jesus to die for the sin of the world, and by faith actions in Jesus, any man can receive the total forgiveness He paid for two thousand years ago. This word *propitiation* means that not only has wrath been removed, but now every good thing that can be said is being said about mankind in Heaven, which means the same thing as this verse: Eph 1:3 "Blessed be the God and Father of our Lord Jesus Christ, who hath blessed us with all spiritual blessings in heavenly places in Christ."

Once you receive that forgiveness, you are made the righteousness of God in Christ Jesus. Rom 10:9 "That if thou shalt confess with thy mouth the Lord Jesus, and shalt believe in thine heart that God hath raised him from the dead, thou shalt be *sozo*/saved. 10 For with the heart man believeth unto righteousness; and with the mouth confession is made unto *soteria*/salvation. 11 For the scripture saith, Whosoever believeth on him shall not be ashamed. 12 For there is no difference between the Jew and the Greek: for the same Lord over all is rich unto all that call upon him. 13 For whosoever shall call upon the name of the Lord shall be *sozo*/saved."

So now that you have believed that God raised Jesus from the dead and confessed with your mouth Jesus as Lord, you receive the gift of righteousness in your spirit given by God, and you have *zoe*/life in your spirit. This is called the new creation or being born again by believing the Word of God. 1 Pet 1:23 "Being born again, not of corruptible seed, but of incorruptible, by the word of God, which *zao*/liveth and abideth for ever. 24 For all flesh is as grass, and all the glory of man as the flower of grass. The grass withereth, and the flower thereof falleth away: 25 but the word of the Lord endureth for ever. And this is the word which by the gospel is preached unto you." You are now newly created of eternal stuff, the Word of God.

So what does all this have to do with hypocrisy? Notice that Jesus called those who judged against others hypocrites because, while they had the position to speak for God, they spoke for the devil instead. In the greatest sense, a hypocrite against God is one who ignores what God accomplished for Himself and man in Jesus Christ. A Christian hypocrite lives their life as if God was not in them and for them in all of life and judges others the same way. Here is the attitude of God: 2 Cor 5:16 "Wherefore henceforth know we no man after the flesh: yea, though we

Understanding How to Avoid Hypocrisy

have known Christ after the flesh, yet now henceforth know we him no more. 17 Therefore if any man be in Christ, he is a new creature: old things are passed away; behold, all things are become new." This is the way a renewed mind in Christ thinks.

Since you are a spirit inhabiting a body and have a soul, what is your real nature? Your ideal state, as designed by God, is for your spirit to be in total unity with Him and totally in charge of your soul and body. Jesus is an example of such a man. For most of us, our soul is in charge and our spirit dead to God until we are born again. Then, until we renew our mind into the Gospel of Christ in us the hope of glory, we still act as mere men. 1 Cor 3:1 "And I, brethren, could not speak unto you as unto spiritual, but as unto carnal, even as unto babes in Christ. 2 I have fed you with milk, and not with meat: for hitherto ye were not able to bear it, neither yet now are ye able. 3 For ye are yet carnal: for whereas there is among you envying, and strife, and divisions, are ye not carnal, and walk as (*mere Gentile*) men?"

As a Christian, are you defined by God based on your imperfect soul or your perfected spirit in Jesus? Here is God's answer: Eph 4:22 "That ye put off concerning the former conversation the old man, which is corrupt according to the deceitful lusts; 23 and be renewed in the spirit of your mind; 24 and that ye put on the new man, which after God is created in righteousness and true holiness."

According to God, if your self-image or self-identification as a Christian is other than God in righteousness and true holiness, you are in disobedience, which is sin and, thus, you are a hypocrite. If you do not like having your wrong ponderings or attitudes called sin, consider this sad fact: 2 Cor 4:3 "But if our gospel be hid, it is hid to them that are lost (*suffering the effects of the law of sin and death and not of zoe/life in the new creation, according to Eph 4:17-18*): 4 in whom the god of this world hath blinded the minds of them which believe not, lest the light of the glorious gospel of Christ, who is the image of God, should shine unto them. 5 For we preach not ourselves, but Christ Jesus the Lord; and ourselves your servants for Jesus' sake." Such is the penalty for not fully integrating the great work of Jesus into your Christian life. That is not just your "church" life, but every part of your life.

[NOTE: Between the self-normalizing subconscious and the devil, we are bombarded with thoughts, as we go through life, especially as we seek to obey God in the Scriptures. Those thoughts, by themselves, are not sin. What *is* sin is failure to obey: 2 Cor 10:5 "Casting down imaginations, and every high thing that exalteth itself against the knowledge of God, and bringing into captivity every thought to the obedience of Christ." Obeying this scripture, along with the other, some one thousand forty-nine commands in the New testament, will keep you busy enough. The goals of this book are for you to recognize what God has said works to His glory in this Universe and how to go about adjusting yourself in cooperation with Holy Spirit, by the Bible, into the glorious Gospel of Jesus Christ. Do not fault the

OK, God, Now What?

Creator for any consequences for failure to obey the written instruction manual. Hos 4:6 "My people are destroyed for lack of knowledge: because thou hast rejected knowledge, I will also reject thee, that thou shalt be no priest to me: seeing thou hast forgotten the law of thy God, I will also forget thy children." Any resistance in you to this reality is a deception that needs to be removed in Jesus. (To do this, see the ten-step process in the Glossary under the heading The Wrath of God.)]

That is right; God treats you just like He does Jesus Christ. So who is double-minded? Is it the one who looks at their sin and imperfections and disowns them and proclaims their real nature is to be just like Jesus Christ? Or is it the one who claims they are a sinner and still on the path to acceptance? The answer is clear: The single-minded with God says, "The old man died in Jesus, and now it is Christ in me that is the real me." Now look for God to build that right path in you by faith actions. Gal 5:4 "Christ is become of no effect unto you, whosoever of you are justified by the law; ye are fallen from grace." [NOTE: For more on this, please see *Discovering Our Redemption* at www.CovenantPeaceMinistries.com.]

So the Christian who goes to the bar to dance and drink in unrighteous activity is being the hypocrite. They are being entirely consistent with who and what they are, as they attend Christian church and praise God the very next day or even that night, as they stop and agree with God that they just did things for which Jesus already died and for which God forgave them two thousand years ago, they cast out any devils associated with it, and then thank God for His forgiveness two thousand years ago and that they are now being healed of both the desire and consequences of their sin. But in the bar or dance hall, they are acting the very opposite of who and what they are. That is where they are being a hypocrite. Therefore, a Christian is a hypocrite when he or she sins, not when they do right.

So, as you hear that voice in your head calling you a hypocrite, as you thank God for those things you do not yet see, or as you praise God in the middle of trials, when nothing seems right, whose voice is that? It is either your corrupted self-normalizing subconscious, trying to get you back to the devil-inspired normal, or it is the devil through one of his agents, trying to stop you from being who and what you really are. So how do you tell the difference? For now, it does not matter. Attack them both with the truth of God's Word (see 1 John 4:1-3).

Fight all those lying inner voices with right faith actions and, instead, obey: James 1:2 "My brethren, count it all joy when ye fall into divers temptations; 3 knowing this, that the trying of your faith worketh patience. 4 But let patience have her perfect work, that ye may be perfect and entire, wanting nothing." Notice that you are applying a good emotion—joy—over the trial, knowing that it is producing the fruit of patience or consistency, so you can set yourself and others free more effectively. Thus, you are overwriting fear with strong, positive emotions and faith actions in God. God commanded this centuries ago; science is just now explaining how it works.

Understanding How to Avoid Hypocrisy

Freedom in Christ and praise to God comes from knowing, to the core of your being: Rom 5:1 "Therefore being justified by faith (*actions*), we have peace with God through our Lord Jesus Christ: 2 by whom also we have access by faith (*actions*) into this grace wherein we stand, and rejoice in hope of the glory of God. 3 And not only so, but we glory in tribulations also: knowing that tribulation worketh patience (*consistency in faith actions*); 4 and patience (*consistency in faith actions*), experience; and experience, hope: 5 and hope maketh not ashamed; because the *agape*/love of God is shed abroad in our hearts by the Holy Ghost which is given unto us. 6 For when we were yet without strength, in due time Christ died for the ungodly."

I now want to give you the entire first chapter of First Peter because it puts all this into perspective. Notice that you are to rejoice even though you have heaviness in your heart due to your present unhappy circumstances, whatever they happen to be. When you do that, you are making a choice of whom and what you believe by faith actions. If you give in to past memories and the training of the devil and keep your mind on the flesh and not the Word of God, you are being a hypocrite to your true self in Jesus. By stirring up yourself by faith actions to get into the mind of Christ in you, you can rejoice anyway, because as you do, you save or renew your own soul. That is your job, with God's help—to clean up your soul to believe God, in His Word, over all the sense evidence that says otherwise. And part of the process is knowing that your faith actions will be tried, and you will overcome, using the weapons of God, and not be a hypocrite and act like those of the world. **Instead, you will identify with exactly what you are now, a new creation in Christ Jesus** whose only goal is to act just like Jesus would in this situation by faith actions.

1 Pet 1:3 "Blessed be the God and Father of our Lord Jesus Christ, which according to his abundant mercy hath begotten us again unto a *zao*/lively hope by the resurrection of Jesus Christ from the dead, 4 to an inheritance incorruptible, and undefiled, and that fadeth not away, reserved in heaven for you, 5 who are kept by the power of God through faith (*actions*) unto *soteria*/salvation ready to be revealed in the last time. 6 Wherein ye greatly rejoice, though now for a season, if need be, ye are in heaviness through manifold temptations: 7 that the trial of your faith (*actions*), being much more precious than of gold that perisheth, though it be tried with fire, might be found unto praise and honour and glory at the appearing of Jesus Christ: 8 whom having not seen, ye *agape*/love; in whom, though now ye see him not, yet believing (*by faith actions*), ye rejoice with joy unspeakable and full of glory: 9 receiving the end of your faith (*actions*), even the *soteria*/salvation of your souls. 10 Of which *soteria*/salvation the prophets have inquired and searched diligently, who prophesied of the grace that should come unto you: 11 searching what, or what manner of time the Spirit of Christ which was in them did signify, when it testified beforehand the sufferings of Christ, and the glory that should follow. 12 Unto whom it was revealed, that not unto themselves, but unto us they did

minister the things, which are now reported unto you by them that have preached the gospel unto you with the Holy Ghost sent down from heaven; which things the angels desire to look into. 13 Wherefore gird up the loins of your mind, be sober, and hope to the end for the grace that is to be brought unto you at the revelation of Jesus Christ; 14 as obedient children, not fashioning yourselves according to the former lusts in your ignorance: 15 but as he which hath called you is holy, so be ye holy in all manner of conversation; 16 because it is written, Be ye holy; for I am holy. 17 And if ye call on the Father, who without respect of persons judgeth according to every man's work, pass the time of your sojourning here in fear: 18 forasmuch as ye know that ye were not redeemed with corruptible things, as silver and gold, from your vain conversation (*manner of life*) received by tradition from your fathers; 19 but with the precious blood of Christ, as of a lamb without blemish and without spot: 20 who verily was foreordained before the foundation of the world, but was manifest in these last times for you, 21 who by him do believe in God, that raised him up from the dead, and gave him glory; that your faith and hope might be in God. 22 Seeing ye have purified your souls in obeying the truth through the Spirit unto unfeigned love of the brethren, see that ye *agape*/love one another with a pure heart fervently: 23 being born again, not of corruptible seed, but of incorruptible, by the word of God, which *zao*/liveth and abideth for ever. 24 For all flesh is as grass, and all the glory of man as the flower of grass. The grass withereth, and the flower thereof falleth away: 25 but the word of the Lord endureth for ever. And this is the word which by the gospel is preached unto you," and by which you are born again.

So now you know that the devil's main temptation is to get you to act like a hypocrite, when things are bad, you fail, or you are tired and feel weak. Hypocritical Christians fear and gladly obey things other than God. Rather than do that, work to let Psalms 23 and 91 become your daily attitude with these kinds of affirmations: Ps 23:4 "Yea, though I walk through the valley of the shadow of death, I will fear no evil: for God *is with me [and in me because of Jesus]*; *His* rod and *His* staff they comfort (*encourage*) me." Ps 91:7 "A thousand shall fall at *my* side, and ten thousand at *my* right hand; but it shall not come nigh *me*. 8 Only with *my* eyes *shall I* behold and see the reward of the wicked. 9 Because *I have* made the Lord, which is my refuge, even the most High, *my* habitation." This will result because all the wicked will be destroyed by me, for I am sent into the Valley to wield the rod and staff of God, just as Jesus did, and to destroy all the works of the devil because: Ps 91:2 "I ... say of the Lord, He is my refuge and my fortress: my God; in him will I trust." Your new attitude is, "Yahoo, things look bad, and the devil is winning, but let us go and make some Peace, because: Rom 16:20 "... the God of peace shall bruise Satan under *my* feet *as shattered glass*. The grace of our Lord Jesus Christ is with *me* (*to know, be and do this*). Amen. (*So be it!*)" That is the attitude of a champion, a champion in Christ, an *agape*/love warrior of the *Zao*/Living God!

Understanding How to Avoid Hypocrisy

Now that is what God calls a single-minded attitude that will stand in the Day of Judgment, not because of your perfection, but because you have learned how incredibly and totally you are loved by God Himself. 1 John 4:17 "Herein is our *agape*/love made perfect, that we may have boldness in the day of judgment: because as he is, so are we in this world. 18 There is no fear in *agape*/love; but perfect *agape*/love casteth out fear: because fear hath torment. He that feareth is not made perfect in *agape*/love. 19 We *agape*/love him, because he first *agape*/loved us."

Now this passage makes more sense: Jude 20 "But ye, *agape*/beloved, building up yourselves on your most holy faith, praying in the Holy Ghost, 21 keep yourselves in the *agape*/love of God, looking for the mercy of our Lord Jesus Christ unto eternal *zoe*/life. 22 And of some have compassion, making a difference: 23 and others *sozo*/save with fear, pulling them out of the fire; hating even the garment spotted by the flesh. 24 Now unto him that is able to keep you from falling, and to present you faultless before the presence of his glory with exceeding joy, 25 to the only wise God our Saviour, be glory and majesty, dominion and power, both now and ever. Amen."

Remember, we are to keep ourselves in the love of God while in the midst of trials (not because we do not have them), because this is how we declare God's love to the enemy of our souls. Phil 1:27 "Only let your conversation (*the words out of your mouth and the actions you do*) be as it becometh the gospel of Christ: that whether I come and see you, or else be absent, I may hear of your affairs, that ye stand fast in one spirit, with one mind striving together for the faith of the gospel; 28 and in nothing terrified by your adversaries: which (*this lack of terror*) is to them an evident token of perdition, but to you of *soteria*/salvation, and that of God. 29 For unto you it is given in the behalf of Christ, not only to believe on him, but also to suffer for his sake; 30 having the same conflict which ye saw in me, and now hear to be in me."

Notice that as you stand in right faith actions, having decided to no longer be run around with a double-mind by the devil, trying to entice you to fear and to walk in evil lust and anger, your standing in Christ by your words and actions proclaims your trust in God and your knowing that all the enemy's ways will one day be destroyed. This is what is described in verse 28 above. This process releases the salvation of God to you now, in this life, and not just later. It also reprograms your heart into the ways of God, so that this can become a right faith action lifestyle and not just a single event.

Notice, again, that one of the ways to show God you love Him is how you stand in trials, by holding on to His Word. James 1:12 "Blessed is the man that endureth temptation: for when he is tried, he shall receive the crown of *zoe*/life, which the Lord hath promised to them that *agape*/love him." 1 Cor 10:13 "There hath no temptation taken you but such as is common to man: but God is faithful, who will not suffer you to be tempted above that ye are able; but will with the temptation also make a way to escape, that ye may be able to bear it (*or go through it to victory on the other side*). 14 Wherefore, my dearly *agape*/beloved, flee from idolatry." [NOTE: Trusting in something else other than God is idolatry. According to this scripture, idolatry keeps us from standing, even though we have a guarantee that we can make it. (Please see the Glossary for the meaning of the word *lambano*, often translated as *receive*. According to the Parable of the Sower and the Seed, you are to *lambano*/receive by faith actions the Word of God to victory. This is one of the key skills of victorious champions in Christ.)]

At first, you will feel strange, as you stand in your faith action weapons of thanksgiving—praise, joy, scripture reading and proclamation, and prayer—even as your mind is being assaulted with fearful and angry thoughts and visions, and your emotions are running amok, enticed with evil lusts. People will enter your life to distract, offend and terrify you. Do these assaults ever go away? No, the devil will try many wiles, but stand on the Word of God by continual faith actions, and the devil will flee eventually. James 4:7 "Submit yourselves therefore to God (*agree to do it God's way*). Resist the devil, and he will flee from you. 8 Draw nigh to God, and he will draw nigh to you. Cleanse your hands, ye sinners; and purify your hearts, ye double minded." Now you can see where the double-minded parts are (when you bring no joy to the Lord in trials) and how to use the Affirmations to become single-minded in the *agape*/love of God through Jesus, the Christ.

Again, another summary from First Peter: 1 Pet 4:1 "Forasmuch then as Christ hath suffered for us in the flesh, **arm yourselves likewise with the same mind** (*as Jesus did*): for he that hath suffered in the flesh hath ceased from sin; 2 that he no longer should *zao*/live the rest of his time in the flesh to the lusts of men, but to the will of God. 3 For the time past of our life may suffice us to have wrought the will of the Gentiles (*those without God and, therefore, with the devil*), when we walked in lasciviousness, lusts, excess of wine, revellings, banquetings, and abominable idolatries: 4 wherein they think it strange that ye run not with them to the same excess of riot, speaking evil of you: 5 who shall give account to him that is ready to judge the quick and the dead."

So what do we do in our "spare time"? We deal with any hardness of heart toward God (double-mindedness, hardness of hearing, evil fear and unbelief) and obey Jesus. Mark 16:14 "Afterward he (*Jesus*) appeared unto the eleven as they sat at meat, and upbraided them with their unbelief and hardness of heart, because they believed not them which had seen him after he was risen. 15 And he said unto them, Go ye into all the world, and preach the gospel to every creature. 16 He that believeth and is baptized shall be *sozo*/saved; but he that believeth not shall be damned. 17 And these signs shall follow them that believe (*with a single heart*); In my name shall they cast out devils; they shall speak with new tongues; 18 they shall take up serpents; and if they drink any deadly thing, it shall not hurt them; they shall lay hands on the sick, and they shall recover. 19 So then after the Lord had spoken unto them, he was received up into heaven, and sat on the right hand of God. 20 And they went forth, and preached everywhere, the Lord working with them, and confirming the word with signs following. Amen."

Notice Jesus' solution for unbelief and hardness of heart: He "chewed them out": Mark 16:14 "Afterward he (*Jesus*) appeared unto the eleven as they sat at

Understanding How to Avoid Hypocrisy

meat, and upbraided them with their unbelief and hardness of heart … ." And what did He exhort and rebuke them for? "… because they believed not them which had seen him after he was risen." Even in the face of miracles, we can miss God and call other witnesses liars. If this is true of lovers of Jesus, how much more of those outside the faith.

Or, as Holy Spirit said: <u>Heb 10:21</u> "And having an high priest over the house of God; 22 let us draw near with a true heart in full assurance of faith (*actions*), having our hearts sprinkled from an evil conscience, and our bodies washed with pure water. 23 Let us hold fast the profession of our faith (*actions*) without wavering; (for he is faithful that promised;) 24 and let us consider one another to provoke unto *agape*/love and to good works (*in continual right faith actions*): 25 not forsaking the assembling of ourselves together, as the manner of some is; but exhorting one another: and so much the more, as ye see the day approaching."

We do this because we see how easy it is to miss the Gospel and, thus, face misery on the Day of Judgment. <u>Rom 1:15</u> "So, as much as in me is, I am ready to preach the gospel to you that are at Rome also. 16 For I am not ashamed of the gospel of Christ: for it is the *dunamis*/power of God unto *soteria*/salvation to every one that believeth (*by faith actions*); to the Jew first, and also to the Greek. 17 For therein is the righteousness of God revealed from faith to faith: as it is written, The just shall *zao*/live (*in miracle power*) by faith (*actions*). 18 For the wrath of God is revealed from heaven against all ungodliness and unrighteousness of men, who hold the truth in unrighteousness." <u>2 Pet 1:12</u> "Wherefore I will not be negligent to put you always in remembrance of these things, though ye know them, and be established in the present truth. 13 Yea, I think it meet, as long as I am in this tabernacle, to stir you up (*to faith actions*) by putting you in remembrance." You can have any opinion or attitude you want now, but on that Day, only God's opinion will stand.

So how do you fight hypocrisy in your own life before you can straighten out others? Consider this faith action medicine: Read Ephesians 1:1-4:16 and pray the prayers in Eph 1 and 3 daily. Obey Eph 4:17-6:24 by mediating on it day and night, visualizing yourself obeying each verse, phrase and concept joyfully and in gladness, just as Jesus would. Then make sure you obey at least one thing every hour of every day. Also use the ten steps for handling sin found in The Wrath of God section in the Glossary. Read the Affirmation Magnets in this book at least once a day. Do this for nine months, and ask others to check your attitude, and tape record your "casual" words on a regular basis.

CHAPTER 15

UNDERSTANDING HOW TO GO TO THE NEXT LEVEL

One could ask, "How is this idea different from positive thinking?" In part, it is not. The righteous by Jesus are the ultimate positive thinkers and speakers. An ultimate command to positive thinking is found in: Phil 4:4 "Rejoice in the Lord alway: and again I say, Rejoice. 5 Let your moderation be known unto all men. The Lord is at hand. 6 Be careful (*anxious, worried or terrified*) for nothing; but in every thing by prayer and supplication with thanksgiving let your *aiteo*/requests be made known unto God. 7 And the peace of God, which passeth all understanding, shall keep your hearts and minds through Christ Jesus. 8 Finally, brethren, whatsoever things are true, whatsoever things are honest, whatsoever things are just, whatsoever things are pure, whatsoever things are lovely, whatsoever things are of good report; if there be any virtue, and if there be any praise, think on these things."

So the major difference between the power of affirmations and positive thinking is that God requires your positive thinking to be the result of your trust and obedience in Him, not yourself, Fate or the Universe. All other methods do not meet His requirements and will not survive the Day of Judgment. But you are free to choose to do whatever you want, up until that Day. That Day appears far off and the consequences remote, but rest assured it is spoken, and it will be, and death will not keep you from it. Rev 1:17 "And when I saw him (*Jesus*), I fell at his feet as dead. And he

Understanding How to Go to the Next Level

laid his right hand upon me, saying unto me, Fear not; I am the first and the last: 18 I am he that *zao*/liveth, and was dead; and, behold, I am *zao*/alive for evermore, Amen; and have the keys of hell and of death." Heb 6:2 "Of the doctrine of baptisms, and of laying on of hands, and of resurrection of the dead, and of eternal judgment." 2 Pet 3:7 "But the heavens and the earth, which are now, by the same word are kept in store, reserved unto fire against the day of judgment and perdition of ungodly men." 2 Cor 5:10 "For we must all appear before the judgment seat of Christ; that every one may receive the things done in his body, according to that he hath done, whether it be good or bad." Rev 20:11 "And I saw a great white throne, and him that sat on it, from whose face the earth and the heaven fled away; and there was found no place for them. 12 And I saw the dead, small and great, stand before God; and the books were opened: and another book was opened, which is the book of *zoe*/life: and the dead were judged out of those things which were written in the books, according to their works. 13 And the sea gave up the dead which were in it; and death and hell delivered up the dead which were in them: and they were judged every man according to their works. 14 And death and hell were cast into the lake of fire. This is the second death. 15 And whosoever was not found written in the book of *zoe*/life was cast into the lake of fire." Acts 17:30 "And the times of this ignorance God winked at; but now commandeth all men every where to repent: 31 because he hath appointed a day, in the which he will judge the world in righteousness by that man whom he hath ordained; whereof he hath given assurance unto all men, in that he hath raised him from the dead."

By the way, in Phil 4:8, that phase *good report* means that no matter how bad it is, with God you can overcome and deliver His glory into the Earth with Him by faith actions. In a good report, giant problems will fall loudly. See Numbers 13 and 14 for more on this matter of a "good report."

All of God's laws are made for man, those we consider natural and those we consider supernatural. To God, they are all one. Consider radio or television or even cell phone waves. They pass around and through us all the time, yet until we turn on a radio or television or our cell phone rings, we do not know it is happening. Such is the world of the spirit. So, to God, there is no distinction, as there is to us. So, for the sake of study, we may separate various aspects, yet to God and our reality, they are all interconnected.

One way to describe God is this: James 1:17 "Every good gift and every perfect gift is from above, and cometh down from the Father of lights, with whom is no variableness, neither shadow of turning." 1 John 1:5 "This then is the message which we have heard of him, and declare unto you, that God is light, and in him is no darkness at all." Deut 32:4 "He is the Rock, his work is perfect: for all his ways are judgment: a God of truth and without iniquity, just and right is he."

Vibration is described by a wave or curve that goes up and down, the up being positive and the down being negative. All vibration has a discontinuity of the positive and negative. The frequency, the distance between two positive peaks, implies a negative bottom in between. This vibration has, within its very nature, a greater and a lesser, or a light (positive) and a dark (negative). But, in God, there is no vibration; He is solid light.

The definition of God is that He is light, with no darkness, i.e., there is no vibration in Him. He is totally positive, with no negative darkness. Not only is God light, He is also *agape*/love. 1 John 4:16 "… God is *agape*/love; and he that dwelleth in *agape*/love dwelleth in God, and God in him." What an invitation, to know God as you walk in *agape*/love, and He walks where you walk!

As God is *agape*/love, we can consider *agape*/love an out-worked extension of this purity, or lack of negativity, in God. But we must work to stay in this *agape*/love. 1 Tim 1:4 "Neither give heed to fables and endless genealogies, which minister questions, rather than godly edifying which is in faith: so do. 5 Now the end of the commandment is *agape*/charity out of a pure heart, and of a good conscience, and of faith unfeigned: 6 from which some having swerved have turned aside unto vain jangling."

All of nature, for this eon, has vibration. What we call "natural law" operates within this vibration and, thus, has its own seed of destruction-negativity or darkness in it. When God is done with the process we now call time, here is His objective, as He Himself spoke it to Moses: Num 14:21 "But as truly as I live, all the earth shall be filled with the glory of the LORD." This is described partially in Revelation chapters 21 and 22.

Notice that God describes Himself as "alive" and, therefore, He is not an inanimate object or force, but a person. The amazing thing is that in Jesus we can operate in the *zoe* life and *agape* love of God, and both the *zoe* and *agape* of God, as well as Holy Spirit who now dwells in the new-creation Christian, likewise, have no vibration. So, to the extent that we operate like Jesus, without vibration or in godly purity, the more we correctly or completely relate to Him. All other lesser levels will one day be destroyed. This level of "natural" or "supernatural" vibration is the realm where the devil, demons and evil spirits freely operate. So, if you are going to deal in the spiritual or the natural world, you may be assured that you will encounter evil spirits. And as long as you operate at any level of "vibration," you are susceptible to attacks and deception from these evil spirits. 1 Pet 5:8 "Be sober, be vigilant; because your adversary the devil, as a roaring lion, walketh about, seeking whom he may devour."

A mind renewed in the Word of God, in the New Testament revelation of Jesus, the Christ, as well as the rest of the Scriptures, are your first line of defense. As Jesus said: John 8:31 "Then said Jesus to those Jews which believed on him, If ye continue in my word, then are ye my disciples indeed; 32 and ye shall know the truth, and the truth shall make you free." Notice that it takes constant repetition of truth in faith actions to make it work, to set and keep you free. That is the purpose of the Affirmations in this book. They are mostly scripture, to keep you in the Word of Christ and trusting God. Because the subconscious knows only the present, many of the affirmations from the Bible are converted to the present tense, as if fully done. Thus, your subconscious will accept that you can now live in that Word. This how you move to the next level in God.

UNDERSTANDING HOW TO GO TO THE NEXT LEVEL

What is amazing is that many of the affirmations needed no change, such as: Gal 2:20 "I am (*have been*) crucified with Christ: nevertheless I *zao*/live; yet not I, but Christ *zao*/liveth in me: and the life which I now *zao*/live in the flesh I *zao*/live by the faith (*actions*) *in* the Son of God, who *agape*/loved me, and gave himself for me. 21 I do not frustrate the grace of God: for if righteousness come by the law, then Christ is dead in vain."

The second part to moving forward is to have some patience as you make and keep your heart pure in Jesus by continual right faith actions. 2 Tim 2:19 "Nevertheless the foundation of God standeth sure, having this seal, The Lord knoweth them that are his. And, Let every one that nameth the name of Christ depart from iniquity. 20 But in a great house there are not only vessels of gold and of silver, but also of wood and of earth; and some to honour, and some to dishonour. 21 If a man therefore purge himself from these, he shall be a vessel unto honour, sanctified, and meet for the master's use, and prepared unto every good work. 22 Flee also youthful lusts: but follow righteousness, faith, *agape*/charity, peace, with them that call on the Lord out of a pure heart (*subconscious mind*). 23 But foolish and unlearned questions avoid, knowing that they do gender strifes. 24 And the servant of the Lord must not strive; but be gentle unto all men, apt to teach, patient, 25 in meekness instructing those that oppose themselves; if God peradventure will give them (*including yourself*) repentance to the acknowledging of the truth; 26 and that they may recover themselves out of the snare of the devil, who are taken captive by him at his will (*because they have the devil's thoughts as strongholds within their conscious and subconscious mind*)." 2 Tim 3:14 "But continue thou in the things which thou hast learned and hast been assured of, knowing of whom thou hast learned them; 15 and that from a child thou hast known the holy scriptures, which are able to make thee wise unto *soteria*/salvation through faith (*actions*) which is in Christ Jesus. 16 All scripture is given by inspiration of God, and is profitable for doctrine, for reproof, for correction, for instruction in righteousness: 17 that the man (*or woman*) of God may be perfect (*mature*), throughly furnished unto all good works." 1 Thes 4:3 "For this is the will of God, even your sanctification, that ye should abstain from fornication: 4 that every one of you should know how to possess his vessel in sanctification and honour; 5 not in the lust of concupiscence, even as the Gentiles which know not God." 1 John 3:2 "*Agape*/beloved, now are we the sons of God, and it doth not yet appear what we shall be: but we know that, when he shall appear, we shall be like him; for we shall see him as he is. 3 And every man that hath this hope in him purifieth himself, even as he (*Jesus*) is pure." 1 Tim 1:5 "Now the end of the commandment is *agape*/charity out of a pure heart, and of a good conscience, and of faith unfeigned: 6 from which some having swerved have turned aside unto vain jangling."

Join in the race to make hearts free from fear, and put on the pure, without vibration, *agape*/love in Christ Jesus. Let's get started! And, in the process, let's get rid of all the "vain jangling."

CHAPTER 16

UNDERSTANDING HOW TO APPROACH HEALING

The New Testament makes it clear that healing, like Jesus performed, is part of the Gospel and part of a renewed mind. Matt 28:18 "And Jesus came and spake unto them, saying, All power is given unto me in heaven and in earth. 19 Go ye therefore, and teach all nations, baptizing them in the name of the Father, and of the Son, and of the Holy Ghost: 20 teaching them to observe all things whatsoever I have commanded you: and, lo, I am with you alway, even unto the end of the world. Amen."

What are some of the things He taught His disciples to do regarding healing? Matt 10:7 "And as ye go, preach, saying, The kingdom of heaven is at hand. 8 Heal the sick, cleanse the lepers, raise the dead, cast out devils: freely ye have received, freely give." Luke 9:1 "Then he called his twelve disciples together, and gave them power and authority (*pre-permission*) over all devils, and to cure diseases. 2 And he sent them to preach the kingdom of God, and to heal the sick." This was His work, as the great Arm of God described in Isaiah 53.

Because of His great compassion, Jesus continued to see the need for more healing, so He added others to do this ministry of healing. Luke 10:1 "After these things the Lord appointed other seventy also, and sent them two and two before his face into every city and place, whither he himself would come. 2 Therefore

Understanding How to Approach Healing

said he unto them ... , 8 And into whatsoever city ye enter, and they receive you, eat such things as are set before you: 9 and heal the sick that are therein, and say unto them, The kingdom of God is come nigh unto you." When these returned in victory, Jesus reaffirmed: Luke 10:19 "Behold, I give unto you power to tread on serpents and scorpions, and over all the power of the enemy: and nothing shall by any means hurt you. 20 Notwithstanding in this rejoice not, that the spirits are subject unto you; but rather rejoice, because your names are written in heaven."

So, for a period of time we see eighty-three people ministering like Jesus, in healing the sick, raising the dead, casting out devils and cleansing the lepers. This was, of course, Jesus, the twelve (including Judas), and then the seventy, and what they were all doing was part of the command included in the Great Commission of Matthew 28.

We must not forget those who used the name of Jesus to do the same things. This was repeated twice in the Scriptures, so we would not miss the message. Mark 9:38 "And John answered him, saying, Master, we saw one casting out devils in thy name, and he followeth not us: and we forbad him, because he followeth not us. 39 But Jesus said, Forbid him not: for there is no man which shall do a miracle in my name, that can lightly speak evil of me. 40 For he that is not against us is on our part." Luke 9:50 "And Jesus said unto him, Forbid him not: for he that is not against us is for us."

This surely makes it appear that if you are doing the same ministry, Jesus will not stop you either. It must be that this is something He wants done—using His name to free any and all people from any and all oppressions of the devil according to: Acts 10:38 "How God anointed Jesus of Nazareth with the Holy Ghost and with power: who went about doing good, and healing all that were oppressed (*under the active dominion, reign or lordship*) of the devil; for God was with him."

This is summarized in this scripture: Mark 16:15 "And he said unto them, Go ye into all the world, and preach the gospel to every creature. 16 He that believeth and is baptized shall be *sozo*/saved; but he that believeth not shall be damned. 17 And these signs shall follow them that believe; In my name shall they cast out devils; they shall speak with new tongues; 18 they shall take up serpents; and if they drink any deadly thing, it shall not hurt them; they shall lay hands on the sick, and they shall recover. 19 So then after the Lord had spoken unto them, he was received up into heaven, and sat on the right hand of God. 20 And they went forth, and preached everywhere, the Lord working with them, and confirming the word with signs following. Amen." Believers do all of these right faith action things.

From the time of the Acts of the Apostles until recent times, there have always been reports of miraculous healings. Today, in the Second and Third Worlds, there are still numerous reports of healings in the name of Jesus Christ. Except for the beginning period of Christianity, there has never been a record of so many signs and wonders being done in the name of Jesus throughout the Earth.

OK, GOD, NOW WHAT?

Holy Spirit fully declares: 1 Cor 2:4 "And my speech and my preaching was not with enticing words of man's wisdom, but in demonstration of the Spirit and of power: 5 that your faith (*actions*) should not stand in the wisdom of men, but in the *dunamis*/(*miracle*) power of God." While many have struggled to get the Gospel truth out, it is fair to say that, in the Western world, for the most part, preaching has emphasized more fully the wisdom of men and not the power of God. In general, Western Christian churches are not places where people go to get healed of blindness or arthritis, cancer or any other infirmity. Yet Jesus said prophetically that this is what believers would do. In the Second and Third Worlds, many do go to Christian churches (of a variety of denominations) for healing, and many are healed in the name of Jesus.

A renewed mind must deal with the fact that we are to grow up into Jesus in "all" respects, and that includes healing and signs and wonders in the name of Jesus. Eph 4:13 "Till we all come in the unity of the faith, and of the knowledge of the Son of God, unto a perfect (*mature*) man, unto the measure of the stature of the fulness of Christ: 14 that we henceforth be no more children, tossed to and fro, and carried about with every wind of doctrine, by the sleight of men, and cunning craftiness, whereby they lie in wait to deceive; 15 but speaking the truth in *agape*/love, may grow up into him in all things, which is the head, even Christ." Jesus healed the sick, and so must those who are like Him. This is made clear in 1 Pet 2:24 "... by his stripes we were healed."

Jesus is ever the Healer, for He cannot change His nature. Heb 13:8 "Jesus Christ the same yesterday, and to day, and for ever." And we have the same Spirit as Jesus had and still has. Gal 4:6 "And because ye are sons, God hath sent forth the Spirit of his Son into your hearts, crying, Abba (*Daddy*), Father." Therefore our inner desire is to walk just like Jesus walked. It takes much negative training or soul corruption to continue to deny this core nature of a Christian.

Based on the historical records (and the Bible is one of the most historically validated ancient documents in existence), ancient Judaism and early Christianity were steeped in the miraculous power of God demonstrated through less-than-perfect men and women. One practical manual on this subject is our *Battle Prayer for Divine Healing, Field Manual 2*. It is not our purpose here to provide the scriptural evidence for healing. I simply offer the fact that the word *Christian*, meaning "a Christ-like one," says it all.

The Affirmations in this book contain numerous references to the fact that each believer is to readily minister healing, according to Mark 16:17-18. Other ancient texts of the first three hundred years of Christianity support that it was the laymen, and not just the leaders, who were known for miracles, thus living out Mark 16:16-18. A renewed mind, with the purpose of operating in the *agape*/love of God, includes releasing this healing ability.

Understanding How to Approach Healing

The Anglican Church studied the powerful events reported in South Africa under the ministry of Dr. John G. Lake around 1910 and, concluding that they were valid, started a healing ministry within that church that continues today. It is known as the Emmanuel Society and the Order of St. Luke. *The Healing Reawakening* by F. MacNutt (Grand Rapids, MI: Chosen Books, 2005) discusses the fact that today, in Africa, a church that cannot deliver healing by the name of Jesus loses attendance. So the Catholic Church is now operating in the-name-of-Jesus miracles there. For more detail on this please examine www.jglm.org, the official web site of John G. Lake Ministries and www.CovenantPeaceMinistries.com. So, without apology, the Affirmations in Christ contain appropriate scriptural confessions, assuming that Mark 16:15-18 is the expected behavior for every Christian, and not just a special few.

One way to describe healing, or any activity that releases the *zoe*/life of God into a situation, is to imagine an irrigation pump. First there is a source of water (the healing *zoe* in the Word of God and in your spirit, with Holy Spirit). Faith is both the hose and the pump. The valve that releases water to flow is your heart, single-minded on healing in compassion and/or authority in Jesus' name. Put the hose to the water, turn on the pump, open the valve and pump life. We are the hose; the pump and the valve is our soul; the *zoe* travels, by faith, through your soul to the one in need. Soul agreement with God, in compassion, authority, righteousness and judgment against the devil, is the pump pressure. Co-laborers, man and God, heal people from the devil's oppressions with God's Holy Spirit *zoe*/life.

The fuel is compassion, authority, righteousness and judgment to make people free, knowing your sins and theirs were remitted in Jesus, and just as you need a spark plug and ignition system to start an engine, your faith action "stirring up" is your ignition system, to light the fire that burns in your soul. That "stirring up" process aligns your heart and your mind, opening the valve with God and His *agape*/love, so that He can flow readily though you. With a heart firmly entrenched in the Word of God (a hose connected to the lake), the valve open and the pump running in faith actions, we release the *zoe* of God to heal, as Jesus did, with our words and/or hands.

Jesus is our example, and we see that He walked in great confidence in God and freely delivered *zoe*/life, God's resurrection power. John 11:33 "When Jesus therefore saw her weeping, and the Jews also weeping which came with her, he groaned (*snorted as a war horse, ready to go to battle, a sign of stirring Himself up*) in the spirit, and was troubled (*stirred, agitated in Himself in indignation*)." This was equivalent to Jesus stirring Himself up in zeal or anger, as the "pump," to push out the *zoe* of God.

Here we see Him continuing in this "stirring-up." Notice, first, the Jews knew God heard Jesus and that He could deliver the *zoe*/life of God at will. John 11:37 "And some of them said, Could not this man, which opened the eyes of the blind, have caused that even this man should not have died? 38 Jesus therefore again groaning in himself (*stirred up, agitated in an aggressive manner, in indignation, to change something*) cometh to the grave. It was a cave, and a stone lay upon it."

Notice the confidence Jesus had with God. John 11:39 "Jesus said, Take ye away the stone. Martha, the sister of him that was dead, saith unto him, Lord, by this time he stinketh: for he hath been dead four days. 40 Jesus saith unto her, Said I not unto thee, that, if thou wouldest believe, thou shouldest see the glory of God? 41 Then they took away the stone from the place where the dead was laid. And Jesus lifted up his eyes, and said, **Father, I thank thee that thou hast heard me. 42 And I knew that thou hearest me always**: but because of the people which stand by I said it, that they may believe that thou hast sent me. 43 And when he thus had spoken, he cried with a loud (*strong and direct*) voice, Lazarus, come forth. 44 And he that was dead came forth, bound hand and foot with graveclothes: and his face was bound about with a napkin. Jesus saith unto them, Loose him, and let him go." The glory of God includes raising the dead.

Jesus was not quiet or subdued throughout this entire process, so a quiet church is not always the right atmosphere to raise the dead or get the power of God moving. Jesus was agitated, stirred up, to fix a wrong and had confidence that God heard Him. We are told that our confidence in God is one of the paths to His being able to answer our *aiteo*/asking (requiring, demanding, expecting, desiring) Him to move in power. 1 John 5:13 "These things have I written unto you that believe on the name of the Son of God; that ye may know that ye have eternal *zoe*/life, and that ye may believe on the name of the Son of God. 14 And this is the confidence that we have in him, that, if we *aiteo*/ask any thing according to his will, he heareth us: 15 and if we know that he hear us, whatsoever we *aiteo*/ask, we know that we have the *aiteo*/petitions that we *aiteo*/desired of him. 16 If any man see his brother sin a sin which is not unto death, he shall *aiteo*/ask, and he shall give him *zoe*/life for them ... ." The issue is our "knowing" that Father God has heard us and will respond to our *aiteo*/request. (Right hearing means that you not only hear, but also obey what you have heard. Thus, in answered prayer, God is responding to you.)

Confidence expressed in our mouth and our actions is the valve. For this to be successful, our subconscious (or heart) needs to cooperate with our intentions and attitude, to deliver healing. Right affirmations are one of God's ways to build these right attitudes. Thanksgiving, praise, proclamation, gladness, enthusiasm, agitation, invigoration, and being stirred up are all parts of the faith-action pump to empower the *zoe*/life to flow where it is needed.

This does not mean just outward invigoration, but can be an attitude of the heart, so that on the outside you appear calm, but on the inside there is a raging furnace of God's *agape*/love, to release His *zoe*/life into the Earth. Rev 1:13 "And in the midst of the seven candlesticks one like unto the Son of man, clothed with a garment down to the foot, and girt about the paps with a golden girdle. 14 His head and his hairs were

UNDERSTANDING HOW TO APPROACH HEALING

white like wool, as white as snow; and **his eyes were as a flame of fire**; 15 and his feet like unto fine brass, as if they burned in a furnace; and his voice as the sound of many roaring waters." You, too, can have the fire of Jesus burning in your heart to release the *zoe* of God. 1 John 4:17 "… because as he is, so are we in this world."

I have observed, with myself and others, that when ministering *zoe*/life, it is best to take a few moments to stir yourself up, to start or to maintain the enthusiasm of Holy Spirit. Often, this is done with a few moments of praise or speaking in tongues, walking and clapping and shouting. To get the "pump" going may require much longer, if you are in a "cold start." Even during periods of long ministry to many people the effective minister will regularly stop ministering and take a few moments to get refreshed and stirred up again into God's enthusiasm. (This is necessary when ministering to large groups of people on a one-by-one basis.) As a normal course of your life, if you stay stirred up into God's *agape*/love all day every day, you can be ready to minister in a moment's notice, as you go about your daily routine.

If you are distracted by what others think (called fear of man) or how inadequate you are (fear of failure), get your mind back on the Lord, who came to destroy the works of the devil and left us with the job of finishing the work. Fear of man is a snare, but with continued use of the Affirmations, you will renew your mind to become a useful co-laborer with God. Since healing and being healed are by grace, you will never be worthy or feel fully adequate, so instead, start praising God for His strength, despite your feelings of inadequacy. Grace is not about you, but about God's goodness, power and love by and through Jesus in you.

The people of Israel were asked to cross the Jordan River and kill giants, but most of them lived a "bad report," and so they died in the wilderness. Ps 78:41 "Yea, they turned back and tempted God, and limited the Holy One of Israel." A bad attitude in mere men stopped God from working. We may have Holy Spirit dwelling within us, but He is still limited by our enthusiasm and confidence in Him. 2 Tim 1:6 "Wherefore I put thee in remembrance that thou stir up (*by continual right faith actions*) the gift of God, which is in thee by the putting on of my hands. 7 For God hath not given us the spirit of fear; but of *dunamis*/power (*miracle ability*), and of *agape*/love, and of a sound mind (*to think and act just like Jesus would*)." Notice that we may have the gift and power of Holy Spirit, but until we get our thinking and our soul with spiritual emotions lined up on the Word of God with right faith actions, He cannot come forth and exercise that *dunamis*/power and *agape*/love, and get us into right Jesus-thinking in the mind of Christ.

One of the goals addressed in this book is that these Affirmations become, not just theory, but reality, and you become deeply conscious of the ever-present Christ in your life for every situation and event—on His terms, not yours. Gal 2:19 "For I through the law am dead to the law, that I might *zao*/live unto God. 20 I am (*have been*) crucified with Christ: nevertheless I *zao*/live; yet not I, but Christ *zao*/liveth in me: and the life which I now *zao*/live in the flesh I *zao*/live by the faith

OK, God, Now What?

(actions) in the Son of God, who *agape*/loved me, and gave himself for me. 21 I do not frustrate the grace of God: for if righteousness come by the law, then Christ is dead in vain." Walking in this is walking in the confidence that Jesus had.

Thus, you can make your faith effective in demonstrating the supernatural power of God, just as Jesus did. 2 Cor 13:5 "Examine yourselves, whether ye be in the faith; prove your own selves. Know ye not your own selves, how that Jesus Christ is in you, except ye be reprobates (*useless, like garbage, ineffective and lacking spiritual power or prayer answers*)?" Philem 6 "That the communication of thy faith may become effectual by the acknowledging of every good thing which is in you in Christ Jesus." 1 Cor 2:5 "That your faith should not stand in the wisdom of men, but in the power of God."

You can take almost any section of the Affirmations and use them to "stir yourself up into God," into enthusiasm with loud words, shouting, proclaiming, clapping, dancing, walking, running, prancing, smiling, singing, jumping, arm waving and yelling. Fullness of joy is not quiet or sad, but full of life and thanksgiving. So delivering the healing of God is part of being like Jesus and walking in His joy.

With the Affirmations, we can keep our heart in the Word of God, as they contain many scriptures on divine healing. As we attach strong positive emotion to the right thoughts and actions to deliver healing, we prepare our heart to cooperate, and not fight us, as we *aiteo* for ourselves or others. Our faith, confidence and courage opens the heart valve to deliver the *zoe*/life God so longs to deliver through each of us in the Body of Christ. Affirmations A-Z and 54-58 are focused on healing and prayer effectiveness.

The following three prayers are for healing from our *Battle Prayer for Divine Healing, Field Manual 2* and have been used successfully by many. With slight adaptations, they will fit any situation that is not like Heaven on Earth. The first and third prayers are based on those from Curry Blake found at www.jglm.org.

To stir yourself up in God with right faith actions, use the Affirmations as strong and bold declarations, with praise and thanksgiving, then say (in *aiteo*) the following prayers. Just as with thanksgiving, joy or praise, in preparation for prayer, you can act your way into believing quicker than you can believe your way into acting. Do this first until you begin to feel it. To stir yourself up in God, say any of the Affirmations until your confidence in God has grown, then pray these prayers singularly or in sequence, as if hitting a rock with a hammer. Jer 23:29 "Is not my word like as a fire? saith the LORD; and like a hammer that breaketh the rock in pieces?"

Father, in the name of Jesus, have Holy Spirit pray through me now and fill me with Your dominion, love and compassion for this situation to victory. Thank You, Father! In the name of Jesus, thank You! Yahoo!

1. **Father, in the name of Jesus, I/we thank You this is already done.** And, Father, in the name of Jesus, right now, for (PERSON'S NAME), I speak to the devil

Understanding How to Approach Healing

and take authority over you, devil, and bind you to obey me, in the name of Jesus. I speak to this (PROBLEM AREA) and I speak to your body, (PERSON'S NAME), and I say, in the name of Jesus Christ of Nazareth, the Lord of Heaven and Earth, that RIGHT NOW all works of (THE PROBLEM) will GO, infection and disease will die, and none of this will ever return. Any pain, I break you and command you to go and never return. In the name of Jesus, fear of this (DISEASE OR PROBLEM) will leave and not ever return RIGHT NOW, in the name of JESUS, and, (PERSON'S NAME), you will be absolutely healed and normal. You and your body will operate normally, and you will do all things well and normally and you will be a testimony to God. In the name of Jesus, so be it. Receive NOW, in the name of Jesus of Nazareth, by His blood and His stripes. Amen/So Be It!

2. **Father, in the name of Jesus**, I take authority over the devil working in (PERSON'S NAME) right now, by the redeeming blood and healing stripes of Jesus, and, in the name of Jesus, just as if Jesus were here right now, I command you, devil, to hear and obey the voice of the Word of God through me and go NOW. Take all your works, IN THE NAME OF JESUS, and GO NOW, and do not come back. Go NOW, in the name of JESUS! (PROBLEM), in the name of Jesus, you hear and obey the voice of the Word of God through me, and you go now. In the name of Jesus, all symptoms, causes, effects and damage, you go NOW, and do not come back. I command, in the name of Jesus, for (PERSON'S NAME)'s body to be made whole. Body, you hear and obey, and be whole, in the name of Jesus. Pain, fear of pain, and fear of this (PROBLEM), in the name of Jesus, you GO NOW. I bless the entire (PERSON'S FAMILY NAME) family, all relatives, generations, relationships and their right worship and finances, now, in the name of Jesus Christ. Furthermore, in the name of Jesus, devil, all income, property and peace you have destroyed, I command you to repay to (PERSON'S) family, seven times to each one it was taken from, per Proverbs 6:31. So, devil, pay and pay NOW, in the name of JESUS. Thank You, Father, in the name of Jesus, for Your Word and Your *agape*/love. Thank You!

3. **(For an individual or group) In Jesus' name, Father**, I thank You, for this is already done, in Jesus, and I say, in the name of Jesus, right now, Sickness and disease, pain, fear of pain and fear of sickness, GO NOW, in the name of Jesus. You will leave this person/these people. I command you now, Loose them. I command healing, RIGHT NOW. Every bodily, spiritual, physical, emotional, and mental need is to be met right now, in Jesus' name. I command physical healing—NOW. I command pain, fear of pain and any other fear to stop—NOW, in Jesus' name. BE WHOLE! Amen and so be it! In the name of Jesus!

OK, God, Now What?

Father, in the name of Jesus Christ of Nazareth, *Yahweh Rapha*, the LORD that heals us, I thank You that You care for us lovingly with *racham*/mercy and *chesed*/*agape*/love. Praise the power to the name of Jesus, at which every knee shall bow and every tongue confess that Jesus Christ is Lord, to Your glory, Father. By Jesus' blood, we are now a royal priesthood for the nations, to show forth Your praises (see 2 Pet 1:9), and I thank You, Father: Col 1:12 … who hath made us meet to be partakers of the inheritance of the saints in light: 13 who hath delivered us from the power of darkness, and hath translated us into the kingdom of *Your agape*/dear Son: 14 in whom we have redemption through his (*Jesus'*) blood, even the forgiveness of sins. Eph 1:7 … according to the riches of *Your* grace; *for* 2 Cor 2:12 now we have received, not the spirit of the world, but the spirit which is of You, *Father* God; that we might know the things that are freely given to us of *You, Father* God, *in Jesus*. Gal 4:6 And because we are sons, *You, Father* God, *have* sent forth the Spirit of *Your* Son into *my* heart, crying, Abba (*Daddy*), Father. 2 Tim 1:7 For *You, Father* God, *have* not given *me* the spirit of fear; but of power (*ability*), and of *agape*/love, and of a sound mind. 2 Cor 1:21 Now he which stablisheth us … in Christ, and hath anointed us, is *You, Father* God; 22 who hath also sealed us, and given the earnest of the Spirit in our hearts. *And, through Jesus, You have commanded us to extend Your kingdom by setting people free of the oppressions of the devil, all of which You paid for with the soul, body and blood of Jesus.* Matt 10:7 And as *I* go, *I* preach, saying, The kingdom of heaven is at hand. 8 *I* heal the sick, cleanse the lepers, raise the dead, cast out devils: for freely *I* have received, freely *I* give. *Thank You, Father. In the name of Jesus, thank You!*

If you do not see the results you need in one hour, repeat three to twenty times an hour, each hour until you do. This is about results and not just saying, "Well, I prayed, let's see what God will do." You are the determining factor, not God. Luke 10:19 "Behold, I give unto **YOU** power (*pre-permission*) to tread on serpents and scorpions, and over all the power of the enemy: and nothing shall by any means hurt you. 20 Notwithstanding in this rejoice not, that the spirits are subject unto you; but rather rejoice, because your names are written in heaven." This word *tread* includes many steps of dominion until the enemy is subdued. What you tolerate you force God to tolerate, until you will tolerate it no longer, until you get stirred up by faith actions into His attitude toward any work of the devil: "Out, in the name of Jesus!"

Keep at it, according to: Luke 18:1 "And he (*Jesus*) spake a parable unto them to this end, that men ought always to pray, and not to faint." Mark 11:24 "Therefore I (*Jesus*) say unto you, What things soever ye *aiteo*/desire (*require, demand and expect as due by covenant promise*), when ye pray, believe (*by faith actions*) that ye receive them, and ye shall have them." Matt 7:11 "If you then, evil as you are, know how

Understanding How to Approach Healing

to give good and advantageous gifts to your children, how much more will your Father Who is in heaven [perfect as He is] give good and advantageous things to those who keep on *aiteo*/asking Him!" AMP

One man took eight hours of constant healing confession to break the flu, and another time it took him only ten seconds. Another took six weeks of thanksgiving to remove a tumor, another thirty seconds. Another straightened club feet in three minutes, and in another case, it took two days of constant commanding battle. The problem was not the issue, but the attitude of the warrior. In all cases, victory went to those who would not give up. According to 1 Corinthians 13, *agape*/love does not give up.

The grace to win comes with working to win. God has done His part: 2 Pet 1:2 "Grace and peace be multiplied unto you through the (*experiential, actually doing it*) knowledge of God, and of Jesus our Lord, 3 according as his divine power hath given unto us all things that pertain unto *zoe*/life and godliness, through the knowledge of him that hath called us to glory and virtue: 4 whereby are given unto us exceeding great and precious promises: that by these ye might be partakers of the divine nature, having escaped the corruption that is in the world through lust."

The milk of the Word is in the teaching; the meat of the Word is in the doing. Right thinking in God's *zoe* gets us to right doing. John 4:34 "Jesus saith unto them, My meat is to do the will of him that sent me, and to finish his work." John 6:38 "For I came down from heaven, not to do mine own will, but the will of him that sent me." Luke 10:19 "Behold, I (*Jesus*) give unto you power (*pre-permission*) to tread on serpents and scorpions, and over all the power of the enemy: and nothing shall by any means hurt you." James 2:26 "For as the body without the spirit is dead, so faith without works is dead also." James 1:12 "Blessed is the man that endureth temptation (*to give up trusting God to fulfill His Word*): for when he is tried (*by the devil in the face of continued delay and trials, while* lambanoing *the grace of God, the gift of righteousness and the promises of God*), he shall receive the crown of *zoe*/life, which the Lord hath promised to them that *agape*/love him." 1 John 5:2 "By this we know that we *agape*/love the children of God, when we *agape*/love God, and keep his commandments. 3 For this is the *agape*/love of God, that we keep his commandments: and his commandments are not grievous. 4 For whatsoever is born of God overcometh the world: and this is the victory that overcometh the world, even our faith (*actions*). 5 Who is he that overcometh the world, but he that believeth that Jesus is the Son of God?" 1 Thes 5:5 "Ye are all the children of light, and the children of the day: we are not of the night, nor of darkness. 6 Therefore let us not sleep, as do others; but let us watch and be sober. 7 For they that sleep sleep in the night; and they that be drunken are drunken in the night. 8 But let us, who are of the day, be sober, putting on the breastplate of faith and *agape*/love; and for an helmet, the hope of *soteria*/salvation. 9 For God hath not appointed us to wrath, but to obtain *soteria*/salvation by our Lord Jesus Christ, 10 who died for us, that, whether we wake or sleep, we should *zao*/live together with him." Eph 5:8 "For ye were sometimes darkness, but now are ye light in the Lord: walk as children of light."

Under Dr. Lake's ministry, a man prayed in English and tongues for twenty hours every day to break a killing plague. At the end of about three weeks, suddenly all the sick were quickly made well in the whole region. More recently, a group of three men stopped a plague in Mexico by praying in tongues for three days and then laying hands on the sick in Jesus' name, according to Mark 16:18. Faint not! Jesus is Lord through us!

We repeat again for emphasis: one man took eight hours of constant healing confession to break the flu in his own body, and another time it took him only ten seconds. One took six weeks of thanksgiving to remove a tumor, another thirty seconds. One straightened club feet in three minutes, and, in another case, it took two days of constant commanding battle. The problem was not the issue, but the attitude of the warrior. In all cases, victory went to those who would not give up. It is a matter of the heart and will. In all cases, it was God's will to heal. The issue and faith-action effort was with the minister, not God.

Our problem is not God. He is our Helper, but we are the ones who have to do the faith-action doing. "Anything between you and a promise of God is a devil, in either lies we believe and/or in active resistance to healing or salvation," (Curry Blake, The Voice of Healing, KWHB Television broadcast, Episode 2, Tulsa, Oklahoma, March 2007). Get rid of the lies with truth and the devils with commands, in the name of Jesus, and you will see godly results. Agree with God that the devil has had his way long enough, and exercise the authority Jesus has given you to set people free.

You will never do enough to be worthy or to deserve to be used by God; it is all by grace, not works. Do the right things, and you will see right results. A large part of believing is in doing right faith actions. What you do is what you really believe. It is a law of the human spirit that you can act yourself into believing quicker than you can believe yourself into acting. Do, and you will see results. 1 Cor 3:9 "For we are labourers together with God: ye are God's husbandry, ye are God's building." 2 Cor 6:1 "We then, as workers together with him, beseech you also that ye receive not the grace of God in vain. 2 For he saith, I have heard thee in a time accepted, and in the day of *soteria*/salvation (*deliverance, healing*) have I succoured thee: behold, now is the accepted time; behold, now is the day of *soteria*/salvation (*deliverance, healing*)."

This means that the Day of Judgment against the devil has already started with Jesus, and it's up to us now to finish the job, so that all men can enjoy the benefits of salvation. James 4:6 "But he giveth more grace. Wherefore he saith, God resisteth the proud, but giveth grace unto the humble. 7 Submit yourselves therefore to God. Resist the devil, and he will flee from you." Eph 5:14 "Wherefore he saith, Awake thou that sleepest, and arise from the dead, and Christ shall give thee light. 15 See

UNDERSTANDING HOW TO APPROACH HEALING

then that ye walk circumspectly, not as fools, but as wise, 16 redeeming the time, because the days are evil. 17 Wherefore be ye not unwise, but understanding what the will of the Lord is."

Here is a description of the disciples, as Jesus fought to get them to believe: Luke 24:41 "And while they yet believed not for joy, and wondered, he said unto them, Have ye here any meat?" Their joy was falsely based on believing that Jesus had not really died and come back as a full and real man. So to prove it, Jesus ate meat with them. Their expectations outside of scripture prevented them from believing the Word of God concerning the death and resurrection of Jesus. When they did believe, then they could walk in this promise: John 16:23 "And in that day ye shall *aiteo*/ask me nothing. Verily, verily, I say unto you, Whatsoever ye shall *aiteo*/ask the Father in my name, he will give it you. 24 Hitherto have ye *aiteo*/asked nothing in my name: *aiteo*/ask, and ye shall receive, that your joy may be full." That is the goal of the Affirmations contained in this book.

Jesus noted faith when He found it, but did not require faith on the part of the one in need in order to exercise His authority and command healing, so Father God could heal by Holy Spirit. About half the recorded miracles of Jesus note the sick one's faith, a few note the faith of one asking for another, and with about half Jesus exercised all the faith to get them healed. For example, in Nain (Luke 7:11-16) Jesus stopped a funeral procession and raised a dead man without anyone asking Him. So when you minister healing for and with Jesus, you treat each case as if you are raising the dead, and if the one in need has faith, that is an extra benefit, but not a requirement. You be like Jesus and have the faith, and you will avoid a lot of inaccurate theology. The Affirmations are designed to help in building this kind of faith.

Unbelief fears that God will not do it; faith believes God will perform His Word. Strong faith believes it so much that you begin giving God thanks and praise that it is already done, even as you *aiteo* Him to do His Word, His covenant promises. God requires that we keep proclaiming His Word, expecting Him to do it over any situation, until it is done. One way to tell a troubled or doubting heart that you do believe is to start the behaviors of confession, thanksgiving, gladness, praise, joy, affirmation and command in God anyway. If you don't feel it, you can do the right behaviors until you do feel it. At the same time, by constant repetition and right behaviors, you are renewing your mind so that your heart is cleansed into agreeing with God on that topic. It is not that we don't have fears and fear attacks; it is how we handle them when they come that matters. Faint not and perform faith actions!

Lord, give us light until we do Your will in thankful joy.

Again, if you have an urgent healing need, please get our book *Battle Prayer for Divine Healing, Field Manual 2*.

Chapter 17

Understanding How to Use the Affirmations

You can use the Affirmations found in this book as part of a short-term, "cramming" program, to deal with an urgent situation, as a long-term obedience commitment to renew your mind, or as a regular refresher once you have achieved a level of confidence that produces results with God. As with anything worthwhile, it will take diligence.

All thoughts that come into our brain send electrical signals throughout our brain system and often to the rest of our body. Anything we say or think has the same effect. When you read something, the same thing happens. Jesus told us that we get in life what we say. If you want a life like Jesus, then you have to speak like Him. John 3:34 "For he whom God hath sent speaketh the words of God: for God giveth not the Spirit by measure unto him." Therefore the Affirmations are to be spoken, not just read silently.

According to modern science, affirmations direct the subconscious on how to help you achieve your goals. As you make continued affirmations, your subconscious helps in two major ways:

1. First, it interprets events according to your affirmations, so that those affirmations are directed to your conscious mind, to help you act in accordance with your affirmations, as the events occur.

Understanding How to Use the Affirmations

2. The second seems to be an integration process in which the subconscious seems to offer up, through the "conscious," helpful thoughts and ideas that keep you moving in the direction consistent with your affirmations.

Right affirmations produce a right consciousness; wrong affirmations produce a wrong consciousness. 1 Tim 1:5 "Now the end of the commandment is *agape*/charity out of a pure heart, and of a good conscience, and of faith unfeigned."

Outside of modern science, as God works in us, we can now "hear" what He is saying with a small inner voice. But just as when Jesus spoke, if your heart is not ready, you cannot "hear" Him—even if He "yells" and uses a whip. Phil 2:12 "Wherefore, my *agape*/beloved, as ye have always obeyed, not as in my presence only, but now much more in my absence, work out your own *soteria*/salvation with fear and trembling. 13 For it is God which worketh in you both to will and to do of his good pleasure. 14 Do all things without murmurings and disputings: 15 that ye may be blameless and harmless, the sons of God, without rebuke, in the midst of a crooked and perverse nation, among whom ye shine as lights in the world; 16 holding forth the word of *zoe*/life; that I may rejoice in the day of Christ, that I have not run in vain, neither laboured in vain."

The vital tool, built into the human, of the subconscious or the heart, is always working. To improve or change your behaviors, new affirmations can add new thought patterns or attitudes and help replace the negative or non-supportive emotions with supportive or positive emotions on past thoughts, attitudes and ideas, to match your new or current affirmations. For example, top athletes use affirmations as part of the process of making their behaviors match the best of behaviors they desire in game or competition events.

God has always had this tool available, so that men could train their subconscious to match their desired behaviors in Him. Josh 1:7 "Only be thou strong and very courageous (*believing in God to perform His Word, or to have faith in God and do the things He requires, expecting Him to do His part*), that thou mayest observe to do according to all the law, which Moses my servant commanded thee: turn not from it to the right hand or to the left, that thou mayest prosper whithersoever thou goest. 8 This book of the law shall not depart out of thy mouth; but thou shalt meditate therein day and night, that thou mayest observe to do according to all that is written therein: for then thou shalt make thy way prosperous, and then thou shalt have good success. 9 Have not I commanded thee? Be strong and of a good courage; be not afraid, neither be thou dismayed: for the Lord thy God is with thee whithersoever thou goest." Notice that we are to make our own way successful in God, by controlling our thinking and keeping it in God. We start by directing the words we put into our mouth and directing our imagination. We are to do all this with constant repetition and positive emotions. This has never changed.

OK, God, Now What?

God has always required that we write His laws on our heart: Prov 7:2 "Keep my commandments, and live; and my law as the apple of thine eye. 3 Bind them upon thy fingers, write them upon the table of thine heart." We now know that the process of "heart-writing" includes diligent repetition and right imagination. Josh 1:7 "Only be thou strong and very courageous (*by continual right faith actions*), that thou mayest observe to do according to all the law, which Moses my servant commanded thee: turn not from it to the right hand or to the left, that thou mayest prosper whithersoever thou goest. 8 This book of the law shall not depart out of thy mouth; but thou shalt meditate therein day and night, that thou mayest observe to do according to all that is written therein: for then thou shalt make thy way prosperous, and then thou shalt have good success."

A key element of the New Covenant in Jesus is that God will write His laws in our inward parts. Heb 8:10 "For this is the covenant that I will make with the house of Israel after those days, saith the Lord; I will put my laws into their mind, and write them in their hearts: and I will be to them a God, and they shall be to me a people: 11 and they shall not teach every man his neighbour, and every man his brother, saying, Know the Lord: for all shall know me, from the least to the greatest. 12 For I will be merciful to their unrighteousness, and their sins and their iniquities will I remember no more. 13 In that he saith, A new covenant, he hath made the first old. Now that which decayeth and waxeth old is ready to vanish away." Since God has made this promise, you can rest assured that it will happen. We are given the opportunity to do it with His help now, or He will do it later. He will walk freely in men who enter His New Covenant in the body and blood of His wonderful Son, Jesus, the Lord, who works to write His laws on their hearts and minds.

Notice how Paul rejoices that he had a part in the process for the Corinthians: 2 Cor 3:3 "Forasmuch as ye are manifestly declared to be the epistle of Christ ministered by us, written not with ink, but with the Spirit of the living God; not in tables of stone, but in fleshy tables of the heart. 4 And such trust have we through Christ to God-ward: 5 not that we are sufficient of ourselves to think any thing as of ourselves; but our sufficiency is of God; 6 who also hath made us able ministers of the new testament; not of the letter, but of the spirit: for the letter killeth, but the spirit giveth *zoe*/life." This is the process of God writing His laws on our inward parts.

God's plan is that now, in this life, we work with His Word and His gifts. Eph 4:11 "And he gave some, apostles; and some, prophets; and some, evangelists; and some, pastors and teachers; 12 for the perfecting of the saints, for the work of the ministry, for the edifying of the body of Christ: 13 till we all come in the unity of the faith, and of the *epignosis*/knowledge (*as a master craftsman*) of the Son of God, unto a perfect man, unto the measure of the stature of the fulness of Christ: 14 that we henceforth be no more children, tossed to and fro, and carried about with every wind of doctrine, by the sleight of men, and cunning craftiness, whereby they lie

Understanding How to Use the Affirmations

in wait to deceive; 15 but speaking the truth in *agape*/love, may grow up into him in all things, which is the head, even Christ: 16 from whom the whole body fitly joined together and compacted by that which every joint supplieth, according to the effectual working in the measure of every part, maketh increase of the body unto the edifying of itself in *agape*/love." Keep your eye on the target, and you have a chance to hit it.

The first step to real freedom, to being all God made you in Christ, is to recognize or acknowledge that we are commanded to control our thoughts as part of the process of growing in Christ and to no longer be a victim of any thought or information that is "just passing through." Often you cannot stop thoughts from coming to you; you cannot control what your eyes see, what smells you smell or what your ears hear; but you can always control how you respond to all this information and the thoughts you are aware of. And you can and must manage such thoughts when they come. 2 Cor 10:5 "Casting down imaginations, and every high thing that exalteth itself against the knowledge of God, and bringing into captivity every thought to the obedience of Christ."

The Affirmations supplied here are controlled words, mostly scripture, modified to the present tense. Your subconscious mind cannot tell the past or the future, and everything, to it, is present, when the thoughts are activated. So when affirmations are recalled by the subconscious or heart, the memory is present tense and accepted as reality now in your cognitive mind for action consistent with the affirmation(s).

The basis for all right behavior is a strong and good self-identity or self-esteem. The Christian has the greatest self-identity that could possibly exist. Eph 4:24 "And that ye put on the new man, which after God is created in righteousness and true holiness." Col 2:9 "For in him (*Jesus*) dwelleth all the fulness of the Godhead bodily. 10 And ye are complete (*have all things to be able to mature into Him in all respects*) in him, which is the head of all principality and power: 11 in whom also ye are circumcised with the circumcision made without hands, in putting off the body of the sins of the flesh by the circumcision of Christ: 12 buried with him in baptism, wherein also ye are risen with him through the faith (*actions*) *in* the operation of God, who hath raised him from the dead. 13 And you, being dead in your sins and the uncircumcision of your flesh, hath he quickened together with him, having forgiven you all trespasses; 14 blotting out the handwriting of ordinances that was against us, which was contrary to us, and took it out of the way, nailing it to his cross; 15 and having spoiled principalities and powers, he made a shew of them openly, triumphing over them in it."

You do not know the real you until you know yourself as a new creature in Christ Jesus. 2 Cor 5:16 "Wherefore henceforth know we no man after the flesh: yea, though we have known Christ after the flesh, yet now henceforth know we him no more. 17 Therefore if any man be in Christ, he is a new creature: old things are passed away; behold, all things are become new." With this as your self-identity, there is nothing that God in you cannot overcome, thus creating Heaven on Earth. 1 John 4:4 "Ye are of God, little children, and have overcome them: because greater is he that is in you, than he that is in the world." Heb 13:5 "... *God* hath said, I will never leave thee, nor forsake thee. 6 So that we may boldly say, The Lord is my helper, and I will not fear what man shall do unto me." Phil 4:13 "I can do all things through Christ which strengtheneth me." Matt 19:26 "But Jesus beheld them, and said unto them, With men this is impossible; but with God all things are possible." Mark 9:23 "Jesus said unto him, If thou canst believe, all things are possible to him that believeth *(by continual right faith actions)*." Luke 18:27 "And he said, The things which are impossible with men are possible with God." Eph 3:20 "Now unto him that is able to do exceeding abundantly above all that we *aiteo*/ask *(by demanding, requiring or expecting as due by covenant promise)* or think, according to the power that worketh in us, 21 unto him be glory in the church by Christ Jesus throughout all ages, world without end. Amen."

So, in order to control and build righteous memories and righteous emotions, you can speak to yourself the truth of God's love in the present tense, and your subconscious will start to build that truth into your entire mind. But it will take effort. Notice this command: Jude 20 "But ye, *agape*/beloved, building up yourselves on your most holy faith, praying in the Holy Ghost, 21 keep yourselves in the *agape*/love of God, looking for the mercy of our Lord Jesus Christ unto eternal *zoe*/life. 22 And of some have compassion, making a difference: 23 and others *sozo*/save with fear, pulling them out of the fire; hating even the garment spotted by the flesh. 24 Now unto him that is able to keep you from falling, and to present you faultless before the presence of his glory with exceeding joy, 25 to the only wise God our Saviour, be glory and majesty, dominion and power, both now and ever. Amen."

This is a start-and-grow-by-doing life. You can act your way into right believing much faster than you can believe your way into right acting. As an act of your will and intention, start doing the right things, and eventually you will "be" the right things. As Smith Wigglesworth (who had a very miraculous ministry) once said: "If the Spirit is not moving, I move the Spirit" (Curry Blake, The Voice of Healing, KWHB Television Broadcast, Episodes 1 and 2, Tulsa, Oklahoma, March 2007). Or, as Holy Spirit commands: 2 Tim 1:6 "Wherefore I put thee in remembrance that thou stir up [*by faith actions*] the gift of God, which is in thee by the putting on of my hands. 7 For God hath not given us the spirit of fear; but of *dunamis*/power *(miracle ability)*, and of *agape*/love, and of a sound mind *(like Jesus has)*." Thus, you will become expert at controlling your thoughts and purposely doing thanksgiving, praise and joy without feeling, often against great emotional and mental resistance, until you and God get in agreement in your heart. Just like the need to bathe daily, this battle will never really end until Revelation 21 and 22 come to pass.

Understanding How to Use the Affirmations

So read, speak and do the right things of right faith actions until you are in agreement with them, knowing you are re-prioritizing what your subconscious or heart will recall to various events in your life. This may take one second or one hundred years; it all depends on what you and others have built into your subconscious in your life up until now. Phil 3:13 "Brethren, I count not myself to have apprehended: but this one thing I do, forgetting those things which are behind, and reaching forth unto those things which are before, 14 I press toward the mark for the prize of the high calling of God in Christ Jesus."

Speak in the present tense, and your mind will obey in the present tense those memories with the greatest emotional content. So, add strong positive emotional actions as you read the Affirmations. These include thanks, joy, respect, gratitude, praise, acceptance and love. Thoughts and memories move to the higher recall priority by strong emotional content and repetition. As you add repetition and high emotional content, these are the thoughts and attitudes that you will respond with first when faced with the various situations of life. Keep repeating the Affirmations daily so that they remain in priority over the many negative or neutral daily events as they occur, thus obeying Philippians 4:6-9, Titus 3:8 and Philemon 6.

The full set of Affirmation Magnets take two and a half to four hours to make, depending on how fast you speak and how much you meditate on them as you say them. The more you can repeat them each day, the better. Add variety by saying them with more emotion, and stop for a time of thanksgiving and praise. Aim for at least two hours a day spent in this way. Less time per day will mean slower and weaker results, and more is definitely better. Remember, you are receiving information and thoughts all day long. This prepares you to accept the help Holy Spirit is shedding abroad into your heart on a continual basis, but because of hardness of heart toward Him, you cannot "hear" Him to obey. Unless you take your God-given right and command to manage your thoughts and behavior, others will manage your thoughts and behavior for you. In this case, God is your Helper and not your "Doer." On the Day of Judgment, you will not be able to point a finger at God and accuse Him of not helping you, but you will moan in agony over all the times you ignored His help.

Typically, most people start the morning in faith that God is using this exercise in His Word to change them, with a half hour to three hours of the Affirmations, followed by prayer, including tongues. Then they meditate, or chew on the Scriptures throughout the day. Try turning various affirmations and scriptures into songs, and sing them to yourself throughout the day. Then repeat or make new scriptural affirmations before going to sleep at night. We highly recommend going to sleep listening to scripture, usually the New Testament letters or scripture songs. [The musical group, Son of Korah, has done a great job of setting the Psalms to modern music. Visit their website at http://www.sonsofkorah.com. With Internet word searches, you can find other sources of scripture songs or scriptures in song.]

OK, GOD, NOW WHAT?

The best path seems to be to first focus on speaking the Affirmations through at least one session a day, and, as you do, trust God to get what you need into you. Expect at least one scripture to come more alive to you as you speak. If none does, trust that Holy Spirit is working anyway, and pick one yourself to focus on. This is an attitude of letting the Word work on you, rather than you working or laboring in the Word to gain understanding. Also add in two hours of tongues per day.

Some aspects of the Affirmations is like riding a train or a bus and looking out the window at the countryside. You cannot stop and look more closely; you just keep moving. For later sessions in the day, walk the journey, stopping on certain scriptures and really "chewing" on them. Over time (obviously with a labor in faith actions), you will get your heart more singled-minded on God through His Word and actually become a living "word of God" yourself. This is also included in the definition of what it means to be a Christian, a "Christ-like" one, the Word of God being made flesh in you as well.

In John 5:15-34, Jesus looked at all of the Old Testament and concluded that He could do those things He saw His Father do, including raise the dead. This is keeping your eye on the goodness of the Lord, for Jesus is the "exact representation," the true message of who and what Father God is. Where your eye is, this is where your heart will be as well. You can build value in the Earth of the earthly or of the heavenly. What you ponder on and speak of shows where your heart really is. Matt 6:19 "Lay not up for yourselves treasures upon earth, where moth and rust doth corrupt, and where thieves break through and steal: 20 but lay up for yourselves treasures in heaven, where neither moth nor rust doth corrupt, and where thieves do not break through nor steal: 21 for where your treasure is, there will your heart be also. 22 The light of the body is the eye: if therefore thine eye be single, thy whole body shall be full of light. 23 But if thine eye be evil, thy whole body shall be full of darkness. If therefore the light that is in thee be darkness, how great is that darkness! 24 No man can serve two masters: for either he will hate the one, and love the other; or else he will hold to the one, and despise the other. Ye cannot serve (*set your life source on and* zao *in both*) God and mammon."

The very lifestyle of the natural or worldly man brings a curse. Jer 17:5 "Thus saith the LORD; Cursed be the man that trusteth in man, and maketh flesh his arm, and whose heart departeth from the LORD. 6 For he shall be like the heath in the desert, and shall not see when good cometh; but shall inhabit the parched places in the wilderness, in a salt land and not inhabited. 7 Blessed is the man that trusteth (*by continual faith actions*) in the LORD, and whose hope the LORD is. 8 For he shall be as a tree planted by the waters, and that spreadeth out her roots by the river, and shall not see when heat cometh, but her leaf shall be green; and shall not be careful in the year of drought, neither shall cease from yielding fruit. 9 The heart is deceitful above all things, and desperately wicked: who can know it? 10 I the LORD

Understanding How to Use the Affirmations

search the heart, I try the reins, even to give every man according to his ways, and according to the fruit of his doings."

Verses 7, 9 and 10 above show that what we really trust in is a matter of the heart. The wise man asks God to use His Word to evaluate where his heart really is. Ps 139:23 "Search me, O God, and know my heart: try me, and know my thoughts: 24 and see if there be any wicked way in me, and lead me in the way everlasting."

While the Christian is "complete in Christ," there is a lot of work between what we are made (complete) and how we really walk (perfection into the maturity of Christ): Eph 4:15 "But speaking the truth in *agape*/love, may grow up into him in all things, which is the head, even Christ." Our great tool is the written Word of God. Heb 4:11 "Let us labour [*in continual right faith actions*] therefore to enter into that rest, lest any man fall after the same example of unbelief. 12 For the word of God is quick, and powerful, and sharper than any twoedged sword, piercing even to the dividing asunder of soul and spirit, and of the joints and marrow, and is a discerner of the thoughts and intents of the heart. 13 Neither is there any creature that is not manifest in his sight: but all things are naked and opened unto the eyes of him with whom we have to do." See also Psalm 119. This is not to be done merely in the letter, which leads to death, but in the Spirit, which leads to *zoe*/life.

The first "trap" to pass is to not get caught up in the Law, religious observance, and to honor God with the lips and not the heart. Rom 7:5 "For when we were in the flesh, the motions of sins, which were by the law, did work in our members to bring forth fruit unto death. 6 But now we are delivered from the law, that being dead wherein we were held; that we should serve in newness of spirit, and not in the oldness of the letter." 2 Cor 3:3 "Forasmuch as ye are manifestly declared to be the epistle of Christ ministered by us, written not with ink, but with the Spirit of the *zao*/living God; not in tables of stone, but in fleshy tables of the heart. 4 And such trust have we through Christ to God-ward: 5 not that we are sufficient of ourselves to think any thing as of ourselves; but our sufficiency is of God; 6 who also hath made us able ministers of the new testament; not of the letter, but of the spirit: for the letter killeth, but the spirit giveth *zoe*/life. 7 But if the ministration of death, written and engraven in stones (*through Moses*), was glorious, so that the children of Israel could not stedfastly behold the face of Moses for the glory of his countenance; which glory was to be done away: 8 how shall not the ministration of the spirit be rather glorious? 9 For if the ministration of condemnation be glory, much more doth the ministration of righteousness (*by grace, through faith in Jesus*) exceed in glory [*manifested in the Earth*]."

One measure of walking in the Spirit is what parts of the New Testament you actually walk in, that is, what scriptures can be used to describe the consistent elements of your life, i.e. your heart. There is a great deal of remedial work necessary for an adult who has not heard and obeyed with glad diligence the following scriptures: Eph 5:15 "See then that ye walk circumspectly, not as fools, but as wise, 16 redeeming the time, because the days are evil. 17 Wherefore be ye not unwise, but understanding what the will of the Lord is. 18 And be not drunk with wine, wherein is excess; but be (*continually being*) filled with the Spirit; 19 speaking to yourselves in psalms and hymns and spiritual songs, singing and making melody in your heart to the Lord; 20 giving thanks always for all things unto God and the Father in the name of our Lord Jesus Christ; 21 submitting yourselves one to another in the fear of God." Phil 4:4 "Rejoice in the Lord alway: and again I say, Rejoice. 5 Let your moderation be known unto all men. The Lord is at hand. 6 Be careful (*anxious, worried, fearful, terrified*) for nothing; but in every thing by prayer and supplication with thanksgiving let your *aiteo*/requests be made known unto God. 7 And the peace of God, which passeth all understanding, shall keep your hearts and minds through Christ Jesus. 8 Finally, brethren, whatsoever things are true, whatsoever things are honest, whatsoever things are just, whatsoever things are pure, whatsoever things are lovely, whatsoever things are of good report; if there be any virtue, and if there be any praise, think on these things. 9 Those things, which ye have both learned, and received, and heard, and seen in me, do: and the God of peace shall be with you." Col 3:14 "And above all these things put on *agape*/charity, which is the bond of perfectness. 15 And let (*make*) the peace of God rule in your hearts, to the which also ye are called in one body; and be ye thankful. 16 Let (*make*) the word of Christ dwell in you richly in all wisdom; teaching and admonishing one another in psalms and hymns and spiritual songs, singing with grace in your hearts to the Lord. 17 And whatsoever ye do in word or deed, do all in the name of the Lord Jesus, giving thanks to God and the Father by him." 1 Thes 5:14 "Now we exhort you, brethren, warn them that are unruly, comfort the feebleminded, support the weak, be patient toward all men. 15 See that none render evil for evil unto any man; but ever follow that which is good, both among yourselves, and to all men. 16 Rejoice evermore. 17 Pray without ceasing. 18 In every thing give thanks: for this is the will of God in Christ Jesus concerning you. 19 Quench not the Spirit. 20 Despise not prophesyings. 21 Prove all things; hold fast that which is good. 22 Abstain from all appearance of evil. 23 And the very God of peace sanctify you wholly; and I pray God your whole spirit and soul and body be preserved blameless unto the coming of our Lord Jesus Christ. 24 Faithful is he that calleth you, who also will do it." Heb 3:12 "Take heed, brethren, lest there be in any of you an evil heart of unbelief, in departing from the *zao*/living God. 13 But exhort one another daily, while it is called To day; lest any of you be hardened through the deceitfulness of sin. 14 For we are made partakers of Christ, if we hold the beginning of our confidence stedfast unto the end." Heb 10:22 "Let us draw near with a true heart in full assurance of faith, having our hearts sprinkled from an evil conscience, and our bodies washed with pure water. 23 Let us hold fast the profession of our faith (*actions*) without wavering; (for he is faithful

Understanding How to Use the Affirmations

that promised;) 24 and let us consider one another to provoke unto *agape*/love and to good works: 25 not forsaking the assembling of ourselves together, as the manner of some is; but exhorting one another: and so much the more, as ye see the day approaching." Mark 16:15 "And he (*Jesus*) said unto them, Go ye into all the world, and preach the gospel to every creature. 16 He that believeth and is baptized shall be *sozo*/saved; but he that believeth not shall be damned. 17 And these signs shall follow them that believe; In my name shall they cast out devils; they shall speak with new tongues; 18 they shall take up serpents; and if they drink any deadly thing, it shall not hurt them; they shall lay hands on the sick, and they shall recover. 19 So then after the Lord had spoken unto them, he was received up into heaven, and sat on the right hand of God. 20 And they went forth, and preached everywhere, the Lord working with them, and confirming the word with signs following. Amen." Rom 15:19 "Through mighty signs and wonders, by the *dunamis*/power of the Spirit of God; so that from Jerusalem, and round about unto Illyricum, I have fully preached the gospel of Christ." 1 Cor 2:4 "And my speech and my preaching was not with enticing words of man's wisdom, but in demonstration of the Spirit and of *dunamis*/power: 5 that your faith should not stand in the wisdom of men, but in the *dunamis*/power of God." 2 Tim 1:6 "Wherefore I put thee in remembrance that thou stir up [*by faith actions*] the gift of God, which is in thee … . 7 For God hath not given us the spirit of fear; but of *dunamis*/(*miracle*) power, and of *agape*/love, and of a sound mind."

So that we do not become confused about what *dunamis*/power Holy Spirit is talking about: Luke 6:17 "And he (*Jesus*) came down with them, and stood in the plain, and the company of his disciples, and a great multitude of people ... which came to hear him, and to be healed of their diseases; 18 and they that were vexed with unclean spirits: and they were healed. 19 And the whole multitude sought to touch him: for there went *dunamis*/virtue out of him, and healed them all." Acts 6:8 "And Stephen, full of faith and *dunamis*/power, did great wonders and miracles among the people." Acts 8:6 "And the people with one accord gave heed unto those things which Philip spake, hearing and seeing the miracles which he did. 7 For unclean spirits, crying with loud voice, came out of many that were possessed with them: and many taken with palsies, and that were lame, were healed."

For a significant remedial program, I suggest a daily program that consists of the following: saying the Our Father and Psalms 23 and 91 upon rising, the entire Affirmations three times, fifty to seventy-five of the Psalms, three chapters of Proverbs, three chapters of the Gospels, Galatians through to Colossians, three chapters of the rest of the New Testament, and at least one chapter of the Old Testament. Also include prayer and fasting. The total time would be about nine to twelve hours a day: six hours of the Affirmations at one and a half to two hours each, two to three hours with the Psalms and Proverbs, two hours in the New Testament and other scriptures. Now you have an idea of what Jesus was doing in all-night prayer. It probably included much scripture recitation and singing.

The scripture Affirmations contained in this book, combined with fasting, directly attack unbelief. According to Mark 16, believers will lay hands on the sick, and they will recover. When the disciples could not cast out a demon, first Jesus showed the will of God by healing the boy Himself. Matt 17:19 "Then came the disciples to Jesus apart, and said, Why could not we cast him out? 20 And Jesus said unto them, Because of your unbelief: for verily I say unto you, If ye have faith (*actions*) as a grain of mustard seed, ye shall say unto this mountain, Remove hence to yonder place; and it shall remove; and nothing shall be impossible unto you. 21 Howbeit this kind (*of unbelief*) goeth not out but by prayer and fasting." Fasting can subdue your soul to hear and believe more.

The Greek word for *belief* is the verb form of the noun *faith*, with the root meaning of "obey" by faith actions. Jewish prayer was mostly praying the Scriptures back to God, for Him to perform, so pray for God to reveal Himself to you in scripture. You can add fasting to your prayer and affirmations, with this book as a guide, to let the Word of God wash out unbelief and faithlessness from your heart and then act with thanks, praise, joy, faith, courage, persistence and confidence in God as you minister. Feelings will come later.

Note what Jesus said in the next verse: Matt 17:21 "Howbeit this kind goeth not out but by prayer and fasting." When He said "this kind," He was not referring to the demons, but to their unbelief, for faith allows God to move, not just fasting.

Jewish prayer focuses on praying the Scriptures, so fasting with scripture-based prayer or scripture recitation or public scripture reading is a way to get rid of unbelief and, thus, build faith or believing by continual faith actions. Fasting is a form of afflicting or humbling your soul or heart, mind, will and emotions to right or godly thinking. When you are in unbelief or despair, your soul is in need of "saving." James 1:21 "Wherefore lay apart all filthiness and superfluity of naughtiness, and *lambano*/receive [*by faith actions*] with meekness the engrafted word, which is able to *sozo*/save your *psuche*/souls (*hearts, minds, wills and emotions; lives*)."

So we see several ways to build faith. First, you must hear the Word of God. You build in Christ the clear truth into your heart by constant repetition and positive emotional behaviors. Next you start to believe God enough to put the words of His promises in your mouth and speak them to the situation, despite the evils and fear-pressures you are feeling. This can be your first acting to right believing rather than waiting to "feel ready" to say them. You start doing, and the victory in Jesus feelings may eventually line up. And, finally, you look at the impossibilities of the situation, see the answer in your mind's eye, and give God joyous thanksgiving, praise and triumph, calling those things that be not as though they were, knowing

Understanding How to Use the Affirmations

that God is able, will do it, and cannot lie. Persuade yourself, by His Bible truths. Build your heart confidence/faith in God that He already paid for it in Jesus, and Christ is in you to do it. The last step is to keep working the law of faith actions until you see the answer.

How long should this last, to see the benefits of the Affirmations? That is impossible to answer, as it depends upon:

a) your past,
b) your present and
c) how you respond to the issues of life every day.

So whether a one-day-, a weekend-, a week-, a several week-, a month-, a twelve month- or a seven-year-advance, you will be in charge of your own destiny with and in God. He will help you, as you labor diligently. He will even show you how to have fun, as you give thanks and rejoice, when you do not feel like it.

For each thought or idea, minimum results come in twenty-one days, with some double-minded freedom in ninety days. Right maintenance for a right life, according to the Scriptures, requires three to five hours a day spread over six to eight time blocks or sessions and one day a week, the Sabbath, with almost no other words except scripture spoken in gladness and child-like rejoicing. If your children are not happy and rejoicing in God with you all day long, you are not celebrating the Sabbath correctly. This is a life-maintenance program, not a special "season" of effort.

Why is there no prayer listed in the remedial program? Because:

A) The Affirmations, Psalms and various scripture readings already have prayer in them.
B) As your heart gets re-prioritized, you will find yourself praying and doing for others more often.
C) As you follow this faith-action program, say one to four years, you will find that scripture meditation (muttering, chanting and singing), prayer and thanksgiving, will become part of your every-moment existence.
D) Because you are praying and loving in God more (you will see so many answers to prayer you will pray and see God move even without conscious action on your part); it will become who and what you are, a functional son of God, acting as Jesus would on the Earth today.
E) Just as Jesus explained in the Parable of the Sower (Matthew 13, Mark 4, and Luke 8), the devil will attack the Word in you, and you will have lots to pray about and, thus, you will be constantly looking at God's words, to reaffirm His promises into your heart, and *aiteo*/asking HIM to perform it, as you battle the devil with faith actions.

OK, God, Now What?

If this is not enough, then I suggest our other study materials: *Faith Evidence, Freedom in a Snake-Bitten World, Discovering Our Redemption* and the *Battle Prayer for Divine Healing, Field Manual 2*, as additional tools.

The issue is: will you obey the God of *agape*/love or the devil, who only comes to rob, kill and destroy? You, as a Christian, are the Body, the flesh of Jesus on the Earth. You are receiving writing on your heart all day by your thoughts, your emotions, your words, your actions, and by what your senses experience. But who is running your life: Hollywood, your feeling or emotions, CNN, your bank account or God? You must decide to control what is in your heart. As you make these Affirmations, as you control the words out of your mouth, and as you obey God in glad obedience, you will write His *agape*/love onto your own heart and into those you help.

Ultimately the right faith action behaviors that will result in eternal-value gold, silver and jewels on the Day of Judgment will come from a single-minded-in-God heart. And with a single-minded-in-God heart, you will have greater "faith" results. James 1:5 "If any of you lack wisdom, let him *aiteo*/ask of God, that giveth to all men liberally, and upbraideth not; and it shall be given him. 6 But let him *aiteo*/ask in faith (*actions*), nothing wavering. For he that wavereth [*in faith actions*] is like a wave of the sea driven with the wind and tossed. 7 For let not that man think that he shall receive any thing of the Lord. 8 A double minded man is unstable in all his ways." Notice that God defines anything that is not like Jesus as being "unstable."

Faith means you give glad thanksgiving to God over the answer before you see the answer and in spite of all the apparent reasons the answer cannot happen. Faith action lasts or continues at least one second longer than it takes for the answer to bear fruit.

Whether you are aware of it or not, what you are saying in the Affirmations is being written into your subconscious. Everything you experience is being recorded in your memory every day and night. But only that experienced with emotion and repetition are made more significant, for ready recall. The Affirmations allow you to choose what is written in your heart. Rest assured, if you do not choose God's Word, the devil is offering his lies instead. Either titillation or cogitative choice determine the intensity of the emotion for each memory, thought or idea.

Remember, what is repeated (and with great emotion) is given priority, but it still takes twenty-one days of repetition to build the new thoughts, forty days to build a new mindset or attitude, and ninety days of repetition to subdue thoughts you no longer want. So, for the entire ninety days, you may face great resistance, barrages of second thoughts and confusion as you speak the Affirmations. While these times may vary for you, typically it takes at

Understanding How to Use the Affirmations

least four days to start the neural connection, twenty-one days to fully build the new thought connections, forty days to integrate them, and at least ninety days to subdue the old, when you specifically attack them.

Here are those minimum times summarized:

a) At least 4 days continuous repetition to start to build new neural connections
b) At least 21 continuous days to fully grow neural connections (4 plus 17 more days)
c) At least 40 continuous days to integrate the thought with your other thoughts (21 plus 19 more days)
d) At least 90 days continuous to reassign old memory emotions and heal corrupt or "leaky" neural connections (40 plus 50 more days).

Less diligence and persistence can make the processes take much longer. It can take less time, depending on how many right thoughts, scriptures, attitudes and confessions you already have in your heart. There is always more to be had, until you walk just like Jesus. Phil 3:12 "Not as though I had already attained, either were already perfect: but I follow after, if that I may apprehend that for which also I am apprehended of Christ Jesus. 13 Brethren, I count not myself to have apprehended: but this one thing I do, forgetting those things which are behind, and reaching forth unto those things which are before, 14 I press toward the mark for the prize of the high calling of God in Christ Jesus." Remember, Jesus spent significant time alone, part of which I believe included His own affirmations.

All of this conflict or challenge takes place based on how our minds operate without the influence of the devil. Add the devil, defending his strongholds—by blasting you with more conflicting thoughts, visions, memories, and emotions, even physical distractions through people, animals, strange "feelings," lusts and weather—and this can be quite a battle. It is often helpful to speak the Affirmations directly to the devil with the attitude of, "This is the real me, and you will not defeat what God has made me to be, in the name of Jesus."

This is a battle we are called to fight, so do not faint, but get with the program! 1 Pet 1:13 "Wherefore gird up the loins of your mind, be sober, and hope to the end for the grace that is to be brought unto you at the revelation of Jesus Christ." 2 Cor 10:3 "For though we walk in the flesh, we do not war after the flesh: 4 (for the weapons of our warfare are not carnal, but mighty through God to the pulling down of strong holds;) 5 casting down imaginations, and every high thing that exalteth itself against the knowledge of God, and bringing into captivity every thought to the obedience of Christ." That voice telling you this is too hard is not from God. That voice saying, "I want this; let's go," is God. The blessings belong to those who overcome, and you are made an overcomer in Jesus.

But long-lasting godly change only occurs as your attitudes line up with God and are kept strong through regular repetition and strong emotion. Remember, evil fear is the strong emotion of this world, along with inferiority and insecurity, and *agape*/love the strong emotion of God, along with God's power and connection. Whose company will you keep, the way of the righteous or the way of the wicked? The way of *agape*/love or the way of evil fear? Every moment you are in agreement with one or the other, and every moment of the day something is being written in your heart. The company you keep defines much of this. Prov 1:29 "For that they hated knowledge, and did not choose the fear of the LORD: 30 they would none of my counsel: they despised all my reproof. 31 Therefore shall they eat of the fruit of their own way, and be filled with their own devices. 32 For the turning away of the simple shall slay them, and the prosperity of fools shall destroy them. 33 But whoso hearkeneth unto me shall dwell safely, and shall be quiet from fear of evil." Prov 2:20 "That thou mayest walk in the way of good men, and keep the paths of the righteous. 21 For the upright shall dwell in the land, and the perfect shall remain in it. 22 But the wicked shall be cut off from the earth, and the transgressors shall be rooted out of it." Prov 3:33 "The curse of the LORD is in the house of the wicked: but he blesseth the habitation of the just. 34 Surely he scorneth the scorners: but he giveth grace unto the lowly. 35 The wise shall inherit glory: but shame shall be the promotion of fools." Prov 4:18 "But the path of the just is as the shining light, that shineth more and more unto the perfect day. 19 The way of the wicked is as darkness: they know not at what they stumble." Prov 16:25 "There is a way that seemeth right unto a man, but the end thereof are the ways of death." Ps 26:1 "Judge me, O LORD; for I have walked in mine integrity: I have trusted (*by continual faith actions*) also in the LORD; therefore I shall not slide. 2 Examine me, O LORD, and prove me; try my reins and my heart. 3 For thy *chesed*/lovingkindness is before mine eyes: and I have walked in thy truth. 4 I have not sat with vain persons, neither will I go in with dissemblers. 5 I have hated the congregation of evil doers; and will not sit with the wicked." 1 Cor 15:33 "Be not deceived: evil communications corrupt good manners (*attitudes toward yourself, others and life in general*)." 2 Tim 2:16 "But shun profane and vain babblings: for they will increase unto more ungodliness. 17 And their word will eat as doth a canker." Heb 12:15 "Looking diligently lest any man fail of the grace of God; lest any root of bitterness springing up trouble you, and thereby many be defiled." 2 Pet 2:18 "For when they speak great swelling words of vanity, they allure through the lusts of the flesh, through much wantonness, those that were clean escaped from them who live in error. 19 While they promise them liberty, they themselves are the servants of corruption: for of whom a man is overcome,

Understanding How to Use the Affirmations

of the same is he brought in bondage. 20 For if after they have escaped the pollutions of the world through the knowledge of the Lord and Saviour Jesus Christ, they are again entangled therein, and overcome, the latter end is worse with them than the beginning." Heb 3:12 "Take heed, brethren, lest there be in any of you an evil heart of unbelief, in departing from the living God. 13 But exhort one another daily, while it is called To day; lest any of you be hardened through the deceitfulness of sin. 14 For we are made partakers of Christ, if we hold the beginning of our confidence stedfast unto the end."

Other approaches to mind renewing mix the Psalms with the Affirmations as part of a regular routine. Aim for ten to fifty psalms a day. You can mix and match, as works for you. If you want to change your behaviors, you must think differently. To think differently, you start by what you allow your mouth to speak. Ps 45:1 "My heart is inditing a good matter: I speak of the things which I have made touching the king: my tongue is the pen of a ready writer." 2 Sam 23:2 "The Spirit of the LORD spake by me, and his word was in my tongue."

Go through the New Testament and first ask God to build in you what you see you need, or to remove what you do not want. Command the desired things to come and the wicked to go. Then make that scripture an affirmation to expand your daily confessions.

When you read, you activate your vision or imagination in both your conscious and subconscious mind. When you speak, you activate your vision, your hearing, and, by vibration and with your lips moving, your touch and motion. You are still leaving out smell and taste. The more senses you can add with the thought, the stronger it is in your conscious and subconscious, i.e., the easier it is recalled, as triggering information comes in. Therefore even silently moving your lips as you read is more powerful than reading silently without motion. Remember, the cognitive mind retention is three to five days at best. A few hours or days of intense focus can produce temporary results in the cognitive mind. For long-term retention and behavior change, it must be built in the subconscious also.

The more thanksgiving, joy, gladness and fun you can add to the process, the stronger and the better the behavioral changes. Remember, the stronger the emotion the greater the priority your subconscious assigns to a memory to recall it quickly. The quicker it is recalled, as triggering information comes in, the more you will act like Jesus in any given situation. So judging by the hard biology of modern science, for you to build a new thought with the desired emotion takes twenty-one days of constant repetition with emotions to make it a permanent part of your heart. And it takes ninety days to subdue wrong or evil thoughts.

Those "second thoughts" or double-minded thoughts that come moments later, as you start to think or do right, as guided by Holy Spirit, are either not fully subdued old thoughts or the devil, both reacting to the initial thoughts that you accept. As you keep subduing the old thoughts, i.e., re-assigning new, like-Jesus-would-have emotions to them, even if the devil launches those evil or limiting thoughts at you, you will not respond the same, and will ultimately become single-minded in what God has said and be able to walk in true *agape*/love.

As you become aware of those second thoughts (typically negative, but sometimes wildly foolish and/or lustful), do not ignore them, but rather obey Philippians 4:6-9 and attack them with prayer, for God to fix them, and then speak good confessions with thanksgiving, to confirm His love as greater than the fear in those negative thoughts. So whether those second thoughts are valid warnings, your corrupted subconscious or demonic trickery, your answer is the same. Obey Philippians 4:6 and get into vibrant thanksgiving for God's victory over any obstacle.

Also remember, your subconscious cannot tell if you are faking the emotion or not as you speak the Affirmations, so forced or mechanical laughter looks the same to the unconscious mind as real laughter. Fake dancing and shouting is the same as real dancing and shouting to the heart. While you are "faking it," your subconscious (or the devil) may tell you, "This is not real." In either case, this is a lie, as science has now proven that, whether is it faked or not, such thoughts, with emotion, are stored at a higher priority level for recall. Keep going anyway, reminding yourself that you may not be fully integrated with right emotions and truth, but you will be more integrated as and after you "fake it." This is part of the process of you controlling your thoughts and not just "taking" any thought that comes along.

The command to rejoice is found some one hundred and ninety-two times in the Bible, and to give thanks or thanksgiving some hundred times. In no case does it say you have to "feel like it first." The closest it gets is for you to call to remembrance those things that help you make the decision to do the behaviors of rejoicing and/or thanksgiving. Ps 107:21 "Oh that men would praise the LORD for his *chesed*/goodness, and for his wonderful works to the children of men! 22 And let them sacrifice the sacrifices of thanksgiving, and declare his works with rejoicing."

What many assume was standard or colloquial talk by Jesus was actually Him describing what people of His day understood: you are not the thoughts that come to you or you have in your heart; you are what you keep, obey or *lambano* to speaking and doing. Matt 6:25 "Therefore I say unto you, **Take no thought** for your life, what ye shall eat, or what ye shall drink; nor yet for your body, what ye shall put on. Is not the life more than meat, and the body than raiment?" Matt 6:31 "Therefore **take no thought**, saying, What shall we eat? or, What shall we drink? or, Wherewithal shall we be clothed?" Mark 13:11 "But when they shall lead you, and deliver you up, **take no thought** beforehand what ye shall speak, neither do ye premeditate: but whatsoever shall be given you in that hour, that speak ye: for it is not ye that speak, but the Holy Ghost." Luke 12:22 "And he said unto his disciples, Therefore I say unto you, **Take no thought** for your life, what ye shall eat; neither

UNDERSTANDING HOW TO USE THE AFFIRMATIONS

for the body, what ye shall put on." All of these are commands from Jesus not to let evil fear have dominion in your thought life.

As you progress, in a panic situation, you will become aware that you are asking Holy Spirit for scripture to activate in your memory. The more fun and positive you have made these Affirmations and other scripture memorization, the easier this will be. He will give you words to attack the situation, to bring the glory of God. As soon as you hear it, internalize it and apply it to your situation, with a present tense affirmation. Again, the more gladness and thanksgiving you can "fake," the quicker you will come into agreement with Holy Spirit within you, and set yourself free from fear, because panic is really fear. This is one way to "stir yourself up" into Holy Spirit, that is, to think, act and emote like He does.

Ps 16:11 "Thou wilt shew me the path of life: in thy presence is fulness of joy; at thy right hand there are pleasures for evermore." As you walk in this joy and confidence in God, you will now activate what some call "The Law of Attraction." Yes, you do get what you say in this Universe. Jesus said it, and science is now proving it. The more positive things you say, the more positive becomes your heart. The more positive your heart in Jesus, the more positive you are in God's help and strength, and the more you will be positive in all situations. The more positive you are, the more others will want to be around you and can safely send their friends to be around you. And the more people and answers God sends to you, the better you will be able to relate successfully to and with them. The fruit of all this is that you will operate less and less in a "froward mouth," and, instead, in more blessing.

As God has always said: Prov 2:10 "When wisdom entereth into thine heart, and knowledge is pleasant unto thy soul; 11 discretion shall preserve thee, understanding shall keep thee: 12 to deliver thee from the way of the evil man, from the man that speaketh froward things; 13 who leave the paths of uprightness, to walk in the ways of darkness; 14 who rejoice to do evil, and delight in the frowardness of the wicked; 15 whose ways are crooked, and they froward in their paths: 16 to deliver thee from the strange woman, even from the stranger which flattereth with her words; 17 which forsaketh the guide of her youth, and forgetteth the covenant of her God." Prov 3:32 "For the froward is abomination to the LORD: but his secret (*way of speaking*) is with the righteous. 33 The curse of the LORD is in the house of the wicked: but he blesseth the habitation of the just. 34 Surely he scorneth the scorners: but he giveth grace unto the lowly. 35 The wise shall inherit glory: but shame shall be the promotion of fools."

As a new start, for most people, plan to do this for about six to twelve months before you will begin to notice, or even better, others begin to notice your new attitudes. As you become more confident in God in the process, you will also notice more immediate and more powerful prayers and answers to prayer, as you reprogram your inner man to think more like Heaven, and, thus, obey: Philem 6 "That the communication of thy faith may become effectual by the acknowledging of every good thing which is in you in Christ Jesus."

Heaven is waiting on us to release the glory of God's promises into the Earth. Matt 16:19 "I will give you the keys of the kingdom of heaven; and whatever you bind (declare to be improper and unlawful) on earth must be what is already bound in heaven; and whatever you loose (declare lawful) on earth must be what is already loosed in heaven [Isa 22:22]." AMP 2 Cor 1:20 "For all the promises of God in him (*Jesus*) are yea, and in him Amen, unto the glory of God by us." God is eagerly waiting to send His promises to Earth when you call. Holy Spirit longs to deliver them as we *aiteo* the Father.

As you continue to renew your mind with continual and diligent right faith actions into the New Testament revelation of Christ in you the hope of glory, you also will break out more often into thanks, praise and joy and walk more as what you are, a true Champion in Christ, in any situation by the grace of God. And God, with you as His co-laborer, will have united your heart, and you will become one with Him. 1 Cor 3:7 "So then neither is he that planteth any thing [*in affirmations*], neither he that watereth [*in glad affirmations*]; but God that giveth the increase [*to God-level results*]."

Thus, you will work with God to fulfill the New Covenant. Heb 10:15 "Whereof the Holy Ghost also is a witness to us: for after that he had said before, 16 This is the covenant that I will make with them after those days, saith the Lord, I will put my laws into their hearts, and in their minds will I write them; 17 and their sins and iniquities will I remember no more. 18 Now where remission of these is, there is no more offering for sin." Jesus did the remitting of sin part; we are to do the mind renewing part based on His work in this life. If not, He will do the rest of the mind renewing on the Day of Judgment. It's your call.

[NOTE: For specific and urgent needs, I suggest that you pray this prayer for God to go directly to your heart and get you clean in critical areas now: Father, in the name of Jesus, 2 Thes 3:5 "... direct *my heart* into the *agape*/love of God, and into the patient waiting for Christ, *so that I overcome to Your glory in this situation*."]

What is there left for God to do? He has given "all things." What is left after "all?" The next verse gives the key. 2 Pet 1:5 "And beside this, **giving all diligence** ...." That means you do not stop until you win or overcome. That is the attitude of *agape*/love. That is the attitude of a champion, an overcomer in Christ.

As Jesus said: Rev 2:7 "He that hath an ear, let him hear what the Spirit saith unto the churches; To him that **overcometh** will I give to eat of the tree of *zoe*/life, which is in the midst of the paradise of God." Rev 2:11 "He that hath an ear, let him hear what the Spirit saith unto the churches; He that **overcometh** shall not be hurt of the second death." Rev 2:17 "He that hath an ear, let him hear what the Spirit saith unto the churches; To him that **overcometh** will I give to eat of the hidden manna, and will give him a white stone, and in the stone a new name written, which no man knoweth saving he that *lambano*/receiveth it." Rev 2:26 "And he that **overcometh**, and keepeth my works (*guards them and does not let them escape*) unto the end, to him will I give power over the nations: 27 and he shall rule them with a rod of iron; as the vessels of a potter shall they be broken to shivers: even as I *lambano*/received of my Father. 28 And I will give him the morning star. 29 He that hath an ear, let him hear what the Spirit saith unto the churches." Rev 3:5 "He that **overcometh**, the same shall be clothed in white raiment; and I will not blot out his name out of the book of *zoe*/life, but I will confess his name before my Father, and before his angels. 6 He that hath an ear, let him hear what the Spirit saith unto the churches." Rev 3:12 "Him that **overcometh** will I make a pillar in the temple of my God, and he shall go no more out: and I will write upon him the name of my God, and the name of the city of my God, which is new Jerusalem, which cometh down out of heaven from my God: and I will write upon him my new name. 13 He that hath an ear, let him hear what the Spirit saith unto the churches." Rev 3:21 "To him that **overcometh** will I grant to sit with me in my throne, even as I also overcame, and am set down with my Father in his throne. 22 He that hath an ear, let him hear what the Spirit saith unto the churches."

The **overcoming One** is within us. 1 John 4:4 "Ye are of God, little children, and have **overcome** them: because greater is he that is in you, than he that is in the world." The greater One is within the Christian, as soon as they are born again. This is not a development process of adding things that were not there before. Col 2:10 "And ye are complete in him, which is the head of all principality and power." Like a perfect, newborn baby, all the parts and potential are there, ready for maturation by instruction and right doing. Right instruction always leads to right behaviors or actions.

Godly instruction is an information and aligning process, getting us to the point that we can hear and cooperate with the *zao*/living God within us, Christ the hope of glory. 2 Cor 4:7 "But we have this treasure in earthen vessels, that the excellency of the power may be of God, and not of us." 2 Tim 2:15 "Study (*with much diligent effort*) to shew thyself approved unto God, a workman that needeth not to be ashamed, rightly dividing the word of truth [*unto miracle manifestation*]." 2 Tim 3:15 "And that from a child thou hast known the holy scriptures, which are able to make thee wise unto *soteria*/salvation through faith (*actions*) which is in Christ Jesus. 16 All scripture is given by inspiration of God, and is profitable for doctrine, for reproof, for correction, for instruction in righteousness: 17 that the man [*or woman*] of God may be perfect, throughly furnished unto all good works."

As we reprogram and keep our heart and our mind to hear the Lord within us, we will do what He asks and do it with His attitudes and heart. It is the Word of God, in cooperation with Holy Spirit, that sorts this out for us. Heb 4:12 "For the word of God is quick, and powerful, and sharper than any twoedged sword, piercing even to the dividing asunder of soul and spirit, and of the joints and marrow, and is a discerner (*judge*) of the thoughts and intents of the heart. 13 Neither is there any creature that is not manifest in his sight: but all things are naked and opened unto the eyes of him with whom we have to do."

And here is a key part: 1 Thes 4:4 "That every one of you should know how to possess his vessel in sanctification and honour." 2 Tim 2:19 "Nevertheless the foundation of God standeth sure, having this seal, The Lord knoweth them that are his. And, Let every one that nameth the name of Christ depart from iniquity. 20 But in a great house there are not only vessels of gold and of silver, but also of wood and of earth; and some to honour, and some to dishonour. 21 **If a man therefore purge himself from these, he shall be a vessel unto honour**, sanctified, and meet for the master's use, and prepared unto every good work. 22 Flee also youthful lusts: but follow righteousness, faith (*actions*), *agape*/charity, peace, with them that call on the Lord out of a pure heart. 23 But foolish and unlearned questions avoid, knowing that they do gender strifes. 24 And the servant of the Lord must not strive; but be gentle unto all men, apt to teach, patient, 25 in meekness instructing those that oppose themselves; if God peradventure will give them repentance to the acknowledging of the truth; 26 and that they may recover themselves out of the snare of the devil, who are taken captive by him at his will." 1 John 3:2 "*Agape*/beloved, now are we the sons of God, and it doth not yet appear what we shall be: but we know that, when he shall appear, we shall be like him; for we shall see him as he is. 3 **And every man that hath this hope in him purifieth himself, even as he is pure."**

A measure of your purity of heart is how willing you are to purge your vessel for the Master's use. John 7:16 "Jesus answered them, and said, My doctrine is not mine, but his that sent me. 17 If any man will do his will, he shall know of the doctrine, whether it be of God, or whether I speak of myself." John 3:19 "And this is the condemnation, that light is come into the world, and men *agape*/loved darkness rather than light, because their deeds were evil. 20 For every one that doeth evil hateth the light, neither cometh to the light, lest his deeds should be reproved. 21 But he that doeth truth cometh to the light, that his deeds may be made manifest, that they are wrought in God." Eph 5:8 "For ye were sometimes darkness, but now are ye light in the Lord: walk as children of light: 9 (for the fruit of the Spirit is in all goodness and righteousness and truth;) 10 proving what is acceptable unto the Lord. 11 And have no fellowship with the unfruitful works of darkness, but rather reprove them. 12 For it is a shame even to speak of those things which are done of them in secret. 13 But all things that are reproved are made manifest by the light: for whatsoever doth make manifest is light. 14 Wherefore he saith, Awake thou that sleepest, and arise from the dead, and Christ shall give thee light. 15 See then that ye walk circumspectly, not as fools, but as wise, 16 redeeming the time, because the days are evil. 17 Wherefore be ye not unwise, but understanding what the will of the Lord is. 18 And be not

Understanding How to Use the Affirmations

drunk with wine, wherein is excess; but be (*continually being*) filled with the Spirit; 19 speaking to yourselves in psalms and hymns and spiritual songs, singing and making melody in your heart to the Lord; 20 giving thanks always for all things unto God and the Father in the name of our Lord Jesus Christ; 21 submitting yourselves one to another in the fear of God."

Hear the great lament of Jesus: Matt 13:14 "And in them is fulfilled the prophecy of Esaias, which saith, By hearing ye shall hear, and shall not understand; and seeing ye shall see, and shall not perceive: 15 for this people's heart is waxed gross, and their ears are dull of hearing, and their eyes they have closed; lest at any time they should see with their eyes, and hear with their ears, and should understand with their heart, and should be converted, and I should *iaomai*/heal (*physically and prosper*) them." 3 John 2 "*Agape*/beloved, I wish (*pray*) above all things that thou mayest prosper and be in health, even as thy soul prospereth."

For those struggling with the Old Testament versus the New, every New Testament verse referencing the Scriptures meant only the Old Testament, as the New Testament was codified or established much later, after all the gospels and letters were written. 2 Tim 3:14 "But continue thou in the things which thou hast learned and hast been assured of, knowing of whom thou hast learned them; 15 and that from a child thou hast known the holy scriptures, which are able to make thee wise unto *soteria*/salvation through faith (*actions*) which *are* in Christ Jesus. 16 All scripture is given by inspiration of God, and is profitable for doctrine, for reproof, for correction, for instruction in righteousness: 17 that the man [*or woman*] of God may be perfect, throughly furnished unto all good works." Matt 22:29 "Jesus answered and said unto them, Ye do err, not knowing the scriptures, nor the power of God." Rom 15:4 "For whatsoever things were written aforetime were written for our learning, that we through patience and comfort of the scriptures might have hope." This includes the psalms. Eph 5:19 "Speaking to yourselves in psalms and hymns and spiritual songs, singing and making melody in your heart to the Lord."

Notice that Peter considered Paul's writing as being equivalent to scripture. 2 Pet 3:16 "As also in all his (*Paul's*) epistles, speaking in them of these things; in which are some things hard to be understood, which they that are unlearned and unstable wrest, as they do also the other scriptures, unto their own destruction."

Part of the purpose of tongues is to edify or build yourself up in God (1 Cor 14:4, Jude 20). This includes faith and life purpose. We recommend at least two hours daily of hard, loud and fast tongues and/or saying tongues as you read the Affirmations or Scripture. Use the Affirmations and the Psalms with tongues as prayer tools to acquire an ear that can hear to glad obedience, physical healing and godly prosperity in every part of life!

God is direct in telling us to keep working with faith actions and *agape* love works until we get His promises to manifest; we continually make this confession:

OK, God, Now What?
Christian Worker's Confession

Because God commands: <u>1 Cor 15:57</u> "But thanks be to God, which giveth us the victory through our Lord Jesus Christ. 58 Therefore, my *agape*/beloved brethren, be ye stedfast, unmovable, always abounding in the *(faith-action)* work of the Lord, forasmuch as ye know that your *(faith-action)* labour is not in vain in the Lord."

Therefore I will stay to win; I will not give up; I will keep proclaiming Jesus' great name in faith actions until His and my enemies bow in defeat and submission to the glory of God. <u>Eph 3:10</u> "To the intent that now unto the principalities and powers in heavenly places might be known by the church the manifold wisdom of God, 11 according to the eternal purpose which he purposed in Christ Jesus our Lord: 12 in whom we have boldness and access with confidence by the faith *(actions) in* him *(Jesus)*."

I will not tolerate the devil and his works to rule anywhere I find them; I will be who Jesus says I am: <u>Luke 10:19</u> "Behold *(stop and make this change your life)*, I give unto you power *(authority, commission, pre-permission and all the resources of heaven)* to tread on *(crush, destroy and remove from power)* serpents and scorpions, and over all the power *(ability and works)* of the enemy: and nothing shall by any means hurt you. 20 Notwithstanding in this rejoice not, that the spirits are subject unto you; but rather rejoice, because your names are written in heaven." Thank You, Jesus! Yahoo!

Knowing God is not teaching you a lesson in troubles; He is encouraging and waiting for you to stand up in Jesus, and teach the devil a lesson.

Knowing the healing is done, now go for it with continued faith actions until you get it.

Knowing this is not about seeing what God will do; it is proclaiming this is what will be by the promise of God and enforcing it with faith actions in and by the name of Jesus until it is manifest, knowing no faith action labor in the Lord is in vain. Thank You, Lord Jesus! Yahoo!

PART II
THE AFFIRMATIONS

Make the following faith-action Affirmations in Christ with glad emotion and, while you are doing it, see or imagine yourself doing or receiving what you are speaking by grace. Make the Affirmation Magnets by speaking out loud, or, at least, silently moving the lips, sometimes fast, for heart writing, and sometimes slower, for revelation and understanding. We need both. Mix and match as seems appropriate.

You are doing several things at once. One is writing God's Word on your heart. Another is seeking God in Spirit and in Truth.

Note: Due to the application modifications to convert many of the scriptures into affirmations, these scriptures then become author paraphrases.

* Get your FREE GIFT of the first Affirmation (A) divided up into ten bite-sized pieces for ease of use and portability. Go to the Contact Us page at www.CovenantPeaceMinistries.com to request your FREE GIFT.

CHAPTER 18

AFFIRMATIONS IN CHRIST
RELEASING GOD'S POWER

A. **Father, in the name of Jesus, use these confessions** and affirmations to help me understand and walk in You and Your great work in Jesus better. I am Your son/daughter. Jesus is my Lord. Jesus uses me to save myself and others. He uses my hands, my mouth, my mind, even my entire life to bring His salvation to the Earth. Thank You, Lord Jesus, for working in me and through me. The same Holy Spirit who dwells in Jesus dwells in me. Any doubt, lie, fear, sin or unbelief in me I command to hear and obey the voice of the Word of God through me and **to go now**, in the name **of Jesus Christ of Nazareth**, my Lord, and to be replaced with truth, faith actions, hope, power, *agape*/love and a sound mind. Mind, you operate in the mind of Christ. Heart, receive only God's truth. Mind of the flesh, you are dead in Christ and have no authority over me. Body, you are whole and right in every way, so do your job. I put on Jesus Christ, I put on His righteousness, I put on His holiness and I put on His salvation. I have everything He has when He was raised from the dead. I am totally healed—spirit, soul and body, mind, heart, will and emotions—into His image. The chastisement of my peace was upon Jesus, the Christ of God and my only Lord, so I freely preach the Gospel, heal the sick, cleanse the lepers, raise the dead, cast out devils, handle poisons or snakes, and walk in blessing and prosperity in every part of life. I am Col 1:12 "giving thanks (*continually*) unto the Father, which hath made *me* meet to be *a partaker* of the inheritance of the saints in light: 13 who hath delivered *me* from the power of darkness, and hath translated *me* into the kingdom of his *agape*/dear Son: 14 in whom *I* have redemption through his blood, even the forgiveness (*remission, removal, purging, obliteration and putting away*) of sins: 15 who is the image of the invisible God, the firstborn of every creature." For greater is Jesus Christ who is in me than he who is in the world. I do all things through Jesus Christ who strengthens me, and Father God meets all my needs, *aiteo*, requirements and demands according to His covenant promises and according to His riches in glory by Christ Jesus, for I am made the righteousness of Father God in Christ Jesus, as a permanent gift, by grace and through faith actions in His blood. Rom 11:29 "For the gifts and calling of God are without repentance." The *agape*/love of God shed by Holy Spirit in my heart directs me to good works and healing all who are oppressed (*under the active rule and lordship*) of the devil, for God is in me and with me in all I do. I delight to do God's will in all ways. I believe Father God, for He and His Word are one. Therefore all things of God's Word are possible to me. As Jesus is, so am I in the world right now. Jesus Christ is in me, so the works of my hands are blessed, for I lay hands on the sick, and they recover totally right then, by Holy Spirit power. Whatever good I do prospers to the goodness of the Lord. I do greater works than Jesus, for He has gone to the Father and has obtained Holy Spirit for me. Jesus speaks through me as I speak rightly, and works healings, miracles, blessings and answers to prayer by me. All things of God are possible to me, for I believe God by faith actions, who cannot lie in His promises. Thank You, Lord Jesus! Yahoo!

B. You, Father God, have made me a son, and because I am a son, You have sent forth the Spirit of Your Son, Jesus Christ, into my heart, crying, Abba, Daddy, Father to You. Right now, by You, Father God, empowering my word, I am pulling down every evil stronghold, casting out every vain imagination and every high thing in me that exalts itself against the knowledge of You, Father God, and bringing into captivity my every thought into the obedience of Christ, and walking in glad agreement with Holy Spirit. Eph 1:17 … The God of my Lord Jesus Christ, the Father of glory, *has given me His* spirit of wisdom and revelation in the knowledge of him: 18 the eyes of *my* understanding *continuously* being enlightened; *and I continuously grow in knowing* what is the hope of his calling, and what the riches of the glory of his inheritance in the saints, 19 and what is the exceeding greatness of his power *to me who believes by faith actions*, according to the working of his mighty power, 20 which he wrought in Christ, when he raised him from the dead, and set him at his own right hand in the heavenly places, 21 far above all principality, and power, and might, and dominion, and every name that is named, not only in this world, but also in that which is to come: 22 and hath put all things under his feet, and gave him to be the head over all things to the church *of which I am a part*, 23 which is his body, the fulness of him that filleth all in all. *My heart is filled with the triumph of Christ in the call of God in my life! Yahoo! Yahoo! Yahoo!*

C. **God gives me His Spirit** without measure, for He gives me His words, and I speak them by faith actions, in *agape*/love, and the Lord confirms these words with signs abundantly following. Every day, in every way, I am getting better and better, for I continually grow in the knowledge of God in godliness and *zoe*/life. 1 Tim 2:3 For this is good and acceptable in the sight of God our Saviour; 4 who will have all men to be *sozo*/saved, and to come unto the knowledge of the truth [*and to receive the* agape/*love of the truth unto salvation*]. 5 For there is one God, and one mediator between God and men, the man Christ Jesus; 6 who gave himself a ransom for all, to be testified in due time. 7 Whereunto I am ordained a preacher, and an apostle, (I speak the truth in Christ, and lie not;) a teacher ... in faith (*actions*) and verity (*truth*). Heb 10:12 ...This man, *Jesus Christ,* after he had offered one sacrifice for sins for ever, sat down on the right hand of God; Heb 9:26 ... now once in the end of the world hath he appeared to put away sin by the sacrifice of himself. 27 And as it is appointed unto men once to die, but after this the judgment: 28 so Christ was once offered to bear the sins of many; and unto them that look for him shall he appear the second time without sin unto *soteria*/salvation. Heb 1:3 Who being the brightness of *Father God's* glory, and the express image of his person, and upholding all things by the word of his power, when he had by himself purged our sins, sat down on the right hand of the Majesty on high; 1 John 3:5 and *I* know that he was manifested to take away our sins; and in him is no sin. Rev 1:5 ... Jesus Christ, who is the faithful witness, and the first begotten of the dead, and the prince of the kings of the earth. Unto him that *agape*/loved us, and washed (*dissolved, put off and destroyed from us*) our sins in his own blood, 6 and hath made us kings and priests unto God and his Father; to him be glory and dominion for ever and ever. Amen. Eph 4:20 *For I* have ...so learned Christ; 21 ... *I* have heard him, and have been taught by him, as the truth is in Jesus: 22 that *I* put off concerning the former conversation the old man, which is corrupt according to the deceitful lusts; 23 and *am* renewed in the spirit of *my* mind; 24 and that *I continuously* put on the new man, which after *Father* God is created in righteousness and true holiness. 25 Wherefore putting away lying, *I* speak *to* every man truth *as my* neighbour: for we are members one of another. *I may* 26 be angry, and sin not:

OK, God, Now What?

I let not the sun go down upon *my* wrath: 27 neither give *I* place to the devil. *Knowing that Father has said that* 28 let him that stole steal no more: but rather let him labour, working with his hands the thing which is good, that he may have to give to him that needeth. *Therefore I* 29 let no corrupt communication proceed out of *my* mouth, but that which is good to the use of edifying, that it may minister grace unto the hearers. 30 And grieve not the Holy Spirit of God, whereby *I am* sealed unto the day of redemption. *I* 31 let all bitterness, and wrath, and anger, and clamour, and evil speaking, be put away from *me*, with all malice: 32 and *I am* kind to *others*, tenderhearted, forgiving *others*, even as God for Christ's sake hath forgiven *me*. 5:1 ... Therefore *I labor in faith actions by the grace of God to be a* follower *(imitator)* of God, as *an agape*/dear *child*; 2 and walk in *agape*/love, as Christ also hath *agape*/loved us, and hath given himself for us an offering and a sacrifice to God for a sweetsmelling savour. *Father God* agape/*loves me, just like He loves Jesus. Praise You, Father, for the wonderful* agape/*love You have for me in Jesus. Thank You! Yahoo! Yahoo!*

D. Father, You are causing me to trust You with all my heart in faith actions. You are uniting my heart to fear Your name. By You working in me, I do not lean on my own understanding, but I acknowledge You in all my ways, and You are directing my paths to Your glory. Right now You are filling me with Your words of peace, salvation, reconciliation, forgiveness, redemption, adoption, mercy, grace, truth and help, for I open my mouth, and You fill my lips, and I speak Your words in *agape*/love to Your glory. You, Holy Spirit, are my Helper. I am a co-worker with God for good. Eph 4:13 *As* we all come in the unity of the faith, and of the knowledge of the Son of God, unto a perfect man, unto the measure of the stature of the fulness of Christ. 2 Cor 10:4 For *this weapon of confession is* mighty through *You, Father* God, to the pulling down of strong holds; 5 casting down imaginations, and every high thing that exalteth itself against the knowledge of *You, Father* God, *in me*, and bringing into captivity *my* every thought to the obedience of Christ. *Thank You, Father, for the wonderful work You are doing. In the name of Jesus, thank You. Lord, be magnified. Thy kingdom come. Thy will be done on Earth as it is in Heaven. Thank You, Father. In Jesus' name, thank You.*

E. I have power in the name of Jesus for Gal 4:4 ... when the fulness of the time was come, God sent forth his Son, made of a woman, made under the law, 5 to redeem them that were under the law, that we might receive the adoption of sons. 6 And because *we* are sons, God hath sent forth the Spirit of his Son into *our* hearts, crying, Abba (*Daddy*), Father. 7 Wherefore *I am* no more a servant, but a son; and if a son, then an heir of God through Christ, *and a joint heir with Jesus as* Rom 8:17 ... children/*sons*, then heirs; heirs of God, and

Affirmations in Christ

joint-heirs with Christ ... *Jesus is my King, and I am made a king for Him.* Eccl 8:4 Where the word of a king is, there is power .... *When I speak in the name of Jesus, there is God's power.* Rom 5:17 For if by one man's offence death reigned *as king* by one; much more *I* which *lambano/receive* [*in faith actions*] abundance of grace and of the gift of righteousness ... *reign as a king* in *zoe*/life by one, Jesus Christ, Rev 1:5 ... who is the faithful witness, and the first begotten of the dead, and the prince of the kings of the earth. Unto him that *agape*/loved us, and washed us from our sins in his own blood, 6 and hath made *me a king and a priest* unto God and his Father; to him be glory and dominion for ever and ever. Amen. *All praise to* 1 Tim 6:14 ... our Lord Jesus Christ: 15 ... who is the blessed and only Potentate, the King of kings, and Lord of lords; 2 Cor 1:19 for the Son of God, Jesus Christ, ... was not yea and nay, but in him was yea. 20 For all the promises of God in him are yea, and in him Amen, unto the glory of God by us. 21 Now he which stablisheth us *together* in Christ, and hath anointed *me*, is *Father* God; 22 who hath also sealed *me*, and given the earnest of the Spirit in *me to fulfill my part in this promise*: Isa 49:24 Shall the prey be taken from the mighty, or the lawful captive delivered? 25 But thus saith the Lᴏʀᴅ, Even the captives of the mighty shall be taken away, and the prey of the terrible shall be delivered: for I will contend with him that contendeth with thee, and I will save thy children. *So I speak* Acts 14:3 ... boldly in the Lord, which *gives* testimony unto the word of his grace, and *grants* signs and wonders to be done by *my* hands. *As it is with Jesus, so it is with me, for* Luke 4:18 the Spirit of the Lord is *also* upon me, because he hath anointed (*called, qualified and enabled*) me to preach the gospel to the poor; he hath sent me to heal the brokenhearted, to preach deliverance to the captives, and recovering of sight to the blind, to set at liberty them that are bruised, 19 to preach the acceptable year of the Lord. ... *For* 21 ... this *is the* day *of salvation in which* this scripture *is* fulfilled .... 2 Cor 5:14 For the *agape*/love of Christ constraineth *me*; because *I* thus judge, that if one died for all, then were all dead: 15 and that he died for all, that they which *zao*/live should not henceforth *zao*/live unto themselves, but unto him which died for them, and rose again. 16 Wherefore henceforth know *I* no man after the flesh: yea, though *I* have known Christ after the flesh, yet now henceforth know *I* him no more. 17 Therefore if any man be in Christ, he is a new creature: old things are passed away; behold, all things are become new. 18 And all things are of God, who hath reconciled us to himself by Jesus Christ, and hath given to *me* the ministry of reconciliation; 19 to wit, that God was in Christ, reconciling the world unto himself, not imputing their trespasses unto them; and hath committed unto *me* the word of reconciliation. 20 Now then *I am an ambassador* for Christ, as though God did beseech *all men* by *me*: *I* pray *for each one* in Christ's stead, *all men be*

OK, God, Now What?

reconciled to God. 21 For *You, Father, have* made *Jesus* to be sin for us, who knew no sin; that we might be made the righteousness of *You, Father* God, in him. 6:1 *I* then, as *worker* together with him, beseech *all men* also that *they* receive not the grace of *You, Father* God in vain. 2 (For *You say*, I have heard thee in a time accepted, and in the day of *soteria*/salvation have I succoured thee: behold, now is the accepted time; behold, now is the day of *soteria*/salvation.) 2 Cor 3:5 Not that *I am* sufficient of *myself* to think any thing as of *myself*; but *my* sufficiency is of God; 6 who also hath made *me an* able *minister* of the new testament; not of the letter, but of the spirit: for the letter killeth, but the spirit giveth *zoe*/life. *For by grace I* 1 Cor 3:16 know *that I am a* temple of God, and that the Spirit of God dwelleth in *me*. Rom 5:1 Therefore being justified by faith (*actions*), *I* have peace with God through our Lord Jesus Christ: 2 by whom also *I* have access by faith (*actions*) into this grace wherein *I* stand, and rejoice in hope of the glory of God. 3 And not only so, but *I* glory in tribulations also: knowing that tribulation worketh patience; 4 and patience, experience; and experience, hope (*joyful expectation of coming good*): 5 and hope maketh not ashamed; because the *agape*/love of God is shed abroad in *my heart* by the Holy Ghost which is given unto *me*. 6 For when we were yet without strength, in due time Christ died for the ungodly. *By the grace of God* 1 Cor 2:16 ... *I* have the mind of Christ. 1 Cor 1:30 For of *Father God am I* in Christ Jesus, who of God is made unto *me* wisdom, and righteousness, and sanctification, and redemption: 31 that, according as it is written, He that glorieth, let him glory in the Lord. *I therefore continually* 2 Cor 13:5 examine *myself*, whether *I* be in the faith (*facts*); *proving myself*. *Knowing myself*, how that Jesus Christ is in *me*, except *I* be *reprobate (useless and ineffective in my faith, worthy to be cast away)*. *So my spirit thinks like Jesus* 2 Tim 1:7 for God hath not given *me* the spirit of fear; but of power, and of *agape*/love, and of a sound mind. 8 *So I am not* ashamed of the testimony of our Lord, nor *any of* his *prisoners*: but *am a* partaker of the afflictions of the gospel according to the power of God; 9 who hath *sozo*/saved *me*, and called *me* with an holy calling, not according to *my* works, but according to his own purpose and grace, which was given *me* in Christ Jesus before the world began, 10 but is now made manifest by the appearing of our Saviour Jesus Christ, who hath abolished death, and hath brought *zoe*/life and immortality to light through the gospel. 2 Cor 4:6 For God, who commanded the light to shine out of darkness, hath shined in *my heart*, to give the light of the knowledge of the glory of God in the face of Jesus Christ. 7 *And I* have this treasure in *an* earthen *vessel*, that the excellency of the power may be of God, and not of *me*. *So, like Jesus in faith actions, God's power is in me to exercise the triumph of Jesus by faith actions. Praise You, Lord Jesus, for Your triumphant victory! Yahoo! Yahoo! Yahoo! You are in me to reign through me! Yahoo!*

Affirmations in Christ

F. For Jesus is my one and only Lord <u>Rom 3:25</u> whom *Father* God hath set forth to be a propitiation through faith in his blood, to declare his righteousness for the remission of sins that are past, through the forbearance of *Father* God; 26 to declare, I say, at this time his righteousness: that *Father God* might be just, and the justifier of him which believeth in Jesus. <u>1 John 2:2</u> And he is the propitiation (*the satisfaction and payment in full*) for *my* sins: and not for *mine* only, but also for the sins of the whole world. *Father God is building in me the revelation unto my walking in* agape/*love that* <u>Rom 4:5</u> *for* to him that worketh not, but believeth on him that justifieth the ungodly, his faith is counted for righteousness. 6 Even as David also describeth the blessedness of the man, unto whom God imputeth righteousness without works, 7 saying, Blessed are they whose iniquities are forgiven, and whose sins are covered. 8 Blessed is the man to whom the Lord will not impute sin. *Therefore as I am in Jesus, Father God does not count my sins against me,* <u>Gal 3:8</u> and the scripture, foreseeing that God would justify the heathen through faith, preached before the gospel unto Abraham, saying, In thee shall all nations be blessed. 9 So then they which be of faith (*actions*) are blessed with faithful Abraham. *I am of faith actions and blessed with faithful Abraham in Jesus.* <u>Rom 5:17</u> For if by one man's offence death reigned *as king* by one; much more they which (*continually*) *lambano*/receive [*by faith actions*] abundance of grace and of the gift of [*permanent*] righteousness shall reign *as kings* in *zoe*/life by one, Jesus Christ. <u>Eph 2:4</u> For *Father* God, who is rich in mercy, for his great *agape*/love wherewith he *agape*/loved us, 5 even when we were dead in sins, hath quickened us together with Christ, (by grace *am I sozo*/saved;) 6 and hath raised *me* up together, and made *me* sit together in heavenly places in Christ Jesus: 7 that in the ages to come he might shew the exceeding riches of his grace in his kindness toward *me* through Christ Jesus. 8 For by grace *am I sozo*/saved through faith (*actions*); and that not of *myself*: it is the gift of *Father* God: 9 not of works, lest any man should boast. 10 For *I am Father God's* workmanship, created in Christ Jesus unto good works, which *Father* God hath before ordained that *I* should walk in them. 11 Wherefore *by grace I* remember, that *I*, being in time past *a Gentile* in the flesh, who *is* called Uncircumcision by that which is called the Circumcision in the flesh made by hands; 12 that at that time we were without Christ, being aliens from the commonwealth of Israel, and strangers from the covenants of promise, having no hope, and without *Father* God in the world: 13 but now in Christ Jesus *we* who sometimes were far off are made nigh by the blood of Christ. 14 For he is our peace, who hath made both one, and hath broken down the middle wall of partition between us; 15 having abolished in his flesh the enmity, even the law of commandments contained in ordinances; for to make in himself of twain one new man, so making peace; 16 and that he might reconcile both unto *Father*

OK, God, Now What?

God in one body by the cross, having slain the enmity thereby: 17 and came and preached peace to *us* which were afar off, and to them that were nigh. 18 For through him we both have access by one Spirit unto the Father. *Therefore I am blessed and highly favored of God to bless and be a blessing. Good things happen to me, and I make good things happen for others. And I am made, by Father's grace, to be just like my elder brother Jesus, to preach* Acts 10:36 the word which God sent unto the children of Israel, preaching peace by Jesus Christ: (he is Lord of all:) ... , 38 *for* Father God *has* anointed *me in* Jesus of Nazareth with the Holy Ghost and with power: *and I go* about doing good, and healing all that are oppressed (*under the active rule and lordship*) of the devil; for *Father* God *is* with *me, for I am brought nigh by the blood of Jesus.* Acts 13:37 *For Jesus*, whom God raised again, saw no corruption. 38 *For I make* it known ... that through this man, *Jesus,* is preached unto *all* the forgiveness (*remission, purging, putting away and obliteration*) of sins: 39 and by him all that believe are justified from all things, from which *we* could not be justified by the law of Moses. Mark 16:15 *And I* go into all the world, and *I* preach the gospel to every creature. 16 He that believeth and is baptized shall be *sozo*/saved; but he that believeth not shall be damned. 17 And these signs *follow me* that *believes* (*in faith actions*); in *the* name *of Jesus I* cast out devils; *I* speak with new tongues; 18 *I* take up serpents; and if *I* drink any deadly thing, it shall not hurt *me; I* lay hands on the sick, and they ... recover *totally. Because* 19 ... the Lord *Jesus* ... *has been received* up into heaven, and *sits* on the right hand of God, *I do even greater works than Jesus and I* 20 *go* forth, and *I preach* everywhere, *in word and good deeds,* the Lord working with *me,* and confirming the word with signs following, *just as Father God wants all His sons. Amen. For* 1 John 4:4 *I am* of God, *one of His* little children, *a son of God,* and have overcome *the lie of the devil*: because greater is he that is in *me,* than he that is in the world. *For by Father God's spirit of wisdom and revelation I* 1 Cor 3:16 know ... *I am a* temple of *Father* God, and that the Spirit of God dwelleth in *me.* 1 John 3:20 For if *my un-renewed* heart condemns me [*due to my sins or sense of unworthiness, or sin consciousness and forgetting that my sins were purged, washed, destroyed, dissolved and purified two thousand years ago by Jesus through the cross*], God is greater than *my* heart, and knoweth all things *that my sins are purged, washed, destroyed, dissolved and purified. By grace, knowing that I am* 21 *agape*/beloved, if *my* heart condemn *me* not, *or I remember my former purging, washing, destruction, dissolution and purification of all sins,* then have *I* confidence toward *Father* God. 22 And whatsoever *I aiteo*/ask (*by demanding as due by covenant promise*), *I* receive of him, because *I* keep his commandments, and do those things that are pleasing in his sight. 23 And this is his commandment, That *I* should believe (*in faith actions*) on the name of his Son Jesus Christ, and *agape*/love one another, as he gave us commandment. 24 And he that keepeth his commandments dwelleth in him, and he in him. And hereby *I* know that he abideth in *me*, by the Spirit which he hath given *me*. *Knowing* Acts 3:12 ... *while men may* marvel *at the confirming signs and wonders the Lord does at my word or touch* or why look *they* so earnestly on *me*, as though by *my* own power or holiness *I* had made ... *healing miracles or wonders, knowing that it is the name of Jesus* Acts 3:16 ... through faith (*actions*) in his name *that* hath made *any sign and wonder, and not my holiness or power. For* Eph 1:7 in *Jesus I* have redemption through his blood, the forgiveness (*remission, purging, putting away and obliteration*) of sins, according to the riches of *Father God's* grace; Eph 1:13 in whom *I* also trusted, after that *I* heard the word of truth, the gospel of our *soteria*/salvation: in whom also after that *I* believed, *I was* sealed with that holy Spirit of promise, 14 which is the earnest of our inheritance until the redemption of the purchased possession, unto the praise of *Father's* glory. Phil 4:19 *And* my *Father* God shall supply all *my* need (*aiteo*), according to his riches in glory by Christ Jesus, a*nd perfect that which concerneth me and mine*. 20 Now unto God and our Father be glory for ever and ever. Amen. *Who lets us direct Him in faith actions by our thoughts, words, hands and deeds, for He is in me and with me. Thank You, Father! In the name of Jesus of Nazareth, the Christ, thank You! Almighty God, thank You! In the name of Jesus, thank You! Yahoo!*

G. **For by the grace of God I proclaim the grace of God,** Acts 20:32 and ... commend *everyone* to God, and to the word of his grace, which is able to build *us* up, and to give *us* an inheritance among all them which are sanctified (*purified and made holy*). John 1:12 *For* as many as *lambano*/received (*hold on to, cling to and stand in*) him, to them gave he power to become the sons of God, even to them that believe on his name: 13 which were born, not of blood, nor of the will of the flesh, nor of the will of man, but of God. 14 And the Word was made flesh, and dwelt among *the first believers*, (and *they* beheld his glory, the glory as of the only begotten of the Father,) full of grace and truth. ... 17 For the law was given by Moses, but grace and truth came by Jesus Christ. Rom 5:15 *For* not as the offence, so also is the free gift. For if through the offence of one many be dead, much more the grace of God, and the gift by grace, which is by one man, Jesus Christ, hath abounded unto many. 16 And not as it was by one that sinned, so is the gift: for the judgment was by one to condemnation, but the free gift is of many offences unto justification. 17 For if by one man's offence death reigned (*as king*) by one; much more *I, as one* which *lambano*/receives [*by faith actions*] abundance of grace and of the gift of [*permanent*] righteousness ... *reigns as a king for my Lord Jesus Christ* in *zoe*/life by one, Jesus Christ [*to bring the Kingdom of God to Earth as it is in Heaven, just as Jesus did.*] 18 Therefore as by the offence of one judgment came upon all men to condemnation; even so by the righteousness of one the free gift came upon all men unto justification of *zoe*/life. 19 For as by one man's disobedience many were made sinners, so by the obedience of one shall many be made [*new creatures that are permanently*] righteous. 20 Moreover the law entered, that the offence might abound. But where sin abounded, grace did much more abound: 21 that as sin hath reigned *as king* unto death, even so might grace reign *as a king in me* through *the gift of* righteousness unto eternal *zoe*/life by Jesus Christ our Lord. *I therefore* Rom 15:19 through mighty signs and wonders, by the power of the Spirit of God; so that from *home*, and round about unto *all the world*, I ... fully *preach* the gospel of Christ. *For* Rom 16:20 ... the God of peace *bruises* Satan under *my* feet *as shattered glass*. The grace of our Lord Jesus Christ *is* with *me* [*to know, be and do this*]. Amen. Acts 15:12 ... declaring what miracles and wonders God *has* wrought among *all men* by *me*. Acts 19:11 And God *does* special miracles by *my hands*: 12 so that from *my* body *are* brought unto the sick handkerchiefs or aprons, and the diseases *depart* from them, and the evil spirits *go* out of them, 2 Cor 12:12 ... in signs, and wonders, and mighty deeds [*because God's grace reigns through me*]. *Knowing that* Gal 3:5 he therefore that ministereth to *us* the Spirit, and worketh miracles among *us*, doeth he it *not* by the works of the law, *but* by the hearing of faith [*that no man is justified by the works of the law but by the faith of Jesus Christ*]. *As Holy Spirit has said:* Acts 13:38 Be it known unto you therefore, men and brethren, that through this man (*Jesus of Nazareth, the Christ*), is preached unto you the forgiveness (*remission, purging, obliteration and putting away*) of sins: 39 and by him all that believe are justified from all things, from which *we* could not be justified by the law of Moses. Acts 10:43 To him give all the prophets witness, that through his name whosoever believeth in him shall receive remission (*purging, removal, obliteration and putting away*) of sins. Ps 143:2 ... For in thy sight shall no man living be justified. Rom 8:3 For what the law could not do, in that it was weak through the flesh, God sending his own Son in the likeness of sinful flesh, and for sin, condemned sin in the flesh: 4 that the righteousness of the law might be fulfilled in us, who walk not after the flesh, but after the Spirit. *As the Word of God says*: Rom 10:4 For Christ is the end of the law for righteousness to every one that believeth (*in faith actions*). 5 For Moses describeth the righteousness which is of the law, That the man which doeth those things shall *zao*/live by them. 6 But the righteousness which is of faith (*actions*) speaketh on this wise, Say not in thine heart, Who shall ascend into heaven? (that is, to bring Christ down from above:) 7 or, Who shall descend into the deep? (That is, to bring up Christ again from the dead.) 8 But what saith it? The word is nigh thee, even in thy mouth, and in thy heart: that is, the word of faith, which we preach; 9 that if thou shalt confess with thy mouth the Lord Jesus, and shalt believe in thine heart that God hath raised him from the dead, thou shalt be *sozo*/saved. 10 For with the heart man believeth unto righteousness; and with the mouth confession is made unto *soteria*/salvation.

Affirmations in Christ

11 For the scripture saith, Whosoever believeth on him shall not be ashamed. 12 For there is no difference between the Jew and the Greek: for the same Lord over all is rich unto all that call upon him. 13 For whosoever shall call upon the name of the Lord shall be *sozo*/saved. *As Philip preached Jesus to the eunuch, starting with Isaiah 53,* Acts 8:37 and Philip said, If thou believest with all thine heart, thou mayest. And *the eunuch* answered and said, I believe that Jesus Christ is the Son of God. 1 John 4:14 And we have seen and do testify that the Father sent the Son to be the Saviour of the world. 15 Whosoever shall confess that Jesus is the Son of God, God dwelleth in him, and he in God. 1 John 5:4 For whatsoever is born of God overcometh the world: and this is the victory that overcometh the world, even our faith (*actions*). 5 Who is he that overcometh the world, but he that believeth (*by continual right faith actions*) that Jesus is the Son of God? 1 John 5:11 And this is the record, that God hath given to us eternal *zoe*/life, and this *zoe*/life is in his Son. 12 He that hath the Son hath *zoe*/life; and he that hath not the Son of God hath not *zoe*/life. 13 These things *did John write* unto *us* that believe on the name of the Son of God; that *we* may know that *we* have eternal *zoe*/life, and that *we* may believe (*in faith actions*) on the name of the Son of God. *Jesus, You are the Son of God. I have eternal zoe/life in You. Almighty God dwells in me and moves, in the name of Jesus, in faith actions by me. Thank You, Father! Yahoo! Lord, You are good, and Your mercy is everlasting! Yahoo!*

H. For I preach the Heb 2:3 ... great *soteria*/salvation; which at the first began to be spoken by the Lord, and was confirmed unto *those* that heard him; 4 God also bearing *me* witness, both with signs and wonders, and with divers miracles, and gifts of the Holy Ghost, according to his own will *as He delights in doing this through me.* Gal 2:16 Knowing that a man is not justified by the works of the law, but by the faith of Jesus Christ, even *I* have believed in Jesus Christ, that *I* might be justified by the faith of Christ, and not by the works of the law: for by the works of the law shall no flesh be justified. ... 19 For I through the law am dead to the law, that I might *zao*/live unto God. 20 I am (*have been*) crucified with Christ: nevertheless I *zao*/live; yet not I, but Christ *zao*/liveth in me: and the life which I now *zao*/live in the flesh I *zao*/live by the faith (*actions*) *in* the Son of God, who *agape*/loved me, and gave himself for me. 21 I do not frustrate the grace of God: for if righteousness come by the law, then Christ is dead in vain. *By this justification, the zoe/life of Jesus is in me, to will and to do of the Father's good pleasure, including raising the dead.* Acts 26:18 To open *the* eyes *of Jew and Gentile*, and to turn them from darkness to light, and from the power (*authority, jurisdiction or force*) of Satan unto God, that they may receive forgiveness (*deliverance, remission, pardon and liberty*) of sins, and inheritance among them which are sanctified (*purified and made holy*) by faith that is in *Jesus*. 1 Cor 15:1 ... I declare ... the gospel which I *preach* unto

OK, God, Now What?

all, which also *we* have *lambano*/received, and wherein *we* stand; 2 by which also *we* are *(continually being) sozo*/saved, as *we* keep in memory what I *preach* unto *all*, unless *we* have believed in vain. 3 ... How that Christ died for our sins according to the scriptures; 4 and that he was buried, and that he rose again the third day according to the scriptures: 5 and that he was seen of Cephas, then of the twelve: 6 after that, he was seen of above five hundred brethren at once .... 7 After that, he was seen of James; then of all the apostles. ... 17 And if Christ be not raised, *our* faith is vain; *we* are yet in *our* sins. 18 Then they also which are fallen asleep in Christ are perished. 19 If in this *zoe*/life only we have hope in Christ, we are of all men most miserable. 20 But now is Christ risen from the dead, and become the firstfruits of them that slept. 21 For since by man came death, by man came also the resurrection of the dead. 22 For as in Adam all die, even so in Christ shall all be made alive. <u>Rom 4:24</u> But for us also, to whom it shall be imputed *for righteousness*, if we believe on him that raised up Jesus our Lord from the dead; 25 who was delivered for our offences, and was raised again for our justification. <u>Rom 6:22</u> But now being made free from sin, and become servants to God, *we* have *our* fruit unto holiness, and the end everlasting *zoe*/life. 23 For the wages of sin is death; but the gift of God is eternal *zoe*/life through Jesus Christ our Lord. <u>Luke 24:46</u> And *Jesus* said unto them, Thus it is written, and thus it behoved Christ to suffer, and to rise from the dead the third day: 47 and that repentance and remission of sins should be preached in his name among all nations, beginning at Jerusalem. ... 49 And, behold, I *(Jesus)* send the promise of my Father upon you: but tarry ye in the city of Jerusalem, until ye be endued with *dunamis*/power *(ability)* from on high. *Holy Spirit now dwells in me in power.* <u>Acts 17:30</u> And the times of this ignorance God winked at; but now commandeth all men every where to repent: 31 because he hath appointed a day, in the which he will judge the world in righteousness by that man whom he hath ordained; whereof he hath given assurance unto all men, in that he hath raised him from the dead. *That is* <u>Rom 2:16</u> in the day when God shall judge the secrets of men by Jesus Christ according to *the* gospel. *Praise You, Lord Jesus!*

I. <u>1 Cor 3:6</u> I *plant, and water, others plant and water;* but God *gives* the increase. 7 So then neither is he that planteth any thing, neither he that watereth; but God that giveth the increase. 8 Now he that planteth and he that watereth are one: and every man shall receive his own reward according to his own labour. 9 For *I am a laborer* together with God: *they* are God's husbandry, *they* are God's building. 10 According to the grace of God which is given unto me, as a wise masterbuilder, I *continue* the foundation, and *build* thereon. But *I* take heed how *I build* thereupon. 11 For other foundation can no man lay than that is laid, which is Jesus Christ. 12 Now if any man build upon this foundation gold, silver, precious stones, wood, hay, stubble; 13 every man's work shall be made manifest: for the day shall declare it, because it shall be revealed by fire; and the fire shall try every man's work of what sort it is. 14 If any man's work abide which he hath built thereupon, he shall receive a reward. 15 If any man's work shall be burned, he shall suffer loss: but he himself shall be *sozo/ saved; yet so as by fire. For I* 16 know ... that *I am* the temple of God, and that the Spirit of God dwelleth in *me.* 2 Cor 5:9 Wherefore *I* labour, that, whether present or absent, *I* may be accepted of him. 10 For we must all appear before the judgment seat of Christ; that every one may receive the things done in his body, according to that he hath done, whether it be good or bad. 11 Knowing therefore the terror of the Lord, *I* persuade men; but *I am* made manifest unto God; and I trust also are made manifest in *the* consciences *of those who hear and see me.* Gal 4:4 But when the fulness of the time was come, *Father* God sent forth his Son, made of a woman, made under the law, 5 to redeem them that were under the law, that we might receive the adoption of sons. 6 And because *we* are sons, God hath sent forth the Spirit of his Son into *our* hearts, crying, Abba (*Daddy*), Father. 7 Wherefore *I am* no more a servant, but a son; and if a son, then an heir of God through Christ. *I am* agape/*loved and liked by God, who sent His Son to die for me. I am loved by God! Yahoo!*

J. Gal 3:8 **And the scripture**, foreseeing that God would justify the heathen through faith, preached before the gospel unto Abraham, saying, In thee shall all nations be blessed. 9 So then they which be of faith (*actions*) are blessed with faithful Abraham. *Therefore I am blessed with Abraham.* 10 For as many as are of the works of the law are under the curse: for it is written, Cursed is every one that continueth not in all things which are written in the book of the law to do them. 11 But that no man is justified by the law in the sight of God, it is evident: for, The just shall *zao*/live (*in miracle power*) by faith (*actions*). 12 And the law is not of faith: but, The man that doeth them shall *zao*/live in them. 13 Christ hath redeemed us from the curse of the law, being made a curse for us: for it is written, Cursed is every one that hangeth on a tree: 14 that the blessing of Abraham might come on the Gentiles through Jesus Christ; that we might receive the promise of the Spirit through faith. *Therefore I have Holy Spirit of God as a gift by Jesus Christ. For I* Rom 6:3 **know** ... that so many of us as were baptized into Jesus Christ were baptized into his death. 4 Therefore we are buried with him by baptism into death: that like as Christ was raised up from the dead by the glory of the Father, even so we also should walk in newness of *zoe*/life (*now*). 5 For if we have been planted together in the likeness of his death, we shall be also in the likeness of his resurrection: 6 **knowing** this, that our old man is crucified with him, that the body of sin might be destroyed, that henceforth we should not serve sin. 7 For he that is dead is freed from sin. 8 Now if we be dead with Christ, we believe (*by faith actions*) that we shall also *zao*/live with him: 9 **knowing** that Christ being raised from the dead dieth no more; death hath no more dominion over him. 10 For in that he died, he died unto sin once: but in that he *zao*/liveth, he *zao*/liveth unto God. 11 **Likewise I reckon** *myself* to be dead indeed unto sin, but *zao*/alive unto God through Jesus Christ our Lord. *Knowing, by the grace of Father God, that* Rom 13:10 *agape*/love worketh no ill to his neighbour: therefore *agape*/love is the fulfilling of the law. 11 And that, knowing the time, that now it is high time to awake out of sleep: for now is *my soteria*/salvation nearer than when *I* believed. 12 The night is far spent, the day is at hand: *I* therefore cast off the works of darkness, and *I* put on the armour of light. 13 *I, by the grace of God working in me,* walk honestly, as in the day; not in rioting and drunkenness, not in chambering and wantonness, not in strife and envying. 14 *And I put* on the Lord Jesus Christ, and make not provision for the flesh, to fulfil the lusts thereof. Eph 4:22 *I* put off concerning the former conversation the old man, which is corrupt according to the deceitful lusts; 23 and *am* renewed in the spirit of *my* mind; 24 and that *I* put on the new man *in the attitude of my heart that I am a new creation in Jesus,* which after God is created in righteousness and true holiness [*and no longer a mere human, but my new nature is just like Jesus'*]. 25 Wherefore putting away lying, *I* speak ... truth with *my* neighbour: for we are members one of another. ... 29 *I* let no corrupt communication proceed out of *my* mouth, but that which is good to the use of edifying, that it may minister grace unto the hearers. 30 And grieve not the Holy Spirit of God, whereby *I am* sealed unto the day of redemption. *Therefore I do acts of* agape/*love by obeying Him.* Matt 10:7 And as *I* go, *I* preach, saying, The kingdom of heaven is at hand. *I* 8 heal the sick, cleanse the lepers, raise the dead, cast out devils: freely *I* have *lambano*/received, freely *I* give. *For not with my holiness, but by the name of Jesus and faith actions in the name of Jesus, I deliver Father God to do the works He has longed to do by His Spirit, who dwells in me and is greater than he who is in the world, and by which I zao/live by faith actions to Father's glory as the king and priest Jesus has made me to be. Thank You, Father, in Jesus' name! Thank You! Thank You! Thank You! Yahoo!*

K. **2 Thes 1:11** Wherefore *I pray that You, Father* God, *in the name of Jesus*, would count *me* worthy of this calling, and fulfil all the good pleasure of *Your* goodness, and the work of faith (*actions*) with power 12 that the name of our Lord Jesus Christ may be glorified in *me*, and *me* in him, according to the grace of our God and the Lord Jesus Christ. Phil 1:9 And this I pray, that *my agape*/love may abound yet more and more in knowledge and in all judgment; 10 that *I* may approve things that are excellent; that *I* may be sincere and without offence till the day of Christ; 11 being filled with the fruits of righteousness, which are by Jesus Christ, unto the glory and praise of *You, Father* God. Col 1:9 ... That *I, Father, in the name of Jesus,* might be filled with the knowledge of *Your* will in all wisdom and spiritual understanding; 10 that *I* might walk worthy of the Lord unto all pleasing, being fruitful in every good work, and increasing in the knowledge of *You, Father* God; 11 strengthened with all might, according to *Your* glorious power, unto all patience and longsuffering with joyfulness; 12 giving thanks *(continuously)* unto *You,* the Father, which hath made us meet to be partakers of the inheritance of the saints in light: 13 who hath delivered us from the power of darkness, and hath translated us into the kingdom of *Your agape/*dear Son: 14 in whom we have redemption through his blood, even the forgiveness *(remission, purging, obliteration and putting away)* of sins: 15 who is the image of *You, Father,* the invisible God, the firstborn of every creature: 16 for by *Jesus* were all things created, that are in heaven, and that are in earth, visible and invisible, whether they be thrones, or dominions, or principalities, or powers: all things were created by *Jesus,* and for *Jesus:* 17 and *Jesus* is before all things, and by *Jesus* all things consist. 18 And *Jesus* is the head of the body, the church: who is the beginning, the firstborn from the dead; that in all things *Jesus* might have the preeminence. 19 For it pleased *You,* the Father, that in *Jesus* should all fulness dwell; 20 and, having made peace through the blood of *Jesus'* cross, by *Jesus* to reconcile all things unto *Yourself;* by *Jesus,* I say, whether they be things in earth, or things in heaven. *Thank You, Father God! Thank You! In the name of Jesus, thank You! Yahoo!*

L. **Eph 3:14** **For this cause** I bow my knees unto *You,* the Father of our Lord Jesus Christ, 15 of whom the whole family in heaven and earth is named, 16 that *You, Father,* would grant *me,* according to the riches of *Your* glory, to be strengthened with might by *Your* Spirit in *my* inner man; 17 that Christ may dwell in *my heart* by faith *(actions);* that *I,* being rooted and grounded in *agape/*love, 18 may be able to comprehend with all saints what is the breadth, and length, and depth, and height; 19 and to know the *agape/*love of Christ, which passeth knowledge, that *I* might be filled with all the fulness of *You, Father* God. 20 Now unto *You, Father,* that *are* able to do exceeding abundantly above all that *I aiteo/*ask *(by demanding as due by covenant promise)* or think, according to the power that worketh in *me,* 21 unto *You* be glory in the church by Christ Jesus throughout all ages, world without end. Amen. **Eph 4:4** There is one body, and one Spirit, even as *we* are called in one hope of *our* calling; 5 one Lord, one faith, one baptism, 6 one God and Father of all, who is above all, and through all, and in *us* all. 7 But unto every one of us is given grace according to the measure of the gift of Christ. *I, therefore,* Col 1:12 *give* thanks *(continually)* unto *You,* the Father, *through the name of Jesus Christ, my Lord,* which hath made *me* meet *(qualified and able by grace)* to be *a partaker* of the inheritance of the saints in light: *for it is You, Father,* 13 who hath delivered *me* from the power of

OK, God, Now What?

darkness, and hath translated *me* into the kingdom of *Your agape*/dear Son: 14 in whom *I* have redemption through his *(Jesus')* blood, even the forgiveness *(payment unto remission, purging, obliteration and putting away)* of sins: 15 who is the image of *You*, the invisible God, the firstborn of every creature: 16 for by *Jesus* were all things created, that are in heaven, and that are in earth, visible and invisible, whether they be thrones, or dominions, or principalities, or powers: all things were created by *Jesus*, and for *Jesus*: 17 and *Jesus* is before all things, and by *Jesus* all things consist. 18 And *Jesus* is the head of the body, the church: who is the beginning, the firstborn from the dead; that in all things *Jesus* might have the preeminence. 19 For it pleased *You*, the Father, that in *Jesus* should all fulness dwell; 20 and, having made peace through the blood of *Jesus'* cross, by *Jesus* to reconcile all things unto *Yourself*; by *Jesus*, I say, whether they be things in earth, or things in heaven. 21 And *I*, that *was* sometime alienated and *an enemy* in *my* mind by wicked works, yet now hath *Jesus* reconciled *me to You, Father God,* 22 in the body of his flesh through death, to present *me* holy and unblameable and unreproveable in *Your* sight: 23 *so* I continue in the faith *(actions)* grounded and settled, and *I am* not moved away from the hope of the gospel *(of Christ in me the hope of Your glory in me and through me)*, which *I* have heard, and ... *I* am made a minister. 2 Cor 5:7 For *I* walk by faith *(actions)*, not by sight: *I gladly call those things that be not yet of His promises as if they are until I see God do them. Thank you, Father! In the name of Jesus, thank You! Thank You, Lord Jesus, for Your mighty work! Thank You for Your* agape/love! *Glory! Yahoo!*

M. Just like Jesus, wherever I am I deliver the reconciliation of Father God; I heal the sick, cleanse the lepers, raise the dead, cast out demons, to proclaim the sovereignty of God in action. God heals as I lay hands or speak words of *zoe*/life. God does special miracles through me. I do greater works than Jesus because He has gone to the Father. I am sent as Jesus was sent to speak God's words in fullness. John 3:34 For he whom God hath sent speaketh the words of God: for God giveth not the Spirit by measure unto *me*. *So no disease, infirmity, death, lack, terror or destruction is able to stand before me, in the name of Jesus. God gives me His Spirit without measure, to speak His words of reconciliation through the blood of Jesus Christ.* 2 Cor 5:21 For he hath made *Jesus* to be sin for us who knew no sin; that we might be made the righteousness of God in him. Luke 4:18 The Spirit of the Lord is upon me, because he hath anointed me to preach the gospel to the poor; he hath sent me to heal the brokenhearted, to preach deliverance to the captives, and recovering of sight to the blind, to set at liberty them that are bruised, 19 to preach the acceptable year of the Lord, *now*. 2 Cor 4:6 For God, who commanded the light to shine out of darkness, hath shined in *my heart*, to give the light of the knowledge of the glory of God in the face of Jesus Christ. 7 *And I* have this treasure in *an* earthen *vessel*, that the excellency of the power may be of God, and not of *me*. 8 *As a warrior of Holy Spirit, to bring Heaven to Earth, I am* troubled on every side, yet not distressed; *I am* perplexed, but not in despair; 9 persecuted, but not forsaken; cast down, but not destroyed; 10 always bearing about in the body the dying of the Lord Jesus, that the *zoe*/life also of Jesus might be made manifest in *my* body. 2 Cor 3:17 Now the Lord is that Spirit: and where the Spirit of the Lord is, there is liberty (*to be all God wants me to be by Holy Spirit in me*). 18 But we all, with open face beholding as in a glass (*mirror*) the glory of the Lord (*within us*), are changed into the same image from glory to glory, even as by the Spirit of the Lord. Col 1:27 To whom God *makes* known *through me* what is the riches of the glory of this mystery… , which is Christ in *us*, the hope of glory: 28 whom *I* preach, warning every man, and teaching every man in all wisdom; that we may present every man perfect (*mature*) in Christ Jesus. 2 Cor 1:3 Blessed be God, even the Father of our Lord Jesus Christ, the Father of mercies, and the God of all comfort; 4 who comforteth *me* in all *my* tribulation, that *I* may be able to comfort them which are in any trouble, by the comfort wherewith *I myself am* comforted of God. 5 For as the sufferings of Christ abound in *me*, so *my* consolation also aboundeth by Christ. *For* Ps 31:23 *I* love the LORD, *as one of* his saints: for the LORD preserveth the faithful, and plentifully rewardeth the proud doer. 24 *I am* of good courage, and he shall strengthen *my* heart, *as I* hope in the LORD (*who raises the dead*). *Knowing* Ps 27:13 I had fainted, unless I had believed (*in faith actions*) to see the goodness of the LORD in the land of the living. *But no matter what, I do see the goodness of the Lord in the land of the living. I therefore* 14 wait on the LORD (*by entwining Him into every part of my life continually in faith actions*): so *I am* of good courage (*by faith actions*), and he *strengthens my* heart: wait (*entwine by faith actions*), I say, on the LORD. *For* Eph 6:10 finally … I *am* strong in the Lord, and in the power of his might [*by faith actions*]. 11 *I* put on the whole armour of God, that *I* may be able to stand against the wiles of the devil. 12 For *I* wrestle not against flesh and blood, but against principalities, against powers, against the rulers of the darkness of this world, against spiritual wickedness in high places. 13 Wherefore *I* take unto *myself* the whole armour of God, that *I* may be able to withstand in the evil day, and having done all, to stand. 14 *I* stand [*by faith actions*] therefore, having *my* loins girt about with truth, and having on the breastplate of righteousness; 15 and *my* feet shod with the preparation of the gospel of peace; 16 above all, *I continually take* the shield of faith (*actions*), wherewith *I* shall be able to quench all the fiery darts of the wicked. 17 And *I* take the helmet of salvation, and the sword of the Spirit, which is the word of God: 18 *I am* praying always with all prayer and supplication in the Spirit, and watching thereunto with all perseverance and supplication for all saints; 19 and for (*myself and other Gospel preachers*), that utterance may be given unto *us*, that *we* may open *our mouths* boldly, to make known the mystery of the gospel, 20 ... that therein *we* may speak boldly, as *we* ought to speak. *Knowing* <u>Acts 10:38</u> how *You, Father* God, *have* anointed *me in* Jesus of Nazareth with the Holy Ghost and with power: *so I go* about doing good, and healing all that *are* oppressed (*under the active rule and lordship*) of the devil; for *You, Father* God, *are* with *me*. <u>Rom 15:19</u> Through mighty signs and wonders, by the power of the Spirit of God; so that from *home* and round about *all the world*, I ... fully *preach* the gospel of Christ. <u>Matt 10:7</u> And as *I* go, *I* preach, saying, The kingdom of heaven is at hand. 8 *With Jesus beside the Father, I* heal the sick, cleanse the lepers, raise the dead, cast out devils: freely *I* have *lambano*/received, freely *I* give, *in every city or place, in the name of Jesus Christ*. <u>Mark 16:15</u> As Jesus said, *by Jesus through Holy Spirit, I* go into all the world, and *by Jesus through Holy Spirit, I* preach the gospel to every creature. 16 He that believeth and is baptized shall be *sozo*/saved, *by Jesus through Holy Spirit*; but he that believeth not shall be damned. 17 And, *by Jesus through Holy Spirit, to the glory of Father God,* these signs follow *me* that *believes* (*in faith actions*); in *the* name *of* Jesus I cast out devils, *by Jesus through Holy Spirit*; *I* speak with new tongues, *by Jesus through Holy Spirit*; 18. *I* take up serpents, *by Jesus through Holy Spirit*; and if *I* drink any deadly thing, it shall not hurt *me*, *by Jesus through Holy Spirit*; *I* lay hands on the sick, and they ... recover *totally, by Jesus through Holy Spirit.* 19 ... The Lord *Jesus* ... was received up into heaven, and *sits* on the right hand of God. 20 *I go* forth, and *I preach* everywhere, *by Jesus through Holy Spirit*, the Lord *Jesus* working with *me*, and confirming the word with signs following, *by Jesus through Holy Spirit, to the glory of Father God*. Amen! *Lord Jesus, You accomplished Your great work! You have obtained Holy Spirit for us. You, Lord Jesus, are the Administrator of Holy Spirit, and we, Your Body, administer Holy Spirit on the Earth for and with You in faith actions. Thank You for this calling. Thank You for Your great work. Thank You, Lord Jesus, thank You! Hallelujah! Yahoo! God, You are good! Your mercy is everlasting! Yahoo!*

N. **Father, in the name of Jesus**, give me Your spirit of wisdom and revelation in the knowledge of You, with the eyes of my understanding being enlightened so that I walk to Your glory by Jesus Christ, knowing that <u>2 Pet 1:2</u> grace and peace *are* multiplied unto *us* through the knowledge of *You, Father* God, and of Jesus our Lord, 3 according as, *in Jesus, Your* divine power hath given unto us all things that pertain unto *zoe*/life and godliness, through the knowledge of *You, Father*, that have called us to glory and virtue: 4 whereby are given unto us, *in Jesus*, exceeding great and precious promises: that by these *we* might be partakers of the divine nature, *in Jesus*, having escaped the corruption that is in

AFFIRMATIONS IN CHRIST

the world through lust. 5 And beside this, *I, by Your Spirit, give* all diligence, *that I* add to *my* faith *(actions)* virtue; and to virtue knowledge; 6 and to knowledge temperance; and to temperance patience; and to patience godliness; 7 and to godliness brotherly kindness; and to brotherly kindness *agape*/charity. *So that* 8 ... these things *are in me*, and abound, *so that* they make *me* that *I* shall neither be barren nor unfruitful in the knowledge of our Lord Jesus Christ. *Knowing, unto being zealous for good works, by faith actions in* agape/*love, that* 9 ... he that lacketh these things is blind, and cannot see afar off, and hath forgotten that he was purged from his old sins. *So, Father, open my eyes, cause me to see afar off and keep me in remembrance that I have been purged from my old sins by the blood of Jesus.* 10 Wherefore the rather, *Father, build in me the knowing, so that I* give diligence to make *my* calling and election sure, *in abounding in the manifestation of Your divine nature through me, to the knowing that, as I do* these things, *I* shall never fall: 11 for so an entrance shall be ministered unto *me* abundantly into the everlasting kingdom of our Lord and Saviour Jesus Christ, *to the praise of Your glory. Father, keep me in right remembrance of these things, unto glad obedience in* agape/*love. Thank You, Father! In the name of Jesus, thank You!* 12 Wherefore I will not be negligent to put *myself and others* always in remembrance of these things, though *we* know them, and be established in the present truth [*in this Day of Salvation in the remission of sins through the blood of Jesus Christ.*] *So that I soften my heart, so I hear You in Your Word and know the greatness of Your power, so that I* <u>Matt 13:15</u> ... should see with *my* eyes, and hear with *my* ears, and should understand with *my* heart, and should be converted, and *You* should heal *me in any area* <u>2 Pet 1:9</u> *that I* lack in the things (*of Your divine nature or godliness, so I am no longer*) blind, and cannot see afar off, *or forget* that *I* was purged from *my* old sins [*in Your mighty work in Jesus*]. *So I am one that believes and to whom You have revealed the greatness of the power of Your Arm, for:* <u>Isa 53:1</u> Who hath believed (*by faith actions*) our report? and to whom is the arm of the LORD revealed? 2 For he shall grow up before him as a tender plant, and as a root out of a dry ground: he hath no form nor comeliness; and when we shall see him, there is no beauty that we should desire him. 3 He is despised and rejected of men; a man of sorrows, and acquainted with grief: and we hid as it were our faces from him; he was despised, and we esteemed him not. 4 Surely he hath *nasa*/borne our griefs *and infirmities*, and *cabal*/carried our sorrows *and sicknesses*: yet we did esteem him stricken, smitten of God, and afflicted. 5 But he was wounded for our transgressions, he was bruised for our iniquities: the chastisement of our peace was upon him; and with his stripes we are healed. 6 All we like sheep have gone astray; we have turned every one to his own way; and the LORD hath laid on him the iniquity of us all. 7 He was oppressed, and he was afflicted, yet he opened not his mouth: he is brought as a lamb to the slaughter, and as a sheep before her shearers is dumb, so he openeth not his mouth. 8 He was taken from prison and from judgment: and who shall declare his generation? for he was cut off out of the land of the living: for the transgression of my people was he stricken. 9 And he made his grave with the wicked, and with the rich in his death; because he had done no violence, neither was any deceit in his mouth. 10 Yet it pleased the LORD to bruise him; he hath put him to grief (*and sickness*): when thou shalt make his soul an offering for sin, he shall see his seed, he shall prolong his days, and the pleasure of the LORD shall prosper in his hand. 11 He shall see of the travail of his soul, and shall be satisfied: by his knowledge shall my righteous servant justify many; for he shall *cabal*/bear their iniquities. 12 Therefore will I divide him a portion with the great, and he shall divide the spoil with the strong; because he hath poured out his soul unto death: and he was numbered with the transgressors; and he *nasa*/bare the sin of many, and made intercession for the transgressors. *So I say continually*: **Ps 103:1** Bless the LORD, O my soul: and all that is within me, bless his holy name. 2 Bless the LORD, O my soul, and forget not all his benefits: 3 who forgiveth all thine iniquities; who healeth all thy diseases; 4 who redeemeth thy life from destruction; who crowneth thee with *chesed*/lovingkindness and *racham*/tender mercies; 5 who satisfieth thy mouth with good things; so that thy youth is renewed like the eagle's. 6 The LORD executeth righteousness and judgment [*by our faith actions*] for all that are oppressed. 7 He made known his ways unto Moses, his acts unto the children of Israel. 8 The LORD is merciful and gracious, slow to anger, and plenteous in *chesed*/mercy. 9 He will not always chide: neither will he keep his anger for ever. 10 He hath not dealt with us after our sins; nor rewarded us according to our iniquities. 11 For as the heaven is high above the earth, so great is his *chesed*/mercy toward them that fear him. 12 As far as the east is from the west, so far hath he removed our transgressions from us. 13 Like as a father pitieth his children, so the LORD pitieth them that fear him. 14 For he knoweth our frame; he remembereth that we are dust. 15 As for man, his days are as grass: as a flower of the field, so he flourisheth. 16 For the wind passeth over it, and it is gone; and the place thereof shall know it no more. 17 But the *chesed*/mercy of the LORD is from everlasting to everlasting upon them that fear him, and his righteousness unto children's children; 18 to such as keep his covenant, and to those that remember his commandments to do them. 19 The LORD hath prepared his throne in the heavens; and his kingdom ruleth over all. 20 Bless the LORD, ye his angels, that excel in strength, that do his commandments, hearkening unto the voice of his word. 21 Bless ye the LORD, all ye his hosts; ye ministers of his, that do his pleasure. 22 Bless the LORD, all his works in all places of his dominion: bless the LORD, O my soul. *Bless You, O loving Father, in the name of Jesus! Bless You, O Lord Jesus! Hallelujah! God, You are good! Your mercy is everlasting! Yahoo!*

Affirmations in Christ

O. **By the grace of God, knowing that Jesus,** 1 Pet 2:24 who his own self bare our sins in his own body on the tree, that we, being dead to sins, should *zao*/live unto righteousness: by whose stripes *we* were healed. 25 For *we* were as sheep going astray; but now *I have* returned unto the Shepherd and Bishop of *our* souls. Eph 1:12 That we should be to the praise of his glory, *by trusting* in Christ, 13 ... after that *I* heard the word of truth, the gospel of *our soteria*/salvation: in whom also after that *I* believed, *I was* sealed with that holy Spirit of promise, 14 which is the earnest of our inheritance until the redemption of the purchased possession, unto the praise of his glory. *That by me, Father* Col 1:27 ... God would make known what is the riches of the glory of this mystery among *all peoples*; which is Christ in you, the hope of glory. Rom 15:19 Through mighty signs and wonders, by the power of the Spirit of God; so that from *home* unto *the world* I fully *preach* the gospel of Christ. Rom 1:16 For I am not ashamed of the gospel of Christ: for it is the power of God unto *soteria*/salvation to every one that believeth; to the Jew first, and also to the Greek. 17 For therein is the righteousness of God revealed from faith to faith: as it is written, The just shall *zao*/live (*unto miracle power*) by faith (*actions*). 1 John 3:8 ... For this purpose the Son of God was manifested *in me*, that he might destroy the works of the devil [*though me*]. Rom 16:20 And the God of peace *bruises* Satan under *my* feet *as shattered glass*. The grace of our Lord Jesus Christ *is* with *me* [*to know, will, be and do this*]. Amen. Heb 3:1 Wherefore, *as one of the* holy brethren, partakers of the heavenly calling, *I* consider the Apostle and High Priest of *my* profession (*confession*), Christ Jesus; ... 8 *and I* harden not *my heart*, as in the provocation, in the day of temptation in the wilderness (*when many times things looked bad, as if the Word and love of God were going to fail*): ... *so I enter in by believing God to perform and confirm His Word, no matter what the circumstances, knowing that* **Ps 23:1** the Lord is my shepherd; I shall not want, 2 he maketh me to lie down in green pastures: he leadeth me beside the still waters. 3 He restoreth my soul: he leadeth me in the paths of righteousness for his name's sake. 4 Yea, though I walk through the valley of the shadow of death, I will fear no evil: for thou art with me; thy rod and thy staff they comfort me. 5 Thou preparest a table before me in the presence of mine enemies: thou anointest my head with oil; my cup runneth over. 6 Surely goodness and *chesed*/mercy shall follow (*pursue and overtake*), me all the days of my life: and I will dwell in the house of the Lord for ever. *For* 1 John 4:4 *I am* of God, *one of His* little children (*a full adopted son of God*), and have overcome *the devil and all his works*: because greater is he that is in *me*, than he that is in the world. Heb 10:35 I cast not away therefore *my* confidence, which hath great recompence of reward. 36 For *I* have need of patience, that, after *I* have done the will of God, *I* might receive the promise. 37 For yet a little while, and he that shall come will come, and will not tarry. *Knowing that* 38 now the just shall *zao*/live *(unto miracle power)* by faith *(actions)*: but if any man draw back *[from faith actions]*, my soul shall have no pleasure in him. 39 But *I am* not of them who draw back unto perdition; but of them that believe *(by faith actions)* to the *sozo*/saving of the soul. Heb 11:1 Now faith *in Father God, in His Word,* is the substance *and the strength* of things hoped for *(the joyful expectation of coming good),* the evidence of things not seen. 2 For by it *I obtain* a good report. 2 Cor 4:13 *And I,* having the same spirit of faith *(actions),* according as it is written, I believed and therefore have I spoken; *I* also believe *(by faith actions),* and therefore speak *[God's Word of salvation, knowing He will perform it].* 1 Cor 15:10 *For* by the grace of God I am what I am *[born again of God]*: and his grace which was bestowed upon me was not in vain; but I labour more abundantly than they all: yet not I, but the grace of God which *is* with me. *Knowing,* Gal 2:19 for I through the law am dead to the law, that I might *zao*/live unto God. 20 I am *(have been)* crucified with Christ: nevertheless I *zao*/live; yet not I, but Christ *zao*/liveth in me: and the life which I now *zao*/live in the flesh I *zao*/live by the faith *(actions) in* the Son of God, who *agape*/loved me, and gave himself for me. 21 I do not frustrate the grace of God: for if righteousness come by the law, then Christ is dead in vain. John 14:12 Verily, verily, *Jesus has said* unto *me,* that *continually believe (by faith actions),* The works that *He did* shall *I* do also; and greater works than these shall *I* do; because *Jesus has gone unto* Father. 13 And whatsoever *I* shall *aiteo*/ask *(by demanding, expecting as due by covenant promise)* in *His* name, that will *Jesus* do, that the Father may be glorified in the Son. *For He said:* 14 If ye shall *aiteo*/ask *(by demanding, expecting as due by covenant promise)* any thing in my name, I will do it. *And not my holiness, but the name of Jesus and faith actions to and in the name of Jesus makes people and situations whole, to the glory of You, Father God.* 2 Thes 1:11 Wherefore *I* pray that *You, Father,* our God, would count *me* worthy of this calling, and fulfil all the good pleasure of *Your* goodness, and the work of faith *(actions)* with power: 12 that the name of our Lord Jesus Christ may be glorified in *me,* and *me* in him, according to the grace of our God and the Lord Jesus Christ. Heb 13:20 Now *You, Father,* the God of peace, that brought again from the dead our Lord Jesus, that great shepherd of the sheep, through the blood of the everlasting covenant, 21 make *me* perfect in every good work to do *Your* will, working in *me* that which is wellpleasing in *Your* sight, through Jesus Christ; to whom be glory for ever and ever. Amen. *Thank You, Father! You are working in and for me to my good! You agape/love me! You call me valuable to You! Thank You for the value You set on me, Jesus! Thank You, Jesus, for ransoming me by Your blood! Thank You! Yahoo!*

P. Father, by You I preach Your Word that You reign through us. Acts 10:36 The word which *You* sent unto the children of Israel, preaching peace by Jesus Christ: (he is Lord of all:) ... 38 how *You* anointed Jesus of Nazareth with the

Affirmations in Christ

Holy Ghost and with power: who went about doing good, and healing all that were oppressed (*under the active rule and lordship*) of the devil; for *You were* with him. 1 Pet 2:24 Who his own self bare our sins in his own body on the tree, that we, being dead to sins, should *zao*/live unto righteousness: by whose stripes *we* were healed. Ps 18:27 For thou wilt save the afflicted people; but wilt bring down high looks. 28 For thou wilt light my candle: the LORD my God will enlighten my darkness. 29 For by thee I ... run through a troop; and by my God I *leap* over a wall. 30 As for God, his way is perfect: the word of the LORD is tried: he is a buckler to all those that trust (*by faith actions*) in him. 31 For who is God save the LORD? Or who is a rock save our God? 32 It is God that girdeth me with strength, and maketh my way perfect. 33 He maketh my feet like hinds' feet, and setteth me upon my high places. 34 He teacheth my hands to war, so that a bow of steel is broken by mine arms. 35 Thou hast also given me the shield of thy salvation: and thy right hand hath holden me up, and thy gentleness hath made me great. 36 Thou hast enlarged my steps under me, that my feet *do* not slip. *By Your warrior heart in me,* 37 I *pursue* mine enemies, and *overtake* them: neither *do* I turn again till they *are* consumed. 38 I *wound* them that they *are* not able to rise: they *fall* under my feet, *in Jesus' name*. 39 For thou hast girded me with strength unto the battle: thou hast subdued under me *all the work of the enemy* that *rises* up against me. 40 Thou hast also given me the necks of mine enemies [*the devil and his works*]; that I might destroy them that hate me. 41 They *cry*, but there *is* none to save them: even unto the LORD, but *You answer* them not. 42 ... I beat them small as the dust before the wind: I ... cast them out as the dirt in the streets. Rom 15:13 Now *You, Father,* the God of hope fill *me* with all joy and peace in believing (*faith actions*), that *I* may abound in hope, through the power of the Holy Ghost. 2 Tim 2:3 *I* therefore endure hardness, as a good soldier of Jesus Christ. 1 Tim 1:18 ... That *I*, by *the prophecies and promises of God, might* war a good warfare; 19 holding faith (*actions*), and a good conscience ... . *For I use the shield of faith actions to quench the fiery darts and fears of the enemy, knowing*: Ps 27:1 The LORD is my light and my salvation; whom shall I fear? The LORD is the strength of my life; of whom shall I be afraid? Ps 42:11 Why art thou cast down, O my soul? and why art thou disquieted within me? hope thou in God: for I shall yet praise him, who is the health of my countenance, and my God. *I proclaim, in the name of Jesus by faith actions, I am strong in the Lord and in the power of His might and that* Phil 4:13 I can do all things through Christ which strengtheneth me. *For You said:* Joel 3:10 ... Let the weak say, I am strong. *I am strong in the Lord, for this is my true born-again nature, just like my elder brother, Jesus, in the power of Holy Spirit.* Ps 112:7 I shall not be afraid of evil tidings: *my* heart is fixed, trusting (*by continual faith actions*) in the LORD. 8 *My* heart is established, *I shall not be afraid, until I see my desire upon my enemies. For* Ps 46:1 God is our refuge and strength, a very present help in trouble. 2 Therefore will not we fear, though the earth be removed, and though the mountains be carried into the midst of the sea; 3 though the waters thereof roar and be troubled, though the mountains shake with the swelling thereof. Selah. Phil 4:13 I can do all things through Christ which strengtheneth me. Ps 27:13 I had fainted, unless I had believed (*by faith actions*) to see the goodness of the LORD in the land of the living. *I say* 14 wait on the LORD (*entwine Him into every part of your life in faith actions*): be of good courage (*by faith actions*), and he shall strengthen thine heart: wait (*entwine, trust by continual faith actions*) I say, on the LORD. *Therefore I do not faint, but am strong in His strength in me, proclaiming in absolute certainty that He will perform His Word, I will see the goodness of the Lord in the land of the living, and I am in joyful thanksgiving, knowing He confirms His Word of grace through me. Yahoo!* Phil 1:6 Being confident of this very thing, that he which hath begun a good work in *me* will perform it until the day of Jesus Christ. *Yahoo! For You, Father* Heb 1:1 God, who at sundry times and in divers manners spake in time past unto the fathers by the prophets, 2 *have* in these last days spoken unto us by *Your* Son, whom *You have* appointed heir of all things, by whom also *You* made the worlds; 3 who being the brightness of *Your* glory, and the express image of *Your* person, and upholding all things by the word of his power, when he had by himself purged our sins, sat down on the right hand of *You*, the Majesty on high; … 13 *for* to which of the angels said *You* at any time, Sit on my right hand, until I make thine enemies thy footstool? *With Jesus at Your right hand,* Rom 16:20 … *You, Father*, the God of peace, shall bruise Satan under *my* feet *as shattered glass, as I preach Your Kingdom, heal the sick, cleanse the lepers, raise the dead and cast out devils.* The grace of our Lord Jesus Christ is with *me* [*to know, be and do this*]. Amen. … 25 Now to *You, Father*, that is of power to stablish *me* according to *Your* gospel, and the preaching of Jesus Christ, according to the revelation of the mystery, which was kept secret since the world began, 26 but now is made manifest, and by the scriptures of the prophets, according to the commandment of *You*, the everlasting God, made known to all nations for the obedience of faith (*actions*): 27 to *You, Father* God, only wise, be glory through Jesus Christ for ever. Amen. *Hallelujah! Yahoo! Lord, You are good! Your mercy is everlasting! And Your truth endureth to all generations! Yahoo!*

Q. **I am sent of God to do the works of Jesus.** As a believer: Mark 16:17 And these signs shall follow them that believe; in *Jesus'* name *I, as a believer*, cast out devils; *I, as a believer*, speak with new tongues; 18. *I, as a believer*, take up serpents; and if *I, as a believer*, drink any deadly thing, it shall not hurt *me*; *I, as a believer*, lay hands on the sick, and they shall recover *totally*. *For I constantly walk in the absolute certainty and* Luke 10:19 behold *that I have* power (*author-*

Affirmations in Christ

ity, commission, pre-permission and the resources of Heaven) to tread on serpents and scorpions, and over all the power of the enemy: and nothing shall by any means hurt *me*. 20 Notwithstanding in this *I* rejoice not, that the spirits are subject unto *me*; but rather *I* rejoice, because *my name is* written in heaven. *I am equipped and commanded to walk as Jesus walked*. 1 John 2:5 But whoso keepeth his word, in him verily is the *agape*/love of God perfected: hereby know we that we are in him. 6 He that saith he abideth in him ought himself also so to walk, even as he walked. *I am to follow or imitate God as Jesus did*. Eph 5:1 Be ye therefore followers (*imitators*) of God, as *agape*/dear (*loved*) children; 2 and walk in *agape*/love, as Christ also hath *agape*/loved us, and hath given himself for us an offering and a sacrifice to God for a sweetsmelling savour. 1Cor 2:4 And my speech and my preaching *are* not with enticing words of man's wisdom, but in demonstration of the Spirit and of power: 5 that *our* faith should not stand in the wisdom of men, but in the power of God. ... 12 Now *I* have received, not the spirit of the world, but the spirit which is of God; that *I* might know the things that are freely given to us of God. *I am made for and get zoe/life for anyone in any sin or any effect of sin, including sickness or disease, for* 1 John 5:16 if any man see his brother sin a sin which is not unto death, he shall *aiteo*/ask (*by demanding as due by covenant promise*), and *therefore Father God shall give me zoe*/life for them ... . *By the grace of God, I do not let sin, sickness or disease rule in me or others*. Rom 6:14 For sin shall not have dominion over you: for ye are not under the law, but under grace. *I am to zao/live for God to serve others*. Rom 8:2 For the law of the Spirit of *zoe*/life in Christ Jesus hath made me free from the law of sin and death. 2 Cor 5:15 And that he died for all, that they which *zao*/live should not henceforth *zao*/live unto themselves, but unto him which died for them, and rose again, *and do greater works than Jesus, as Jesus said*: John 14:12 Verily, verily, I say unto you, He that believeth (*by faith actions*) on me, the works that I do shall he do also; and greater works than these shall he do; because I go unto my Father. 13 And whatsoever ye shall *aiteo*/ask (*by requiring, demanding and expecting as due by covenant promise*) in my name, that will I do, that the Father may be glorified in the Son. 14 If ye shall *aiteo*/ask (*by requiring, demanding and expecting as due by covenant promise*) any thing in my name, I will do it. *I obey Jesus to see answered* aiteo/*asking, requiring, demanding and expecting as due by covenant promise*. John 16:23 ... Verily, verily, I (*Jesus*) say unto you, Whatsoever ye shall *aiteo*/ask (*by requiring, demanding and expecting as due by covenant promise*) the Father in my name, he will give it you. *So I* 24 ... *aiteo*/ask (*by requiring, demanding and expecting as due by covenant promise, in Jesus' name*), and I receive, that *my* joy may be full. *God's very nature is to heal the sick, so it is my new-creation nature also*. Ps 103:2 Bless the LORD ... 3 who forgiveth all *my* iniquities; who healeth all *my* diseases;

OK, God, Now What?

4 who redeemeth *my* life from destruction; who crowneth *me* with *chesed/*lovingkindness and *racham/*tender mercies; 5 who satisfieth *my* mouth with good things; so that *my* youth is renewed like the eagle's. 6 The LORD executeth righteousness and judgment *through me* for all that are oppressed. *As a part of Jesus' Body, I do what Jesus would do in proclaiming and demonstrating* <u>Acts 10:36</u> the word which God sent unto the children of Israel, preaching peace by Jesus Christ: (he is Lord of all:) 38 how God anointed Jesus of Nazareth with the Holy Ghost and with power: who went about doing good, and healing all that were oppressed (*by the active reign, lordship and power*) of the devil; for God was with him. 39 And *we believe the* witnesses of all things which he *(Jesus)* did both in the land of the Jews, and in Jerusalem; whom they slew and hanged on a tree: 40 him God raised up the third day, and shewed him openly; 41 not to all the people, but unto witnesses chosen before of God, even to *the early disciples,* who did eat and drink with him after he rose from the dead. 42 And he *(Jesus)* commanded *me, by them,* to preach unto the people, and to testify that it is he which was ordained of God to be the Judge of quick and dead. 43 To him give all the prophets witness, that through his name whosoever believeth in him shall receive remission (*purging, obliteration, removal and putting away*) of sins. <u>2 Cor 1:21</u> Now he which stablisheth us, *including me,* in Christ, and hath anointed *me,* is God; 22 who hath also sealed us, and given the earnest of the Spirit in our hearts. *Therefore my new spirit thinks like Jesus:* <u>Gal 4:6</u> And because ye are sons, God hath sent forth the Spirit of his Son into *my heart,* crying, Abba (*Daddy*), Father. <u>2 Tim 1:7</u> For God hath not given *me* the spirit of fear; but of *dunamis/*power (*ability*), and of *agape/*love, and of a sound mind *to walk in* agape *love, just as Jesus did.* <u>Rom 13:14</u> *So I* put on the Lord Jesus Christ, and make not provision for the flesh, to fulfil the lusts thereof. *I am called by Father God to* agape/*love Him, and others for Him with all kinds of good works, just like Jesus did, so Father's* agape/*love can be seen in the Earth.* <u>1 John 4:17</u> Herein is our *agape/*love made perfect, that we may have boldness in the day of judgment: because as he is, so are we in this world. 18 There is no fear in *agape/*love; but perfect *agape/*love casteth out fear: because fear hath torment. He that feareth is not made perfect in *agape/*love. *Therefore I always focus by faith actions on the* agape/*love the Father has for me and through me for others, knowing all the requirements have been met in Jesus.* <u>Isa 53:4</u> Surely he hath *nasa/*borne our griefs *and infirmities,* and *cabal/*carried our sorrows *and sicknesses:* yet we did esteem him stricken, smitten of God, and afflicted. 5 But he was wounded for our transgressions, he was bruised for our iniquities: the chastisement of our peace was upon him; and with his stripes we are healed. 6 All we like sheep have gone astray; we have turned every one to his own way; and the LORD hath laid on him the iniquity of us all. ... 10 Yet it pleased the LORD to bruise him; he hath put him to grief (*and sickness*): when thou shalt make his soul an offering for sin, he shall see his seed, he shall prolong his days, and the pleasure of the LORD shall prosper

Affirmations in Christ

in his hand. 11 He shall see of the travail of his soul, and shall be satisfied: by his knowledge shall my righteous servant justify many; for he shall *cabal*/bear their iniquities. *Praise God! I am justified by faith in the mighty work of Jesus! He is making me to know and understand this, so I walk in Him and His triumph by faith actions more and more every day! Praise You, Lord Jesus Christ, King of Kings and Lords of Lords! Praise Your great work in the cross! Praise You! Thank You, Father! In the name of Jesus, thank You for Your great work in Jesus! Hallelujah! Yahoo! Lord, You are good! Your mercy is everlasting! Yahoo!*

R. Just like Jesus, *I am* given the Spirit of Jesus to be just like Jesus, a vessel of God's love to man. Gal 4:6 And because ye are sons, God hath sent forth the Spirit of his Son into *our* hearts, crying, Abba (*Daddy*), Father. Gal 3:26 For ye are all the children, *sons* of God by faith (*actions*) in Christ Jesus. Gal 2:20 I am (*have been*) crucified with Christ: nevertheless I zao/live *the zoe/life of Jesus*; yet not I, but Christ zao/liveth in me *to walk like He walked*: and the life which I now zao/live *of Jesus' agape* in the flesh I zao/live [*of walking like Jesus in power,* agape/love, *sound mind, grace and truth, doing good, and healing those oppressed of the devil by, for, through and with Father God, by and in His Spirit, because of the terrible sacrifice and mighty work in the soul-life, body and blood of Jesus, His Firstborn,* Agape/Beloved *Son, and I zao/live this*] by the faith (*actions*) *in* the Son of God, who *agape*/loved me, and gave himself for me. 21 I do not frustrate the grace of God: for if righteousness come by the law, then Christ is dead in vain. Rom 8:26 Likewise the Spirit also helpeth (*me to stand for God, against*) *my* infirmities (*weaknesses*): for *when I* know not what *I* should pray for as *I* ought: the Spirit itself maketh intercession for *me* with groanings which cannot be uttered. 27 And he that searcheth the hearts knoweth what is the mind of the Spirit, because he maketh intercession for the saints according to the will of God. 28 And *by grace I* know that all things work together for good to them that *agape*/love God, to them who are the called according to his purpose. 29 For whom he did foreknow, he also did predestinate to be conformed to the image of his Son, that he might be the firstborn among many brethren. 30 Moreover whom he did predestinate, them he also called: and whom he called, them he also justified: and whom he justified, them he also glorified. 31 What shall *I* then say to these things? If God be for *me*, who can be against *me*? 32 He that spared not his own Son, but delivered him up for us all, how shall he not with him also freely give us all things? 33 Who shall lay any thing to the charge of God's elect? It is God that justifieth. 34 Who is he that condemneth? It is Christ that died, yea rather, that is risen again, who is even at the right hand of God, who also maketh intercession for *me*. Rom 5:1 There-

OK, GOD, NOW WHAT?

fore being justified by faith (*actions*), *I* have peace with God through our Lord Jesus Christ: 2 by whom also *I* have access by faith (*actions*) into this grace wherein *I* stand, and rejoice in hope of the glory of God. 2 Cor 5:21 For *Father* God hath made *Jesus* to be sin for us, who knew no sin; that we might be made the righteousness of *Father* God in *Jesus*. 2 Cor 1:19 For the Son of God, Jesus Christ, who was preached ... by *Paul* ... was not yea and nay, but in him was yea. 20 For all the promises of God in *Jesus* are yea, and in him Amen, unto the glory of God by us. 21 Now he which stablisheth *me* in Christ, and hath anointed *me*, is God; 22 who hath also sealed *me*, and given the earnest of the Spirit in *my heart*. Thus Isa 11:2 ... the spirit of the LORD *rests upon me in Jesus*, the spirit of wisdom and understanding, the spirit of counsel and might, the spirit of knowledge and of the fear of the LORD; 3 and *makes me* of quick understanding in the fear of the LORD: and *I do* not judge after the sight of *my* eyes, neither reprove after the hearing of *my* ears: 4 but with righteousness *I* judge the poor, and reprove with equity for the meek of the earth: and *I* smite the earth with the rod of *my* mouth, and with the breath of *my* lips *I* slay the wicked. 5 And righteousness shall be the girdle of *my* loins, and faithfulness the girdle of *my* reins. Luke 4:18 The Spirit of the Lord is upon me, because he hath anointed me to preach the gospel to the poor; he hath sent me to heal the brokenhearted, to preach deliverance to the captives, and recovering of sight to the blind, to set at liberty them that are bruised, 19 to preach the acceptable year of the Lord. Acts 10:38 ... God *has* anointed *me in* Jesus of Nazareth with the Holy Ghost and with power: *so I go* about doing good, and healing all that *are* oppressed (*under the active rule and lordship*) of the devil; for God *is* with *me*. ... 40 God raised up *Jesus* the third day, and shewed him openly; 41 not to all the people, but unto witnesses chosen before of God, even to *those disciples*, who did eat and drink with him after he rose from the dead. 42 And he commanded us to preach unto the people, and to testify that it is *Jesus* which was ordained of God to be the Judge of quick and dead. 43 To him give all the prophets witness, that through his name whosoever believeth in him shall receive remission (*purging, obliteration and putting away*) of sins. Acts 26:18 To open *the* eyes *of all mankind*, and to turn them from darkness to light, and from the power (*authority*) of Satan unto God, that they may receive forgiveness (*remission, purging, obliteration and putting away*) of sins, and inheritance among them which are sanctified by faith (*actions*) that *are* in *Jesus*. Gal 3:27 For as many of *us* as have been baptized into Christ have put on Christ. *I continuously renew my mind by putting on Jesus to glorify God.* Eph 4:21 ... As the truth is in Jesus: 22 *I* put off concerning the former conversation the old man, which is corrupt according to the deceitful lusts; 23 and *am* renewed in the spirit of *my* mind; 24 *by putting* on the new man,

Affirmations in Christ

which after God is created in righteousness and true holiness. *My true, bornagain nature is to walk just like Jesus, knowing* Rom 13:10 *agape*/love worketh no ill to his neighbour: therefore *agape*/love is the fulfilling of the law. 11 And that, knowing the time, that now it is high time to awake out of sleep: for now is *my soteria*/salvation nearer than when *I* believed. 12 The night is far spent, the day is at hand: *I* therefore *continuously* cast off the works of darkness, and ... *I continuously* put on the armour of light. 13 *I continuously walk* honestly, as in the day; not in rioting and drunkenness, not in chambering and wantonness, not in strife and envying. 14 *I continuously* put on the Lord Jesus Christ, and make not provision for the flesh, to fulfil the lusts thereof. *I continuously strive to walk in Holy Spirit by faith actions, for* 2 Cor 3:17 now the Lord is that Spirit: and where the Spirit of the Lord is, there is liberty *to be all I am in God*. 18 *So I*, with open face beholding as in a glass (*mirror*), *seeing myself filled with* the glory of the Lord, *I am* changed into the same image from glory to glory, even as by the Spirit of the Lord. *I* Col 3:9 lie *to no one*, seeing that I have put off the old man with his deeds; 10 and have put on the new man, which is renewed in knowledge after the image of *Father God* that created *me anew in Jesus*: 11 where there is neither Greek nor Jew, circumcision nor uncircumcision, Barbarian, Scythian, bond nor free: but Christ is all, and in all. *I* 12 put on therefore, as the elect of God, holy and *agape*/beloved, bowels of mercies, kindness, humbleness of mind, meekness, longsuffering; 13 forbearing one another, and forgiving one another, if any man have a quarrel against any: even as Christ forgave *me*, so also do *I*. 14 And above all these things *I put* on *agape*/charity (*actions*), which is the bond of perfectness. 15 And *I let* the peace of God rule in *my heart*, to the which also *I am* called in one body; and *I am* thankful. 16 *I* let the word of Christ dwell in *me* richly in all wisdom; teaching and admonishing *myself and* one another in psalms and hymns and spiritual songs, singing with grace in *my heart* to the Lord. 17 And, *by the grace of God working in me*, whatsoever *I* do in word or deed, *I* do all in the name of the Lord Jesus, giving thanks to God and the Father by him. 1 Cor 15:10 *For* by the grace of God I am what I am: and his grace which was bestowed upon me was not in vain; but I *labor [in faith actions]* more abundantly than they all: yet not I, but the grace of God which *is* with me. *Thank You, Father God, Father of Lights, Father of Love and Truth! Thank You, in the name of Jesus! Thank You! Glory to Your goodness to me in Jesus! Yahoo!*

S. **By the grace of God working in me** I Phil 2:3 let nothing be done through strife or vainglory; but in lowliness of mind *I esteem others* better than *myself*. 4 *I* look ... on *mine* own things, but ... also on the things of others. 5 *I* let this mind be in *me* which was also in Christ Jesus: 6 who, being in the form of God, thought it not robbery to be equal with God: 7 but made himself of no reputation, and took upon him the form of a servant, and was made in the likeness of men: 8 and being found in fashion as a man, he humbled himself, and became obedient unto death, even the death of the cross. ... 12 Wherefore, *as one of the agape/*beloved, as *I* always *obey*, *I* work out *my* own *soteria*/salvation with fear and trembling. 13 For it is God which worketh in *me* both to will and to do of his good pleasure. 14 *I* do all things without murmurings and disputings: 15 that *I* may be blameless and harmless, *a son* of God, without rebuke, in the midst of a crooked and perverse nation, among whom *I* shine as *a light* in the world; 16 holding forth the word of *zoe*/life; that I may rejoice in the day of Christ, that I have not run in vain, neither laboured in vain. Phil 3:8 Yea ... I count all things *of this world* but loss for the excellency of the knowledge of Christ Jesus my Lord: ... that I may win Christ, 9 and be found in him, not having mine own righteousness, which is of the law *or works*, but that which is through the faith of Christ, the righteousness which is of God by faith (*actions*): [*and not by the holiness which I walk in more of every day*]. 10 That I may know him, and the power of his resurrection, and the fellowship of his sufferings, being made conformable unto his death; 11 if by any means I might attain unto the resurrection of the dead. 12 Not as though I had already attained, either were already perfect: but I follow after, if that I may apprehend that for which also I am apprehended of Christ Jesus. 13 ... I count not myself to have apprehended: but this one thing I do, forgetting those things which are behind, and reaching forth unto those things which are before, 14 I press toward the mark for the prize of the high calling of God in Christ Jesus [*in continual right faith actions*]. *I delight to do Your will, O God! Praise to You! I am agape/loved by You forever! Yahoo!*

T. **1 Pet 1:13 Wherefore,** *in cooperation with Holy Spirit,* **I gird** up the loins of *my* mind, *am* sober, and hope to the end for the grace that is to be brought unto *me* at the revelation of Jesus Christ; 14 as *an* obedient *child*, not fashioning *myself* according to the former lusts in *my* ignorance: 15 but as he which hath called *me* is holy, so *I am* holy in all manner of conversation; 16 because it is written, Be ye holy; for I am holy. *And, Father, in the name of Jesus, keep me* Eph 6:10 ... strong in *You*, and in the power of *Your* might. *To* 11 *continuously* keep on *Your* whole armour [*in faith actions*], *Father* God, that *I* may be able to stand against the wiles of the devil. 12 For *I* wrestle not against flesh and blood, but against principalities, against powers, against the rulers of the darkness of this world, against spiritual wickedness in high places. 13 Wherefore *I keep* unto *myself* the whole armour of *You, Father* God, that *I* may be able to withstand in the evil day, and having done all, to stand. 14 *I* stand [*in continual faith actions*] therefore, *keeping my* loins girt about with truth, and *keeping* on the breastplate of righteousness; 15 and *keeping my* feet shod with the preparation of the gospel of peace; 16 above all, *keeping* the shield of faith (*actions*), wherewith *I* shall be able to quench all the fiery darts of

Affirmations in Christ

the wicked. 17 And *keeping* the helmet of *soteria*/salvation, and the sword of the Spirit, which is the word of God: 18 praying always with all prayer and supplication in the Spirit, and watching thereunto with all perseverance and supplication for all saints; 19 and *I pray, Father, in the name of Jesus, that* utterance may be given unto me, that I may open my mouth boldly, to make known the mystery of the gospel, 20 ... that therein I may speak boldly, as I ought to speak. 2 Cor 10:3 For though we walk in the flesh, we do not war after the flesh: 4 (for the weapons of our warfare are not carnal, but mighty through *You, Father* God, to the pulling down of strong holds;) 5 casting down imaginations, and every high thing that exalteth itself against the knowledge of *You, Father* God, and bringing into captivity every thought to the obedience of Christ; 6 and having in a readiness to revenge all disobedience, when *my* obedience is fulfilled. 2 Tim 1:2 ... Grace, mercy, and peace, from God the Father and Christ Jesus our Lord *to me*. ... 6 Wherefore I put *myself* in *continual* remembrance that *I* stir up [*by faith actions*] the gift of God, which is in *me* .... 7 For God hath not given *me* the spirit of fear; but of *dunamis*/power (*miracle ability*), and of *agape*/love, and of a sound mind, *to think and do as Jesus would*. ... 12 for I know whom I have believed, and am persuaded that he is able to keep that which I have committed unto him against that day. *I therefore* 13 hold fast the form of sound words, which *I have* heard of [*the Gospel*], in faith and *agape*/love (*actions*) which is in Christ Jesus. *For Jesus commanded:* Luke 10:19 Behold, I give unto you power (*authority, commission, pre-permission and the resources of Heaven*) to tread on serpents and scorpions, and over all the power of the enemy: and nothing shall by any means hurt you. 20 Notwithstanding in this rejoice not, that the spirits are subject unto you; but rather rejoice, because your names are written in heaven. 2 Tim 2:14 Of these things *I* put (*myself and those that hear me*) in remembrance, charging *all of us* before the Lord that *we* strive not about words to no profit, but to the subverting of the hearers. *I* 15 study (*in thoughtful and diligent labor*) to shew *myself* approved unto God, a workman that needeth not to be ashamed [*by grace in Holy Spirit of wisdom and revelation in the knowledge of Him, with the eyes of my understanding being enlightened to*] rightly dividing the word of truth. ... 23 But foolish and unlearned questions *I* avoid, knowing that they do gender strifes. 24 And, *I, as a* servant of the Lord, *do* not strive; but *am* gentle unto all men, apt to teach, patient, 25 in meekness instructing those that oppose themselves; if God peradventure will give them repentance to the acknowledging of the truth; 26 and that they may recover themselves out of the snare of the devil, who are taken captive by him at his will. John 8:31 *For I believe on Jesus, and I continue in His* Word, *so I am one of His* disciples indeed; 32 and *I, by Spirit of Truth,* shall know the truth, and the truth shall make *me* free, *to be and do all that Father has for me. For* 2 Tim 3:16 all scripture is given by inspiration of God, and is profitable for doctrine, for reproof, for correction, for instruction in righteousness: 17 that *I, as a* man/woman of God, may be perfect,

OK, God, Now What?

throughly furnished unto all good works. 1 John 5:11 *I believe the witness of God in His Son Jesus and no longer call God a liar but only true in all things,* ... *that God hath given to us eternal zoe/life, and this zoe/life is in his Son.* 13 ... *I know that I have eternal zoe/life, and that I may believe (by faith actions) on the name of the Son of God. So, Father, keep me in Your Spirit of wisdom and understanding in You so that if none go with me, I know that* 2 Tim 4:17 notwithstanding the Lord *stands* with me, and *strengthens* me; that by me the preaching might be fully known, and that all *men* might hear [*unto glad obedience the glorious gospel of Christ in us the hope of glory*]: and I *am* delivered out of the mouth of the lion. 18 And the Lord shall deliver me from every evil work, and will preserve me unto his heavenly kingdom: to whom be glory for ever and ever. Amen. Rom 15:17 I ... glory through Jesus Christ in those things which pertain to God. 18 ... To make *all men* obedient, by word and deed, 19 through mighty signs and wonders, by the power of the Spirit of God; so that from *home and into all the world I* fully *preach* the gospel of Christ, Mark 16:20 ... the Lord working with *me*, and confirming the word [*of His grace*] with signs following. Amen. 1 Tim 1:17 Now unto the King eternal, immortal, invisible, the only wise God, be honour and glory for ever and ever. Amen. Jude 24 Now unto him that is able to keep *me and is keeping me* from falling, and to present *me* faultless before the presence of his glory with exceeding joy, 25 to the only wise God our Saviour, be glory and majesty, dominion and power, both now and ever. Amen. *Yahoo! Jesus, You are in me. Hallelujah! Thank You, Father God, in the name of Jesus, Thank You! Lord, You are good! Your mercy is everlasting! Yahoo!*

U. **For I know** Eph 5:8 *I was* sometimes darkness, but now *by the new creation, I am* light in the Lord: *by the grace of God ever with me, I* walk as *a child* of light: 9 *and continually grow* the fruit of the Spirit ... in all goodness and righteousness and truth. [Gal 5:22 *For* the fruit of the Spirit is (*actions of*) *agape*/love, joy, peace, longsuffering, gentleness, goodness, faith, 23 meekness, temperance: against such there is no law. 24 And, *because I am* Christ's, I have crucified the flesh with the affections and lusts. 25 *So I ever grow in living* in the Spirit, *so I also* walk in the Spirit. 26 *I am* not desirous of vain glory, *I do not* provoke one another *to evil but to do* agape/love, *I do not* envy *others.*] Instead, *I walk in* agape/ love *and am continually* 10 proving *and demonstrating* what is acceptable unto the Lord. 11 And *I* have no fellowship with the unfruitful works of darkness, but rather *I* reprove them. 12 For it is a shame even to speak of those things which are done of them in secret. 13 *For I know* all things that are reproved are made manifest by the light: for whatsoever doth make manifest is light. 14 Wherefore he saith, Awake thou that sleepest, and arise from the dead, and Christ shall give thee light. *So I readily acknowledge my sins as purged in*

Affirmations in Christ

Jesus, make any right restitutions or reconciliations, give grace to others and receive my healing given two thousand (2000) years ago. 15 *So* I walk circumspectly, not as *a rebel or a fool*, but as wise *unto God, knowing the wisdom of God is greater than silver or jewels; so I grow continually in wisdom, knowledge and understanding, and am constantly* 16 redeeming the time, because the days are evil. 17 Wherefore *I am* not unwise, but understanding what the will of the Lord is. 18 And *I do* not *get* drunk with wine, wherein is excess; but *I am continually being* filled with the Spirit [*by faith actions*]; 19 speaking to *myself and others* in psalms and hymns and spiritual songs, singing and making melody in *my* heart to the Lord; 20 giving thanks always for all things unto God and the Father in the name of our Lord Jesus Christ; 21 submitting *myself*; one to another in the fear of God. Eph 4:20 *For I have so* learned Christ; 21 ... as the truth is in Jesus: 22 that *I continually* put off concerning the former conversation the old man, which is corrupt according to the deceitful lusts; 23 and *am continually* renewed in the spirit of *my* mind *in the Word of Christ and my new creation*; 24 and *I continually* put on, *and stay in* the new *creation* man, which after God is created in righteousness and true holiness. 25 Wherefore putting away lying, *I* speak ... truth with *my every* neighbour: for we are members one of another. *And I work and live zealously in doing good works, in faith actions working by* agape/*love, to the glory of God the Father, through Jesus, my Lord, by His Spirit. Whenever fear, doubt or unbelief comes on me I am* Phil 4:6 ... careful for nothing (*I do not tolerate fear or anxiety in anything, even though they seem logical and real*); but in every thing by prayer and supplication with thanksgiving *I* let *my aiteo*/requests be made known unto God [*by proclaiming His promises and* aiteo/*asking, by requiring, demanding and expecting as due by covenant promise His answer unto joyful thanksgiving, for I* lambano/*receive it by faith actions, knowing I will possess it*]. 7 And the peace of God, which passeth all understanding, *keeps my heart and mind* through Christ Jesus. 8 Finally, *and above all else* ... , whatsoever things are **true**, whatsoever things are **honest**, whatsoever things are **just**, whatsoever things are **pure**, whatsoever things are **lovely**, whatsoever things are of **good report**; if there be any **virtue**, and if there be any **praise**, *I* think on these things *constantly*. *Grace and peace to victory is in me from God my Father,* Rev 1:5 and from Jesus Christ, who is the faithful witness, and the first begotten of the dead, and the prince of the kings of the earth. Unto him that *agape*/loved us, and washed us from our sins in his own blood, 6 and hath made us kings and priests unto God and his Father; to him be glory and dominion for ever and ever. Amen. Rev 5:9 And they sung a new song, saying, Thou art worthy to take the book, and to open the seals thereof: for thou wast slain, and hast redeemed us to God by thy blood out of every kindred, and tongue, and people, and nation; 10 and hast made us unto our God kings and priests: and we shall reign on the earth. (Rom 5:17 ... *For I hold on to, cling to and will not let go, I lambano/receive [by faith actions] abundance of grace and of the [permanent] gift of righteousness* ...) ... 12 Saying with a loud voice, Worthy is the Lamb that was slain to receive power, and riches, and wisdom, and strength, and honour, and glory, and blessing. *Thank You, Father! Lord, be magnified! Blessed be the name of the Lord! Praise to You, Lord Jesus Christ, and Your mighty work, for You got the job done, to the glory of God our Father! Hallelujah!*

V. **Father, I thank You that You are getting me to rest in You** and believe that as I *aiteo*, I do trust that You hear me, Jesus hears me and Holy Spirit hears me, and I believe You because You said whatever I *aiteo*/ask in the name of Jesus, Jesus will do. I do not just try, but I do trust You by honoring Your Word in faith actions. I will have what I *aiteo* in the name of Jesus because You *agape*/love people and cannot lie. I speak to the mountains and You do move them in Your covenant promises. I do rest in You to fulfill Your Word on my lips and in my heart. Thank You! Oh, God of truth and without iniquity, thank You!

W. **I know and give thanks in the wonder that** I am given the Spirit of Jesus to be just like Jesus, a vessel of God's love to man. Gal 4:6 And because ye are sons, God hath sent forth the Spirit of his Son into our hearts, crying, Abba (*Daddy*), Father. Gal 3:26 For ye are all the children (*sons*) of God by faith (*actions*) in Christ Jesus. Gal 2:20 I am (*have been*) crucified with Christ: nevertheless I *zao*/live *the zoe/life of Jesus*; yet not I, but Christ *zao*/liveth in me *to walk like He walked*: and the life which I now *zao*/live *of Jesus'* agape in the flesh I *zao*/live *the nature of Jesus* by the faith (*actions*) *in* the Son of God, who *agape*/loved me, and gave himself for me. 21 I do not frustrate the grace of God: for if righteousness (*unity with God unto* zoe *life*) come by the law, then Christ is dead in vain. Rom 5:1 Therefore being justified by faith (*actions*), *I* have peace with God through our Lord Jesus Christ: 2 by whom also *I* have access by faith (*actions*) into this grace wherein *I* stand, and rejoice in hope of the glory of God. 2 Cor 5:21 For *Father God* hath made *Jesus* to be sin for us, who knew no sin; that we might be made the righteousness of God in him. 2 Cor 1:19 For the Son of God, Jesus Christ, who was preached ... by Paul ... was not yea and nay, but in him was yea. 20 For all the promises of God in him are yea, and in him Amen, unto the glory of God by us. 21 Now he which stablisheth *me* in Christ, and hath anointed *me*, is God; 22 who hath also sealed *me*, and given the earnest of the Spirit in *my heart*. Thus Isa 11:2 ... the spirit of the Lord *rests* upon *me in Jesus*, the spirit of wisdom and understanding, the spirit of counsel and might, the spirit of knowledge and of the fear of the Lord; 3 and *makes me* of quick understanding in the fear of the Lord: and *I do* not judge after the sight of *my* eyes, neither reprove after the hearing of *my* ears: 4 but with righteousness *I* judge the poor, and reprove with equity for the meek of the earth: and *I* smite the earth with the rod of *my* mouth, and with the breath of *my* lips *I* slay the wicked. 5 And righteousness shall be the girdle of *my* loins, and faithfulness (*in continual faith actions*) the girdle of *my* reins. Luke 4:18 The Spirit of the Lord is upon me, because he hath anointed me to preach the gospel to the poor; he hath sent me to heal the brokenhearted, to preach deliverance to the captives, and recovering of sight to the blind, to set at liberty them that are bruised, 19 to preach the acceptable year of the Lord. *I preach that*: Acts 13:38 Be it known unto you therefore, men and brethren, that through this man (*Jesus*) is preached unto you the forgiveness (*remission, purging, obliteration and putting away*) of sins: 39 and by him all that believe are justified from all things, from which ye could not be justified by the law of Moses. Acts 10:38 ... God *has* anointed *me in* Jesus of Nazareth with the Holy Ghost and with power: so *I* go about doing good, and healing all that are oppressed (*under the active rule and lordship*) of the devil; for God is with *me*. Acts 10:43 To him (*Jesus*) give all the prophets witness, that through his name whosoever believeth in him shall receive remission (*purging, obliteration and putting away*) of sins. *And God is with me* Acts 26:18 to open *the* eyes *of all mankind*, and to turn them from darkness to light, and from the power of Satan unto God, that they may receive forgiveness (*remission, purging, obliteration and putting away*) of sins, and inheritance among them which are sanctified by faith (*actions*) that *are* in *Jesus*. Gal 3:27 For as many of us as have been baptized into Christ have put on Christ. *I renew my mind by putting on Jesus to glorify God.* Eph 4:21 ... As the truth is in Jesus: 22 *I* put off concerning the former conversation the old man, which is corrupt according to the deceitful lusts; 23 and *am* renewed in the spirit of *my* mind; 24 by putting on the new man (*by continual right faith actions*), which after God is created in righteousness and true holiness. *Knowing* Rom 13:10 *agape*/love worketh no ill to his neighbour: therefore *agape*/love is the fulfilling of the law. 11 And that, knowing the time, that now it is high time to awake out of sleep: for now is *my soteria*/salvation nearer than when *I* believed. 12 The night is far spent, the day is at hand: *I* therefore cast off the works of darkness, and ... put on the armour of light. 13 *I* walk honestly, as in the day; not in rioting and drunkenness, not in chambering and wantonness, not in strife and envying. 14 *I* put on the Lord Jesus Christ (*in my self-concept by continual right faith actions*), and make not provision for the flesh, to fulfil the lusts thereof. Col 3:9 *I* lie to *no one*, seeing [*in the new birth*], that *I* have put off the old man with his deeds; 10 and have put on the new man, which is renewed in knowledge after the image of him that created him: 11 where there is neither

OK, God, Now What?

Greek nor Jew, circumcision nor uncircumcision, Barbarian, Scythian, bond nor free: but Christ is all, and in all. 12 *I* put on (*in my mind and attitude*) therefore, as the elect of God, holy and *agape*/beloved, bowels of mercies, kindness, humbleness of mind, meekness, longsuffering; 13 forbearing one another, and forgiving one another, if any man have a quarrel against any: even as Christ forgave *me*, so also do *I*. 14 And above all these things *I* put on *agape*/charity, which is the bond of perfectness. 15 And *I* let the peace of God rule in *my heart*, to the which also *I am* called in one body; and *I am* thankful. 16 *I* let the word of Christ dwell in *me* richly in all wisdom; teaching and admonishing *myself and* one another in psalms and hymns and spiritual songs, singing with grace in *my heart* to the Lord. 17 And [*by the grace of God working in me*] whatsoever *I* do in word or deed, *I* do all in the name of the Lord Jesus, giving thanks to God and the Father by him. Phil 3:8 Yea … I count all things of this world but loss for the excellency of the knowledge of Christ Jesus my Lord: … that I may win Christ, 9 and be found in him, not having mine own righteousness, which is of the law *or works*, but that which is through the faith of Christ, the righteousness which is of God by faith (*actions*): 10 that I may know him, and the power of his resurrection, and the fellowship of his sufferings, being made conformable unto his death; 11 if by any means I might attain unto the resurrection of the dead. 12 Not as though I had already attained, either were already perfect: but I follow after, if that I may apprehend that for which also I am apprehended of Christ Jesus. 13 … I count not myself to have apprehended: but this one thing I do, forgetting those things which are behind, and reaching forth unto those things which are before, 14 I press toward the mark for the prize of the high calling of God in Christ Jesus [*in continual faith actions*]. Jude 24 Now unto him that is able to keep *me* from falling, and to present *me* faultless before the presence of his glory with exceeding joy, 25 to the only wise God our Saviour, be glory and majesty, dominion and power, both now and ever. Amen. *Lord, glorify Your name through me! Thank You, Father, in the name of Jesus, thank You! Yahoo! Lord, You are good! Your mercy is everlasting! Yahoo!*

X. **Father, in the name of Jesus, the Baptizer** with Holy Spirit and fire, give abundant manifestations of Your Spirit, including words of wisdom, knowledge, faith, healings, working of miracles, prophecy, discerning of spirits, diverse kinds of tongues, interpretation of tongues, dead raising, creative restorations, wholeness and special miracles and works. Stir me that I 1 Cor 12:31 … covet earnestly *unto effective faith actions* the best gifts: *and walk by Your Spirit in the* more excellent way *of* agape/love. So that I 1 Cor 14:1 follow after *agape*/charity, and desire spiritual gifts, but rather that *I* may prophesy *to the edification of the church. And devote myself to prayer and the ministry of the Word, in the unity of the Spirit, in the bond of peace. Father, teach me to walk*

Affirmations in Christ

in the glad assurance that I have the same Spirit You gave Jesus, so that I gladly confess, 2 Cor 13:5 *knowing* ...that Jesus Christ is in *me, as by Your grace I am not reprobate (useless in my faith in You, Father God), but I am proclaiming*: Luke 4:18 The Spirit of the Lord is upon me, because he hath anointed me to preach the gospel to the poor; he hath sent me to heal the brokenhearted, to preach deliverance to the captives, and recovering of sight to the blind, to set at liberty them that are bruised, 19 to preach the acceptable year of the Lord. 2 Cor 6:2 (For he saith, I have heard thee in a time accepted, and in the day of *soteria*/salvation have I succoured thee: behold, now is the accepted time; behold, now is the day of *soteria*/salvation.) Acts 10:38 How *that You, Father God, anoint us in* Jesus of Nazareth with the Holy Ghost and with power: *so we go* about doing good, and healing all that *are* oppressed (*under the active reign and lordship*) of the devil; for *You, Father God are* with *us in Jesus just like You are with Jesus.* 1 John 4:17 Herein is our *agape*/love made perfect, that we may have boldness in the day of judgment: because as he is, so are we in this world. *For* 1 John 4:4 ye are of God, little children, and have overcome them: because greater is he that is in you, than he that is in the world. *And, Father, get me to know that* Gal 4:3 even so we, when we were children, were in bondage under the elements of the world: 4 but when the fulness of the time was come, *You, Father God,* sent forth *Your* Son, made of a woman, made under the law, 5 to redeem them that were under the law, that we might receive the adoption of sons. 6 And because *we* are sons, *You, Father God, have* sent forth the Spirit of *Your* Son into *our* hearts, crying, Abba, (*Daddy*) Father. 7 Wherefore *I am* no more a servant, but a son; and if a son, then an heir of *You, Father God,* through Christ. *Father, reveal the glory of Your inheritance in us that* Phil 3:14 *we* press toward the mark for the prize of the high calling of *You, Father* God, in Christ Jesus, *so that we walk in Your total and complete remission unto redemption in Jesus, that we might* agape/*love You totally. For Jesus said*: John 17:22 And the glory which thou gavest me I have given them; that they may be one, even as we are one: 23 I in them, and thou in me, that they may be made perfect in one; and that the world may know that thou hast sent me, and hast *agape*/loved them, as thou hast *agape*/loved me. Rom 15:6 That *we* may with one mind and one mouth glorify God, even *You,* the Father of our Lord Jesus Christ. 7 Wherefore receive *we* one another, as Christ also received us to the glory of God. 1 Cor 10:31 Whether therefore *we* eat, or drink, or whatsoever *we* do, *we* do all to the glory of God. *Father, give us Your Spirit of wisdom and revelation in the knowledge of You, that we might behold Your glory in the face of Jesus in us, that we might be changed.* 2 Cor 3:17 Now the Lord is that Spirit: and where the Spirit of the Lord is, there is liberty. 18 But we all, with open face beholding as in a glass (*mirror*) the glory of the Lord, are changed into the same image from glory to glory, even as by the Spirit of the Lord. *And, Father, keep us so that we* 2 Cor 4:5 …preach not ourselves, but Christ Jesus the Lord; and ourselves *as* servants for Jesus' sake. 6 For God, who commanded the light to shine out of darkness, hath shined in our hearts, to give the light of the knowledge of the glory of God in the face of Jesus Christ. 7 But we have this treasure in earthen vessels, that the excellency of the power may be of God, and not of us. *Father, in the name of Jesus, give me Your Spirit of wisdom and revelation in the knowledge of You, with the eyes of my understanding being enlightened, so that I,* Eph 6:10 finally, *as one of the* brethren, *am* strong in *You,* and in the power of *Your* might *(by continual right faith actions), that I* 11 put on the whole armour of God, that *I* may be able to stand against the wiles of the devil, *knowing* 12 *that* we wrestle not against flesh and blood, but against principalities, against powers, against the rulers of the darkness of this world, against spiritual wickedness in high places. 13 Wherefore *I* take unto *myself* the whole armour of God, that *I* may be able to withstand in the evil day, and having done all, to stand. *So I resist the devil, knowing he will flee from me as I* 14 stand (*by faith actions*) therefore, having *my* loins girt about with truth, and having on the breastplate of righteousness; 15 and *my* feet shod with the preparation of the gospel of peace; 16 above all, taking the shield of faith (*actions*), wherewith *I* shall be able to quench all the fiery darts of the wicked. 17 And *continually taking* the helmet of *soteria*/salvation, and the sword of the Spirit, which is the word of God: *so that I am* 18 praying always with all prayer and supplication in the Spirit, and watching thereunto with all perseverance and supplication for all saints; 19 and for *all preachers,* that utterance may be given unto *us,* that *we* may open *our* mouths boldly, to make known the mystery of the gospel, 20 … that therein *we* may speak boldly, as *we* ought to speak. 2 Thes 1:11 Wherefore *I pray* that *You, Father,* our God, would count *me* worthy of this calling, and fulfil all the good pleasure of *Your* goodness, and the work of faith (*actions*) with power: 12 that the name of our Lord Jesus Christ may be glorified in *me,* and *me* in him, according to the grace of our God and the Lord Jesus Christ. *Thank You, Father, in the name of Jesus Christ, thank You! Jehovah the Good, God the Good, Elohim the Good, Adonai the Good, Jesus the Good, Holy Spirit the Good, Father the Good. Hallelujah! Jesus is Lord! Yahoo!*

Y. **Father, You have shown Yourself as He who raises the dead.** When the widow's son died, Your prophet Elijah called on You: 1 Kings 17:20 "And he cried unto the Lord, and said, O Lord my God, hast thou also brought evil upon the widow with whom I sojourn, by slaying her son?" And Your resounding answer was NO! And then You commanded one who thought like You to pray until that boy was raised. Father, in the name of Jesus, You know where I am, what I have done, what You can do through me, and that You have made me one of Your own through Jesus

Affirmations in Christ

Christ my Lord. Make me one who You can think and fight through to heal the sick, raise the dead, cleanse the lepers, cast out devils and proclaim and deliver freedom to the lawful and unlawful prisoners of any kind. I want to be one whom You can work with and through. Be my strength, my courage, my help, my wisdom and my *agape*/love in Your work. Just as when the man of God, Elijah, demanded the last water and food of the widow You had commanded to house and feed him, and she faced her fears and put her eyes on You and Your supply. She gave Elijah her last, and they were all fed, as You promised, for a whole year. In the same way, teach me to face my fears of lack and not enough so that I look to You rather than the situation. And when I start to sink, as I look at circumstances, just as Peter did, as he walked on the water with Jesus, send me Your living Word that picks me up and gets me back on faith actions in You. I proclaim my testimony is: Ps 107:20 "He sent his word, and healed them, and delivered them from their destructions. 21 Oh ... *and I* praise the LORD for his *chesed*/goodness, and for his wonderful works to the children of men! 22 And *I* sacrifice the sacrifices of thanksgiving, and declare his works with rejoicing." Heb 13:15 "By *Jesus Christ I* therefore ... offer the sacrifice of praise to *You, Father* God, continually, that is, the fruit of *my* lips, giving thanks to *Your* name. 16 *And I* do good and *do* communicate *in good and generous works and deliver Your salvation to all those in need, especially those in need of healing, I* forget not: for with such sacrifices *I know You, Father* God, *are* well pleased." Father, Your anointing abides on me and teaches me to walk like Jesus. For 1 John 2:27 "... the anointing which *I* have received of *You, Father,* abideth in *me,* and *I* need not that any man teach *me, so I look to You, teaching me through Your Word and Your teachers for me*: but as the same anointing teacheth *me* of all things, and is truth, and is no lie, and even as it hath taught *me to renew my mind, I* shall abide in *You, as I walk in You, knowing*: 1 Cor 1:21 "Now he, which stablisheth us ... in Christ, and hath anointed us, is *You, Father* God; 22 who hath also sealed us, and given the earnest of the Spirit in our hearts." And I 1 John 3:1 "behold, what manner of *agape*/love *You,* the Father, *have* bestowed upon us, that we should be called the sons of *You, Father* God: therefore the world knoweth us not, because it knew *Jesus* not. As the 2 *agape*/beloved, now are we the sons of *You, Father* God, and it doth not yet appear what we shall be: but we know that, when *Jesus* shall appear, we shall be like him; for we shall see him as he is. 3 And every man that hath this hope in him purifieth himself, even as he is pure." So, Father, as I work out my own salvation in fear and trembling, to purify myself by Your grace, I know, Gal 2:19 "for I through the law am dead to the law, that I might *zao*/live unto *You, Father* God, *just as Jesus did for*: 20 I am (*have been*) crucified with Christ: nevertheless I *zao*/live; yet not I, but Christ *zao*/liveth in me: and the life which I now *zao*/live in the flesh I *zao*/live by the faith (*actions*) *in* the Son of God, who *agape*/loved me, and gave himself for me. 21 I do not frustrate the grace of *You, Father* God:

OK, GOD, NOW WHAT?

for if righteousness come by the law, then Christ is dead in vain." Father, in the name of Jesus, <u>Deut 31:6</u> "*I am* strong (*in Your strength for me*) and of a good courage (*in faith actions*), I fear not (*by considering only failure*), nor *am I* afraid (*or allow myself to be harassed by the evil power*) of *any evil situation or people*: for *You, Father,* the LORD *my* God, *You* it is that *do* go with *me*, *You* will not fail *me*, nor forsake *me*." In the name of Jesus, I take authority over and command all evil fear to leave me now, and I command my inner man to rise up and think the thoughts of God and His goodness toward me by faith actions. Father, by Your grace, <u>2 Cor 10:3</u> "for though *I* walk in the flesh, *I* do not war after the flesh: 4 (for the weapons of *my* warfare are not carnal, but mighty through *You, Father* God, to the pulling down of strong holds;) 5 casting down imaginations, and every high thing that exalteth itself against the knowledge of *You, Father* God, and bringing into captivity *my* every thought to the obedience of Christ," to stop all evil thoughts and only allow myself to <u>Phil 4:4</u> "rejoice in the Lord alway: and again I say, Rejoice. 5 *I let my* moderation be known unto all men. *For I am continually knowing the* Lord is at hand (*in power and authority*). 6 *I am* careful (*anxious, fearful or worried*) for nothing; but in every thing by prayer and supplication with thanksgiving *I let my aiteo*/requests be made known unto God. 7 And the peace of God, which passeth all understanding, shall keep *my heart* and *mind* through Christ Jesus. 8 Finally, *as one of the* brethren *in the Lord,* whatsoever things are **true**, whatsoever things are **honest**, whatsoever things are **just**, whatsoever things are **pure**, whatsoever things are **lovely**, whatsoever things are of **good report**; if there be any **virtue**, and if there be any **praise**, *I only* think on these things. 9 Those things, which *I* have both learned, and received, and heard, and seen in *Jesus and of God's goodness in the Scriptures, I* do: and the God of peace *to victory over any oppression, reign or lordship of the devil* shall be with *and operate in me*." And You are released by me, as I control my mind to think like You, my Father God. So when I am harassed with dreadful fear, I fill my mind by continual faith actions with confidence in You, Father, and Your goodness toward me. For I am saved by Your loving grace, Father God, through faith actions, and I am made Your righteousness in Jesus, to be an imitator of You in Jesus. Praise You, Father, that You get me to cooperate more and more with Holy Spirit to *zao*/live the *zoe*/life of Jesus in me to Your good pleasure. Thank You, Father, in the Name of Jesus, thank You! Hallelujah! Jesus is Lord! Jesus, You are mighty, awesome and wonderful! Glory to You! Jesus, You are Lord! Yahoo! Lord, You are good! Your mercy is everlasting and Your truth endureth to all generations! Yahoo! Yahoo!

Z. **I am born again** after the image of Father God in Christ Jesus, and I delight to do the will of God. Anything in me that resists the will of God is not of me, and Father, in the name of Jesus, build in me to Rom 6:3 **know** ... that so many of us as were baptized into Jesus Christ were baptized into his death. 4 Therefore we are buried with him by baptism into death: that like as Christ was raised up from the dead by the glory of *You, the Father*, even so we also should walk in newness of *zoe*/life *now*. 5 For if we have been planted together in the likeness of his death, we shall be also in the likeness of his resurrection: *Father, build in me the* 6 **knowing** this, that our old man is crucified with him, that the body of sin might be destroyed, that henceforth we should not serve sin. 7 For he that is dead is freed from sin. 8 Now if we be dead with Christ, we believe that we shall also *zao*/live with him. *Build in me the* 9 **knowing** that Christ being raised from the dead dieth no more; death hath no more dominion over him. 10 For in that he died, he died unto sin once: but in that he *zao*/liveth, he *zao*/liveth unto *You, Father* God. 11 Likewise *I* **reckon** *myself* to be dead indeed unto sin, but *zao*/alive unto *You, Father* God, through Jesus Christ *my* Lord. 12 *I* let not sin therefore reign in my mortal body. *Rather, by the grace of You, Father God, I acknowledge my sins and all works of the devil in me, and I therefore* Rom 13:12 ... cast off the works and lies of darkness, and put on the armour of light. 13 *I* walk honestly, as in the day; not in rioting and drunkenness, not in chambering and wantonness, not in strife and envying. 14 But *I* put on the Lord Jesus Christ, and make not provision for the flesh, to fulfil the lusts thereof, *and I put on Jesus Christ now. Father God is conforming me to the image of His Son, Jesus Christ, for I renew the spirit of my mind. I delight to do His will in all ways,* Phil 2:15 that *I* may be blameless and harmless, *a son* of God, without rebuke, in the midst of a crooked and perverse nation, among whom *I* shine as a light in the world; 16 holding forth the word of *zoe*/life ... . Eph 2:4 *For Father* God, who is rich in mercy, for his great *agape*/love wherewith he *agape*/loved us, 5 even when we were dead in sins, hath quickened us together with Christ, (by grace *am I sozo*/saved;) 6 and hath raised *me* up together, and made *me* sit together in heavenly places in Christ Jesus. *So I walk in Father God's righteousness in Christ Jesus, to bring Heaven to Earth in righteousness, peace and joy by dunamis power, agape love and operate in the mind of Christ by faith actions, to think, speak and do as Jesus would, no matter where I am.* Col 3:1 "For *I am* risen with Christ, and *I do* seek those things which are above, where Christ sitteth on the right hand of God. 2 *I* set *my* affection on things above, not on things on the earth. 3 For *I am* dead, and *my zoe*/life is hid with Christ in God. Col 2:9 For in Jesus dwelleth all the fulness of the Godhead bodily. 10 And we are complete in him, which is the head of all principality and power: 11 in whom also we are circumcised with the circumcision made without hands, in putting off the body of the sins of the flesh by the circumcision of Christ: 12 buried with him in baptism, wherein also ye are risen with him through the faith of the operation of God, who hath raised him from the dead. *I fear not, and I am not afraid.* Deut 31:6 *I am strong (in the Lord's strength for me) and of a good courage (in faith actions), I fear not (by considering only failure), nor am I afraid (or allow myself to be harassed by the evil power) of the devil and his agents: for You, Father, the Lord my God, You, O God, it is You, Father, that do go with me; You, Father God, will not fail me, nor forsake me. Therefore I keep in faith actions until I see the promise fulfilled:* 1 Cor 15:57 But thanks be to God, which giveth us the victory through our Lord Jesus Christ. 58 Therefore, as *one of the agape/*beloved brethren, *I am* stedfast, unmovable, always abounding in the *(faith action)* work of the Lord, forasmuch as I know that *my (faith-action)* labour is not in vain in the Lord. *By Your grace I* 1 Pet 1:18 ... know that *I* was not redeemed with corruptible things, as silver and gold, from *my* vain conversation received by tradition from *my* fathers; 19 but with the precious blood of Christ, as of a lamb without blemish and without spot: 20 who verily was foreordained before the foundation of the world, but was manifest in these last times for *me*, 21 who by him do believe in God, that raised him up from the dead, and gave him glory; that *my* faith and hope *(actions)* might be in God. 22 Seeing, *by Your grace, I continually* purify *my* soul in obeying the truth through the Spirit unto unfeigned *phileo/*love of the brethren, *I see that I agape/*love one another with a pure heart fervently: 23 being born again, not of corruptible seed, but of incorruptible, by the word of God, which *zao/*liveth and abideth for ever, *knowing* 24 for all flesh is as grass, and all the glory of man as the flower of grass. The grass withereth, and the flower thereof falleth away: 25 but the word of the Lord endureth for ever. *And this is the Word which by the Gospel is preached unto me, and so that I* 2 Pet 3:18 ... grow in grace, and in the knowledge of our Lord and Saviour Jesus Christ. To him be glory both now and for ever. Amen, *and that* Jude 20 ... *I, as agape/*beloved, therefore, *by His Spirit, am continually* building up *myself* on our most holy faith *(actions)*, praying in the Holy Ghost, 21 keeping *myself* in the *agape/*love of *You, Father* God, looking for the mercy of our Lord Jesus Christ unto eternal *zoe/*life: 22 and of some *I* have compassion, making a difference: 23 and others *I sozo/*save with fear, pulling them out of the fire; hating even the garment spotted by the flesh. 24 Now unto him that is able to keep *me* from falling, and to present *me* faultless before the presence of his glory with exceeding joy, 25 to the only wise God our Saviour, be glory and majesty, dominion and power, both now and ever. Amen. *Thank You, Father God, that You set my value as worth the spirit, soul, body and blood of Jesus to redeem me and make me Yours. You agape/love me! I am loved! I am known and still loved. Thank You, Father, in the name of Jesus, thank You! Hallelujah! Jesus is Lord! Jesus, You are mighty, awesome and wonderful! Glory to You, Lord! Hallelujah! Hallelujah! Yahoo! You are in me to reign through me! And I am in You to reign through You, by faith actions. Yahoo! Lord, You are good! Your mercy is everlasting! And Your truth endureth to all generations! Yahoo! Yahoo!*

Affirmations in Christ

Godly Prosperity

1. <u>Matt 6:24</u> *I know that* **no man can serve two masters**: for either he will hate the one, and *agape*/love the other; or else he will hold to the one, and despise the other. Ye cannot serve God and mammon. *So I love and serve only God and, therefore, men through Jesus Christ,* 25 *for I* take no thought for *my psuche*/life (*soul*), what *I* shall eat, or what *I* shall drink; nor yet for *my* body, what *I* shall put on. *My psuche*/life (*soul*) *is* more than meat, and *my* body *more* than raiment. *For I* 26 behold the fowls of the air: for they sow not, neither do they reap, nor gather into barns; yet *my* heavenly Father feedeth them. *I am* much better *to God* than they. 27 *For I know that by* taking thought *I* cannot add one cubit unto *my* stature. 28 And *so I take no* thought for raiment. *Instead I* consider the lilies of the field, how they grow; they toil not, neither do they spin: 29 *for I know,* that even Solomon in all his glory was not arrayed like one of these. 30 Wherefore, if God so clothe the grass of the field, which to day is, and to morrow is cast into the oven, shall he not much more clothe *me, for I am of great joyful* faith, *for I know I am loved by the Almighty God who cannot lie*. 31 Therefore *I take* no thought, saying, What shall we eat? or, What shall we drink? or, Wherewithal shall we be clothed? 32 (for after all these things do the Gentiles seek:) for *my* heavenly Father knoweth that *we* have need of all these things. 33 *So I* seek first the kingdom of God, and his righteousness; and all these things shall be added unto *me*. 34 *I* take therefore no thought for the morrow: for the morrow shall take thought for the things of itself. Sufficient unto the day is the evil thereof. <u>Eph 2:8</u> For by grace *I am sozo*/saved through faith; and that not of *myself*: it is the gift of *Father* God: 9 not of works, lest any man should boast. *So I make my boast in Father God, and not what I do right.* 10 For *I am Father God's* workmanship, created in Christ Jesus unto good works, which *Father* God hath before ordained that *I* should walk in them. *Therefore I call those things of God's promises that be not yet as though they were, in the name of Jesus, for I speak, believing I receive them unto praise and glad thanksgiving, and I shall see the goodness of the Lord in the land of the living. Hallelujah! Thank You, Lord Jesus!*

2. <u>Mark 11:22</u> "*As* **Jesus has commanded us,** *I* have faith (*actions*) in God *and the faith of God*. 23 For verily *Jesus said unto us,* that whosoever shall say unto this mountain (*or any difficult, improbable or impossible situation*), Be thou removed, and be thou cast into the sea; and shall not doubt in his heart, but shall believe (*by faith actions*) that those things which he saith shall come to pass; he shall have whatsoever he saith. 24 Therefore *Jesus said unto us,* What things soever ye *aiteo*/desire (*require, demand and expect as due by covenant promise*), when ye pray, believe (*by faith actions*) that ye receive them, and ye shall have them."

OK, God, Now What?

Therefore I *aiteo*/ask (require, demand and expect) God to fulfill His covenant promises by saying, in the name of Jesus, to any unhappy or evil situation, that it be removed and made a blessing, knowing that Father God has heard me, in the name of Jesus, that He will not withhold any good thing from me, so I do not doubt God in His promises, and I am believing in thanksgiving and joy, knowing that I shall have it. Eph 2:8 "For by grace *I am sozo*/saved through faith; and that not of *myself*: it is the gift of *Father* God: 9 not of works, lest any man should boast. *So I make my boast in Father God, and not what I do right.* 10 For *I am Father God's* workmanship, created in Christ Jesus unto good works, which *Father* God hath before ordained that *I* should walk in them." Therefore I call those things of God's promises that be not yet as though they were, in the name of Jesus, for I speak, believing in faith actions I receive them in faith working by *agape*/love unto praise and glad thanksgiving, and I shall see the goodness of the Lord in the land of the living. Hallelujah! Thank You, Lord Jesus! Yahoo!

3. **So I continually say, expecting God to make it for me, that today my net** worth is $_____, I am now earning $_____ a year from my investments, ventures, and businesses, and I am saving $_____ a year. I am joyfully giving 10 percent of my income to my favorite charities, and another 10 percent to my church, and I cheerfully help widows and orphans in their distress. Life, at the summit in Jesus, is sweet and satisfying, and I bless God in all I do. I grow in the true knowledge of God through Jesus Christ more and more every day. Thank You, Father, for performing Your Word in me and mine, to Your glory. Eph 2:8 "For by grace *I am sozo/saved* through faith; and that not of *myself*: it is the gift of *Father* God: 9 not of works, lest any man should boast. *So I make my boast in Father God, and not what I do right.* 10 For *I am Father God's* workmanship, created in Christ Jesus unto good works, which *Father* God hath before ordained that *I* should walk in them." Therefore I call those things of God's promises that be not yet as though they were, in the name of Jesus, for I speak, believing I receive them unto praise and glad thanksgiving, and I shall see the goodness of the Lord in the land of the living. No matter the situation, good always comes to me; I always walk in glad expectation in Jesus. Thank You, Father, in the name of Jesus Christ, my Lord and my Shepherd, thank You. Yahoo! Yahoo! Yahoo!

4. **I do not tolerate unforgiveness in my life** for Mark 11:25 ... when *I pray, I forgive, if I have ought against any [or if any have ought against me]: that my Father also which is in heaven may forgive me my trespasses. Knowing* 26 but if *I* do not forgive, neither will *my* Father which is in heaven forgive *my* trespasses, *and I will walk in the reaping of the flesh what I sow to the flesh*. So I keep

Affirmations in Christ

short accounts with God and men, and therefore <u>Matt 5:44</u> *as Jesus has commanded, I agape/love my enemies, I bless them that curse me, I do good to them that hate me*, and pray for them which despitefully use *me*, and persecute *me*; 45 that *I may be [in thought, word and deed] a child* of *my* Father which is in heaven: for he maketh his sun to rise on the evil and on the good, and sendeth rain on the just and on the unjust. <u>1 Pet 3:10</u> *So I* will *agape*/love *zoe*/life, *and will see good days, so I* refrain *my* tongue from evil, *and my* lips … speak no guile: 11 *I do* eschew *(avoid)* evil, *and instead gladly do good; I do* seek peace, and ensue *(gladly pursue)* it. <u>Ps 34:15</u> For the eyes of the Lord are over the righteous *in Jesus*, and his ears are open unto *my* prayers: 16 but the face of the Lord is against them that do evil *[to let them walk in the fruit of their ways]*. Therefore <u>Rom 12:14</u> *I have mercy on them and* bless them which persecute *us*: *I* bless, and curse not. 15 *I* rejoice with them that do rejoice, and weep with them that weep. 16 *I am of the same mind of Christ* one toward another. *I* mind not high things *[of evil and pride]*, but condescend to men of low estate. *I am not* wise in *my* own conceits. 17 *I* recompense to no man evil for evil. *I* provide things honest in the sight of all men. 18 … *As* much as lieth *of Christ in me, I live* peaceably with all men. 19 *As one of the* dearly *agape*/beloved, *I do not* avenge *myself*, but rather give place unto wrath: for it is written, Vengeance is mine; I will repay, saith the Lord. 20 Therefore if *my* enemy hunger, *I* feed him; if he thirst, *I* give him drink: for in so doing *I* shalt heap coals of fire on his head. 21 *I will not be* overcome of evil, but *I always* overcome evil with good. *For I do not get offended or bitter at God, for I know every evil is from the devil in some way, and God, who cannot lie and cannot fail, is always my Helper to get me to overcome to total triumph in Jesus. So I thankfully and gladly* lambano God in all His promises, and I do see His goodness, for nothing of God's promises is impossible to me in Jesus, for I believe that no evil report can stand, but I believe and gladly obey God in faith actions to overcoming in Jesus. **<u>Ps 112:1</u>** Praise ye the Lord. *I am* blessed *for I fear* the Lord, *I delight* greatly in his commandments. 2 *My* seed shall be mighty upon earth: the generation of the upright shall be blessed. 3 Wealth and riches shall be in *my* house, *I handle prosperity well and wisely to the glory of God through my Lord Jesus Christ*: and *my* righteousness *in Jesus* endureth for ever. 4 Unto *me*, the upright *in Jesus*, there ariseth light in the darkness: *I am* gracious, and full of compassion, and righteous. 5 *I, as a good man, shew* favour, *and lend*: *I* guide *my* affairs with discretion. 6 Surely *I* shall not be moved for ever: *for I am one of* the righteous *in Jesus that are* in everlasting remembrance. 7 *I am* not afraid of evil tidings: *my* heart is fixed, trusting *(by faith actions)* in the Lord. 8 *My* heart is established, *I* shall not be afraid, until *I* see *my* desire upon *my* enemy *[the devil and all his works]*. 9 *I disperse, I give* to the poor; *my* righteousness *in Jesus* endureth for ever; *my* horn shall be exalted with honour. 10 The wicked shall see it, and be grieved; he shall gnash with his teeth, and melt away: the desire of the wicked shall perish. *Yahoo! Father, this is the Day of Your Salvation, and I am glad, and I rejoice in You by Jesus Christ! Thank You, Father, for Your goodness to me! Yahoo!*

5. **By the grace of God through my Lord Jesus Christ** I am living the life of my dreams. Love, laughter, and unbridled passion fuel my life and turn my dreams into reality. I am grateful for my vibrant health and high energy, and for the health and happiness of my _____ and my children. My family and I grow closer and wiser every day, sharing God's *agape*/love, *zoe*/life, joy and possibility with all those we love and care for. I effectively love my _____ more and more every day, to her/his/their joy and the joy of my children _____. My heart and my head are soaring with possibility and opportunity. I see and deliver potential where others only see loss. I am blessed and grateful for my whole life and everything in it. I count it all joy in all temptations and trails, knowing glad and joyous patience and consistency in God are building me into Jesus. I cheerfully feed the hungry, cloth the naked, visit widows and orphans in their distress, keep myself unstained from the evil of the world and the *agape*/love of money, and I Luke 6:28 "bless them that curse *me*, and pray for them which despitefully use *me*," knowing the Lord will execute judgment for me. Good always comes to me in Jesus; every cloud is loaded with silver and gold for me. Yahoo! Father, this is the Day of Your Salvation, and I am glad, and I rejoice in You by Jesus Christ!

6. **I am a genius and I use God's wisdom daily.** I give myself permission to be powerful in God by Jesus Christ by faith actions. Josh 1:5 There shall not any man be able to stand before *me or terrify me* all the days of *my* life: as God [*is with Jesus, the Son of God, so He is*] with *me: God* will not fail *me*, nor forsake *me*. 6 *I stay* strong *in the Lord* and *am* of a good courage: for unto this people shall *I* divide for an inheritance the land, which *Father God* sware unto *our* fathers to give *us*. 7 [*I focus on Him and His promises to*] only be (*of fearless confidence*), strong and very courageous, that *I may* observe to do according to all the *Bible*, which *Jesus* commanded [*me to love one another, and believe on the name of Jesus Christ*]: *I* turn not from it to the right hand or to the left, that *I may* prosper whithersoever *I go*. 8 ... the *Bible* does not depart out of *my* mouth; but *I* meditate therein day and night, that *I may* observe to do according to all that is written therein: for *I do* make *my* way prosperous *in God*, and *I do* have good success. *I obey Father God for* 9 *He has* commanded *me, so I am* strong [*in the Lord and in the power of His might, and in His wisdom, knowledge and understanding*], and *I am continually* of a good courage [*in*

Affirmations in Christ

glad cooperation with Holy Spirit, edifying and giving grace to others as I speak]; I will not be afraid, neither will I be dismayed: for the Lord *my God is with me whithersoever I go. So I believe by faith actions on and in the name of my Lord Jesus Christ, I know that I have eternal zoe/life, and I agape/love as Jesus agape/loves to excellence in every part of life. I freely preach the Word of God and He confirms it with signs and wonders. God confirms His covenant of peace and abundance in and through me. Father God, in the name of Jesus, thank You! Yahoo!*

7. **I have absolute certainty** in my ability from, by and with God to generate any amount of income I choose in godly obedience. God is my Rock, and in Him do I trust by faith actions. I live in God's favor. God consistently sends all the right people to help me grow my life, faith in God and businesses. I am a brilliant and savvy <u>businessman/woman</u>, and I have everything it takes right now to grow each of my companies to a billion-dollar company. I have all the talent, intelligence, resources, and money I need to create this new masterpiece. I readily link good emotions to my righteous affirmations and produce godly results. God continually overflows my life with His divine appointments, to meet our and other's needs, to His glory in every part of life.

8. **I am always calm, succinct, happy** and outstanding when speaking, being interviewed or presenting a seminar or keynote. I am superior in effective communication in all styles and situations, in which my listeners hear or my readers read what I am saying, to clear understanding, and they feel what I am feeling. I am a master presenter and persuader on and off the platform, using superior salting and word pictures. I am superior in the language of *agape*/love in all situations to the glory of God. It is so much fun! I proclaim the Word of God just like Jesus did, and He confirms it with signs and wonders. I easily and pleasantly show men and women how to work more with God in every part of their lives. I make knowledge and wisdom acceptable so that people desire it. I eat healthy and diet and exercise to keep my weight to a size _____. And I identify, attack and destroy all fears that keep me overweight or unhealthy and replace them with right thoughts, words, attitudes and actions. I am good at losing excess weight and staying in great shape and attitude. I eat to live for health and wellness, and keep my appetites under control by focusing on better rewards, to the glory of God.

9. **I am a person of action and accomplishment.** I use time very wisely and effectively. In every situation, I do the right things rightly, with the right godly priorities. I take time to mutter-meditate on God's Word three times each day. I am very effective with accomplishment and people. I take the time to

acknowledge, honor and relate to people in all situations. I accomplish three major things a day that move my life and my businesses forward. I pray first, and then I move. I pray on the run and in quiet times. I do not get lost in clutter, but am superior in establishing clarity, priorities, accomplishments and relationships that effectively move things forward, for I have great favor with God, who loves me, and with people, for I am blessed and highly favored of God. Glory to You, Father! Yahoo!

10. **I speak words of comfort and encouragement easily** and graciously, so they are received and acted upon to godly results. I make truth exciting and delightful. In every situation, I see and am able to gladly inspire others to exceed what they are now doing. I reset myself and others to greater possibilities and then deliver on them day by day. I quickly and rightly identify limiting beliefs and false stories in myself and others, and help myself and others move past them effectively. I am an extraordinary win-win-win negotiator, and people like dealing with me. I always keep my priorities with God, wife/husband, family, country, health, business and ministry in right order. I graciously identify, destroy and replace all unrighteous limiting beliefs in myself and others.

11. **Whenever fear, doubt or unbelief come** on me, I am Phil 4:6 "… careful for nothing (*I do not tolerate fear, worry or anxiety in anything, even though they seem logical and real*); but in every thing by prayer and supplication with (*joyous and exuberant*) thanksgiving *I* let *my aiteo*/requests be made known unto God [*by proclaiming His promises and* aiteo/ask (*requiring, demanding and expecting as due by covenant promise His answer*), *in the name of Jesus, unto joyful thanksgiving for I* lambano/*receive it, knowing I will possess it.*] 7 And the peace of God, which passeth all understanding *keeps my heart and mind* through Christ Jesus. 8 Finally, *and above all else* …whatsoever things are **true**, whatsoever things are **honest**, whatsoever things are **just**, whatsoever things are **pure**, whatsoever things are **lovely**, whatsoever things are of **good report**; if there be **any virtue**, and if there be **any praise**, *I* think on these things *constantly*." Prov 3:3 "*I do not let chesed*/mercy and truth forsake *me: instead I* bind them about *my* neck; *I* write them upon the table of *my* heart: So *I* find favour and good understanding in the sight of God and man. 5 *I* trust (*by faith actions*) in the LORD with all *my* heart; and *I* lean not unto *my* own understanding. 6 In all *my* ways *I* acknowledge him, and he *directs my* paths. 7 *I am* not wise in *my* own eyes: *I* fear the LORD, and *I* depart from evil. 8 *It is* health to *my* navel, and marrow to *my* bones. 9 *I* honour the LORD with *my* substance, and with the firstfruits of all *my* increase:

10 so *my* barns *are* filled with plenty, and *my* presses ... burst out with new wine." I righteously inspire others to also attack and destroy their fears and grow in *agape*/love in and by Jesus Christ. Yahoo! Father, this is the Day of Your Salvation, and I am glad, and I rejoice in You by Jesus! Thank You, Father, in Jesus' name, for Your goodness to me! Yahoo!

12. **Because Jesus became a curse for me**, and I am in Him by the grace of Father God through faith, and not my works, Deut 28:3 "*I am* blessed ... in the city, and *I am* blessed ... in the field. 4 *I am* blessed *in* the fruit of *my* body, and the fruit of *my* ground, and the fruit of *my* cattle, the increase of *my* kine, and the flocks of *my* sheep. 5 Blessed *are my* basket and *my* store. 6 *I am* blessed ... when *I come* in, and *I am* blessed ...when *I go* out. 7 The Lord shall cause *my* enemies that rise up against *me* to be smitten before *my* face: [*for I stand in His grace and His strength in faith actions*] and they shall come out against *me* one way, and flee before *me* seven ways. 8 The Lord ... *commands* the blessing upon *me* in *my* storehouses, and in all that *I* set *my* hand unto; and he ... *blesses me* in the land which the Lord *my* God giveth *me*. 9 The Lord ... establishes *me* an holy people unto himself, as he hath sworn unto *me in Jesus, for Jesus has kept* the commandments of the Lord *my* God *for me*, and *walked* in his ways *for me*, and *by His grace I do keep the commandments of God, and I do walk in His ways more and more every day, by Him working in me in Jesus*. 10 And all people of the earth see that *I am* called by the name of the Lord; and they *are* afraid of *me*. 11 And the Lord *makes me and those with me* plenteous in goods, in the fruit of *my* body, and in the fruit of *my* cattle, and in the fruit of *my* ground, in the land which the Lord sware unto *my* fathers to give *me*, [*for the Lord delights that I prosper and be in health, and my soul prospers in Him*]. 12 The Lord *opens* unto *me* his good treasure, the heaven to give the rain unto *my* land in his season, and to bless all the work of *my* hand: and *I* lend unto many nations, and *I do* not borrow. 13 And the Lord *makes me* the head, and not the tail; and *I am* above only, and *I am not* beneath ... ," for I get all the blessing of the righteous 2 Cor 5:21 "for *Father God* hath made *Jesus* to be sin for *all mankind*, who knew no sin; that *I* might be made the righteousness of *Father God in Jesus*." I walk in the continual triumph of Christ in every part of life. I am gladly generous with the abundance God gives to me, and I gladly and cheerfully care for the poor, and I also teach them in the ways of God that they may prosper in God's covenant of abundance in Jesus. Yahoo!

13. **I am working with more partners** and owning much more of the projects I work on. I structure win-win-win deals with people who can deliver in quality and quantity. I effectively program my unconscious parts to fulfill all God

has for me in every part of life, and I train and educate others to do so also. I live each day with passion and purpose. I am a success in all I do. I respect my abilities, and I always fulfill my potential. I always have enough money for all I need, for my family, God and my businesses. I achieve all my goals and dreams. When it is easy, I am grateful to God and the people He used to make it easy for me and us. I immediately respond with thanksgiving, praise, and joy in the Lord. When it is unclear or difficult, I respond immediately with thanksgiving, praise, joy and *aiteo* until I see the answer come. I never give up, and I always keep working, learning and understanding to find the paths for success in and by Jesus. No matter how great, hard or impossible, no matter the strife and confusion, no matter how short or long, I trust God for wisdom and miracles. Phil 1:28 "And in nothing *am I* terrified by my adversaries: which is to them an evident token of perdition (*their total removal or sudden cooperation*), but to *me* of *soteria*/salvation, and that of God." I am totally confident in God working through me in every aspect of life. I am an excellent businessman/woman. I am wealthy and successful, every day, in all that I do. I encourage myself and others daily with joy in the Lord. For: **Ps 121:1** "I *do* lift up mine eyes unto the hills, from whence cometh my help. 2 My help cometh from the Lord, which made heaven and earth. 3 He will not suffer *my* foot to be moved: he that keepeth *me and mine* will not slumber. 4 Behold, he that keepeth Israel shall neither slumber nor sleep. 5 The Lord is *my* keeper: the Lord is *my* shade upon *my* right hand. 6 The sun shall not smite *me* by day, nor the moon by night. 7 The Lord shall preserve *me and mine* from all evil: he shall preserve *my* soul. 8 The Lord shall preserve *my* going out and *my* coming in from this time forth, and even for evermore." And I know: Ps 27:13 "I had fainted, unless I had believed to see the goodness of the Lord in the land of the living. [*So I continually trust in* aiteo, *thanksgiving, praise and joy, and I continually confess I will see the goodness of the Lord in the land of the living. This is how I*] 14 wait (*entwine by faith actions*) on the Lord: *I am* of good courage, and he shall strengthen *my* heart: wait (*entwine by continual faith actions*), I say, on the Lord" to myself and all those with me. So I Ps 31:23 "… love the Lord, *as one of* his saints: for the Lord preserveth the faithful, and plentifully rewardeth the proud doer. *So, by His grace in me,* 24 *I stay of* good courage (*in faith actions*), and he shall strengthen *my* heart, *for I am one* that *hopes* in the Lord." Praise the name of Jesus and the power of His Word. Praise You, Lord God Almighty, who is my strength and my victory. Thank You, Father God. In the name of Jesus, thank You. Yahoo!

14. **I meet my obligations and keep my promises.** People meet me and want to and do make business with me. I work well with people, and people work well with me. I make all at ease that are around me. I am gracious and courte-

ous in all my manners. I do not lord over any, but esteem others better than myself, and give them honor in all I do. I communicate vision that causes people to want to join me and make my dreams into reality and blessings for all. I live at peace with all men, especially my family. I attract people to me who love me, respect me and act in my best interests; and I do this easily for others. I quickly understand other people's good visions and dreams, and help them achieve them, so they make me wealthy and are glad to do it. I see issues well ahead of time and put things in place to handle them and make them blessings. People are amazed at how well things go when I am part of the project. I do not expect failure, but I know there will be challenges to overcome, and God is there for, through, by and with me to success and victory to make Heaven on Earth in every part of life. I expect success with effort, and plan well each activity and mitigate risks in a superior manner and extraordinarily well. I look for deeper causes and address them properly. No matter what, I focus on outcomes, learning and improvement, again and again. Whether the opportunity is simple or complex, I build teams that are world experts with world standards of excellence and effectiveness at whatever we do—in our personal lives, our families, our relationships, our businesses and our ministries—all to the glory of God through Jesus Christ.

15. **I use my wealth and prosperity very wisely.** Like Job, I *lambano*/hang on to God, no matter what, and I am blessed to be the richest and most prosperous man/woman in the East/_____. I have all the resources necessary to fulfill any and all of my spiritual and business goals and dreams. Making money excites me and energizes me to love and serve God more. I am a powerful and resourceful creator with God, to His glory. I have absolute certainty in all of God's promises to me, and therefore in my ability for Him to work through me, to generate any amount of blessing, power of God, income and prosperity I choose, for I am blessed and highly favored of God in Jesus. Praise the Lord for His goodness to me. I am loved of God.

16. **By the grace of God, I have all the resources I need right now** to become a multimillionaire. I have great abundance flowing into my businesses, which affords every luxury that I and my _____ desire. I am an organized, proactive, wise, disciplined, talented, innovative, personable and intelligent businessperson and man/woman of God in Jesus, continuously applying sound and honest living and business practices. I make God in the Bible desirable to all men and women. Yahoo! Father, this is the Day of Your Salvation, and I am glad, and I rejoice in You by Jesus Christ! Yahoo!

17. **Through Father God, in Jesus, I am a powerful and resourceful creator**, attracting all the wealth and opportunities I need for me to produce my financial success. I have all the skills, intelligence, godly wisdom, contacts, relationships, right deal making and money I need right now to create an incredible masterpiece with each of my businesses and ministries. In Jesus I deserve to earn money easily, and in abundance and to live totally paid in full on all accounts, and with money flowing to me from expected and unexpected sources, for God is with me in all I do. Any work of my hands is blessed to abundance and joyful godliness by grace. I stay in and abide in Jesus continually. Praise You, Father God, for Your wonderful love, grace and truth in Jesus. Praise You, Father God!

18. **I attract and develop teams and team members** of extraordinary godliness, skills, talents and abilities to create successful businesses and godly enterprises. I develop wise counselors and use them rightly all the time. I quickly spot wrong thoughts and separate them from good warning thoughts, and handle them well. I do not get angry easily, and when I do I resolve it quickly, so the devil has no victory in me. By Jesus, I labor by faith actions in *agape*/love to bring happiness, abundance and prosperity in Jesus. By grace and knowing I am a new creation in Christ Jesus, made in righteousness and true holiness, I continuously walk in Holy Spirit righteousness, peace, joy, *dunamis*/power, *agape*/love, the sound mind of Christ, mercy, grace and truth by His Word. God responds to my *aiteo*/asking that my joy may be full in Him by Jesus. I accomplish all my life goals with ease in God's peace, no matter how great the challenge, because I know they require battles, and I am an *agape* love warrior. Ps 34.19 "Many are the afflictions of the righteous, [*but by the righteousness of Jesus,*] the Lord delivers *me* [*to His abundance*] in every one [*and I set others free*]." Even on the busiest of days, I constantly add value to people's lives in honoring and encouraging them. Amazing Jesus lives in me! I am hardened to troubles and cling to God like a rock, no matter how great or long the challenge, for God continually says to me: Isa 43:1 "But now thus saith the Lord that created thee, O Jacob, and he that formed thee, O Israel, Fear not: for I have redeemed thee, I have called thee by thy name; thou art mine. 2 When thou passest through the waters, I will be with thee; and through the rivers, they shall not overflow thee: when thou walkest through the fire, thou shalt not be burned; neither shall the flame kindle upon thee. 3 For I am the Lord thy God, the Holy One of Israel, thy Saviour ... ." I continually focus on this promise of God for me and mine: Isa 41:9 "Thou whom I have taken from the ends of the earth, and called thee from the chief men thereof, and said unto thee, Thou art my servant; I have chosen thee, and not cast thee away. 10 Fear thou not; for I am with thee: be not dismayed; for I am thy God: I will strengthen thee; yea, I will help thee; yea, I

will uphold thee with the right hand of my righteousness. 11 Behold, all they that were incensed against thee shall be ashamed and confounded: they shall be as nothing; and they that strive with thee shall perish. 12 Thou shalt seek them, and shalt not find them, even them that contended with thee: they that war against thee shall be as nothing, and as a thing of nought. 13 For I the Lord thy God will hold thy right hand, saying unto thee, Fear not; I will help thee. 14 Fear not, thou worm Jacob, and ye men of Israel; I will help thee, saith the Lord, and thy redeemer, the Holy One of Israel. 15 Behold, I will make thee a new sharp threshing instrument having teeth: thou shalt thresh the mountains, and beat them small, and shalt make the hills as chaff. 16 Thou shalt fan them, and the wind shall carry them away, and the whirlwind shall scatter them: and thou shalt rejoice in the Lord, and shalt glory in the Holy One of Israel." Therefore I stay strong in the strength of the Lord, to go through the temptations, trials, tests, troubles and battles of life, to bring Heaven to Earth. I use glad diligence, godly wisdom and excellence in every part of life, along with thanksgiving, praise, joy, mercy, grace, truth, Scripture and *aiteo*, as weapons of God to bring Heaven to Earth and to keep myself and others encouraged in the Lord. Great is our God, the only God of salvation! Great is Jesus, my King! Great are You, O Lord! Great are You, O God! Great are You, Jehovah the Good! Yahoo!

19. **I have complete freedom over my time.** God gives me His wisdom and priorities, and I always work as He directs. I am a genius in all business deals and structures. People pay me great sums to help them solve problems and to grow their businesses. I am a genius, and I use God's wisdom every moment. Day by day, in every way, I am getting more like my Lord Jesus Christ in every way. I am inquisitive, creative, looking for deeper causes, judge righteously, of great godly faith, forgiving, *agape*/loving, fun-loving, Christian and adventurous. I have God's extraordinary ability to accomplish everything He has for me. I have Holy Spirit's extraordinary ability to get God's desires for me and accomplish them with Him. I am known as a godly man/woman of prayer to Almighty God in the name of Jesus. I am committed, determined and passionate about what I do. I feel good and do the right things to stay feeling good. I am full of right energy to do right. I am made, by grace, a partaker, unified with and an extension of Jesus in Holy Spirit for God on the Earth. Yahoo! Father, this is the Day of Your Salvation, and I am glad, and I rejoice in You by Jesus Christ! Yahoo! Yahoo! Yahoo!

20. **I am very focused and persistent**. I have tremendous energy and focus for achieving all my life and business goals in God. Each of my businesses and Christian ministries is a masterpiece of what God can do in a man/woman

through Jesus Christ. I laugh often and readily as a good medicine to my body and to help others. Yahoo! (Now laugh.)

21. **I meditate daily on God in His Word** all day long and stay in constant contact and sync with Holy Spirit in faith actions for every part of life, including an abundance of signs and wonders, confirming the truth of the full Gospel of Jesus Christ. I always have crystal clarity of purpose and focus. I always have good answers, no matter how great the problem. I am slow to speak and quick to listen, yet I am good on my feet in new and strange situations. I turn vain and hostile remarks and attitudes into blessing and friendship. I give honor and receive honor well. I am continually thankful to God for Jesus in me, for no matter what happens, I abide in Jesus and make sure His words abide in me by faith actions, to produce the fruits of Jesus in every part of life, with no evil fear, for I know that apart from Jesus I can do no good thing, and I am in Jesus forever. Hallelujah! Yahoo! (Now laugh.)

22. **I use visualization and emotions in a godly way** for every task given me, or I chose to do. 2 Cor 3:17 "Now the Lord is that Spirit: and where the Spirit of the Lord is, there is liberty *(for me to be and do what God has called me to do)*. 18 *For I*, with open face beholding as in a glass *(mirror)* the glory of the Lord *manifesting in and through me in any situation, I am* changed into the same image from glory to glory, *and faith to faith,* even as by the Spirit of the Lord *to produce God's goodness for and with Him.*" I visualize all that I desire of God's goodness, for I continually delight myself in the Lord, and He gives me the desires of my heart. I have complete control over manifesting His will on the Earth in faith actions, for I am blessed in all I do. Therefore I stand by the Word of God in the strength of the Lord, in faith actions working by *agape* love, and destroy every enemy that rises up against me and mine. I am a good workman in the Lord. I subdue the devil and his works, in faith working by *agape* love, and I build the Kingdom of God, in faith working by *agape* love, and good continually comes to me. I am made for and win victory by Jesus in extraordinary and impossible situations. All right things work well and appear to come easily for me, for challenges do not frustrate or confuse me, but are what I easily and readily overcome to the glory of God through His Son, my Lord Jesus Christ, knowing deep in my heart: Isa 54:17 "No weapon that is formed against *me* shall prosper; and every tongue that shall rise against *me* in judgment thou shalt condemn. This is the heritage of the servants of the Lord, and their righteousness is of me, saith the Lord." The evil of the world and fear do not hinder or offend me, for I am perfected in God's *agape*/love every day, to walk in the triumph of my Lord Jesus Christ, to make the world a better place for Him. I enjoy great challenges and opportunity, and I deliver great results, for God

is with me in all I am and all I do, for He never leaves me or forsakes me in Jesus. I stay in constant thanksgiving, praise, joy and *aiteo*. I am always of good report, knowing God will get me to overcome. Praise You, Father, for the name of Jesus, at which every knee must bow and every tongue confess that Jesus is Lord. For You tell us, by Your Word that: Phil 2:9 "… *You, Father God, also have* highly exalted *Jesus,* and given him a name which is above every name: 10 that at the name of Jesus every knee should bow, of things in heaven, and things in earth, and things under the earth; 11 and that every tongue should confess that Jesus Christ is Lord, to the glory of *You,* God the Father." Eph 1:20 "Which *You, Father God,* wrought in Christ, when *You* raised him from the dead, and set *Jesus* at *Your* own right hand in the heavenly places, 21 far above all principality, and power, and might, and dominion, and every name that is named, not only in this world, but also in that which is to come: 22 and *You, Father God, have* put all things under his feet, and gave *Jesus* to be the head over all things to the church, 23 which is his body, the fulness of him that filleth all in all." Praise You, Father, that every word of Yours has the power to make it come to pass. Thank You for *zoe* life in Jesus, the peace of Jesus, the name of Jesus, the Scriptures that cannot be broken and the blood of Jesus that redeemed me. Thank You, Father! In the name of Jesus, thank You!

23. **I attract very lucrative projects** with well-funded founders and investors. I have great favor with God and man. God loves me. People love my work and gladly pay my fees and costs. I deliver more than they expected, and I do it gladly. We develop instant rapport and work well together. They pass on other people to work with me and make sure I am integrated into the team. I am very well recognized and rewarded for my involvement. I have great favor, and good deals come to me, with money to pay me and to reward me, and I am well paid and well rewarded with participation. I provide extraordinary service and advice that is well appreciated. I readily attract the right investors who add value and funding in a positive manner. Investors come looking for me for opportunities, and I do a superior job for them. Wealthy people like me and trust me. I find good projects for them to invest in, and they do invest in them. I get great finder's fees, legally, in all situations. Investors want to be part of any project I am involved in. I operate in the highest integrity with God and men at all times. Yahoo!

24. **I feel happy and at peace with myself in Jesus.** I give myself permission to be powerful in God and with man. I have absolute certainty about my ability to generate any amount of blessing, power of God, prosperity or income I choose. I constantly attract all the right people to help me grow my businesses and ministries. I am a brilliant and savvy businessman/woman and co-laborer with Holy Spirit. I have all the talent, intelligence, resources and money I need.

I am a master at what I do. I stand easily before kings and queens and give them God's *agape*/love and wisdom for great problems, and they follow what I say to great, godly success, and I make the world a better place continually.

25. **Affirming and doing the right things** comes easily and naturally to me. I make my faith-action affirmations in God at least three times each day, to the glory of God, through and by Jesus Christ, my One and Only Lord, who lives and reigns through me to the glory of God the Father, the only wise God and source of all good, light and truth and who makes me stand in Him. My heart gladly meditates on God and His goodness to me continually. Yahoo! Jesus is my Lord and I am His *agape*/beloved brother/sister. Praise the Lord Jesus Christ! Praise the extreme goodness of our Father God who dwells in me by His Spirit because of the mighty and awesome work of Jesus, my Lord and Lord of all! Yahoo! Father, this is the Day of Your Salvation, and I am glad, and I rejoice in You by Jesus Christ! Hallelujah! Hallelujah! Yahoo!

26. **For I know** Eph 5:8 *I was* **sometimes darkness**, but now, *by the new creation, I am* light in the Lord: *by the grace of God ever with me I* walk as *a child* of light: 9 *and continually grow* the fruit of the Spirit ... in all goodness and righteousness and truth. [Gal 5:22 *For I work with and in the Lord to grow* the fruit of the Spirit, *which* is (*actions of*) *agape*/love, joy, peace, longsuffering, gentleness, goodness, faith, 23 meekness, temperance: *knowing* against such there is no law. 24 And *because I am* Christ's, I have crucified the flesh with the affections and lusts. 25 *So I ever grow in living* in the Spirit, *by His Scriptures, so I also* walk in the Spirit. 26 *I am* not desirous of vain glory, *I do not* provoke one another *to evil but to do* agape/*love and good works*]; *I do not* envy one another. *Instead I walk by faith actions working in* agape *love, and I am continually* 10 proving (*and demonstrating*) what is acceptable unto the Lord. 11 And *I* have no fellowship with the unfruitful works of darkness, but rather *I* reprove them. 12 For it is a shame even to speak of those things which are done of them in secret. 13 *For I know* all things that are reproved are made manifest by the light: for whatsoever doth make manifest is light. 14 Wherefore he saith, Awake thou that sleepest, and arise from the dead, and Christ shall give thee light. *So I readily acknowledge my sins and that they were purged in the blood of Jesus two thousand years ago, cast out the devils associated with them, put on the new man in Jesus as my true nature,* lambano/*receive God's mercy and* agape/*love, make any right restitutions or reconciliations, and give effective grace to others, knowing I am fully healed by Jesus' stripes in God's grace. So I walk by faith actions and not by sight.* 15 *So I* walk circumspectly, not as (*a rebel or*) *a fool*, but as wise [*unto God, knowing the wisdom of God is greater than silver or jewels, so I grow continually in*

Affirmations in Christ

wisdom, knowledge and understanding of God, and I am constantly] 16 redeeming the time, because the days are evil. 17 Wherefore *I am* not unwise, but understanding what the will of the Lord is. 18 And *I do* not *get* drunk with wine, wherein is excess; but *I am (continually being)* filled with the Spirit; 19 speaking to *myself and others* in psalms and hymns and spiritual songs, singing and making melody in *my* heart to the Lord; 20 giving thanks always for all things unto God and the Father in the name of our Lord Jesus Christ; 21 submitting *myself;* one to another in the fear of God. *Hallelujah! Hallelujah! Hallelujah!*

27. <u>Eph 4:20</u> *For I have so* **learned Christ**; 21 ... as the truth is in Jesus: 22 that *I (continually)* put off concerning the former conversation the old man, which is corrupt according to the deceitful lusts; 23 and *am (continually)* renewed in the spirit of *my* mind *(in the Word of Christ and my new creation)*; 24 and *I (continually)* put on, *and stay in* the new *(creation)* man *(by faith actions)*, which after God is created in righteousness and true holiness *(to operate and act just like Jesus in all my ways)*. 25 Wherefore putting away lying, *I* speak ... truth with *my every* neighbour: for we are members one of another. ... 29 *I* let no corrupt communication proceed out of *my* mouth, but that which is good to the use of edifying, that it may minister grace unto the hearers, 30 and grieve not the Holy Spirit of God, whereby *I am* sealed unto the day of redemption. 31 *I* let all bitterness, and wrath, and anger, and clamour, and evil speaking, be put away from *me*, with all malice: 32 and *I am* kind one to another, tenderhearted, forgiving one another, even as God for Christ's sake hath forgiven *me*. *And I work and live zealously in doing good works in faith actions working by agape/love, to the glory of God the Father, through Jesus, my Lord, by His Spirit. Yahoo!*

28. <u>1 Tim 2:1</u> *For myself, and also when together with others,* I exhort therefore, that, first of all, supplications, prayers, intercessions, and giving of thanks, be made for all men; 2 for kings, and for all that are in authority; that we may lead a quiet and peaceable *bios*/life in all godliness and honesty. 3 For this is good and acceptable in the sight of God our Saviour; 4 who will have all men to be *sozo*/saved, and to come unto the knowledge of the truth *and* [<u>2 Thes 2:10</u> ... to *lambano*/receive the *agape*/love of the truth, that they might be *sozo*/saved]. 5 For there is one God, and one mediator between God and men, the man Christ Jesus; 6 who gave himself a ransom for all, to be testified in due time. ... 8 *I (myself pray often, and) exhort that* men pray every where, lifting up holy hands, without wrath and doubting. 9 In like manner also, that women adorn themselves in modest apparel, with shamefacedness and sobriety; not with broided hair, or gold, or pearls, or costly array; 10 but (which becometh women professing godliness) with good *Jesus* works. *I do this in the wisdom of Holy Spirit, firm or gentle, speaking the truth in agape/love, and giving grace by operating in the Gospel, not in the wisdom of men, but by the power of God. Yahoo! Father, this is the Day of Your Salvation, and I am glad, and I rejoice in You by Jesus! Yahoo! Lord, You are good! Your mercy is everlasting! Yahoo! Yahoo!*

29. **Grace and peace to victory** is in me from God my Father, Rev 1:5 "and from Jesus Christ, who is the faithful witness, and the first begotten of the dead, and the prince of the kings of the earth. Unto him that *agape*/loved us, and washed (*dissolved, put off and destroyed from us*) our sins in his own blood, 6 and hath made us kings and priests unto God and his Father; to him be glory and dominion for ever and ever. Amen." Phil 4:19 "*And because the Lord Jesus is my righteousness and my Shepherd,* my God *supplies* all *my* need (*prayer,* aiteo/ *requiring, demanding and expecting as due according to His covenant promises*) according to his riches in glory by Christ Jesus *for I shall not lack of any good thing.* 20 Now unto God and our Father be glory for ever and ever. Amen." Matt 7:11 "*For* if *I* then, … know how to give good gifts unto *my* children, how much more shall *my* Father which is in heaven give good things to *me* that *aiteo*/asks (*requires, demands and expects as due by covenant promise*) of him *by speaking into being what I want of God's covenant promises in the name of Jesus*?" For Jesus said: John 16:23 "… Verily, verily, I say unto you, Whatsoever ye shall *aiteo*/ask (*require, demand and expect as due by covenant promise*) the Father in my name, he will give it you. *So I* 24 … *aiteo*/ask (*require, demand and expect as due by covenant promise*) *in the name of Jesus,* and *I* receive, that *my* joy may be full." So I speak in the name of Jesus to *aiteo*/ask (command, require, demand and expect as due by covenant promise) of my Father God, by speaking to those things that be now not yet as though they were in the name of Jesus. And I do greater things than Jesus because He has gone to the Father. Thank You, Father, in the name of Jesus Christ, thank You! Yahoo!

30. **Father, in Jesus' name,** show me and get me to do what I need to do today in Your priority, and get me and each one of us to overcome evil fear in any form by faith actions. I proclaim, for each one, group and organization, that we walk in righteousness, peace, joy, *dunamis*/power, *agape*/love, godly sound mind, mercy, grace and truth in Holy Spirit in the name of Jesus. Father, make it so. Thank You, Father, in the name of Jesus, thank You! Yahoo!

Myself: _____

Spouse/future mate: _____

Affirmations in Christ

Children: _____

Family: _____

Friends: _____

Government: (*leaders, wars, issues*)

_____

_____

_____

Country: _____

Local and universal Church: (*list churches, and leaders*)

_____

_____

_____

_____

_____

Businesses: (*list companies, people involved and any issues*)

    A. _____

    B. _____

    C. _____

    D. _____

    E. _____

    F. _____

OK, God, Now What?

G. _____

H. _____

I. _____

Ministry/good works: (*Yours and others*)

_____

_____

_____

Other: (*Whoever else is on your heart*)

Jerusalem, Israel_____

_____

_____

_____

31. <u>Phil 2:3</u> I let nothing be done through strife or vainglory; but in lowliness of mind *I* esteem *others* better than *myself*. 4 *I* look not on *just my* own things, *and* also on the things of others. 5 *I* let (*make*) this mind be in *me by Holy Spirit within me*, which was also in Christ Jesus: 6 who, being in the form of God, thought it not robbery to be equal with God: 7 but made himself of no reputation, and took upon him the form of a servant, and was made in the likeness of men: 8 and being found in fashion as a man, he humbled himself, and became obedient unto death, even the death of the cross. *Thank You, Lord Jesus Christ!* 9 Wherefore God also hath highly exalted *Jesus*, and given him a name which is above every name: 10 that at the name of Jesus every knee should bow, of things in heaven, and things in earth, and things under the earth; 11 and that every tongue should confess that Jesus Christ is Lord, to the glory of God the Father. 12 Wherefore, *as one of God's agape*/beloved, *I* always *obey*, not *just in the presence of others, but always*, *I* work out *my* own *soteria*/salvation with fear and trembling *before God*. 13 For it is God which worketh in *me* both

Affirmations in Christ

to will and to do of his good pleasure. 14 *I* do all things without murmurings and disputings: 15 that *I* may be blameless and harmless, *a son of God*, without rebuke, in the midst of a crooked and perverse nation, among whom *I* shine as *a light* in the world; 16 holding forth the word of *zoe*/life; that I may rejoice in the day of Christ, that I have not run in vain, neither laboured in vain. Deut 28:14 And *I do* not go aside from any of the words *of the Lord by the grace of Jesus in me*, to the right hand, or to the left, *I do not* go after other gods to serve them. ... 47 Because *I serve (worship and* zao) the LORD *my* God with joyfulness, and with gladness of heart, for the abundance of all things; *for I do not forget the Lord, for it is God that gives me power to attain wealth. By His grace I am faithful and diligent in all His labors for me, and I am continually thankful for all His prosperity to me.* Rom 8:31 What shall *I* then say to these things? If God be for *me*, who can be against *me*? 32 He that spared not his own Son, but delivered him up for us all, how shall he not with him also freely give *me* all things? 33 Who shall lay any thing to the charge of *me, one of* God's elect? It is God that justifieth (*makes me His righteousness in Jesus forever, as one of His sons*). 34 Who is he that condemneth? It is Christ that died, yea rather, that is risen again, who is even at the right hand of God, who also maketh intercession for *me*. 1 John 2:14 *I* ... am strong *in the Lord and the power of His might*, and the word of God abideth in *me*, and *I* have overcome the wicked one. 15 *I agape*/love not the world, neither the things that are in the world. *For* if any man *agape*/love the world, the *agape*/love of the Father is not in him. *And I keep myself in the agape/love of God through Jesus at all times.* 16 For all that is in the world, the lust of the flesh, and the lust of the eyes, and the pride of *bios*/life, is not of the Father, but is of the world. 17 And the world passeth away, and the lust thereof: but he that doeth the will of God abideth for ever. *So I continually strive to walk in Holy Spirit power, agape/love and the mind of Christ, through my Lord Jesus Christ. Hallelujah! Yahoo! Father, this is the Day of Your Salvation, and I am glad, and I rejoice in You by Jesus Christ! Hallelujah! Lord, You are good! Jesus, You reign through me! Yahoo!*

32. Ps 23:4 "Yea, though I walk through the valley of the shadow of death, I will fear no evil: for *God is* with me (*and in me because of Jesus*); *His* rod and *His* staff they comfort (*and encourage*) me." Ps 91:7 "A thousand shall fall at *my* side, and ten thousand at *my* right hand; but it shall not come nigh *me*. 8 Only with *my* eyes shalt *I* behold and see the reward of the wicked [*devil and all his works*]. 9 Because *I have* made the LORD, which is my refuge, even the most High, *my* habitation." Because all the works

of the devil will be destroyed by me, for I am sent into the Valley of the Shadow of death to wield the rod and staff of God, by faith actions, working by *agape*/love, just as Jesus did, to destroy all the works of the devil, in and by the name of Jesus Christ. Because Ps 91:2 "I ... say of the LORD, He is my refuge and my fortress: my God; in him do *I* trust." Yahoo, things may look bad. It may look like the devil is winning, but I say, "Let us go and make some Peace in Jesus!" Because: Rom 16:20 "...the God of peace shall bruise Satan under *my* feet *as shattered glass. The grace of our Lord Jesus Christ is* with *me [to know, be and do this]. Amen, so be it."* Yahoo! Father, this is the Day of Your Salvation, and I am glad, and I rejoice in You by Jesus Christ! Thank You, Father, in the name of Jesus Christ. Thank You! Hallelujah! Father, You reign through me, in and by Jesus Christ! Hallelujah!

33. James 1:2 *I* count it all joy (*in faith actions*) when *I* fall into divers temptations (*trials, tests, bad news, evil reports, lack, delays, confusions and strife*); 3 knowing this, that the trying of *my* faith worketh patience (*consistency, standing in grace, faithfulness and reliability*). 4 *So* I let patience (*consistency, standing in grace, faithfulness and reliability*) have her perfect work *in me*, that *I* may be perfect (*mature*) and entire, wanting nothing. *Knowing that* 5 *if I* lack wisdom (*on what to do to succeed, to overcome by Jesus in any evil situation*), *I aiteo*/ask (*require, demand and expect as due by covenant promise*) of God, that giveth to all men liberally, *including me*, and upbraideth not; and it shall be given *me*. 6 *So I aiteo/* ask (*require, demand and expect as due by covenant promise of God*) *in the name of Jesus in faith, as evidenced by thanksgiving, praise, gladness and joy, knowing He hears me because of Jesus, so I stand and fight the devil with* nothing wavering *in my thanksgiving, praise, gladness, joy, consistency, faithfulness, reliability and confessions of praise and confidence in God by His Word. So I stay single minded in and on Jesus like a rock as I* Mark 11:22 ... have faith (*actions*) in God, *and gladly operate in the faith actions of God, so I* say to any mountain (*trial, test, tribulation or unhappy situation*), Be thou removed—*go away*, and *be made a blessing*; and *I do not* doubt in *my* heart, but *I* believe *unto thanksgiving, praise and joy* that those things which *I do say* shall come to pass; *I* shall have whatsoever *I say of God's covenant promises in the name of Jesus*. 24 *For Jesus said*, What things soever *I aiteo*/desire (*require, demand and expect as due of God's covenant promises, which are His perfect will, and I know He hears*), when *I* pray, *I* believe (*unto thanksgiving, praise and joy*) that *I lambano*/receive them, and *I* shall have (*posses*) them. 1 John 5:14 And this is the confidence that *I* have in him, that, if *I aiteo*/ask any thing according to his will, he heareth *me*: 15 and *I* know that he *hears me*, whatsoever *I aiteo*/ask (*by keeping on requiring, demanding and expecting as due of His covenant promises*), *therefore I* know that *I* have the petitions that *I aiteo/*

desired (*required, demanded and expected as due of His covenant promises*) of him, *because His covenant promises are His perfect will in any situation, and I will have them as* I lambano *them in thanksgiving, praise and joy, and I draw upon His agape/ love, faithfulness and indwelling Holy Spirit as a fully-funded bank account.* James 1:9 *So when things look bad, as if the love and power of God have failed,* I rejoice in that *I am chosen and* exalted *to stand in Jesus against any evil and bring Heaven to Earth now. ... For I know that I am* 12 blessed *as I endure* temptation: for when *I am* tried, *I shall* lambano/receive the crown of zoe/life, which the Lord hath promised to them that *agape*/love him. 13 *I do not say, in these temptations, trials and tests, that* I am tempted of God: for God cannot be tempted with evil, neither tempteth he any man: 14 but *I know when I am* tempted *to doubt God by evil intensity, delay and harassment of fear and dread, the devil is tempting me to be* drawn away of *my* own lust, and enticed. 15 Then when lust hath conceived, it bringeth forth sin: and sin, when it is finished, bringeth forth death. 16 *So I do not err, for as one of the agape*/beloved brethren, *I know that* 17 every good gift and every perfect gift is from above, and cometh down from the Father of lights, with whom is no variableness, neither shadow of turning. 18 Of his own will begat he *me* with the word of truth ... 19 Wherefore, *as one of the agape*/beloved brethren, *I am* swift to hear, slow to speak, slow to wrath: 20 for the wrath of man worketh not the righteousness of God. 21 Wherefore *I* lay apart all filthiness and superfluity of naughtiness, and *lambano*/receive with meekness the engrafted word, which is able to *sozo*/save *my soul unto thankful and glad godly patience, praise and faithfulness.* 22 For I am a doer of the word; [one Rom 5:17 ... which (*continually*) *lambano*/receives [*by faith actions*] abundance of grace and of the *permanent* gift of righteousness *to* reign in *zoe*/life by one, Jesus Christ, *no matter what the devil does in the Valley of the Shadow of Death, and thus keep myself from being deceived.*] 25 *So* I look into the perfect law of liberty *of righteousness in Christ Jesus to* agape/love *others as myself for Father God, and continue* therein, *and* being not a forgetful hearer, but a doer of the work [*of counting it all joy in all temptations, trials and tests*], I shall be blessed *to see the glory of God, as* I lambano *God in His Word by continual faith actions, to overcome in any evil situation for myself and others.* 26 *... So* I bridle my tongue, *and keep my heart from being deceived and, instead, walk in* 27 pure religion and undefiled before God and the Father ... , *by visiting* the fatherless and widows in their affliction, and *keeping myself* unspotted from the world. 1 John 5:11 And this is the record, that God hath given to us eternal *zoe*/life, and this *zoe*/life is in his Son. 12 He that hath the Son hath *zoe*/life; and he that hath not the Son of God hath not *zoe*/life. 13 These things have *been* written unto *me* that *believe* on the name of the Son of God; that *I* may know that *I* have eternal *zoe*/life, and that *I* may believe on the name of the Son of God, *to* agape/love *God by* standing in evil days to overcome, and to agape/love my neighbor as a way to agape/love God. 1 Cor 15:10 *For by the grace of God I am what I am, a new creation in Christ Jesus: and his grace which was bestowed upon me was not in vain; but I labor more abundantly than they all, to walk in all the ways of God, including never getting offended or bitter in God, but always counting it all joy in temptation, trial or test, and giving thanks and praise in all things, in the strength of the Lord: yet not I, but the grace of God which is with me. Thank You, Holy Spirit! You are my strength! Thank You, Father God, and thank You, Lord Jesus Christ, for the gift of Holy Spirit dwelling in me! Thank You! Thank You for agape/loving me! Thank You!*

34. **I am a Christian, called to be a** businessperson, for finance and business is in every part of life, and I am born of Holy Spirit of God. I am a child of God. Gal 2:20 "I am *(have been)* crucified with Christ: nevertheless I zao/live; yet not I, but Christ zao/liveth in me: and the life which I now zao/live in the flesh I zao/live by the faith *(actions) in* the Son of God, who agape/loved me, and gave himself for me. 21 I do not frustrate the grace of God: for if righteousness come by the law, then Christ is dead in vain." So I am righteous by faith in the Son of God, Jesus, my Lord, whom Father God raised from the dead, and not my works. I am born again of the nature of God; in every way He is manifesting His zoe/life in me to will and to do of His good pleasure, and to be everything good, perfect, pure, lovely, just, of good report and of great integrity. I am agape/loved. God rejoices over me with joy. God is helping me in all ways. Father continually sends me His wisdom and divine appointments for every aspect of my life, and by His grace I receive them, bless them and make them blessings for others. No matter how distracted or tired I feel, I rise up and delight myself in the Lord. Whatever the situation I do not accuse and stop at finding fault, but get the wisdom of Father God to heal and deliver the situation to His glory, in faith actions working by agape/love. Thank You, Holy Spirit! Yahoo!

35. **I am a Christian businessman/woman**, ethical, moral and righteous in all my dealings. I help people in business situations. I am an agent of God's love. I make money for good. God teaches me to prosper. 2 Chron 26:5 "... *I always and continually seek God (by faith actions) ... and God makes me to prosper.*" Deut 8:18 "*I continually* remember the LORD *my* God: for it is he that giveth *me* power to get wealth, that he may establish his covenant *through me* which he sware unto *my* fathers ... ." I walk in: Prov 10:22 "The blessing of the LORD, it maketh *me and mine* rich, and he addeth no sorrow with it." For the Lord's plan and desire for me is that: 3 John 2 "*I, as one of the agape/beloved, that* above all things *I may* prosper and be in health, even as *my* soul prospereth. 3 ... And I walk in the truth*" and the agape/love of the truth in all aspects of our great

salvation in Jesus. I operate in God's Spirit of excellence in all things. I make win-win-win deals in every possible situation. I encourage everyone I meet and relate to. I am happy and confident of God's leading and helping me in every way to do His will. I am unstoppable in God to make Heaven on Earth. I can do what I dream to do, for I dream godly dreams. I sow clear, godly goals. I have wonderful goals of God. It is so much fun, joy and excitement to walk in His *agape*/love, not by sight, but in faith actions working by *agape*/love. Hallelujah! Lord, You are good! Yahoo!

36. **I care about people, and people care about me**. I like people. I relate well to people. I am friendly, active, energetic, positive, creative, faithful, understanding, optimistic, gladly diligent and reliable. I keep my word to my own hurt, so I am careful in what I say. I love Father God and hear and gladly obey His Word by His Spirit dwelling in me. I am thankful to God all the time; and I give thanks by Christ Jesus in all situations, knowing that giving thanks with excitement is always the will of God for me. I walk in smiles all day, every day. I am humorous. I am a good friend and give praise often. I layer every criticism with blessing and praise and give grace for God's best answer, no matter what. Every day in every way I am getting better and better in every way. Ps 147:11 "The Lord taketh pleasure in *me* for *I fear* him, *I hope* in his *chesed*/mercy." Ps 100:5 "For the Lord is good; his *chesed*/mercy is everlasting; and his truth endureth to all generations." I walk in His meekness. When things do not go right, per His Word, I immediately turn to Him and seek Him by faith actions, and He gives me His wisdom to prosper in the situation and with the people involved. I regularly stop during the day and get out of my seat to give thanks and rejoice in the Lord. I delight in knowing Jesus in spirit and in truth by faith actions. I walk in the joy of the Lord, knowing: Phil 4:13 "I can do all things through Christ which strengtheneth me." Neh 8:10 "… For the joy of the Lord is *my* strength." So no matter how bad it gets in any evil day, taking the Word of God as my sword in faith actions, I keep myself stirred up in God by thinking on the wonderful things He has given me in Jesus, the dominion of His name, and give thanks, dance and rejoice to victory over any work of the devil, in the name of Jesus, knowing Jesus is Lord of Heaven and Earth. I magnify Jesus, who does triumph through me. Yahoo! Lord, You are good! Yahoo! Yahoo!

37. **I have the best deal in the Universe**; the God of the Universe has chosen me in His Son Jesus and put His love on me. I am looked after and cared for by God Himself. He has completed everything I will ever need in Jesus for me. My blessing include (*make your own list for today*):

_____

_____

_____

_____

_____

_____

38. By grace I weigh _____. I control my eating. I lost/gained the _____ I needed to weigh _____. I diet as necessary to keep at _____. I exercise in some way daily to keep in good physical shape. I eat only nutritious, good foods. I eat what my body needs. I like myself. I am a <u>man/woman</u> of faith actions. I study, learn and obey God's Word as a doer of the Word. I praise, pray, rejoice and worship the Lord God every day, all day long, good or bad. And, whether I am doing well or not, I hold on to Father God in His Word no matter what, to the terror of my enemies. <u>Rom 5:8</u> *For* God commendeth his *agape*/love toward us, in that, while we were yet sinners, Christ died for us. 9 Much more then, being now justified by his blood, we shall be *sozo*/saved from wrath through him. 10 For if, when we were enemies, we were reconciled to God by the death of his Son, much more, being reconciled, we shall be *sozo*/saved by his *zoe*/life. 11 And not only so, but we also joy in God through our Lord Jesus Christ, by whom we have now received the atonement (*reconciliation*). <u>Rom 8:35</u> Who shall separate us from the *agape*/love of Christ? shall tribulation, or distress, or persecution, or famine, or nakedness, or peril, or sword? 36 As it is written, For thy sake we are killed all the day long; we are accounted [*by our enemies*] as sheep for the slaughter. 37 Nay, in all these things we are more than conquerors [*over these enemies*] through him that *agape*/loved us. 38 For I am persuaded, that neither death, nor *zoe*/life, nor angels, nor principalities, nor powers, nor things present, nor things to come, 39 nor height, nor depth, nor any other creature, shall be able to separate us from the *agape*/love of God, which is in Christ Jesus our Lord. *I am* agape/*loved! And, in that* agape/*love, I triumph over the devil and all his work, in the name of Jesus! And in that* agape/*love, I* agape/*love people with the* agape/*love of Jesus. Hallelujah! Hallelujah! Yahoo!*

39. I plan and make all commitments ahead of time, knowing Jesus is Lord indeed. I keep my word to my own hurt. I make only valid promises. I always think things

Affirmations in Christ

through. I speak only as necessary. I make both long- and short-term plans to keep the vision in focus, for me and all my partners. I listen, watch, observe and learn. I sell well. I negotiate well any issue. I work hard. I work smart. I work efficiently. I use time exceedingly well. I am a rainmaker. I create and find deals and make them happen, creating blessing for all involved. I work as a team leader. I respect people, and I am a good manager. I am a good judge of character and can enroll people into good godly visions that get implemented. I build people up for their good. I am fearless and bold. I am firm and confident. I am fair and just. I am honest. I am diplomatic. I am a team leader and a team builder. I continually think about how to give (and do give) words of grace in any situation, that encourage people to do the will of God gladly. Lord, You are good! Yahoo!

40. **I manage my budgets actively** and by looking to the future. I make profit in all my passive and active businesses. I am a blessing to all who deal with me in any way. I bless all who deal with me in any way. I am faithful, reliable, competent and smart. I am intelligent, calm, kind, generous and courageous and relentless in bringing God's best to any situation. I walk in *agape*/love and keep myself stirred up to walk in the Kingdom of God, to walk in righteousness, peace, joy, *dunamis*/power, *agape*/love, sound mind, mercy, grace and truth in Holy Spirit, in the name of Jesus. Praise You, Father, for Christ in me! I act wisely. I talk wisely. I think wisely. I Prov 7:4 "say unto (*God's*) wisdom [*in His Word*], Thou art my sister; and call understanding [*of the ways of God*] my kinswoman." I spend money wisely. I delay instant gratification; I bring in wonderful long-term results. I sow long-term seeds, in faith actions working by *agape*/love. Praise You, Father, for Christ in me the hope of Your glory! Hallelujah! Holy Spirit is using me to demonstrate the best in a Christian businessman/woman and prophet. I love my family and relate to each one as a wonderful gift and lovingly help mature them in Jesus, knowing Jesus is my Lord and Judge. Lord, You are good! Yahoo!

41. **I make God and the Bible exciting** and joyous for my family and loved ones: I am blessed with my (family): _____

_____

_____

_____

_____.

I am blessed in every way. I prosper and am in health as my soul is prosperous in the Lord. If it is to be, it is up to me in Jesus, for Father God has already done His part. I now do my part. I am courageous and bold in God, and He strengthens me. Heb 4:11 *"I labour therefore to enter into that rest of God; [I fight and overcome unbelief with prayer, including tongues, aiteo, proclamation, fasting, thanksgiving, praise, joy and worship in spirit and truth, and rightly dividing His Word of truth in the Scriptures by Holy Spirit.]* 12 For the word of God is quick, and powerful, and sharper than any twoedged sword, piercing even to the dividing asunder of soul and spirit, and of the joints and marrow, and is a discerner of the thoughts and intents of the heart. 13 Neither is there any creature that is not manifest in his sight: but all things are naked and opened unto the eyes of him with whom we have to do. 14 Seeing then that *I* have a great high priest, that is passed into the heavens, Jesus the Son of God, *I* hold fast *my* profession *in Him as my Lord and my Savior, my in-dwelling King."* For greater is He, Jesus Christ by His Spirit that is in me, than he that is in the world. I walk in the active awareness and glad obedience of Jesus' presence, Lordship, *agape*/love, victory and triumph in faith actions more every day.

42. **The Lord Jesus brings me good business** deals, deals so good I don't even have to work at them to make money. I AM SUCCESSFUL IN EVERY PART OF LIFE TO GOD'S GLORY. I am successful spiritually and physically. I am successful emotionally and relationally. I am successful in my family and financially. I am successful in God, by Holy Spirit, in the name of Jesus Christ, my Lord and my righteousness. The Lord sends out His angels to bring me good deals and wisdom. I have God's wisdom in dealing with every part of life. I am prepared more every day in every way to be a righteous, godly businessman/woman, _____, husband/wife, father/mother, brother/sister, uncle/aunt, cousin, friend, worker and minister of the Gospel in faith actions working by *agape*/love, to the glory of Father God, by Jesus Christ, in the grace of Holy Spirit.

43. **I deal well with difficult people**. I mollify the angry and move the slow; I am an expert at the soft answer that turns away wrath. I am diplomatic. I listen well. I pause before I speak. I praise specific acts. I praise often. I am thankful to God and people. I am a "can-do" man/woman. I am an expert at effectively exhorting and encouraging others to move forward in their lives, God and in our projects. I never murmur or complain. Instead, I seek the Lord in faith actions, get His instruction, and gladly do what He says with Him.

44. **I have an incredible, wonderful sense** of timing and appropriate urgency and priorities. I do the right things rightly. I bring solutions to problems and

help deliver them. I act as quickly as needed, in God's wisdom. I act ahead of time. I think through ahead of time. I make lists of all possible actions. I think on paper. Hab 2:2 "And the LORD answered me, and said, Write the vision, and make it plain upon tables, that he may run that readeth it." I am very patient and prudent. I easily enroll and keep people enrolled in my projects, for I know that with the help of others I can do so much more. Therefore I respect and honor people at all times. Lord, You are good! Yahoo!

45. **I am a free flow of God's wisdom** and knowledge, because I learn and do the actions as necessary for success in knowing Jesus, in knowing Father God, in knowing Holy Spirit, in knowing the promises of God, in family success, in business success, in people success, in ministry success and in creative success.

46. **I am persistent. I wait. I plan.** I perform and I invest successfully for the long term. I deal in twenty-year time frames. I build for generations, today and tomorrow. I am responsible for my life, therefore I call on God by the name of Jesus, and I have faith actions in Him. I can do it! I have all things pertaining to *zoe*/life and godliness. Every job or relationship is an assignment from God to bring His glory to that situation and make Heaven on Earth by faith actions. I regularly find and am given good business deals. I am an expert in money management and financing. I manage and pay my bills on time. I manage my personal finances for profit. I keep an excellent credit rating. I talk easily and readily with bankers, business, scientific, engineering, medical, governmental and church leaders of all kinds. I treat each person as a gift of God. I have so much good business that I can freely give good deals to others. I am blessed in all aspects of money growth. Lord, You are good! Yahoo!

47. **I make $ _____ this year.** I am an excellent employee, contractor, partner and boss. The Lord creates events so that my bosses, partners and employees are blessed that they have me. I do the right things rightly at the right time, and I teach others to do the same. I plan in detail every event. The Lord fills in every loose end and encourages both my study and my confidence in Him. I keep my heart clean with His Word every day. I do well in my job; and I do well in my businesses. I do well in my family; and I do well in Christian ministry. I manage all parts of my life in proper order. The Lord opens right doors for me and closes doors that are not for me. **Ps 23:1** "The LORD is my shepherd; I shall not want. 2 He maketh me to lie down in green pastures: he leadeth me beside the still waters. 3 He restoreth my soul: he leadeth me in the paths of righteousness for his name's sake. 4 Yea, though I walk through the valley of the shadow of death, I will fear no evil; for thou are with me;

for thy rod and thy staff they comfort (*and encourage*) me. 5 Thou preparest a table before me in the presence of mine enemies: thou anointest my head with oil; my cup runneth over. 6 Surely goodness and *chesed*/mercy shall follow, (*pursue and overtake*) me all the days of my life: and I will dwell in the house of the LORD for ever." Because Jesus is my Shepherd, I meet, become friends with and work with all the necessary people to make me succeed in my jobs, relationships, ministries and businesses. Praise Father God's grace! Gal 2:19 "For I through the law am dead to the law, that I might *zao*/live unto God. 20 I am (*have been*) crucified with Christ: nevertheless I *zao*/live; yet not I, but Christ *zao*/liveth in me: and the life which I now *zao*/live in the flesh I *zao*/live by the faith (*actions*) *in* the Son of God, who *agape*/loved me, and gave himself for me. 21 I do not frustrate the grace of God: for if righteousness come by the law, then Christ is dead in vain." Praise God, for His promises are for me in Jesus, in spite of me, but because of Jesus! Lord, You are good! Yahoo!

48. I am helping people and making the world a better place in everything I do. I make enough money from my businesses so that I will double my job income by _____. I love only my wife/husband. I love my children. I like myself. I am loved and I am lovable. The God of All Love redeemed me with the soul, flesh and blood of His Son, Jesus my Lord. Thank You, Father God, in the name of Jesus, Thank You! I am knowing You in spirit and in truth more every day! Father, You have set my value as worth the soul, spirit, body and blood of Jesus. Thank You for making me awesome and valuable in You! Thank You for putting me in the triumph of Jesus! Yahoo! Yahoo! Yahoo!

49. I concentrate on solving problems and making things better. I find excellent solutions. I work with others to find even better solutions. I act on solutions. I count all problems as joy, knowing that Father God is working in each one of them for my and our good. I know each problem has a lesson, and I learn the lessons from each event, each problem or difficulty. Every problem is given me to believe God and to co-labor with Father God to overcome, to His glory in Jesus. I humble myself to co-labor with Him. I am getting the lessons necessary for me and mine to accomplish my and our goals and calling of God. I use every event as part of a process to improve me in God. I learn from them, and I see them through Jesus' eyes. 1 Cor 10:13 "There hath no temptation taken *me* but such as is common to man: but God is faithful, who will not suffer *me* to be tempted above that *I am* able; but will with the temptation also make a way *for me* to escape, that *I* may be able to bear it [*unto triumph in Him*]. 14 Wherefore, *as one of the* dearly *agape*/beloved, *I* flee from idolatry." And *I am diligent in my heart to have no other source than Father God, who gives me all things to enjoy.* Rom 8:28 "For I know that all things work together for good to them that *agape*/love God, to them who are the called according to his purpose." I am called according to His purpose in *zoe* life in Christ Jesus, and I love God by *lambano*ing His Word in continual faith actions, counting it all joy, and loving others in the midst of trails to release His *zoe*/life. I get wisdom straight from the mouth of God in His Word and by His Spirit; and I obey that wisdom gladly. I seek the Lord regularly. I turn to prayer first. I follow the Lord. I cut through the demonic confusions and perversions, to see God's will and glory in each event and situation. Since God is for me, who can be against me? God is on my side, who can I fear? I am so loved that Father God sent Jesus to die for me, and to heal and prosper every part of my life. I love obedience to the Lord. I am blessed of God. I am born again, and my whole house (with extended family) shall be *sozo*/saved, for I believe by faith actions on Jesus. Jesus is my Lord and Lord of all my life in every way. I gladly walk in all His ways, in the fear of the Lord, just like Jesus. Praise God for His awesome work in me, to know Him in me more and more. Praise the Lord Jesus in me!

50. **I am bold, strong and courageous** in the Lord. I am confident Father God is getting me everything I need to be a success. I am a giver and doer of good. I know the Lord, and I love the Lord. I hold on to God in His promises like a rock. I face fear in any form readily, in the *agape*/love and strength of the Lord. I am brave, eager and wise. I face evil fear with love, faith actions, preparation, activity, thanksgiving, praise, *aiteo* prayer and walk in the Kingdom of God in Holy Spirit righteousness, peace, joy, power, *agape*/love, sound mind, mercy, grace and truth. I seek God for wisdom in all things and for anything. God freely gives me the wisdom to do the things necessary for the best results. God gets through to me what I am to do; and I carefully and gladly do those things He wants, for I am born of *agape*/love. Thank You, Father! Yahoo!

51. **God is for me**. God is my Helper and my Friend; and I am a friend and helper to Him. I am brave and bold in Jesus. Nothing can stand against me for Father God, the God of the Universe, is with me. I count fear as joy because I see the glory and *agape*/love of the Lord triumph over all fear by my faith actions. I know I am loved, and perfect love casts out fear. Praise You, Lord! You are for me! I am prosperous in all aspects of life. I am a success in You. I am a success in Jesus. I am unbeatable in, through, by and with Christ. I am unstoppable in all parts of life to God's glory, and to bring Heaven to Earth. I am always moving forward in Jesus. I believe I can make good out of any situation. I see good and opportunity in each problem. I am healthy, fit, and feel good. I exercise. I am wealthy in love, faith actions, the power of God and finances. I like me. I *zao* and breathe God, in all situations, to His glory. Yahoo!

52. **Every rest or delay is preparing me** to move. I am a man/woman of faith and action. I fast and pray. I give alms and forgiveness readily. I am one of God's peacemakers. I worship Him and rejoice in spirit and truth. I invest well, and I manage well. I love well, and I work well, for I am born again of God by grace through Jesus Christ my Lord. I like me. God likes me. I love me. God loves me. I am the head and not the tail. I see ahead of others and get God's wisdom for success and faithful endurance to thanksgiving and joy. I lend to others. I am blessed and highly favored of God. Father God is for me to succeed! I am the apple of His eye! If God sees anyone, He sees me and mine, to our good. I gladly stay in the Word of Christ in all situations by faith actions. I obey God by trying every thought to see if it is of God in Jesus, and then I obey Him. Praise the power of God by His Spirit in me! Yahoo!

53. **I am unstoppable in Jesus!** I work well with people, and people work well with me. I like everyone I meet and work with. I see their value, as God sees their value. I am an excellent negotiator. I get excellent terms. I get excellent prices. I find out what the other party wants, why and when, and then I make win-win deals. I am persistent. I pull victory from defeat. I pull success from failure. I think, and then I act. I am a son of God by grace through faith in Jesus Christ and His blood, justified, glorified, sealed with Holy Spirit unto the Day of Redemption, to subdue and establish dominion for God in every part of life. I am perfected in *agape*/love, and I wash out fear every day by faith actions, to the glory of God, and keep myself in knowing His *agape*/love and goodness toward me and all mankind by faith actions. By Jesus, I am His agent, His representative, His extension on Earth, for I know: 1 John 4:17 "Herein is *my agape*/love made perfect, that *I* may have boldness in the day of judgment: because as he is, so *am I* in this world." I am likable and people like me. People help me. I defuse hostility. I settle problems. I see issues from the other person's viewpoint. I meet their needs. I get along with difficult people. I ask excellent questions. I first restate the views and issues of the unhappy and disputers, to clarify and seek to understand their point of view, and then I work with them to find solutions. I win and keep people's trust. I build instant rapport. I win friends and influence people easily. I am good on my feet in strange situations and always say things to add God's grace to the situation. I am a good friend. I like me. I am blessed! Father God is working on me and in me, both to will and to do of His good pleasure, for my success in Jesus! God *agape*/loves me so much He sent Jesus to die for me in *agape*/love! Thank You, Father, for writing my name in Heaven!

Affirmations in Christ

54. I am connected to God in Jesus, and an extension of Father God in Jesus by Holy Spirit on the Earth now. For in this Day of Salvation I know John 14:20 ...that *Jesus is in the Father, and I am in Jesus, and Jesus is in me.* 21 *I have* Jesus' commandments, and *I keep* them, *to walk in* agape/loving *Him: knowing that as I walk in* agape/love *that I agape/love Jesus, and I am agape/loved of our Father God, and Jesus will agape/love me, and will manifest Himself to* [*me in relationship, signs, wonders and confirming His Word of grace*]. *I study to make myself approved as a superior workman in preaching and delivering the grace of God by the name of Jesus.* Acts 14:3 *For wherever I abide I am continually* speaking boldly in the Lord, which *gives* testimony unto the word of his grace, and *grants* signs and wonders to be done by *my* hands, *words and thoughts. I am of the* 1 John 3:21 agape/beloved, if [*because of my faith actions in the propitiation in the blood of Jesus*], *my* heart condemns me not, *thus I* have confidence toward God. *And I continually walk in great confidence in God in His Word.* 22 And whatsoever *I* aiteo/ask (*demand, require and expect as due by covenant promise*), *I* lambano/receive of him, because *I* keep his commandments, and do those things that are pleasing in his sight [*by believing that He is, and that He is a rewarder of me that diligently seeks Him*]. 23 And this is his commandment, That *I* should believe on the name of his Son Jesus Christ, and *agape*/love one another, as he gave us commandment. *And I keep myself in the Word of Christ: of Christ in me the hope of glory. Continually* 2 Cor 13:5 *I* examine *myself*, whether *I* be in the faith; *I* prove *my own self to see if I am,* ... *knowing* how that Jesus Christ is in *me* ... , *to keep my faith powerful and effective in the supernatural power of God, to demonstrate the Kingdom of God as Jesus and the early believers and apostles did, and other believers do. For Holy Spirit* 1 John 5:13 ... *has* written unto *me* that *continually believe* on the name of the Son of God, *Jesus Christ of Nazareth;* that *I* may know that *I* have eternal zoe/life, and that *I am freely encouraged by Holy Spirit to use and* believe on the name of the Son of God. 14 And this is the confidence that *I* have in him, that, if *I* aiteo/ask (*demand, require, and expect*) any thing according to his will, *His covenant promises,* he heareth *me:* 15 and *I* know that he *hears me in thoughts, words and acts of* agape/love *of* whatsoever *I* aiteo/ask (*keep on demanding, requiring, and expecting as due by covenant promise*) *for myself, mine or others, I* know that *I* have the petitions that *I* aiteo/desired (*demanded, required and expected*) of him, *because He hears me to perform His Word. And thus* zoe/life *flows through me as a river of* zao/*living waters to make Heaven on Earth, to set people free in any situation, and I continually* aiteo/ask *and keep on asking* (*demanding, requiring and expecting*) *God to perform His covenant promises.* John 3:34 For *I* whom God hath sent, *I* speak the words of God: for God giveth not the Spirit by measure unto *me. For Jesus said to me:* Matt 18:18 Truly I (*Jesus*) tell you, whatever *I* forbid and declare to be improper and unlawful on earth must be what is already forbidden in heaven *as decreed by Father's covenant promises in the Scriptures,* and whatever *I loose,* permit and declare proper and lawful on earth must be what is already permitted in heaven *as decreed by Father's covenant promises in the Scriptures.* AMP *And thus I fulfill,* Matt 6:9 *for I continually* after this manner therefore pray... : Our Father which art in heaven. Hallowed be thy name. 10 Thy kingdom come. Thy will be done in earth, as it is in heaven. 11 Give us this day our daily *physical, soulish and spiritual* bread. *For* Eph 1:3 blessed be the God and Father of our Lord Jesus Christ, who hath blessed us with all spiritual blessings in heavenly places in Christ, *for me to bring and to make Heaven on Earth by* aiteo/*asking (continually demanding, requiring and expecting Him to perform His covenant promises) in faith actions working by* agape/*love. So I* Matt 10:7 preach, saying, The kingdom of heaven is at hand. *And He confirms His words of grace of His reconciliation in Jesus so that when I* 8 heal the sick, *Jesus heals them now, when I* cleanse the lepers, *Jesus cleanses them now; when I* raise the dead, *Jesus raises them now; when I* cast out devils, *Jesus casts them out now, when I restore the maimed, Jesus restores the maimed:* for freely I have lambano/ received, freely I give. *Praise God! I refuse to be harassed by dread or fear when I aiteo or pray. Instead I live in the moment, with absolute certainty that God cannot lie. He will move, as I aiteo in the name of Jesus for Him, for Jesus paid for our healing with His stripes, Holy Spirit dwells in me, and for every situation, God wants more good than I can think or imagine, and no situation is greater than God who raises the dead and makes the blind to see.* Matt 17:20 And Jesus *continually says* unto me, ... For verily I (*Jesus*) say unto you, If ye have faith (*actions*) as a grain of mustard seed, ye shall say unto this mountain, Remove hence to yonder place; and it shall remove; and nothing shall be impossible unto you. *And I am of great faith actions and confidence in God because I am redeemed by the blood of Jesus, and by His grace I do speak and those mountains do move in the name of Jesus. So I aiteo, knowing* Luke 1:37 for with God nothing is ever impossible and no word from God shall be without power or impossible of fulfillment. AMP Jer 1:12 *For* the Lord *says* unto me, Thou hast well seen: for I will hasten my word to perform it. 2 Cor 5:17 Therefore if any man be in Christ, he is a new creature: old things are passed away; behold, all things are become new. 18 And all things are of God, who hath reconciled us to himself by Jesus Christ, and hath given to *me* the ministry of reconciliation; 19 to wit, that God was in Christ, reconciling the world unto himself, not imputing their trespasses unto them; and hath committed unto *me* the word of reconciliation. 20 Now then *I am an ambassador* for Christ, as though God did beseech *all men* by *me*: I pray *them* [*in words and deeds of Holy Spirit*], in Christ's stead, be ye reconciled to God. 21 For *Father God* hath made *Jesus* to be sin for us, who knew no sin; that we might be made the righteousness of God in him. 6:1 *I,* then, as *a worker (and co-laborer*) together with *Father God*, beseech *all men* also that *they* receive not the grace of God in vain. 2 (For *Father God* saith, I have heard thee in a time accepted, and in the day of *soteria*/salvation have I succoured thee: behold, now is the accepted time; behold, now is the day of *soteria*/salvation.) *Praise God for the name of Jesus and faith in that name by which we must be sozo/saved. Praise You, Father God, for Your Word and Your* agape/love *to me. Thank You!*

55. **When I *aiteo*/pray for needs, Father God meets them.** Phil 4:13 "I can do all things through Christ which strengtheneth me. ... 19 *For* my God shall supply all *my* need (aiteo *demands per His covenant promises, for they are all Yes and Amen in Christ Jesus,*) according to his riches in glory by Christ Jesus. 20 Now unto God and our Father be glory for ever and ever. Amen." For I walk in great confidence in God in His Word, in great faith in Jesus, in great confidence in the work of Jesus by the cross, in great confidence, courage, faith and boldness in the name of Jesus to extend His Kingdom of *agape*/love on the Earth. Phil 2:10 "That at the name of Jesus every knee should bow, of things in heaven, and things in earth, and things under the earth; 11 and that every tongue should confess that Jesus Christ is Lord, to the glory of God the Father." Acts 3:16 "And his name, *the name of Jesus of Nazareth,* through faith (*actions*) in his name, *makes anyone I minister to* strong, *healed, whole, safe and delivered of any oppression of the devil, and those who* see and know: yea *we all confess*: the faith which is by *Jesus* hath given *this person or these people* this perfect soundness *of the glory of God by Holy Spirit* in the presence of them all." James 4:6 "But *God* giveth more grace. Wherefore he saith, God resisteth the proud, but giveth grace unto the humble. *I humble myself by doing it God's way and 7 I* submit *myself* therefore to God, *by resisting* the devil *and not the people in the situation*, and he, *the devil,* will flee from *me.*" For Jesus commanded that I constantly: Luke 10:19 "behold, *am aware of, focus on and have confidence in that fact that,* Jesus gave unto *me exousia*/power (*authority, commission, pre-permission and the resources of Heaven*) to tread on serpents and scorpions, and over all the *dunamis*/power (*ability*) of the enemy: and nothing shall by any means hurt *me.* 20 Notwithstanding in this *I* rejoice not, that the spirits are subject unto *me;* but rather *I* rejoice, because *my name is* written in heaven." Hallelujah! Glory to God! So, in any situation, I keep focused on being an extension of God's *agape*/love, by the gift of righteousness and the abundance of grace, to the measure of Christ and by Holy Spirit within me. For I can do nothing to be worthy of the power of God and His indwelling Holy Spirit in me, and no sin is so great that He has not already paid for it with the blood of Jesus. And just like my Brother, my Example whom I am to imitate, my Lord Jesus, whose

I am and whom I serve in righteousness, peace and joy in Holy Spirit, Acts 10:38 "... God anointed *me in* Jesus of Nazareth with the Holy Ghost and with power: *and I go* about doing good, and healing all that *are* oppressed (*under the active rule and lordship*) of the devil; for God *is* with *me.*" And He is with me to do even greater works than Jesus, because Jesus has risen and sits at the right hand of the Father now. I am part of Jesus and, by grace, I do what Jesus would do the way He would do it, and He does it though me. I know this because the Bible says so. I am redeemed by the blood of Jesus, the Lamb of God, who took away the sin of the world. Jesus got the job done, the power of sin and death has been broken, and He is seated in Heaven with the Father, and I am there with Him, by grace, to minister His reconciliation on Earth now. I have a calling and a destiny that few dream of, and it is already mine to walk in Jesus. Eph 2:8 "For by grace *I am sozo/* saved through faith; and that not of *myself*: it is the gift of God: 9 not of works, lest any man should boast. 10 For *I am Father God's* workmanship, created in Christ Jesus unto good works, which *Father* God hath before ordained that *I* should walk in them." And by His grace and the gift of righteousness I do walk in them. Glory to God, who is able to mature me into Jesus, and is maturing me in Jesus, to His glory! Praise You, O God!

56. I minister God's salvation in the *zoe* of God by "breathing in" the attitude of God's promises in confident faith actions working by *agape*/love against the devil and his works, and for those who need the blessing, by delivering God's *zoe* life in faith actions, knowing: John 16:11 ... the ruler (evil genius, prince) of this world [Satan] is judged and condemned and sentence already is passed upon him. AMP So I continually Luke 10:19 behold (*and I am continually filled with the conscious presence of Jesus and His dominion in me*), *for Jesus has* given unto *me* power (*authority, commission, pre-permission and the resources of Heaven*), to tread on serpents and scorpions, and over all the power (*ability*) of the enemy: and nothing shall by any means hurt *me.* 20 Notwithstanding in this *I* rejoice not, that the spirits are subject unto *me*; but rather *I* rejoice, because *my name is* written in heaven. Col 1:12 *So I am* giving thanks (*continually*) unto the Father, which hath made *me* meet to be *a partaker* of the inheritance of the saints in light: 13 who hath delivered *me* from the power of darkness, and hath translated *me* into the kingdom of his *agape*/dear Son: 14 in whom *I* have redemption through his blood, even the forgiveness (*remission, purging, obliteration and putting away*) of sins. Rev 1:5 ... Jesus Christ, who is the faithful witness, and the first begotten of the dead, and the prince of the kings of the earth. Unto him that *agape*/loved us, and washed us from our sins in his own blood, 6 and hath made us kings and priests unto God and his Father; to him be glory and dominion for ever and ever. Amen. ... 17 ... And he (*Jesus*) ... *says to us*, Fear not; I am the first and the last: 18 I am he that *zao*/liveth, and was dead; and, behold, I am *zao*/alive for evermore, Amen; and have the keys of hell and of death. *So I continually bless the* LORD, Ps 103:3 who forgiveth all ... iniquities; who healeth all ... diseases; 4 who redeemeth *my* life from destruction; who crowneth *me* with *chesed*/lovingkindness and *racham*/tender mercies; 5 who satisfieth *my* mouth with good things; so that *my* youth is renewed like the eagle's. 6 The LORD executeth righteousness and judgment [*through me*] for all that are oppressed. *I am a master of any devil or work of the devil, for* 1 John 4:4 *I am* of God, *one of His* little children, and have overcome *the devil's lies and works*: because greater is he that is in *me*, than he that is in the world. Ps 108:13 Through God we shall do valiantly: for he it is that shall tread down our enemies [*through us*]. Ps 144:1 Blessed be the LORD my strength, which teacheth my hands to war, and my fingers to fight, Ps 145:12 to make known to the sons of men his mighty acts, and the glorious majesty of his kingdom. 13 Thy kingdom is an everlasting kingdom, and thy dominion endureth throughout all generations. 14 The LORD upholdeth all that fall, and raiseth up all those that be bowed down. Ps 91:13 *I do* tread upon the lion and adder: the young lion and the dragon *do I* trample under feet. *And Jesus is in me, for me to command the will of God in any situation, and as I command, in the name of Jesus, our Father,* Rom 16:20 ...the God of peace, bruises Satan under *my* feet *as shattered glass*. The grace of our Lord Jesus Christ *is* with *me* [*to know, be and do this*]. Amen. *For the* LORD *says:* Hos 13:14 I will ransom them from the power of the grave; I will redeem them from death: O death, I will be thy plagues; O grave, I will be thy destruction: repentance shall be hid from mine eyes. *Praise God, I have redemption in the blood of Jesus, by faith!* 2 Tim 1:7 For God hath not given *me* the spirit of fear; but of *dunamis*/power, and of *agape*/love, and of a sound mind. 1 Tim 6:12 *I* fight the good fight of faith (*actions*), *I* lay hold on eternal *zoe*/life, whereunto *I am* also called ... . Eph 6:10 ... *I am* strong in the Lord, and in the power of his might, *declaring and preaching His Word of saving grace,* Acts 14:3 ... speaking boldly in the Lord, which *gives* testimony unto the word of his grace, and *grants* signs and wonders to be done by *my* hands [*words and actions*]. Phil 2:5 That *I* may be blameless and harmless, *a son* of God, without rebuke, in the midst of a crooked and perverse nation, among whom *I* shine as *a light* in the world; 16 holding forth the word of *zoe*/life *in Jesus*. Acts 19:12 So that from *my* body *are* brought unto the sick handkerchiefs or aprons, and the diseases *depart* from them, and the evil spirits *go* out of them. *For* <u>Mark 16:20</u> ... the Lord *is* working with *me*, and confirming the word *of His grace and zoe/life* with signs following. Amen. *So be it!* <u>Acts 10:42</u> And he *(Jesus)* commanded *me* to preach unto *all* people, and to testify that it is he which was ordained of God to be the Judge of quick and dead. 43 To him give all the prophets witness, that through his name whosoever believeth in him shall receive remission *(purging, removal, obliteration and putting away)* of sins. *Praise the* L<small>ORD</small>! *Praise You, Father, for Jesus! Praise Jesus! He reigns in, with and through me, in* agape/love, *by faith actions. Praise the* L<small>ORD</small>! *Yahoo! Lord, You are good! Your mercy is everlasting! Yahoo!*

57. **I am a Christian, born again** of the eternal and unstoppable Word of God, anointed and sealed with Holy Spirit, redeemed, justified, glorified and a temple of Holy Spirit right now. I have the same Spirit that Jesus has to do the same things as Jesus did, and even greater, for Jesus has gone to the Father. <u>Gal 3:13</u> Christ hath redeemed *me* from the curse of the law, being made a curse for *me*: for it is written, Cursed is every one that hangeth on a tree: 14 that the blessing of Abraham might come on the Gentiles through Jesus Christ; that *I* might receive the promise of the Spirit through faith. <u>Gal 4:4</u> *For* when the fulness of the time was come, God sent forth his Son *(Jesus of Nazareth)*, made of a woman, made under the law, 5 to redeem them that were under the law, that we might receive the adoption of sons. 6 And because [*I have believed God raised Jesus from the dead unto the righteousness of* zoe/life, *and called Jesus as my Lord unto* soteria/salvation], *God has made me a son*, God hath sent forth the Spirit of his Son into *my heart continually*, crying, Abba *(Daddy)*, Father, *that I am* agape/loved *and belong to God as an* agape/beloved *and dear child, the apple of His eye*. 7 Wherefore *I am* no more a servant, but a son; and if a son, then an heir of God through Christ. *And I speak the words of Jesus when I proclaim the Gospel of grace and truth just like He did, for* <u>Luke 4:18</u> the Spirit of the Lord is upon me, because he hath anointed me to preach the gospel to the poor; he hath sent me to heal the brokenhearted, to preach deliverance to the captives, and recovering of sight to the blind, to set at liberty them that are bruised, 19 to preach the acceptable year of the Lord. *For* <u>2 Cor 6:1</u> *I* then, as *a worker* together with *Father God, I* receive not the grace of God in vain. 2 (For he saith, I have heard thee in a time accepted, and in the day of *soteria*/salvation have I succoured thee: behold, now is the accepted time; behold, now is the day of *soteria*/salvation.) *So I* <u>Rom 5:17</u> ... *(continually) lambano*/receive [*by faith actions*] abundance of grace *in* soteria/*salvation* and of the gift of righteousness *to* reign in *zoe*/life by one, Jesus Christ. <u>2 Cor 5:17</u> Therefore if any man be in Christ, he is a new creature: old things are passed away; behold, all things are become new. *So I am a new creation in Christ Jesus, the workmanship of God*. 18 And all things are

Affirmations in Christ

of God, who hath reconciled us to himself by Jesus Christ, and hath given to *me* the ministry of reconciliation; 19 to wit, that God was in Christ, reconciling the world unto himself, not imputing their trespasses unto them; and hath committed unto *me* the word of reconciliation. 20 Now then *I am an ambassador and extension of Heaven on Earth* for Christ, as … God *does* beseech *all people* by *me*: and *I* pray *all people* in Christ's stead, be ye reconciled to God. 21 For *Father* God hath made *Jesus* to be sin for us, who knew no sin; that we might be made the righteousness of *Father* God in *Jesus*. <u>2 Cor 6:1</u> *I* then, as *a worker* together with him, beseech *all people, including myself,* also that ye receive not the grace of God in vain. 2 (For he saith, I have heard thee in a time accepted, and in the day of *soteria*/salvation have I succoured thee: behold, now is the accepted time; behold, now is the day of *soteria*/salvation.) *I keep myself in constant remembrance*: <u>Acts 13:38</u> Be it known unto you therefore, men and brethren, that through this man (*Jesus*) is preached unto you the forgiveness (*remission, purging, obliteration and removal*) of sins: 39 and by him all that believe are justified from all things, from which ye could not be justified by the law of Moses. <u>Acts 10:42</u> And *Father God has* commanded us to preach unto the people, and to testify that it is he, (*Jesus*) which was ordained of God to be the Judge of quick and dead. 43 To him give all the prophets witness, that through his name whosoever believeth in him shall receive remission (*purging, removal, washing, obliteration and putting away*) of sins. Hallelujah! Praise the Living God and His Living Word, Jesus Christ!

58. <u>Ps 91:1</u> "He that dwelleth in the secret place of the most High shall abide under the shadow of the Almighty. 2 I will say of the Lord, He is my refuge and my fortress: my God; in him I *do* trust (*by continual faith actions*). 3 Surely he shall deliver *me* from the snare of the fowler, and from the noisome pestilence. 4 He shall cover *me* with his feathers, and under his wings *I do* trust (*by faith actions*): his truth *is my* shield and buckler. 5 *I am* not afraid for the terror by night; nor for the arrow that flieth by day; 6 nor for the pestilence that walketh in darkness; nor for the destruction that wasteth at noonday. 7 A thousand shall fall at *my* side, and ten thousand at *my* right hand; but it shall not come nigh *me*. 8 Only with *mine* eyes *shall I* behold and see the reward of the wicked. 9 Because *I make* the Lord, which is my refuge, even the most High, *my* habitation; 10 there shall no evil befall *me*, neither shall any plague come nigh *my* dwelling. 11 For he shall give his angels charge over *me*, to keep *me* in all *my* ways. 12 They shall bear *me* up in their hands, lest *I* dash *my* foot against a stone. 13 *I do* tread upon the lion and adder: the young lion and the dragon *I do* trample under feet. 14 *Therefore God says to me:* Because *you have* set *your* love upon me, therefore will I deliver *you*: I will set *you* on high, because *you have* known my name. 15 *You* shall call upon me, and I will answer *you*: I will be with *you* in trouble; I will deliver *you,* and

honour *you*. 16 With long life will I satisfy *you*, and shew *you* my salvation." I do set and keep my love on God, no matter what the temptation, dismay and the pressures of the moment, or the dread and terror of the future, and God will deliver me. I do call on the name of Jesus, and I do bring His salvation to Earth for Him. I do know the name of the Lord and do call on Him often and regularly, and God does answer me with His goodness and blessings. God is with me in trouble. God does deliver me. God does honor me. God does give me a long, full, healthy and satisfying life, and God does show me often and fully His salvation. I am loved by God. Father God sets such great value on me that He had Jesus die to free me from my own sins and the sins of man. I am redeemed by the precious, eternal, awesome, reconciling and devil-overcoming blood of Jesus, because God loves me. I am loved by the God of salvation, the Lord God Almighty. Thank You, Father, in the name of Jesus, thank You!

59. **I am a cheerful giver.** 2 Cor 9:7 "... As *I purpose (rightly) in my* heart, so *I* give; not grudgingly, or of necessity: for God *agape*/loveth *me*, a cheerful giver. 8 And God is able to make all grace abound toward *me*; that *I*, always having all sufficiency in all things, may abound to every good work." I am confident in God and in His Word. My confidence is that God will fulfill His Word no matter what. Good business deals come to me, and I make good deals happen. I am strong in the Lord by continual right faith actions. I am courageous in the Lord by faith actions. I do greater works than Jesus because He has gone to the Father. I am redeemed by the blood of Jesus. I belong to God, and He belongs to me. I make clear, precise goals and objectives. I measure and track goal performance. I make detailed, efficient plans to accomplish my goals. I keep the vision alive in others. I win friends and influence people easily for good. I focus all of my abilities to accomplish my goals and God's goals for me. I continually grow in godliness and *agape*/love, for I constantly seek light from the Lord, look to the Day of Judgment, know my sins are purged in Jesus and put on my new man and nature in Christ Jesus all the time. I concentrate on right goal accomplishment rightly. I regularly make and accomplish clear godly goals. My goals have God's priorities. I actively desire to accomplish my goals and those given me. My goals and plans are measurable with 30- to 90-day to 10- to 30-year time frames. I stretch, develop and increase the best that is in me. I make my heart a happy dwelling place for Holy Spirit. I readily acknowledge God in all my ways, and He gives me the right desires in my heart. Father God directs my steps to His glory by Jesus Christ. I am a miracle worker. I cast out demons. I heal the sick. I raise the dead. I lay hands on the sick and they recover right now. I bring peace where there is hatred and strife. I am a mature Christian. I keep myself in the Word of Christ; and

Affirmations in Christ

I effectively grow myself and others in the *agape*/love of God at all times. People are glad to see me, and I am glad to see them. 1 Tim 6:17 "*I am* rich in this world, *I am* not highminded, nor *do I* trust in uncertain riches, but *I do trust (by faith actions)* in the *zao*/living God, who giveth us richly all things to enjoy; 18 *I do* good, *I am* rich in good works, ready to distribute, willing to communicate; 19 laying up in store for *myself* a good foundation against the time to come, that *I* may lay hold on eternal *zoe* life." 2 Cor 5:7 "For *I* walk by faith *(actions)*, not by sight *(or feelings)*." I give thanks before I see the blessing. Praise the Lord Jesus Christ, King of kings and Lord of lords. Hallelujah!

60. **Father God, who cannot fail** and who cannot lie (for in Him there is no shadow of turning or iniquity, and who is *agape*/love) is for me to succeed in every part of life. Heb 13:6 So that *I* boldly say, The Lord is my helper, and I will not fear ... . Ps 139:14 I will praise thee, (Lord God); for I am fearfully and wonderfully made: marvellous are thy works; and that my soul knoweth right well. 15 My substance was not hid from thee, when I was made in secret, and curiously wrought in the lowest parts of the earth. 16 Thine eyes did see my substance, yet being unperfect; and in thy book all my members were written, which in continuance were fashioned, when as yet there was none of them. 17 How precious also are thy thoughts unto me, O God! how great is the sum of them! 18 If I should count them, they are more in number than the sand: when I awake, I am still with thee. *For You, Father, said*: Jer 1:5 Before I formed thee in the belly I knew thee; and before thou camest forth out of the womb I sanctified thee, and I ordained thee a prophet ... , [king and priest] *unto me, the* Lord. Jer 29:11 For I know the thoughts and plans that I have for you, says the Lord, thoughts and plans for welfare and peace and not for evil, to give you hope in your final outcome. AMP Isa 59:21 As for me, this is my covenant with *you*, saith the Lord; My spirit that is upon thee, and my words which I have put in thy mouth, shall not depart out of thy mouth, nor out of the mouth of thy seed, nor out of the mouth of thy seed's seed, saith the Lord, from henceforth and for ever. Heb 3:14 For *I am* made *a partaker, an extension* of Christ *on Earth, so I* hold ... *my* confidence *(by faith actions)* stedfast unto the end; 15 *so I will* hear *to glad obedience* his voice, *and* harden not *my heart, but keep it strong in the Lord and His truth by faith actions in any provocation of when things look as if the agape/love and power of God are going to fail, for* Phil 4:13 I can do all things through Christ which strengtheneth me. *I am expert at the soft answer that turns away wrath, in myself and in others. I do not get offended, bitter or unforgiving toward God or people when temptations, trials or tests come upon me; instead I* lambano *by faith actions God in His covenant promises, and draw closer to God, and resist, by attacking the devil with* aiteo, *thanksgiving, praise and joy in God, by Jesus*

OK, God, Now What?

Christ, my Lord, who ever says to me: Isa 41:10 Fear not [*in spite of what you see*], for I am with you; do not look around you in terror and be dismayed, for I am your God. I will strengthen and harden you to difficulties, yes, I will help you; yes, I will hold you up and retain you with My [victorious] right hand of rightness and justice. AMP *Therefore, whenever fear, doubt or unbelief comes on me, I am* Phil 4:6 ... careful for nothing (*I do not tolerate fear or anxiety in anything, even though they may seem logical and real*); but in every thing by prayer and supplication with thanksgiving *I* let *my* requests (aiteo/demands) be made known unto God [*by proclaiming His promises and* aiteo/asking (*requiring, demanding and expecting as due by covenant promise*) *His answer, in the name of Jesus, unto joyful thanksgiving, for I* lambano/*receive it by faith actions, knowing I will possess it*]. 7 And the peace of God, which passeth all understanding, *keeps my heart* (*and mind*) through Christ Jesus. 8 Finally, *and above all else* ... , whatsoever things are **true**, whatsoever things are **honest**, whatsoever things are **just**, whatsoever things are **pure**, whatsoever things are **lovely**, whatsoever things are of **good report**; if there be any **virtue**, and if there be any **praise**, *I* think on these things *constantly*. *Grace and peace to victory is in me from God, my Father,* Rev 1:5 and from Jesus Christ, who is the faithful witness, and the first begotten of the dead, and the prince of the kings of the earth. Unto him that *agape*/loved us, and washed (*dissolved, put off and removed from us*) our sins in his own blood, 6 and hath made us kings and priests unto God and his Father; to him be glory and dominion for ever and ever. Amen, *in righteousness, peace and joy in Holy Spirit.* Rev 1:17 And *Jesus keeps His* right hand upon me, saying unto me, Fear not; I am the first and the last: 18 I am he that *zao*/liveth, and was dead; and, behold, I am *zao*/alive for evermore, Amen; and have the keys of hell and of death. *For Jesus said:* John 14:19 ...The world seeth me no more, *for now* ... , because I (*Jesus*) *zao*/live, you ...*zao*/live also. 20 *And every* day *I* ... know *more and more* that *Jesus is* in my Father, and *I am in Jesus,* and *Jesus is in me.* Rev 5:9 And *I sing* a new song, saying, *Lord Jesus, Lamb of God,* Thou art worthy to take the book, and to open the seals thereof: for thou wast slain, and hast redeemed us to God by thy blood out of every kindred, and tongue, and people, and nation; 10 and hast made us unto our God kings and priests: and we shall reign on the earth. [Rom 5:17 *For I know that* by one man's offence death reigned *as king* by one; much more *I, as one* which *holds on to, clings to and will not let go,* (*continually*) lambano/*receives* [*in continual faith actions*] abundance of grace and of the [*permanent*] gift of righteousness, (Rom 11:29 for the gifts and calling of God are without repentance), *I* shall reign in *zoe*/life by one, Jesus Christ, *in faith actions working by* agape/*love.*)] ... 12 Saying with a loud voice, Worthy is the Lamb that was slain to receive power, and riches, and

Affirmations in Christ

wisdom, and strength, and honour, and glory, and blessing. *Grace and peace to me from Father God and Jesus, my Lord. Thank You, Father, in the name of Jesus, thank You! Hallelujah! Yahoo! Father, this is the Day of Your Salvation, and I am glad, and I rejoice in You by Jesus Christ! Hallelujah! Lord God Almighty, You reign through us! Glory to God, who delights in my prosperity! Hallelujah! In the name of Jesus, Hallelujah! Hallelujah! HAL-LE-LU-JAH! YA-HOO! Lord, You are good! Your mercy is everlasting, and Your truth endureth to all generations! Yahoo! Lord, You are good! Yahoo!*

SUGGESTIONS FOR YOUR OWN AFFIRMATIONS: The following blank spaces are for you to write in your own affirmations. Plan them out a little, even put them on a separate piece of paper and use them for a few days to be sure they are as you would like before you write them in the book. You can do as we have done, taking some of your favorite scriptures (perhaps ones that we have not used in the book) and making them into affirmations. Or, another good method, although one that may take a little more time, is to record some answers to prayer that are your testimony or some things God has done that reveal His goodness, and then add some of your favorite relevant scriptures and combine them into an affirmation. Your affirmation might start something like this: "Just as when ... (describe here your answered prayer or act of God's goodness), because God said in ... (list here a scripture or as many as you like that fit)." It is okay to use the same scriptures again and again. The important thing is to make this a tool that works for you.

OK, God, Now What?

AFFIRMATIONS IN CHRIST

OK, God, Now What?

CHAPTER **19**

NOW WHAT?

There is much more to be said on the subject of how to be a champion in Christ, and the Affirmations are only a start. Other tools include Scripture memory cards, the right music and teaching, subliminal tapes and recordings, prayer groups, church activities, missions work, evangelism, healing the sick, etc. The next major step is for you to develop purposes or dreams or visions that bring the Kingdom of God to Earth through you. Whether it is as a janitor or a CEO, all aspects of life fit.

The milk of the Word is in the teaching; the meat of the Word is in the doing. Right thinking in God's *zoe* gets us to right faith-action doing.

In order to accomplish an objective, God says: Hab 2:2 "And the LORD answered me, and said, Write the vision, and make it plain upon tables, that he may run that readeth it." Prov 22:20 "Have not I written to thee excellent things in counsels and knowledge, 21 that I might make thee know the certainty of the words of truth; that thou mightest answer the words of truth to them that send unto thee?" Isa 30:8 "Now go, write it before them in a table, and note it in a book, that it may be for the time to come for ever and ever."

You need a plan and a method to execute that plan to make the dreams and visions God gives into a reality. Whether a regular prayer schedule or building a

OK, God, Now What?

city in the wilderness, the steps are the same. Some wonderful books describe the process to achieve extraordinary results. These books are not particularity Christian in focus, but the techniques described are biblically sound. I recommend any of the books by Steven K. Scott. One of them is *Simple Steps to Impossible Dreams* (New York, NY: Fireside, 1998). Another book I recommend is *Billionaire Secrets to Success* by Bill Bartmann (Dallas, TX: Brown Books Publishing Group, 2005). You will note that Mr. Bartmann's book also contains excellent material on how the subconscious mind works and techniques to properly renew it. Other secular books with detail on how the subconscious works include *The Answer* by John Assaraf and Murray Smith (New York, NY: Atria Books, 2008), *The Brain that Changes Itself* by Norman Doige, M.D. (New York, NY: Penguin Group, 2007) and *Who Switched Off My Brain?* by Dr. Caroline Leaf (Switch On Your Brain USA, 2008).

Additionally, of the generation of Dr. Lake, I recommend highly the works of E.W. Kenyon. His work is foundational on the Pauline Revelation and a "must engraft." He did have a different understanding on the covenant of Abraham, based on a lack of understanding of the original Hebrew and Greek words translated as "new" (see www.JaySnell.org), the spirit and the heart, and how to receive Holy Spirit. Other current authors I highly recommend include Curry Blake, Jay Snell, Kenneth Copeland, Creflo Dollar, Joyce Meyer, Joel Osteen, and, for integration with people and business, John Maxwell and Ken Blanchard.

That you have gotten this far is an indication of one of the ways in which God fulfills His promise: Ps 23:1 "The Lord is my shepherd; I shall not want. 2 He maketh me to lie down in green pastures: he leadeth me beside the still waters. 3 **He restoreth *(rescues, renews, makes right)* my soul**: he leadeth me in the paths of righteousness for his name's sake." The Lord wants to set your soul "aright." As with everything, He is limited to working in the Earth though people, and that includes you. Phil 2:12 "Wherefore, my *agape*/beloved, as ye have always obeyed, not as in my presence only, but now much more in my absence, work out your own *soteria*/salvation with fear and trembling. 13 For it is God which worketh in you both to will and to do of his good pleasure. 14 Do all things without murmurings and disputings: 15 that ye may be blameless and harmless, the sons of God, without rebuke, in the midst of a crooked and perverse nation, among whom ye shine as lights in the world; 16 holding forth the word of *zoe*/life; that I may rejoice in the day of Christ, that I have not run in vain, neither laboured in vain."

Thus, the process the Lord uses to write His laws on and in your heart and mind in this life gets you to actively desire, then agree, and finally become involved in those things it takes to restore-rescue-renew-make right your soul. 1 Cor 15:10 "But by the grace of God I am what I am: and his grace which was bestowed upon me was not in vain; but I laboured more abundantly than they all: yet not I, but the grace of God which was with me."

The thing that will transform you is the same thing that transformed Paul, his new identity in Christ. Gal 1:15 "But when it pleased God, who separated me from my mother's womb, and called me by his grace, 16 to reveal his Son in me, that I might preach him ..." This is the power of the New Testament message of "Christ in you the hope of glory."

The Affirmations major in the New Covenant/New Testament revelation to help you change your self-identity to what God has done in you in the new creation because of the work of Jesus. There is revelation that only comes as you use the Affirmations to renew your mind to this awesome truth. As you make the Affirmations a part of your life, you will place and empower yourself with Holy Spirit to move on to and into your God-given destiny, your path of righteousness for His name's sake. And, just as assuredly, this path of righteousness will lead to combating the devil to bring Heaven to Earth through you, for God renews your soul, so you can fulfill your destiny in Him. **Ps 23:4** "Yea, though I walk through the valley of the shadow of death, I will fear no evil: for thou art with me; thy rod and thy staff they comfort (*encourage*) me. 5 Thou preparest a table before me in the presence of mine enemies: thou anointest my head with oil; my cup runneth over. 6 Surely goodness and *chesed*/mercy shall follow (*pursue and overtake*) me all the days of my life: and I will dwell in the house of the LORD for ever."

As you renew your mind with the Affirmations, you will obey less and less those voices that shout into your mind that this does not apply to you. Keep constantly renewing your mind with promises such as Psalm 91 (here presented as an affirmation):

Ps 91:1 He that dwelleth in the secret place of the most High shall abide under the shadow of the Almighty. 2 I will say of the LORD, He is my refuge and my fortress: my God; in him I *do* trust (*by continual faith actions*). 3 Surely he shall deliver *me* from the snare of the fowler, and from the noisome pestilence. 4 He shall cover *me* with his feathers, and under his wings *I do* trust (*by continual faith actions*): his truth *is my* shield and buckler. 5 *I am* not afraid for the terror by night; nor for the arrow that flieth by day; 6 nor for the pestilence that walketh in darkness; nor for the destruction that wasteth at noonday. 7 A thousand shall fall at *my* side, and ten thousand at *my* right hand; but it shall not come nigh *me*. 8 Only with *mine* eyes *shall I* behold and see the reward of the wicked. 9 Because *I make* the LORD, which is my refuge, even the most High, *my* habitation; 10 there shall no evil befall *me*, neither shall any plague come nigh *my* dwelling. 11 For he shall give his angels charge over *me*, to keep *me* in all *my* ways. 12 They shall bear *me* up in their hands, lest *I* dash *my* foot against a stone. 13 *I do* tread upon the lion and adder: the young lion and the dragon *I do* trample under feet. 14 *Therefore God says to me*, Because *you have* set *your* love upon me, therefore will I deliver *you*: I will set *you* on high, because *you have* known my name. 15 *You* shall call upon me, and I will answer *you*: I will be with *you* in trouble; I will deliver *you*, and honour *you*. 16 With long life will I satisfy *you*, and shew *you* my salvation.

I do set and keep my love on God by continual right faith actions, no matter what the temptation, dismay and the pressures of the moment or the dread and terror of the future, and God will deliver me. I do call on the name of Jesus, and I do bring His salvation to Earth for Him by faith actions. I do know the name of the Lord and do call on Him often and regularly, and God does answer me with His goodness and blessings. God is with me in trouble. God does deliver me. God does honor me, and God does give me a long, full, healthy and satisfying life. God does show me often and fully His salvation. I am loved by God. Father God sets such great value on me that He had Jesus die to free me from my own sins and the sins of man. I am redeemed by the precious, eternal and awesome blood of Jesus because God loves me. I am loved by the God of salvation, the Lord God Almighty. Thank You, Father, in the name of Jesus, thank You!

Part of this ancient technology of mind renewal is regular and constant repetitions of affirmations of God's truth in Jesus. Titus 3:8 "This is a faithful saying, and these things I will that **thou affirm constantly**, that they which have believed in God might be careful to maintain good (*God-level*) works. These things are good and profitable unto men." And Philem 6 "That the communication of thy faith may become effectual by the **(*continual*) acknowledging (*by faith actions*)** of every good thing which is in you in Christ Jesus [*by the new birth*]."

Constant and diligent use of the Affirmation Magnets will help you in this process. Knowing, because God commands: 1 Cor 15:57 "But thanks be to God, which giveth us the victory through our Lord Jesus Christ. 58 Therefore, my *agape*/beloved brethren, be ye stedfast, unmovable, always abounding in the (*faith-action*) work of the Lord, forasmuch as ye know that your (*faith-action*) labour is not in vain in the Lord." Therefore I will stay to win; I will not give up; I will keep proclaiming Jesus' great name in faith actions until His and my enemies bow in defeat and submission to the glory of God.

Knowing to your core: Mark 10:9 "What therefore God hath joined together, let not man put asunder." In the new birth: 1 Cor 6:17 "But he that is joined unto the Lord is one spirit." So your reality becomes identification and unity with Jesus: Gal 2:20 "I am (*have been*) crucified with Christ: nevertheless I zao/live the *zoe/life of Jesus*; yet not I, but Christ zao/liveth in me *to walk like He walked*: and the life which I now zao/live *of Jesus'* agape in the flesh I zao/live *the nature of Jesus* by the faith (*actions*) in the Son of God, who *agape/*loved me, and gave himself for me. 21 I do not frustrate the grace of God: for if righteousness [*unto unity in the Spirit with Jesus*] come by the law, then Christ is dead in vain." 2 Cor 5:21 "For *Father* God hath made *Jesus* to be sin for us, who knew no sin; that we might be made the righteousness (*nature, unity, and* zoe *life*) of God in him."

Keep at the Affirmation Magnets, knowing the constant repetition of the Word of God will renew your mind into the wonder of who you are in the new birth, to the glory of God in this life and the next. This will put you into walking in the true prosperity God so desires, by the immense price of Jesus, for you and yours.

APPENDICES

Glossary Contents

Agape 281

Aiteo 282

Chesed 286

Faith Actions 286

Glory 288

Grace 290

Iniquity 290

Justified; Justification 295

Knowledge; Know; Acknowledge 295

Lambano 297

Mercy 298

Peace 298

Propitiation 301

Racham 301

Redeem; Ransom 302

Remission; Forgiveness 302

Righteousness 305

Sin; Transgressions 311

Son 312

Sozo; Soteria 314

Spirit; Soul; Body/*Bios*; *Psuche* 314

The Wrath of God 320

Zao; Zoe 332

A GLOSSARY OF TERMS

The following are expanded working definitions for everyday use. For more academic definitions, I suggest that you start with *Strong's Exhaustive Concordance*. Also our publications, *Faith Evidence* and *Freedom in a Snake-Bitten World* both have extensive discussions and scripture references for many of these key words.

AGAPE

Agape is a Greek noun (Strong's NT 26, pronounced: ag-ah'pay), *agapao*/ verb (Strong's NT 25) which, in the KJV, is translated as *love* and *charity*, i.e. caring in action, and has within its meaning an aggressive working for another's benefit and total good at your own expense and with no expectation of recognition, appreciation, reciprocation or honor, plus a desire to always be with the one loved. The definition of *charity*, love or *agape* in 1 Corinthians 13 and Romans 12-15 describes the basic nature of God and the true nature of Christians, as born-again ones, what Holy Spirit fills our hearts with, and what we are to walk in. *Agape* always is ever-ready and seeking a way to help or do the one loved good. Because *agape* has an emotional content, it is much like the best of a perfect father's and/or a perfect mother's love. John 3:16 "For God so *agape*/loved the world, that he gave his only begotten Son, that whosoever believeth in him should not perish, but have everlasting *zoe*/life. 17 For God sent not his Son into the world to condemn the world; but that the world through him might be *sozo*/saved." *Agape* does not mean without trouble, but One who is with you in all trouble to help get you out of, or to go successfully through, that trouble. *Agape* is related to the Old Testament word *racham*. *Agape* is translated as "charity" in the KJV because it is not just a feeling, but love in action.

AITEO

Aiteo (Strong's NT 154, pronounced: ahee-teh'-o) is the Greek word translated "ask" or "desire" in many New Testament scriptures related to prayer. It means to ask or demand of one in authority because that one made a promise based on requirements, and now the requirements have been met, so the person is now to give the desired promise. It also includes an intensity or focus in your desire to see the request fulfilled. For example: you are working on a task, and you had promised your little daughter that you would take her for an ice cream cone or some other treat when you were done. You are now done, and your daughter *aiteo*/demands by saying, "You are finished. You said you would take me when you were done. You are done; please take me now." Or, in a legal sense, such as in a situation where you fell behind in your property taxes and, as authorities come to kick you out, you get the money and pay the taxes. Then you wave your paid-up receipt and *aiteo*/say, "I paid my taxes; take your people and go now!" Or you pawned an item, and now you have the money to redeem it. You *aiteo*/say, as you wave the ticket, "Here is the money; give it back—now!" Even if the pawn shop owner had a better offer for it, he must give it back to you. *Aiteo* is not a quiet or polite word in that sense.

In the Scriptures, we base our prayer on the covenant promises of God. This is what God has said He will do. Ps 138:2 "I will worship toward thy holy temple, and praise thy name for thy *chesed*/lovingkindness and for thy truth: for thou hast magnified thy word above all thy name." God's name is our access to Him, and we are to use His name to release His covenant promises, His Word, on the Earth. The general principle is to find a promise of God in the Scriptures and *aiteo* Him to perform it, and, for whatever is resisting it, to *aiteo*/go, and the situation to become as you *aiteo* it, all in Jesus' name.

Those great prayer scriptures in John 14-16 all use this word *aiteo* for "ask." Here is just one. John 14:12 "Verily, verily, I say unto you, He that believeth (*by faith actions*) on me, the works that I do shall he do also; and greater works than these shall he do; because I go unto my Father. 13 And whatsoever ye shall *aiteo*/ask (*require, demand and expect as due by covenant promise*) in my name, that will I do, that the Father may be glorified in the Son." As you see, in this case, wherever the Greek word is *aiteo*, I added in a version of the phrase, *"require, demand and expect as due by covenant promise"* behind the translated word.

Notice, in a cruel example of the use of the word *aiteo*, that once King Herod made a promise, and even if he did not want to keep it, he had to perform upon the *aiteo*/asking because he had made the promise. Mark 6:22 "And when the daughter of the said Herodias came in, and danced, and pleased Herod and them that sat with

A Glossary of Terms

him, the king said unto the damsel, *Aiteo*/ask (*require, demand and expect as due by promise, knowing all the requirements have been met*) of me whatsoever thou wilt, and I will give it thee. 23 And he sware unto her, Whatsoever thou shalt *aiteo*/ask (*require, demand and expect as due by promise, knowing all the requirements have been met*) of me, I will give it thee, unto the half of my kingdom. 24 And she went forth, and said unto her mother, What shall I *aiteo*/ask (*require, demand and expect as due by promise, knowing all the requirements have been met*)? And she said, The head of John the Baptist. 25 And she came in straightway with haste unto the king, and *aiteo*/asked (*required, demanded and expected as due by promise, knowing that all the requirements had been met*), saying, I will that thou give me by and by in a charger the head of John the Baptist. 26 And the king was exceeding sorry; yet for his oath's sake, and for their sakes which sat with him, he would not reject her. 27 And immediately the king sent an executioner, and commanded his head to be brought: and he went and beheaded him in the prison, 28 and brought his head in a charger, and gave it to the damsel: and the damsel gave it to her mother." This is the power of the word *aiteo* and how it is used.

Part of the word *aiteo* is to know that the requirements for the one in authority or control to fulfill the promise has been met. All the requirements for God to fulfill any Scripture promise we require of Him have been fully met in Jesus. 2 Cor 1:19 "For the Son of God, Jesus Christ, who was preached among you by us, even by me and Silvanus and Timotheus, was not yea and nay, but in him was yea. 20 For all the promises of God in him are yea, and in him Amen, unto the glory of God by us. 21 Now he which stablisheth us with you in Christ, and hath anointed us, is God; 22 who hath also sealed us, and given the earnest of the Spirit in our hearts."

So a more complete Christian phrase in prayer, where *aiteo* is used, would be, "require, demand and expect as due by covenant promise, knowing that Jesus has fulfilled all the requirements, and there is no reason not to do it, because the time of God's salvation in any form is now." Your faith is believing by faith actions God will fulfill His Word as you *aiteo*.

Another key in prayer is the statement by God in: Isa 45:11 "Thus saith the Lord, the Holy One of Israel, and his Maker, Ask (*require*) me of things to come concerning my sons, and concerning the work of my hands command ye me." This culminates in the statements: Heb 4:14 "Seeing then that we have a great high priest, that is passed into the heavens, Jesus the Son of God, let us hold fast our profession. 15 For we have not an high priest which cannot be touched with the feeling of our infirmities; but was in all points tempted like as we are, yet without sin. 16 Let us therefore **come boldly** unto the throne of grace, that we may *lambano*/obtain mercy, and find (*perceive*) grace to help in time of need." Rom 8:15 "For ye have not received the spirit of bondage again to fear; but ye have received the Spirit of adoption, whereby we cry, Abba (*Daddy*), Father." Eph 3:11 "According to the eternal purpose which he purposed in Christ Jesus our Lord: 12 in whom we have **boldness and access** with confidence by the faith (*actions*) in him."

OK, God, Now What?

Heb 10:19 "Having therefore, brethren, **boldness to enter** into the holiest by the blood of Jesus, 20 by a new and *zao*/living way, which he hath consecrated for us, through the veil, that is to say, his flesh," Heb 13:6 "So that **we may boldly say**, The Lord is my helper, and I will not fear what man shall do unto me."

Jesus said our joy will include many victories in His name. John 16:24 "Hitherto have ye *aiteo*/asked (*by demanding as due by covenant promise*) nothing in my name: *aiteo*/ask (*by demanding as due by covenant promise*), and ye shall receive, that your joy may be full. 25 These things have I spoken unto you in proverbs: but the time cometh, when I shall no more speak unto you in proverbs, but I shall shew you plainly of the Father. 26 At that day ye shall *aiteo*/ask (*by demanding as due by covenant promise*) in my name: and I say not unto you, that I will pray the Father for you: 27 for the Father himself *agape*/loveth you, because ye have *agape*/loved me, and have believed that I came out from God. 28 I came forth from the Father, and am come into the world: again, I leave the world, and go to the Father." The proof He will is your believing faith actions He will do it.

So we use the intensity of the word *aiteo* in intercession with the Father or in commanding the devil to release a captive or oppressed one, or a sick or broken body to hear and obey and be healed or made whole, in the name of Jesus, knowing all the requirements have been met in Jesus. Faith is believing by faith actions God will do what He said He will do until it is done.

Here is how Jesus met the requirements. Isa 53:4 "Surely he hath borne our griefs (*infirmities*), and carried our sorrows (*sicknesses*): yet we did esteem him stricken, smitten of God, and afflicted. 5 But he was wounded for our transgressions, he was bruised for our iniquities: the chastisement of our peace was upon him; and with his stripes we are healed. 6 All we like sheep have gone astray; we have turned every one to his own way; and the LORD hath laid on him the iniquity of us all .... 11 He shall see of the travail of his soul, and shall be satisfied: by his knowledge shall my righteous servant justify many; for he shall bear their iniquities." This word *justify* in verse 11 is the basis for all the New Testament scriptures on justification, or made-as-if-you-had-never-sinned-or-will-ever-sin-again-and-all-things-healed-to-Father-God's-standard-forever righteousness. The issue for today is not that it is done, but how to speed up the timing, so it is delivered now, and not at some future heavenly state.

Notice there is a speaking to the problem in this kind of *aiteo* prayer that is a key understanding. Mark 11:22 "And Jesus answering saith unto them, Have faith (*actions*) in God. 23 For verily I say unto you, That whosoever shall **say unto this mountain**, Be thou removed, and be thou cast into the sea; and shall not doubt in his heart, but shall believe (*by continual right faith actions*) that those things which he saith shall come to pass; he shall have whatsoever he saith. 24 Therefore I say unto you, What things soever ye *aiteo*/desire (*require, demand and expect as due by covenant promise, knowing all requirements have been met in Jesus*), when ye pray, believe (*by con-*

A Glossary of Terms

tinual faith actions) that ye receive them, and ye shall have them." Our focus is for the end result with the problem gone, and we speak to the problem, the mountain, and command it to move fully, expecting God to empower that word to the end result.

We speak to Father God as our superior, with promises to make good, and we speak to the devil and his works to obey, as under our feet. Notice the commands in the "Our Father" (the Greek imperative, command words are bold and underlined). Matt 6:8 "Be not ye therefore like unto them: for your Father knoweth what things ye have need of, before ye *aiteo*/ask him (*require, demand and expect as due by covenant promise*). After this manner therefore pray ye: Our Father which art in heaven (*meaning pay attention, wake up, hear and listen*), **Hallowed** be thy name. 10 Thy kingdom **come.** Thy will **be done** in earth, as it is in heaven. 11 **Give** us this day our daily bread. 12 And **forgive** us our debts, as we forgive our debtors. 13 And **lead** us not into temptation, but **deliver** us from evil: For thine is the kingdom, and the power, and the glory, for ever. Amen." There is no begging in this prayer, and this is how Jesus said to pray, and how to *aiteo* in prayer to God.

Notice the command in this verse: Acts 16:17 "The same followed Paul and us, and cried, saying, These men are the servants of the most high God, which shew unto us the way of *soteria*/salvation. 18 And this did she many days. But Paul, being grieved, turned and **said to the spirit**, I command thee in the name of Jesus Christ to come out of her. And he came out the same hour." Notice it obeyed within an hour. Not quite instant, but the job got done with a forceful *aiteo*.

Notice the attitude of Jesus, as He laid His hands on a needy woman. Luke 13:11 "And, behold, there was a woman which had a spirit of infirmity eighteen years, and was bowed together, and could in no wise lift up herself. 12 And when Jesus saw her, he called her to him, and said unto her (*in judgment against the devil and his works*), Woman, thou art loosed from thine infirmity. 13 And he laid his hands on her: and immediately she was made straight, and glorified God. 14 And the ruler of the synagogue answered with indignation, because that Jesus had healed on the sabbath day, and said unto the people, There are six days in which men ought to work: in them therefore come and be healed, and not on the sabbath day. 15 The Lord then answered him, and said, Thou hypocrite, doth not each one of you on the sabbath loose his ox or his ass from the stall, and lead him away to watering (*with the attitude of a righteous shepherd*)? 16 And ought not this woman, being a daughter of Abraham, whom Satan hath bound, lo, these eighteen years, be loosed from this bond on the sabbath day?" This speaking to the problem and this "ought not" attitude fits right in with the attitude of *aiteo*.

Jesus used this kind of demand or command prayer in His ministry. John G. Lake discovered that this kind of dominion attitude produced far more results than begging intercession. For a more complete treatment of this, see our materials, *Battle Prayer for Divine Healing, Field Manual 2, Discovering Our Redemption*, and, of course, the writings of John Lake, and the many resources of Curry Blake(www.jglm.org).

Chesed

Chesed (Strong's OT 2617, pronounced: keh'-sed) is an Old Testament word often translated in the KJV as "mercy," "kindness," "loving-kindness," "goodness" or "favor." It is only defined by covenant, which is stronger than a contract or modern marriage, and can never be broken. It is the absolute commitment to fulfill the legal covenant conditions, even at the expense of one's life, as demonstrated by what you actually do or cause to happen. It is to do good, as promised, no matter what. It is only defined by action, not thoughts. The modern world has lost much of this concept, so it is hard to understand in today's Western world-view. 1 Samuel 18 shows David and Jonathan cutting a covenant, and 2 Samuel 9 shows how *chesed* is implemented. In vs. 3, it is called the "*chesed*/kindness of God." It is similar to New Testament *grace* in concept and is always in action and power.

Faith Actions

The Bible word translated as *faith*, *pistis* (Strong's NT 4102), is based on a verb, *pisteuo* (Strong's NT 4100). The original language words of *aman* (Strong's OT 539), and *pisteuo* translated as *believe* are verbs, indicating action, and both mean "continued actions to nurture, maintain and hold in your heart, and against the devil, and the current negative reality and thoughts, the assertions of the promises of God, unto exuberant behaviors." The noun *pistis*, translated as *faith*, means "to be in this holding and nurturing process of *pisteuo* believing. This process or behaviors of *pisteuo-aman* believing are called "faith actions."

This biblical believing, or faith, includes three main elements:

1. The Bible facts of God and His goodness in His Bible promises, especially as seen in our redemption in the work of Jesus, the nature and character of God as seen in Jesus, and the promises of God in the Bible.

2. The exuberant faith or believing actions of applying, celebrating, nurturing and enforcing these facts to the various situations of life BEFORE and UNTIL you see the promises of God manifest on earth in this life, i.e., "not slothful" (Heb 6:12). Note: Doing this element in trials and temptations is included in terms like "having, holding or keeping faith," "trusting God," "standing on the Word," "stirring up," and "loving God."

3. The current status of your strength, nurturing or adherence to faith facts and actions, in the face of conflicting information, feelings and offenses.

The supporting actions of faith or believing are found throughout the Bible and summarized here. These are the things we do that mix the Word of God into our hearts and release *zoe* life for blessing (Heb 4:2). The only faith action that appears to be unique in emphasis in the New Testament is speaking in Holy Spirit tongues, and of course the shift from the repetitive temple sacrifices to the one-time sacrifice of Jesus. Faith actions are what we do in holding, keeping or exercising faith.

A GLOSSARY OF TERMS

Note: The following is not exhaustive and some may be duplicative for clarity.

The basic actions or elements of believing are to take the information of the "faith," in the covenant promises of God (2 Cor 1:20), our Redemption in the blood of Jesus (Eph 1:7; Col 1:14; Heb 9:12-14; Rev 12:11), and established that God is good, His mercy and grace are everlasting, and His truth endures and triumphs over all generations (Ps 100:5; 34:8; 86:5; 118:29), and make this biblical information stir you up into exuberant thanksgiving (2 Cor 4:15; Eph 5:20; Col 1:12; 3:17, 1 Thess 5:18), praise (Heb 13:15), joy (Phil 4:4; 1Thes 5:16), blessings (James 1:9-10), courage (Josh 1:6; Ps 31:24; Acts 28:15), patience/consistency (Luke 21:19; James 1:2, 4; Heb 10:36), magnetizing your heart to God with affirmations of God's truth (Heb 3:1; Ps 1:2; Ps 105:1; Hab 2:2), *aiteo* commands in prayer as if God were speaking through you (2 Cor 4:13; Matt 6:8-13; 7:7-11; John 14:13-14; 15:7-8; 16:23-24; Phil 4:4-9; 2 Cor 4:13; 1 John 5:14-16), right fasting (Matt 6:18), right Holy Communion (1 Cor 11:30), operating gifts of Holy Spirit, especially prophecy and diverse tongues (1 Cor 12 and 14), Bible study and meditation by chewing the Word in your mouth to manifesting every aspect of salvation as needed to show yourself an approved workman of God (2 Tim 2:15, Josh 1:8; Ps 119:97; Ps 143:5) and able to manifest any aspect of salvation as needed (2 Tim 3:15, 2 Cor 1:20; 1 Tim 4:15), right consideration and self-talk, like Abraham did (Rom 4:12-21; Heb 3:1), recalling and telling of God's recorded miracles and testimonies (Ps 77:10-12; 78:3-7; 105:1; 119:99; 111:4; 143:5; 145:12; Isa 38:19; 63:7; Jonah 2:7; Matt 22:29; 2 Cor 1:4; Rev 12:11); active patience in continual faith actions (Rom 5, James 1; Phil 4:4-9), right judgment like Jesus did (Matt 7:2; John 5:30; 7:24 and 12:47), raising/lifting hands to God (Ps 28:2; 63:4; 119:48; 134:2 and Lam 3:41), attacking every worry, fear or anxiety with prayer and thanksgiving (Phil 4:4-9), working faith contracts (Hab 2:2), speaking to yourselves in psalms, hymns and spiritual songs, making melody in your heart to the Lord, giving thanks always for all things of redemption to God the Father in the name of the Lord Jesus, submitting yourselves one to another in the fear of God (Eph 5:19-21), daily exhortations by others or yourself (Heb 3:13), operating all the gifts of Holy Spirit (1 Cor 12 and Rom 12), public reading of the Scriptures (1 Tim 4:13), and doing acts of *agape* love, all in the name of Jesus (Matt 10:8; 22:39; 28:19-20; Mark 12:31, 16:15-20; and Luke 10:9).

Note: **Faith contracts** are a written tool where you gather the appropriate scriptures, summarize your commands, and if people are involved, intercession for them, and then keeping it handy for faith actions until the promise manifests. Put it (or them) in a visible place, and every time you go past it (them), repeat with thanksgiving. You can put these on note cards or your electronic devices to have them with you wherever you go. Even better is scheduled faith action reminders of your faith contract(s) on your electronic devices. Your goal is to do faith actions over each faith contract at least twice a day. More is better.

The acts of *agape* love are listed throughout the Bible. We summarize them as *agape*/loving God continually and exclusively with all your heart, mind, soul, strength, believing on the name of Jesus, loving one another as He does, and doing unto others what you would want done unto you. They are to be built on a foundation of gladly *agape*/loving your parents, spouse, children, neighbors and strangers.

These acts of *agape* love include gifts, alms, hospitality, respect and kindnesses to others, clothing the naked, feeding the hungry, sheltering the destitute, delivering the poor, attacking worry, encouraging and giving grace to others, speaking so others receive grace to be more like Jesus, overcoming evil with good, seeking first the Kingdom of God for yourself to community and national betterment, evangelism, personal piety, blessing those that curse you and praying for them that despitefully use you, including casting out the devil in and over them, helping widows, orphans, the weak and innocent, working godly justice, and producing the signs of true Jesus-believers by operating in the name and power of Jesus to heal the sick, restoring the maimed, blind and deaf, raising the dead, casting out devils and cleansing the lepers as recorded for Jesus and the early believers.

So when someone says, "Have faith," Stand on the promises," "Believe God," or "Trust God," your first response should be to start doing faith actions over scripture facts and God's promises that can apply for that situation, and then commit to a regular schedule of 3-6 hours a day in continual, on a regular daily schedule of multiple events, and as occasion serves, faith actions UNTIL victory. As the psalmist wrote: Psalm 119:164 **"Seven times a day** do I praise Thee for Thy righteous judgments (*against the devil and for my/our/their blessing and prosperity*"). And, of course, see: Eph 5:14-21; Col 3:14-17; 1 Thess 5:16-18; 2 Cor 4:13; Heb 6:12 and Heb 13:15.

GLORY

This word means honor, splendor, shiny, beauty, wealth, the best of, the strength of, or power of, radiance and light. An overall definition is that God's glory is released or dwells when Holy Spirit can freely do all God wants to on the Earth of His goodness through His people, i.e., in you. This includes the Shekinah glory filling a place of worship (Ex 40:34-35, 1 Kings 8:11), clouds, mist, or a light or glow on people such as on Moses and Jesus: Luke 9:29 "And as he (*Jesus*) prayed, the fashion of his countenance was altered, and his raiment was white and glistering. 30 And, behold, there talked with him two men, which were Moses and Elias: 31 who appeared in glory, and spake of his decease which he should accomplish at Jerusalem." The glory of God also includes raising the dead: Rom 6:4 "… as Christ was raised up from the dead by the glory of the Father … ." Holy Spirit and God's manifested glory are tightly linked.

God defines His glory as or it is released by His goodness and His name. Ex 33:18 "And he (*Moses*) said, I beseech thee, shew me thy glory. 19 And he said, I will make all my goodness pass before thee, and I will proclaim the name of the LORD before thee; and will be gracious to whom I will be gracious, and will shew *racham*/mercy on whom I will shew *racham*/mercy. 20 And he said, Thou canst not see my face: for there shall no man see me, and live. 21 And the LORD said, Behold, there is a place by me, and thou shalt stand upon a rock: 22 And it shall come to pass, while

A Glossary of Terms

my glory passeth by, that I will put thee in a clift of the rock, and will cover thee with my hand while I pass by: 23 and I will take away mine hand, and thou shalt see my back parts: but my face shall not be seen." Ex 34:5 "And the LORD descended in the cloud, and stood with him there, and proclaimed the name of the LORD. 6 And the LORD passed by before him, and proclaimed, The LORD, The LORD God, merciful and gracious, longsuffering, and abundant in *chesed*/goodness and truth, 7 keeping *chesed*/mercy for thousands, forgiving iniquity and transgression and sin, and that will by no means clear the guilty (*those who will not confess their sin to God for forgiveness*); visiting the iniquity of the fathers upon the children, and upon the children's children, unto the third and to the fourth generation (*this visiting iniquity to the third and fourth generation was repealed in Ezek 18*). 8 And Moses made haste, and bowed his head toward the earth, and worshipped." This is God's definition of the glory that will one day fill the Earth.

There are two main aspects of glory revealed in the Scriptures: glory that comes from God, and glory that comes from man to God. The word *glory* has the root of "heaviness or weighty," implying the true substance, that which lasts when other things pass away. Thus, all righteous works that survive the Day of Judgment as silver, gold and jewels are the result of the glory of the Lord (Holy Spirit) and you working together to produce them. 1 Cor 3:9 "For we are **labourers together with God**: ye are God's husbandry, ye are God's building." Wood, hay and stubble represent things that are not of His glory.

The amazing thing is that this same word *glory* is used when men praise and exalt, i.e., give glory to either God or other men. The combined effect of the glory of the Lord and the glory of man is found in our thanksgiving, praise, worship and obedience in faith actions. Ps 149:4 "For the LORD taketh pleasure in his people: he will beautify the meek with salvation. 5 Let the saints be joyful in glory: let them sing aloud upon their beds" Even our mouths are described as our glory or the place where our glory is shown or released: Ps 30:12 "To the end that my glory may sing praise to thee, and not be silent. O LORD my God, I will give thanks unto thee for ever." No wonder, when we exalt God, Holy Spirit then inhabits our praise, as He (Holy Spirit) is the administrator of glory or manifestations of God's goodness in the earth. Ps 22:3 "But thou art holy, O thou that inhabitest the praises of Israel." 1 Pet 2:9 "But ye are a chosen generation, a royal priesthood, an holy nation, a peculiar people; that ye should shew forth the praises of him who hath called you out of darkness into his marvellous light: 10 which in time past were not a people, but are now the people of God: which had not obtained mercy, but now have obtained mercy." Rom 6:4 "Therefore we are buried with him by baptism into death: that like as Christ was raised up from the dead by the glory of the Father, even so we also should walk in newness of *zoe*/life." Rom 8:11 "But if the Spirit of him that raised up Jesus from the dead dwell in you, he that raised up Christ from the dead shall also quicken your mortal bodies by his Spirit that dwelleth in you." 2 Cor 3:18 "But we all, with open face beholding as in a glass (*mirror*) the glory of the Lord, are changed into the same image from glory to glory, even as by the Spirit of the Lord." Opposites of God's glory include darkness, sin, iniquity, sickness, disease, misery and death.

GRACE

Grace is the love or goodness of a king or ruler manifested in a situation, based on legal grounds. Grace is granted by one who has power or authority to one who does not and is very similar to being blessed or given kindness/*chesed*, in that it is free, unmerited favor that is aggressively applied to you and does good for you. Grace is the free gift of God, to be, think, act like and produce the results of Jesus in any situation, i.e., the will of Father God on Earth as it is in Heaven. Grace is always given, not earned, and is greater than ever could be earned. You don't have to seek it, although you are required to. It seeks you, to give you total goodness for any need. Grace is how you get the blessing benefit. It is God's free gift, to give you what you do not deserve, to walk into the blessings of God, to the fullness of Christ in us. As we are "*sozo*/saved by grace," grace is God's goodness empowered to produce blessing, after the nature of God, and the result is more than you could ever come close to doing for yourself, but brings Heaven on Earth now and in the future. Eph 4:7 "But unto every one of us is given grace according to the measure of the gift of Christ." All of God's grace is available to us in gift, prayer and faith according to Heb 4:16. Grace has aspects of the Hebrew word *chesed*. We recognize and obtain grace in God by knowing the promises and *lambano*/receiving it by faith actions, knowing that Jesus has already obtained the promise for us, and then thanking God, *in advance*, to see it manifested.

INIQUITY

Iniquity means every aspect of wrong thoughts and words that lead to sin, the sins themselves, their consequences and the punishment due for sin. It also can mean misfortunes that attack you. Iniquity specifically is those thoughts that are not of God and, therefore, lead you to sin in any act of commission (doing) or omission (not doing). This is called a propensity to sin or a wicked, adulterous heart, when you keep them in your mind. Keeping wicked thoughts in your mind is the start of doing evil, i.e., wickedness, evil, against God and His ways, violation of the covenant with God. Isa 59:7 "Their feet run to evil, and they make haste to shed innocent blood: their thoughts are thoughts of iniquity; wasting and destruction are in their paths. 8 The way of peace they know not; and there is no judgment in their goings: they have made them crooked paths: whosoever goeth therein shall not know peace." Ps 36:3 "The words of his mouth are iniquity and deceit: he hath left off to be wise, and to do good."

A hard heart, steeped in iniquity, cannot see the goodness of the Lord. Rom 2:4 "Or despisest thou the riches of his goodness and forbearance and longsuffering; not knowing that the goodness of God leadeth thee to repentance? 5 But after thy hard-

A Glossary of Terms

ness and impenitent heart treasurest up unto thyself wrath against the day of wrath and revelation of the righteous judgment of God." All iniquity and its fruits will be destroyed on the Day of Judgment.

God told King Nebuchadnezzar how to stop the judgment foretold by Daniel. Dan 4:27 "Wherefore, O king, let my counsel be acceptable unto thee, and break off thy sins by righteousness, and thine iniquities by shewing mercy to the poor; if it may be a lengthening of thy tranquility." Notice the cure for sin is to go and do good and righteous works, and the cure for iniquity is to be generous to the poor.

This attitude of lack of generosity, care and concern for the poor was called an evil eye by Jesus. Luke 11:34 "The light of the body is the eye: therefore when thine eye is single, thy whole body also is full of light; but when **thine eye is evil**, thy body also is full of darkness. 35 Take heed therefore that the light which is in thee be not darkness. 36 If thy whole body therefore be full of light, having no part dark, the whole shall be full of light, as when the bright shining of a candle doth give thee light." The Jews understood this evil eye to include stinginess, and it colors everything you see.

Jesus related this directly to what is really in your heart by showing an evil eye to be the fruit of a defiled heart. Mark 7:20 "And he said, That which cometh out of the man, that defileth the man. 21 For from within, out of the heart of men, proceed **evil thoughts**, adulteries, fornications, murders, 22 Thefts, covetousness, wickedness, deceit, lasciviousness, **an evil eye**, blasphemy, pride, foolishness: 23 All these evil things come from within, and defile the man." As in Matthew 15:17-20, evil thoughts indicate an evil eye.

Here is just one of the Proverbs that speak of this. Prov 28:21 "To have respect of persons is not good: for for a piece of bread that man will transgress. 22 He that hasteth to be rich hath an **evil eye**, and considereth not that poverty shall come upon him."

Again, this is the source of problems for us all, in the iniquity of our heart, concerning how we want to be and handle riches. Matt 19:23 "Then said Jesus unto his disciples, Verily I say unto you, That a rich man shall hardly enter into the kingdom of heaven. 24 And again I say unto you, It is easier for a camel to go through the eye of a needle, than for a rich man to enter into the kingdom of God. 25 When his disciples heard it, they were exceedingly amazed, saying, Who then can be *sozo*/saved? [NOTE: Peter understood that *sozo*/salvation included now becoming or working toward or investing to be rich.] 26 But Jesus beheld them, and said unto them, With men this is impossible; but with God all things are possible. 27 Then answered Peter and said unto him, Behold, we have forsaken all, and followed thee; what shall we have therefore? 28 And Jesus said unto them, Verily I say unto you, That ye which have followed me, in the regeneration when the Son of man shall sit in the throne of his glory, ye also shall sit upon twelve thrones, judging the twelve tribes of Israel. 29 And every one that hath forsaken houses, or brethren, or sisters, or father, or mother, or wife, or children, or lands, for my name's sake, shall receive an hundredfold, and shall inherit everlasting *zoe*/life. 30 But many that are first shall be last; and the last shall be first."

This core defilement was the chief issue Jesus had with the religious leaders who wanted praise from men, money and power and manifested a great lack of *agape*/love. It can all be summed up in the word *iniquity* because, as you think so you are. This passage is about being careful not to pick up an evil eye for riches, as a way to be independent of trusting God, by whom you associate with and, thus, become a worker of iniquity. Prov 23:1 "When thou sittest to eat with a ruler, consider diligently what is before thee: 2 and put a knife to thy throat, if thou be a man given to appetite. 3 Be not desirous of his dainties: for they are deceitful meat. 4 Labour not to be rich: cease from thine own wisdom. 5 Wilt thou set thine eyes upon that which is not? for riches certainly make themselves wings; they fly away as an eagle toward heaven. 6 Eat thou not the bread of him that hath **an evil eye**, neither desire thou his dainty meats (*to be like him or to take from him*): 7 for as he thinketh in his heart, so is he: Eat and drink, saith he to thee; but his heart is not with thee."

Of course, the central issue is who is your source, God or the ways of this world, to give you happiness while you are in this world? The issue is not riches, for God wants you rich. The issue is who are you trusting. As you trust in other things than what God defines of value, that is iniquity, and, as you think iniquity, you will do iniquity, for that freedom from trusting God alone now becomes idolatry. As with Abraham, Job and David, seek to honor God and do all to His honor and glory, and He will make you rich and independent of the world systems. A right soul is free from iniquity. 3 John 2 "*Agape*/beloved, I wish above all things that thou mayest prosper and be in health, even as thy soul prospereth." 1 Sam 15:23 "For rebellion is as the sin of witchcraft, and stubbornness is as iniquity and idolatry. Because thou hast rejected the word of the LORD, he hath also rejected thee from being king."

This is seen in Peter's response to Simon, who had become a Christian, but still had a corrupt heart and saw everything as a way to make money and to be rich and well respected. Acts 8:18 "And when Simon saw that through laying on of the apostles' hands the Holy Ghost was given, he offered them money, 19 saying, Give me also this power, that on whomsoever I lay hands, he may receive the Holy Ghost. 20 But Peter said unto him, Thy money perish with thee, because thou hast thought that the gift of God may be purchased with money. 21 Thou hast neither part nor lot in this matter: for thy heart is not right in the sight of God. 22 Repent therefore of this thy wickedness, and pray God, if perhaps the thought of thine heart may be forgiven thee. 23 For I perceive that thou art in the gall of bitterness, and in the bond of iniquity."

Or, as summarized by Paul, money is not the problem. Loving money and what it can do independent of God is the issue with iniquity. 1 Tim 6:9 "But they that will be rich fall into temptation and a snare, and into many foolish and hurtful lusts, which drown men in destruction and perdition. 10 For the *agape*/love of money is

A Glossary of Terms

the root of all evil: which while some coveted after, they have erred from the faith, and pierced themselves through with many sorrows. 11 But thou, O man of God, flee these things; and follow after righteousness, godliness, faith, love, patience, meekness. 12 Fight the good fight of faith (*actions*), lay hold on eternal *zoe*/life, whereunto thou art also called, and hast professed a good profession before many witnesses."

Independence, of course, is what the devil tempted Eve and Adam with in the Garden of Eden. Gen 3:4 "And the serpent said unto the woman, Ye shall not surely die: 5 for God doth know that in the day ye eat thereof, then your eyes shall be opened, and ye shall be as gods, knowing good and evil. 6 And when the woman saw that the tree was good for food, and that it was pleasant to the eyes, and a tree to be desired to make one wise, she took of the fruit thereof, and did eat, and gave also unto her husband with her; and he did eat." They were already like God, in His image, and they lost, not gained, when they manifested iniquity.

The Bible standard is to always control or rein in your thoughts and do not allow them to stray to wickedness or iniquity. 2 Cor 10:5 "Casting down imaginations, and every high thing that exalteth itself against the knowledge of God, and bringing into captivity every thought to the obedience of Christ." Ps 10:4 "The wicked, through the pride of his countenance, will not seek after God: God is not in all his thoughts." Prov 30:32 "If thou hast done foolishly in lifting up thyself, or if thou hast thought evil, lay thine hand upon thy mouth." James 1:14 "But every man is tempted, when he is drawn away of his own lust, and enticed. 15 Then when lust hath conceived, it bringeth forth sin: and sin, when it is finished, bringeth forth death." Another translation uses the word *lawlessness* for *iniquity,* the refusal to obey God's known will in His Word and ways, i.e., disobedience, stubbornness and rebellion.

God's forgiveness in the propitiation of Christ completely blots out iniquities and sin, and heals the punishment or curse due for them. Isa 53:5 "But he was wounded for our transgressions, he was bruised for our iniquities: the chastisement of our peace was upon him; and with his stripes we are healed. 6 All we like sheep have gone astray; we have turned every one to his own way; and the Lord hath laid on him the iniquity of us all. ... 11 He shall see of the travail of his soul, and shall be satisfied: by his knowledge shall my righteous servant justify many; for he shall bear their iniquities."

Our propensity to sin is related to what is in our hearts and what we keep thinking on as acceptable. Matt 15:17 "Do not ye yet understand, that whatsoever entereth in at the mouth goeth into the belly, and is cast out into the draught? 18 But those things which proceed out of the mouth come forth from the heart; and they defile the man. 19 For out of the heart proceed evil thoughts, murders, adulteries, fornications, thefts, false witness, blasphemies: 20 these are the things which defile a man: but to eat with unwashen hands defileth not a man." A stingy man will not give even a penny and praises those who act likewise. This is how men reinforce iniquity among themselves. Prov 23:7 "For as he thinketh in his heart, so is he ... ." The opposite is also true; think mercy, grace and truth, and you will do mercy, grace and truth.

Iniquity is purged by knowing the *chesed*/grace of God, that your sins were purged in Jesus, by the truth, His Word (pray Psalm 119 often), and an absolute assurance that every iniquity will be judged and destroyed on the Day of Judgment, and that while you sin on the earth you are sowing to yourself unrighteousness with its sad and wicked fruit, now and on that Day. Prov 16:6 "By *chesed*/mercy and truth iniquity is purged: and by the fear of the LORD men depart from evil." 2 Pet 1:9 "But he that lacketh these things (*the fruits of abiding in Christ*) is blind, and cannot see afar off, and hath forgotten that he was purged from his old sins [*in the* chesed *of the New Covenant in the blood of Jesus*]."

Facing problems and choosing to trust God in continual faith actions, rather than let the problem win also attacks iniquity. When the people of Israel wandered in the wilderness, there were (10) ten times that it looked as if they were going to die, and each time they blamed God. Still, God saved them, because one man among them sought Him and His goodness. Num 14:22 "Because all those men which have seen my glory, and my miracles, which I did in Egypt and in the wilderness, and have tempted me now these ten times, and have not hearkened to my voice; 23 surely they shall not see the land which I sware unto their fathers, neither shall any of them that provoked me see it."

To fight this, James tells us this same thing in the first chapter of the book that bears his name. Instead of doubting God, we "count it all joy," knowing that He is our helper and our friend. Know this: worldly riches (money, power, armies, etc.) are not your answer, but, rather, knowing God. Jer 9:23 "Thus saith the LORD, Let not the wise man glory in his wisdom, neither let the mighty man glory in his might, let not the rich man glory in his riches: 24 but let him that glorieth glory in this, that he understandeth and knoweth me, that I am the LORD which exercise *chesed*/lovingkindness, judgment, and righteousness, in the earth: for in these things I delight, saith the LORD."

The cure to allowing iniquity to dwell in your heart is the ultimate positive attitude and also attacking fear in any form, as it tries to invade and control your life. Phil 4:4 "Rejoice in the Lord alway: and again I say, Rejoice. 5 Let your moderation be known unto all men. The Lord is at hand. 6 Be careful for nothing; but in every thing by prayer and supplication with thanksgiving let your *aiteo*/requests be made known unto God. 7 And the peace of God, which passeth all understanding, shall keep your hearts and minds through Christ Jesus. 8 Finally, brethren, whatsoever things are true (*the Bible*), whatsoever things are honest, whatsoever things are just, whatsoever things are pure, whatsoever things are lovely, whatsoever things are of good report; if there be any virtue, and if there be any praise, think on these things. 9 Those things, which ye have both learned, and received, and heard, and seen in me, do: and the God of peace shall be with you." Or, as God told Joshua: Josh 1:6

"Be strong and of a good courage: for unto this people shalt thou divide for an inheritance the land, which I sware unto their fathers to give them. 7 Only be thou strong and very courageous, that thou mayest observe to do according to all the law, which Moses my servant commanded thee: turn not from it to the right hand or to the left, that thou mayest prosper whithersoever thou goest. 8 This book of the law shall not depart out of thy mouth; but thou shalt meditate therein day and night, that thou mayest observe to do according to all that is written therein: for then thou shalt make thy way prosperous, and then thou shalt have good success. 9 Have not I commanded thee? Be strong and of a good courage; be not afraid, neither be thou dismayed: for the LORD thy God is with thee whithersoever thou goest."

JUSTIFIED; JUSTIFICATION

This is the legal or governmental process of removing all elements of sin, enmity, loss, wrath and/or alienation, and making one totally blessed, so that good from God is forced upon them, i.e., the process by which one is made righteous. For a Christian, we are justified to be made the righteousness of God in Jesus, in our spirit, by faith that God raised Jesus from the dead. Justification or being justified has a very similar meaning to reconciliation, but is more legal in nature.

In Jesus we are justified to *zoe*/life. Rom 5:15 "But not as the offence, so also is the free gift. For if through the offence of one (*Adam*) many be dead, much more the grace of God, and the gift by grace, which is by one man, Jesus Christ, hath abounded unto many. 16 And not as it was by one that sinned, so is the gift: for the judgment was by one to condemnation, but the free gift is of many offences unto justification. 17 For if by one man's offence death reigned by one; much more they which *lambano*/ receive [*by continual faith actions*] abundance of grace and of the gift of righteousness shall reign in *zoe*/life by one, Jesus Christ.) 18 Therefore as by the offence, *sin,* of one judgment came upon all men to condemnation; even so by the righteousness of one the free gift came upon all men unto justification of *zoe*/life." Justification with God through Jesus does not resolve any reconciliation or restitution you need to make with other humans on Earth. God will give you grace to resolve these earthly issues.

KNOWLEDGE; KNOW; ACKNOWLEDGE

The New Testament Greek root word is *ginosko* (Strong's NT 1097), meaning "knowledge by experience and observation, experiential knowledge or full and complete knowledge or understanding." Another word, *epignosis* (Strong's NT 1922), is an even deeper knowing, a knowledge that perfectly unites the person with the subject at all levels. This is the knowledge from expert, reliable and repeatable doing, not just study or a few practice efforts.

Many swim, but few are Olympic swimmers, and fewer still receive gold medals. Many can read the instructions on how to make a cake, but make a few acceptable cakes, and you may begin to *ginosko* cake making. It takes a master bakery chef with years of experience to make a repeatable and proper cake. This is *epignosis* (or *epiginosko*). In modern times, with our classroom and few laboratory sessions, head or basic familiarization is talked about as knowing, but it does not meet the meaning of the word *ginosko*, much less *epignosis*.

In the Bible sense, it is a knowing that unites with the *zoe*/life of God and produces "God-results" in the Earth. So, whether it is a godly businessman, Samson ripping off doors to a city, or raising the dead, the knowing is only effective if God's life mixes with man's life and produces results on a repeatable or "at will" basis. So this is not the typical educational process, where students can remember a few facts, get all the questions right in Sunday School, or pass a driver's classroom test. Even to eventually obtain a vehicle driver's license and be able to drive independently, a practical demonstration of basic skills and judgment are required. Just reading the Bible may give you familiarization, but not a personal knowledge of God.

In our modern world, many have seen or heard about a subject and, thus, become instant experts. To the Hebrew or Greek mind, however, mere mental recognition was of little performance value. Seeing a master musician or ballerina does not make one an expert in either. You may be an expert watcher or listener but not an expert performer. So, in Christianity, until you can do at will a command or demonstrate reliably a desirable characteristic, you are not yet in the realm of *gnosis*, much less *epignosis*.

For example, praying for the sick is much different than getting the sick healed by prayer. This concept is seen in this scripture: Gen 4:1 "And Adam knew Eve his wife; and she conceived, and bare Cain, and said, I have gotten a man from the LORD." Adam and Eve probably had sex many times, but when that act produced a child, it was called "knowing." A level of knowing comes with sex/*ginosko*, but there is a deeper level of knowing when a man and woman create a child. The first is experiential, but the second produces life in union with God.

The Greek word *epignosis* is such a deep knowing, a full knowing. Eph 4:13 "Till we all come in the unity of the faith, and of the *epignosis*/knowledge of the Son of God, unto a perfect man, unto the measure of the stature of the fulness of Christ." Here this knowledge is not referring to what it takes to be born again. That is a relatively low level of agreement with God. It is miraculous, but it is only a basic beginning. What this scripture is referring to is a "knowledge" that when complete, you cannot tell the person as different from Jesus in their behavior or their operation in the full power of God. This is Bible "*epignosis*/knowing," and God's goal for each of us.

Here are these two concepts in the same scripture: 1 Cor 13:12 "For now we see through a glass, darkly; but then face to face: now I *gnosis*/know in part; but then shall I *epignosis*/know even as also I am *epignosis*/known." We may start at some level of *ginosko*, but the goal is to *epignosis* God. If this seems like splitting hairs, consider: Which would you rather have do a critical brain surgery on you: a medical school student, a resident brain surgeon who has just learned the process, or a fine practicing doctor who has done the procedure hundreds or thousands of times without failure? The medical student has familiarization, and the resident perhaps *ginosko*, but the fine practitioner has *epignosis* of the procedure as a master craftsman.

LAMBANO

Lambano (Strong's NT 2983, pronounced: lam-ban'-o) is a Greek word meaning "to hold on to like a man would hold on to a life preserver when overboard in a raging sea." It is often translated "receive" in the KJV. Here it means "to receive," as if you were a football player trying to catch a ball in the middle of a group of strong defenders. You catch it, and the defenders try to knock and grab the ball from your hand, so you must defend and keep the ball in your hands, even as you run toward the goal. Another meaning is to carry a very heavy item, like a very heavy bucket, carry it no matter how far or difficult the ground and delivering it full and on time. Or "holding on" with continual faith actions is to *lambano* God's Word.

This word *lambano* is a key part of the mysteries of God as revealed by Jesus. There is nothing casual about *lambano*; it is an intense work describing intense action and commitment or single-minded purpose. Look at the way this word is used in the Parable of the Sower and the Seed: Matt 13:11 "He (*Jesus*) answered and said unto them, Because it is given unto you to know the mysteries of the kingdom of heaven, but to them it is not given. 12 For whosoever hath, to him shall be given, and he shall have more abundance: but whosoever hath not, from him shall be taken away even that he hath. 13 Therefore speak I to them in parables: because they seeing see not; and hearing they hear not, neither do they understand. 14 And in them is fulfilled the prophecy of Esaias, which saith, By hearing ye shall hear, and shall not understand; and seeing ye shall see, and shall not perceive: 15 for this people's heart is waxed gross, and their ears are dull of hearing, and their eyes they have closed; lest at any time they should see with their eyes, and hear with their ears, and should understand with their heart, and should be converted, and I should heal them. 16 But blessed are your eyes, for they see: and your ears, for they hear. 17 For verily I say unto you, That many prophets and righteous men have desired to see those things which ye see, and have not seen them; and to hear those things which ye hear, and have not heard them. 18 Hear ye therefore the parable of the sower. 19 When any one heareth the word of the kingdom, and understandeth it not, then cometh the wicked one, and catcheth away that which was sown in his heart. This is he which received seed by the way side. 20 But he that received the seed into stony places, the same is he that heareth the word, and anon with joy ***lambano/receiveth*** it; 21 yet hath he not root in himself, but dureth for a while: for when tribulation or persecution ariseth because of the word, by and by he is offended." In verse 20, he did not hold on to the Word and, instead, let go when he became offended, hurt, impatient, disappointed, resentful or bitter both for attacks and delay. The devil tempts us to be offended at God by calling God unreliable or a liar, just as he did with Adam in the Garden. Or the devil tries to get you to be offended at other people in their failures and sin. Either way, the devil wants you let go of God in His Word, call God a liar, and you bear no fruit.

Consider this passage: John 1:12 "But as many as **lambano/received** him, to them gave he power (*authority*) to become (*operate as*) the sons of God, even to them that believe (*by faith actions*) on his name: 13 which were born, not of blood, nor of the will of the flesh, nor of the will of man, but of God." Notice the level of Christ-like authority you walk in is dependent upon how well the born-again Christian *lambanos* by continual faith actions the Word of God against all resistance, apparent defeats, and supposed delay in God's answer. Here is the same message again: Rom 5:17 "For if by one man's (*Adam's*) offence death reigned by one; much more they which (*continually*) *lambano*/receive [*by continual faith actions*] abundance of grace and of the gift of righteousness shall reign in *zoe*/life by one, Jesus Christ."

MERCY

This is ignoring, forgiving or exonerating all wrongs, so that you do not get the full penalty, wrath or evil you deserve, and/or being given a great good you did not earn and are not worthy of. Lam 3:22 "It is of the LORD's *chesed*/mercies that we are not consumed, because his compassions fail not." 1 Pet 1:3 "Blessed be the God and Father of our Lord Jesus Christ, which according to his abundant mercy hath begotten us again unto a *zao*/lively hope by the resurrection of Jesus Christ from the dead, 4 to an inheritance incorruptible, and undefiled, and that fadeth not away, reserved in heaven for you, 5 who are kept by the power of God through faith (*actions*) unto *soteria*/salvation ready to be revealed in the last time."

PEACE

This word is based on the Hebrew *shalom*, which means calm assurance and confidence in God because all things are working well and in order, with nothing missing, nothing broken and everything producing to the abundance of Heaven on Earth. Peace is not a passive state, similar to being drugged, but a calm assurance that no matter how bad things seem to be, God is making them right, because you have put in process and are continuing to do the things to allow or cause it to happen, i.e., thanksgiving, all kinds of prayer and supplication, praise, alms, legal justice, etc. Phil 4:4 "Rejoice in the Lord alway: and again I say, Rejoice. 5 Let your moderation be known unto all men. The Lord is at hand (*in power and authority*). 6 Be careful for nothing (*no anxiety*); but in every thing by prayer and supplication with thanksgiving let your *aiteo*/requests be made known unto God. 7 And the peace of God, which passeth all understanding (*because you have activated godly faith in thanksgiving and will see the supernatural power of God, in answer to your prayers*), shall keep (*guard, be a fortress around*) your hearts and minds through Christ Jesus. 8 Finally, brethren, whatsoever things are true, whatsoever things are honest, whatsoever things are just, whatsoever things are pure, whatsoever things are lovely, whatsoever things are of good report (*as did Joshua and Caleb, in proclaiming victory over the giants you will destroy, because*

A Glossary of Terms

God is with you); if there be any virtue, and if there be any praise, think on these things. 9 Those things, which ye have both learned, and received, and heard, and seen in me, do: and the God of peace shall be with you." Notice this is actively managing your thoughts and behaviors. The best way to control thoughts is to go and do faith actions and acts of *agape*/love. Controlling your thoughts to right behavior is a learned skill.

The meaning of *peace* also includes the process by which this state is achieved, so it is very closely related to *soteria*/salvation, as a state or condition of being, and to *sozo*/saved/peacemaking in how it is achieved. Rom 16:20 "And the God of peace shall bruise Satan under your feet *as shattered glass*. The grace of our Lord Jesus Christ be with you. Amen." So to give peace and grace means all things working well to produce the blessing of Heaven on Earth, and that you will destroy or shatter seven ways all your enemies, as you fight as Jesus would by faith actions. You will have in abundance all things you need to do this work well in you and yours. (Deut 28:7)

A more complete definition is that peace is the blessing of God to make and enjoy the Kingdom of God, Heaven on Earth, in every aspect of life, and to be doing all the right things to produce Heaven on Earth now, including destroying all your enemies God's way. This process or warrior definition fits right with: John 14:26 "But the Comforter, which is the Holy Ghost, whom the Father will send in my name, he shall teach you all things, and bring all things to your remembrance, whatsoever I have said unto you (*so you can act as Jesus would*). 27 Peace (*the ability to fight and bring Heaven on Earth, as I did*) I leave with you, my peace (*calm assurance in trust in God, and that you are doing all things, as Holy Spirit is helping you, to the glory of Father God, to bring the blessing of Heaven to Earth*) I give unto you: not as the world giveth, give I unto you. Let not your heart be troubled, neither let it be afraid." John 16:33 "These things I have spoken unto you, that in me ye might have peace (*calmness, knowing that Jesus has defeated all your enemies for you, to put them under your feet and bring Heaven on Earth, warring, fighting as Jesus taught us*). In the world ye shall have tribulation: but be of good cheer; I have overcome the world." 1 Cor 15:57 "But thanks be to God, which giveth us the victory through our Lord Jesus Christ. 58 Therefore, my *agape*/beloved brethren, be ye stedfast, unmoveable, always abounding in the (*faith-action*) work of the Lord, forasmuch as ye know that your (*faith-action*) labour is not in vain in the Lord." 2 Cor 2:14 "Now thanks be unto God, which always causeth us to triumph in Christ, and maketh manifest the savour of his knowledge by us in every place." This knowledge includes everything from normal life (clean sheets and efficient garbage collection) to the Lord confirming His word of grace in power (healing the sick, raising the dead, the blind seeing, the lame walking, etc.). So if you think peace is all about your comfort, so you can enjoy the pleasures of this world, you have missed the Gospel of God in Jesus Christ.

Notice how this fits with the "peace," or "peacemaker" mission of Jesus. Acts 10:36 "The word which God sent unto the children of Israel, preaching peace by Jesus Christ: (he is Lord of all:) 37 that word, I say, ye know, which was published throughout all Judaea, and began from Galilee, after the baptism which John preached; 38 how God anointed Jesus of Nazareth with the Holy

Ghost and with power: who went about doing good, and healing all that were oppressed of the devil; for God was with him [*to make peace in this way*]." Luke 4:17 "And there was delivered unto him the book of the prophet Esaias. And when he (*Jesus*) had opened the book, he found the place where it was written, 18 The Spirit of the Lord is upon me, because he hath anointed me to preach the gospel to the poor; he hath sent me to heal the brokenhearted, to preach deliverance to the captives, and recovering of sight to the blind, to set at liberty them that are bruised, 19 to preach (*command, declare, proclaim and demonstrate*) the acceptable year of the Lord."

We have been given that same Spirit of power, *agape*/love and sound mind attitude of an *agape*/love warrior in Jesus. Gal 4:4 "But when the fulness of the time was come, God sent forth his Son, made of a woman, made under the law, 5 to redeem them that were under the law, that we might receive the adoption of sons. 6 And because ye are sons, God hath sent forth the Spirit of his Son into your hearts, crying, Abba (*Daddy*), Father." Peace is knowing that you have done and will continue doing those things that produce Heaven on Earth, to make nothing missing, nothing broken or twisted or out of God's purpose, and all things, including your shattering the devil under your feet, are working well to abundance. This gives you a peace or assurance that the world cannot give.

This also fits right in with the traditional definition of a policeman as a "peace officer," and why we are to pray for the government, according to 1 Tim 2 and: Rom 13:1 "Let every soul be subject unto the higher powers (*government in all forms, as it supports the righteous work of God*). For there is no power but of God: the powers that be are ordained of God. 2 Whosoever therefore resisteth the power, resisteth the ordinance of God: and they that resist shall receive to themselves damnation. 3 For rulers are not a terror to good works, but to the evil. Wilt thou then not be afraid of the power? do that which is good, and thou shalt have praise of the same: 4 for he is the minister of God to thee for good. But if thou do that which is evil, be afraid; for he beareth not the sword in vain: for he is the minister of God, a revenger to execute wrath upon him that doeth evil. 5 Wherefore ye must needs be subject, not only for wrath, but also for conscience sake. 6 For for this cause pay ye tribute also: for they are God's ministers, attending continually upon this very thing. 7 Render therefore to all their dues: tribute to whom tribute is due; custom to whom custom; fear to whom fear; honour to whom honour. 8 Owe no man any thing, but to *agape*/love one another: for he that *agape*/loveth another hath fulfilled the law."

PROPITIATION

When sin is propitiated, all wrath is removed and aggressive blessing is bestowed on the former sinner. If there has been no sin, then aggressive blessing is now bestowed from a previous less-blessed, passive or indifferent position. The Greek word is *hilasterion* (Strong's NT 2435), and means "to conciliate or make propitious" or "to cause good things to come." *Random House Dictionary* defines *propitiation* as: "that which propitiates or to make favorably inclined; appease; conciliate." And *conciliate* means: "1) To overcome the distrust or hostility of; placate; win over: *to conciliate an angry competitor*. 2) To win or gain (goodwill, regard, or favor). 3) To make compatible; reconcile."

The propitiation process removes all issues for disfavor, if any, and institutes or restores one to a favorable position of aggressive good and identification. This could be either to resolve a difficulty, to "bribe" or give a token of love for favor.

Favorable means "now disposed to do well toward and wanting to do well toward." So the new position is not neutral or indifferent, but now is a position in which the one now favorably inclined or conciliated is openly seeking to do well toward the one reconciled, as if to themselves. In the case of a king, the king does not now simply forgive any wrong or ignore you; instead, he looks continually for ways to bless or prosper you in any way he can and takes great delight in the bestowment of these benefits. Of course, when the king has this attitude and the person does come to him for help or a favor of any kind, he will gladly and, with great cheer and joy, do whatever can be done. Rom 3:23 "For all have sinned, and come short of the glory of God; 24 being justified freely by his grace through the redemption that is in Christ Jesus: 25 whom God hath set forth to be a propitiation through faith in his blood, to declare his righteousness for the remission of sins that are past, through the forbearance of God; 26 to declare, I say, at this time his righteousness: that he might be just, and the justifier of him which believeth in Jesus." 1 John 2:1 "My little children, these things write I unto you, that ye sin not. And if any man sin, we have an advocate with the Father, Jesus Christ the righteous: 2 and he is the propitiation for our sins: and not for ours only, but also for the sins of the whole world." Eph 1:3 "Blessed be the God and Father of our Lord Jesus Christ, who hath blessed us with all spiritual blessings in heavenly places in Christ." Rom 5:1 "Therefore being justified by faith, we have peace with God through our Lord Jesus Christ." Our propitiation is complete in Christ, so Holy Spirit can now dwell in and operate through men in spite of our current imperfections.

RACHAM

Racham (Strong's OT 7355, pronounced: raw-kham') is an Old Testament word often translated as "mercy," "tender mercies" or "compassion" in the KJV. *Racham* is a deeper word than mercy, which, in modern usage, is more of a legal term. *Racham* means tender loving care actions, as a mother for a child, who can see no wrong in the child, no matter what it does; love that sees past our sins for our good. *Racham* has all the best of motherhood and fatherhood in its meaning, where love never stops, no matter what their children do, and is similar to the New Testament *agape*/love/charity in concept.

REDEEM; RANSOM

This word means to pay the purchase price in order to take ownership and set under the control of the one who paid the price. Gal 3:13 "Christ **hath redeemed** us from the curse of the law, being made a curse for us: for it is written, Cursed is every one that hangeth on a tree: 14 that the blessing of Abraham might come on the Gentiles through Jesus Christ; that we might receive the promise of the Spirit through faith." 1 Pet 1:18 "Forasmuch as ye know that ye **were not redeemed** with corruptible things, as silver and gold, from your vain conversation received by tradition from your fathers; 19 but with the precious blood of Christ, as of a lamb without blemish and without spot." Rom 3:23 "For all have sinned, and come short of the glory of God; 24 being justified freely by his grace through the **redemption** that is in Christ Jesus: 25 whom God hath set forth to be a propitiation through faith (*actions*) in his blood, to declare his righteousness for the *aphesis*/remission (*removal, obliteration, cancellation and putting away forever*) of sins that are past, through the forbearance of God; 26 to declare, I say, at this time his righteousness: that he might be just, and the justifier of him which believeth (*by faith actions*) in Jesus." Eph 1:7 "In whom **we have redemption** through his blood, the (*aphesis*) forgiveness of sins, according to the riches of his grace." 1 Tim 2:5 "For there is one God, and one mediator between God and men, the man Christ Jesus; 6 who **gave himself a ransom** for all, to be testified in due time." Matt 20:28 "Even as the Son of man came not to be ministered unto, but to minister, and to **give his** *psuche*/life/*soul* **a ransom** for many" (see Isa 53:11).

To think that your purpose in life is your own is the ultimate level of deception. 1 Cor 6:19 "What? know ye not that your body is the temple of the Holy Ghost which is in you, which ye have of God, and ye are not your own? 20 For ye are bought with a price (*the life, body, soul, spirit and blood of Jesus*): therefore glorify God in your body, and in your spirit, which are God's." 1 Cor 7:23 "Ye are bought with a price; be not ye the servants of men." Eph 1:13 "In whom ye also trusted, after that ye heard the word of truth, the gospel of your *soteria*/salvation: in whom also after that ye believed, ye were sealed with that Holy Spirit of promise, 14 which is the earnest of our inheritance until the redemption of the purchased possession, unto the praise of his glory." Peace is in those things that fulfill God's goals to produce Heaven on Earth in you, and in those around you.

As the redeemed, we are now called by God to fulfill His purpose of making Heaven on Earth through Jesus. We will face troubles, as the devil exalts himself against the knowledge of God when God sends us to set others free. Knowing you are bought and not your own is freedom.

REMISSION; FORGIVENESS

The same Greek noun-verb pair is translated in the KJV as remit or forgives. In Greek they have one meaning, in English forgive means to pardon by decision, while remit means to pay in full to remove and release a debt or sin. *Aphiemi* (Strong's NT 863), the verb, has the primary meaning of "to send forth, as in to cry, forgive, forsake, lay aside, leave, let alone, allow, omit, put away, remit, suffer, or yield up." Throughout the New

A Glossary of Terms

Testament *aphiemi* is translated as permit, allow, left, leave, let, send away, neglect, forsake, yield, lay aside, let go, let alone, cry, divorce, put away, and forgive. Thus it is a process or action word to remove and pay a debt or curse.

Aphesis (Strong's NT 859), the noun, means to be in the state or condition of freedom, with past bonds permanently broken and no record remaining. It has to do with the state or condition due to a past action or process of offense or debt dismissal, liberty and deliverance and a passing over of a just and due penalty, i.e., *aphiemi*. In the New Testament, we find *aphesis* translated variously as remission, forgiveness, and liberty. When looked at in context, its primary usage concerning sin is that of remission. As remission of sin, *aphesis* means to be in the state of abatement, alleviation, release, interruption, discharge, obliteration, purging, removal, or cancellation. So sin has no effect, debt or curse due. Both the sin, the record of the sin and the curse due are gone, no longer relevant to the case.

For example, when cancer goes into remission, it means that the symptoms disappear, or it is no longer actively working its destruction on the body, and all medical action stops. In the same way, when there is remission of sin, the symptoms of sin disappear, and sin no longer has power over an individual. The confusion comes as the translators use similar words or the same word (such as forgive and remit) for either Greek word and do not indicate the distinction between the English words. The Greek words are consistent, the English words forgive and remit are not.

The verb *aphiemi* is used one hundred and fifty-six times in the New Testament. When we look at the uses, from the various meanings of *aphiemi*, together with their context, we discover that they portray forgiveness as a judicial act of God, whereby He forgives or pardons us for our acts of transgression by the payment of the blood of Jesus. It is basically a legal transaction which deals with our guilt and removes the penalty for our acts of sin by full payment. When we are convicted of our acts of sin, we confess our sins as paid in Jesus. God responds by judicially forgiving us of our sins, removing our guilt and rescinding the penalty from His side. We see this process in: Acts 8:22 "Repent therefore of this your wickedness, and pray God if perhaps the thought of your heart may be forgiven you"

The noun *aphesis* is used seventeen times in the New Testament. When we put these passages together and look at them, from the various meanings of *aphesis* together with their context, we discover that they portray a state of remission of sin, meaning sin has been removed, along with the defilement of that sin, a removal of all claims due. It results in a deliverance from sin, which, in turn, results in our liberty as the children of God. This remission of sin is usually associated, not with repentance, but, rather, with the baptism of the Holy Spirit (see Acts 2:38), to bring about our cleansing from sin. Hebrews tells us: Heb 9:22 "And according to the law almost all things are purified with blood, and without shedding of blood there is no *aphesis*/remission." Forgiveness has to do with the process for pardon of sins, while remission has to do with the permanent state of purification from sin and the sin nature into the new birth, by the blood of Christ. Luke 24:47 "And that repentance and **remission** of sins should be preached in His name to all nations, beginning at Jerusalem." Acts 5:31 "Him God has exalted to His right hand to be Prince and

OK, GOD, NOW WHAT?

Savior, to give repentance to Israel and *aphesis*/**forgiveness** (*remission*) of sins." Notice, in both of these passages, that Jesus provides both forgiveness and purification, obliteration, removal or remission of sin. (The repentance is to manage your life, knowing that Jesus is the Son of God, Emmanuel and the Remover of sin.)

The difference between forgiveness and remission is the key element between the covenant of Moses (the Old Testament) and the completed covenant of Abraham in Jesus (the New Testament). Under the law of Moses, sins were forgiven and healed, but sins could never be removed or remitted (*aphesis/aphiemi*). This is the meaning of the atonement or covering achieved once a year in Yom Kippur. Here all the sins of the nation were atoned, covered, but not removed. Heb 10:4 "For it is not possible that the blood of bulls and of goats should take away sins. ... 12 But this man, after he had offered one sacrifice for sins for ever, sat down on the right hand of God; 13 from henceforth expecting till his enemies be made his footstool. 14 For by one offering he hath perfected for ever them that are sanctified (*separated from Satan back to God through Jesus, according to Col 1:13*). 15 Whereof the Holy Ghost also is a witness to us: for after that he had said before, 16 This is the covenant that I will make with them after those days, saith the Lord, I will put my laws into their hearts, and in their minds will I write them; 17 and their sins and iniquities will I remember no more. 18 Now where *aphesis*/remission of these is, there is no more offering for sin. 19 Having therefore, brethren, boldness to enter into the holiest by the blood of Jesus ..."

In Jesus, sins are not atoned for, but remitted, propitiated — removed — and the person is prepared for favorable, active and aggressive blessing from God in all ways. Rom 3:23 "For all have sinned, and come short of the glory of God; 24 being justified freely by his grace through the redemption that is in Christ Jesus: 25 whom God hath set forth to be a propitiation through faith in his blood, to declare his righteousness for the *aphesis*/remission of sins that are past, through the forbearance of God; 26 to declare, I say, at this time his righteousness: that he might be just, and the justifier of him which believeth in Jesus." 1 John 2:2 "And he (*Jesus*) is the propitiation for our sins: and not for ours only, but also for the sins of the whole world." God, thus, creates the new birth or new creation, making the believer the righteousness of God in Christ Jesus. This is only possible with the English word *remission*, which is a legal and forever-irrevocable action.

This is what God accomplished in Jesus for all mankind. We enter into it by faith actions (Rom 3), and we operate in it by continual right faith actions. Rom 1:16 "For I am not ashamed of the gospel of Christ: for it is the power of God unto *soteria*/salvation to every one that believeth (*by continual faith actions*); to the Jew first, and also to the Greek. 17 For therein is the righteousness of God revealed from faith to faith: as it is written, The just shall *zao*/live (*in miracle power*) by faith (*actions*)." 2 Cor 3:18 "But we all, with open face beholding as in a glass (*mirror*) the glory of the Lord *in ourselves, in spite of the mind of the flesh*, are changed into the same image from glory to glory, even as by the Spirit of the Lord."

Thus, remission is the legal and permanent removal of sin and consequences in Jesus two thousand years ago. We have now (present tense) remission. But we still sin in the present time, meaning our soul is not yet perfected or matured in Christ. When we acknowledge our sin and thank God for the blood of Jesus, then we implement the remission on that specific act in time. This is the forgiveness referred in 1 John 1:9 and Acts 8:22. Here we are to agree that we sinned (the meaning of confess) and thank God that we have remission. Thus, this *aphiemi*/forgiveness is more about present time soul cleansing, agreeing with God in truth and not the condition of your spirit. Failure to acknowledge that you have sown to the flesh means that you will reap corruption until you or someone else deals with the sin by the body and blood of Jesus or it will be dealt with as sin-works on the Day of Judgment (see Gal 6:1-10 and 1 Cor 3:1-15).

RIGHTEOUSNESS

Biblical righteousness has three principle meanings:

1) Righteous acts or works are acts/results that God does through a person so they are perfectly right with God in every way and survive as gold, silver or jewels on the Day of Judgment. This is to obey and do all of God's commandments completely and gladly.

2) A legal state where the one is made as if they had never sinned or will never sin again. This is like being exonerated in a court of law, until you sin or break the law again. This righteousness is conditional, as it is lost when you sin or violate the law again, and you once again become a criminal or a "sinner," with a penalty due, as described in the Law of Moses. Then righteousness must be restored in some way by an action that exonerates, removes or hides the sin from further legal action or curse, and pays or forgives the penalties/curse due for the sin. This is to be legally forgiven of the sin, but your nature remains the same. If you sin again, it is as if you were never righteous, and the full penalty (death) again applies.

3) To be imputed/given the gift of righteousness, which means it is independent of your behavior. The one who is made righteous to this level can produce no alienation or offence to the court or to the one granting righteousness, no matter what they do, and the one in authority aggressively pours all of the blessing and abundance on them (think spoiled, rich kid with a patient and just father). This righteousness of God does not depend upon your goodness, but Jesus', and is a permanent righteousness. Now your nature/spirit is new, and your sins obliterated once, forever, and you are reconciled to God forever, even if you sin again. You are now separated from your sins or evil works, but, until you apply the benefits of the work of Jesus to your current sins and problems, the devil will still try to apply the law of sin and death to you. This level of righteousness allows you to go to God at any time; you are never unclean before Him. God is in Heaven, you are on Earth. If you as a Christian sin, you are righteous with God before and after you sin, but you have to deal with the consequences of sin committed on Earth or God will deal with it under the New Covenant on the Day of Judgment.

OK, God, Now What?

Under the Law of Moses, sins were covered by the annual atonement, but they were never removed or fully paid for, pending the propitiation of Christ. The sins were forgiven, i.e. the penalty/curse/guilt of the law of sin and death removed, but the effect was the people were made the second type of righteousness, blessed, but conditional on right behavior. If you sinned again, you released death as the penalty for sin again. Jesus brought forgiveness and remission, the obliteration of sin, to make men the righteousness of God in Jesus and is made effective and operational to blessings by continual right faith actions in the work of Jesus by the cross.

In Christ we are made the third kind of righteousness before God. We died with Him, as our sins are paid in full by His suffering and death for us. Col 3:3 "For ye are dead, and your *zao*/life is hid with Christ in God." Rom 6:2 "God forbid. How shall we, that are dead to sin, *zao*/live any longer therein? 3 Know ye not, that so many of us as were baptized into Jesus Christ were baptized into his death?" Gal 2:19 "For I through the law am dead to the law, that I might *zao*/live unto God. 20 I am (*have been*) crucified with Christ: nevertheless I *zao*/live; yet not I, but Christ *zao*/liveth in me: and the life which I now *zao*/live in the flesh I *zao*/live by the faith (*actions*) of (*concerning*) the Son of God, who *agape*/loved me, and gave himself for me. 21 I do not frustrate the grace of God: for if righteousness come by the law, then Christ is dead in vain." Rom 5:9 "Much more then, being now justified by his blood, we shall be *sozo*/saved from wrath through him. 10 For if, when we were enemies, we were reconciled to God by the death of his Son, much more, being reconciled, we shall be *sozo*/saved by his *zoe*/life." Luke 24:47 "And that repentance (*Jesus is Lord and Judge, and everyone will have to deal with Him now and later, and He is your Redeemer, Healer and Judge against the devil and every curse of sin*) and *aphesis*/remission (*removal, purging, washing and putting away*) of sins should be preached in his name among all nations, beginning at Jerusalem."

By this one act of Jesus, sin was remitted once, forever, and we enter into this remission and being made the righteousness of God in Jesus by faith. 2 Cor 5:20 "Now then we are ambassadors for Christ, as though God did beseech you by us: we pray you in Christ's stead, be ye reconciled to God. 21 For he hath made him to be sin for us, who knew no sin; that we might be made the righteousness of God in him." Rom 3:28 "Therefore we conclude that a man is justified by faith without the deeds of the law. 29 Is he the God of the Jews only? is he not also of the Gentiles? Yes, of the Gentiles also: 30 seeing it is one God, which shall justify the circumcision by faith, and uncircumcision through faith." Rom 4:5 "But to him that worketh not, but believeth on him that justifieth the ungodly, his faith is counted for righteousness." Rom 5:1 "Therefore being justified by faith, we have peace with God through our Lord Jesus Christ."

In 1 Cor 6 Paul upbraids the Corinthians for their sin, yet he still proclaims: 1 Cor 6:11 "And such [*functional sinners*] were some of you: but ye are washed, but ye are sanctified, but ye are justified in the name of the Lord Jesus, and by the Spirit of our God." In spite of their current sin, they still possessed the Type 3 righteousness obtained by the name of Jesus and the power of Holy Spirit.

A Glossary of Terms

Under the Law of Moses sin was forgiven and the annual atonement covered sin until Jesus came. This forgiveness brought the peace and prosperity of Israel. *Remission* (NT Greek – *aphesis*) is the removal, purging, washing, obliteration, destruction and putting away of sin, with no evidence that it was ever there or will be again making us righteous, not just forgiven. Rom 3:25 "Whom God hath set forth to be a propitiation through faith in his blood, to declare his righteousness for the *aphesis*/remission (*removal, purging, washing, obliteration and putting away*) of sins that are past, through the forbearance of God; 26 to declare, I say, at this time his righteousness: that he might be just, and the justifier (*the one making righteous*) of him which believeth in Jesus." Heb 9:22 "And almost all things are by the law purged with blood; and without shedding of blood is no *aphesis*/remission." Acts 13:38 "Be it known unto you therefore, men and brethren, that through this man is preached unto you the *aphesis*/forgiveness (*remission, obliteration and putting away*) of sins: 39 and by him all that believe are justified from all things, from which ye could not be justified by the law of Moses." Type 3 is with God, but sin and the curse/guilt of sin must be reconciled on Earth (Type 2).

In Jesus we see the fulfillment of God as our righteousness: Isa 45:24 "Surely, shall one say, in the Lord have I righteousness and strength: even to him shall men come; and all that are incensed against him shall be ashamed. 25 In the Lord shall all the seed of Israel be justified, and shall glory." Jer 23:6 "In his days Judah shall be saved, and Israel shall dwell safely: and this is his name whereby he shall be called, THE LORD OUR RIGHTEOUSNESS." Isa 53:11 "He shall see of the travail of his soul, and shall be satisfied: by his knowledge shall my righteous servant justify (*cleanse and make righteous unto holiness*) many; for he shall *cabal*/bear their iniquities."

This is found in the New Covenant through the blood of Jesus. Heb 8:10 "For this is the covenant that I will make with the house of Israel after those days, saith the Lord; I will put my laws into their mind, and write them in their hearts: and I will be to them a God, and they shall be to me a people: 11 and they shall not teach every man his neighbour, and every man his brother, saying, Know the Lord: for all shall know me, from the least to the greatest. 12 For I will be merciful to their unrighteousness, and their sins and their iniquities will I remember no more." Heb 10:4 "For it is not possible that the blood of bulls and of goats should take away sins. ... 16 This is the covenant that I will make with them after those days, saith the Lord, I will put my laws into their hearts, and in their minds will I write them; 17 and their sins and iniquities will I remember no more. 18 Now where *aphesis*/remission (*removal, purging, washing away, obliteration and putting away*) of these (*unrighteousness, sins and iniquities*) is, there is no more offering for sin. 19 Having therefore, brethren, boldness to enter into the holiest by the blood of Jesus..." To have your unrighteousness removed by faith means you are now righteous in spirit. As you confess your current sins, you give thanks for the forgiveness and remission already given 2000 years ago by faith actions in the work of Jesus by the cross to cleanse and renew your soul.

OK, God, Now What?

And we get it the way it has always been given, by faith actions: Gen 15:6 "And he (*Abraham*) believed in the LORD; and he counted it to him for righteousness." To be righteous means there is now no wrath, only blessing. Rom 5:10 "For if, when we were enemies, we were reconciled to God by the death of his Son, much more, being reconciled, we shall be *sozo*/saved by his *zoe*/life. 11 And not only so, but we also joy in God through our Lord Jesus Christ, by whom we have now received the atonement (*reconciliation, propitiation*)." Eph 2:13 "But now in Christ Jesus ye who sometimes were far off are made nigh by the blood of Christ. 14 For he is our peace ... ." Col 1:20 "And, having made peace through the blood of his cross, by him to reconcile all things unto himself; by him, I say, whether they be things in earth, or things in heaven. 21 And you, that were sometime alienated and enemies in your mind by wicked works, yet now hath he reconciled 22 in the body of his flesh through death, to present you holy and unblameable and unreproveable in his sight."

A key element is to understand that we, as Christians, are different than our works. We ourselves, our spirits, are *sozo*/saved, already judged dead, made righteous unto new *zoe*/life in Jesus by Holy Spirit. A Christian is one who has received that by faith. We are now dead to the Law, so the Law has no force over us, and we were made legally righteous, to the level of Jesus, before God, to walk in the experiential outworking of right acts (Type 1), even though our current walk is not perfect (until we walk just like Jesus). 2 Cor 5:21 "For he (*God*) hath made him (*Jesus*) to be sin for us, who knew no sin; that we might be made the righteousness of God in him (*Jesus*)."

Christian life works and behaviors will be judged for the Type 1 righteousness, per 1 Cor 3:15, by fire on the Day of Judgment. Yet the born-again, new man spirit is *sozo*/saved and survives that fire because of the third type of righteousness, which is by the faith (*actions*) of/in Christ and not our works (Rom 5:10, Rom 10:6-13). What survives that day you get to keep. 1 Cor 3:12 "Now if any man build upon this foundation gold, silver, precious stones, wood, hay, stubble; 13 every man's work shall be made manifest: for the day shall declare it, because it shall be revealed by fire; and the fire shall try every man's work of what sort it is. 14 If any man's work abide which he hath built thereupon, he shall receive a reward. 15 If any man's work shall be burned, he shall suffer loss: but he himself shall be *sozo*/saved; yet so as by fire." If you are a Christian, your sin-works may burn, but not you.

God's solution for us was to include us in the death and resurrection of Jesus. This saves our spirit. Yet we will still have our works or "soul fruit" judged: Matt 16:27 "For the Son of man shall come in the glory of his Father with his angels; and then he shall reward every man according to his works." Rom 2:5 "But after thy hardness and impenitent heart treasurest up unto thyself wrath against the day of wrath and revelation of the righteous judgment of God; 6 who will render to every man according to his deeds." 2 Cor 5:10 "For we must all appear before the judgment seat of Christ; that every one may receive the things done in his body, according to that he hath done, whether it be good or bad."

A Glossary of Terms

All the blessings of God go to the righteous: those who commit no sin in their Earth walk or who are now clean because they have had their sins forgiven (both the sin action and the curse consequence of sin). Type 2, conditional righteousness, depends on you, i.e., your holiness. Type 3 righteousness depends on Jesus' holiness and not yours. If you are a Christian, Type 2 righteousness no longer applies before God, as Type 3 has superseded it. Rom 5:1 "Therefore being justified by faith, we have peace with God through our Lord Jesus Christ." In peace, God only has favor toward us to produce Heaven on Earth. Eph 1:3 "Blessed be the God and Father of our Lord Jesus Christ, who hath blessed us with all spiritual blessings in heavenly places in Christ." 2 Pet 1:2 "Grace and peace be multiplied unto you through the knowledge of God, and of Jesus our Lord, 3 according as his divine power hath given unto us all things that pertain unto *zoe*/life and godliness, through the knowledge of him that hath called us to glory and virtue: 4 whereby are given unto us exceeding great and precious promises: that by these ye might be partakers of the divine nature, having escaped the corruption that is in the world through lust." We escaped that corruption when we were made the righteousness of God in Christ Jesus by faith. This righteousness depends on the holiness of Jesus and not our own, Type 3 with God. But on Earth we have to deal with Type 2.

If we sin, we have a choice. We can agree with what God says in His written Word, the Scriptures, or what Holy Spirit convicts us of. As we see that we sinned and call it sin, we are walking in the light. We are seeing clearly. If we do not call our sin as it is, we are walking in darkness and are still deceived in that sin. If we argue with God over what He calls sin, we put ourselves out of fellowship with Him. When we confess that it indeed was sin, that Jesus died for that sin, and that we already have remission for that sin, then this scripture applies. (Notice the first sign that you are out of fellowship, joyful agreement with God, is when your joy is lessened or gone.) 1 John 1:4 "And these things write we unto you, that your joy may be full. 5 This then is the message which we have heard of him, and declare unto you, that God is light, and in him is no darkness at all. 6 If we say that we have fellowship with him, and walk in darkness, we lie, and do not the truth: 7 but if we walk in the light, as he is in the light, we have fellowship one with another, and the blood of Jesus Christ his Son cleanseth us from all sin. 8 If we say that we have no sin, we deceive ourselves, and the truth is not in us. 9 If we confess our sins, he is faithful and just to *aphiemi*/forgive us our sins, and to cleanse us from all unrighteousness. 10 If we say that we have not sinned, we make him a liar, and his word is not in us. 2:1 My little children, these things write I unto you, that ye sin not. And if any man sin, we have an advocate with the Father, Jesus Christ the righteous: 2 and he is the propitiation for our sins: and not for ours only, but also for the sins of the whole world."

Removal of this lack of fellowship issue by confession and receiving cleansing is also called *aphesis*, remission in 1 John 1:9. The thing that dumbfounds the fleshly mind, which makes actions more important than the Word of God, is that even though you sin, you do not lose the righteousness of God in Christ that you are made in the new birth. The new birth is in your spirit, and perhaps in part of your heart, but not in the rest of your soul. Soul purity is your goal in the Christian life. For the Christian, or one in permanent covenant with God, forgiveness relates to your fellowship or agreement with God as you work out your own salvation in this life. When you receive that forgiveness given 2000 years ago for your present sin, you are then back in fellowship with God, and this is the forgiveness. Thus, you control whether you walk in forgiveness and blessing or not (Type 2 on Earth).

This is the realm of sowing and reaping. Gal 6:7 "Be not deceived; God is not mocked: for whatsoever a man soweth, that shall he also reap. 8 For he that soweth to his flesh shall of the flesh reap corruption; but he that soweth to the Spirit shall of the Spirit reap *zoe* life everlasting." This is a clear warning to the sinning Christian. There are no free sins. All words and actions of the Christian constitute our works. The Christian has been separated from their sin works, but all works will be tried on the last Day.

You do not lose righteousness in your spirit for your present sin, but when you sin, you must deal with the devil and his application of the law of sin and death on the Earth. Likewise, you must also deal with God's law of sowing and reaping. Because of lack of confession and lack of application of communion in the bread and wine in truth and faith, you will reap evil or corruption in your physical body and life, in spite of your spirit righteousness. Holy Spirit is sealed in the Christian unto the Day of Redemption, when God will reap in fullness what He has already paid for. Eph 1:13 "In whom ye also trusted, after that ye heard the word of truth, the gospel of your *soteria*/salvation: in whom also after that ye believed, ye were sealed with that holy Spirit of promise, 14 which is the earnest of our inheritance until the redemption of the purchased possession, unto the praise of his glory." So in spite of the Christian who is not just like Jesus in their walk (anything less is sin), Holy Spirit is not going anywhere. God will get what He paid for.

It is not until you apply the truth of the Gospel of Jesus Christ to your sins and/or the curses operating in your life that you will walk in soul-righteousness and blessing in this life. So this is a case of burn it by the fire of the Gospel now, or it will try to kill you in this life. The spirit-righteousness of God in Christ Jesus in your spirit ensures your final salvation after the Day of Judgment. The reality of your soul-righteousness will determine the quality of your testing on the Day of Judgment.

This explains how the Christian can be the righteousness of God and yet sin, or have sin works. The Christian is separated, sanctified from their sin works and unto God. The source of our sanctification is God, by Jesus, not our works. 1 Cor 1:30 "But of him (*God*) are ye in Christ Jesus, who of God is made unto us wisdom, and righteousness, and sanctification, and redemption." This is part of the Gospel, and is really good news! Rom 6:10 "For in that he (*Jesus*) died, he died unto sin once: but in that he *zao*/liveth, he *zao*/liveth unto God. 11 Likewise reckon ye also yourselves to be dead indeed unto sin, but *zao*/alive unto God through Jesus Christ our Lord."

A Glossary of Terms

Those works in your life that are not just like Jesus would do them will not survive the Day of Judgment, yet God, who cannot lie, says the Christian will. 1 Cor 3:12 "Now if any man build upon this foundation gold, silver, precious stones, wood, hay, stubble; 13 every man's work shall be made manifest: for the day shall declare it, because it shall be revealed by fire; and the fire shall try every man's work of what sort it is. 14 If any man's work abide which he hath built thereupon, he shall receive a reward. 15 If any man's work shall be burned, he shall suffer loss: but he himself shall be *sozo*/saved; yet so as by fire. 16 Know ye not that ye are the temple of God, and that the Spirit of God dwelleth in you?" Eternal salvation with indwelling Holy Spirit comes with being made the Type 3 righteousness of God in Christ Jesus in the new birth. See Glossary "The Wrath of God" for more detail on this.

SIN; TRANSGRESSIONS

Sin is actually missing any mark or path God has set, whether by commission (by what we do) or by omission (by what we do not do). Transgressions or willful sins are those violations of God's law that are knowingly done or discovered after the fact. Sin includes transgressions and also those violations you did not even know you committed. Ignorance of the law does not forgive violations of the law, thus, sin is sin, whether you know you committed it or not, and, thus, requires levels of restitution or payment on Earth and in Heaven. According to Genesis 2:17, the law of sin and death is to do right and be blessed, or to sin and die. Rom 6:23 "For the wages of sin is death; but the gift of God is eternal *zoe*/life through Jesus Christ our Lord." Ezek 18:4 "Behold, all souls are mine; as the soul of the father, so also the soul of the son is mine: the soul that sinneth, it shall die." Rom 1:18 "For the wrath of God is revealed from heaven against all ungodliness and unrighteousness of men, who hold the truth in unrighteousness." Rom 2:9 "Tribulation and anguish, upon every soul of man that doeth evil, of the Jew first, and also of the Gentile."

The penalty for sin is death through the curse, which is death in either a fast or a slow and prolonged form. Deut 28:14 "And thou shalt not go aside from any of the words which I command thee this day, to the right hand, or to the left, to go after other gods to serve them. 15 But it shall come to pass, if thou wilt not hearken unto the voice of the LORD thy God, to observe to do all his commandments and his statutes which I command thee this day; that all these curses shall come upon thee, and overtake thee. ... 61 Also every sickness, and every plague, which is not written in the book of this law, them will the LORD bring upon thee, until thou be destroyed." Gal 3:10 "For as many as are of the works of the law are under the curse: for it is written, Cursed is every one that continueth not in all things which are written in the book of the law to do them."

Christ removes the curse from us, when we sin, to give us the ultimate blessing, God Himself, dwelling in us by His Spirit. Gal 3:13 "Christ hath redeemed us from the curse of the law, being made a curse for us: for it is written, Cursed is every one that hangeth on a tree: 14 that the blessing of Abraham might come on the Gentiles through Jesus Christ; that we might receive the promise of the Spirit through faith." To God, Jesus or Holy Spirit, there is now no legal curse on the Earth for anyone.

SON

In the Bible, the word *son* means much more than just a male child. Instead, it is a title, a position and a description of how one is to act. When a Roman general or governor had an officer who could go and do just as he would have, that officer was called a "son." Thus, to be called a son of God means that God can trust you to act just like He would, if He were there. This explains more of why Jesus came under the title Son of God.

In the Greek New Testament, a definite distinction is drawn between children and sons. Children were products of birth, but sons were mature ones, operating in the potential of their nature. One way to describe this is that, as a son of God, He fully possess your soul or you are "full of" or "filled with" His Spirit. Rom 8:14 "For as many as are led by the Spirit of God, they are the *huios*/sons (*mature ones*) of God. 15 For ye have not received the spirit of bondage again to fear; but ye have received the Spirit of adoption, whereby we cry, Abba (*Daddy*), Father. 16 The Spirit itself beareth witness with our spirit, that we are the *teknon*/children (*birthright, immature ones, toddlers*) of God: 17 and if *teknon*/children (*birthright, immature ones, toddlers*), then heirs; heirs of God, and joint-heirs with Christ; if so be that we suffer with him, that we may be also glorified together."

In the New Testament *teknon* (Strong's NT 5043) occurs one hundred times and is used to give prominence to the fact of birth, and never in reference to Jesus as the Son of God. John 1:12 "But as many as received him, to them gave he power to become the *teknon*/sons (*birthright, immature ones, toddlers*) of God, even to them that believe on his name: 13 which were born, not of blood, nor of the will of the flesh, nor of the will of man, but of God."

Huios (Strong's NT 5207) is used three hundred and eighty-six times in the New Testament, and always in describing Jesus as the *Huios*/Son of God. It is used to describe the dignity or the character of the relationship, which includes unity in carrying out the goals of the father or life source. In this passage, as in Rom 8:14 above, it is clear that a *huios* is one who has matured in Christ. Matt 5:44 "But I (*Jesus*) say unto you, *Agape*/love your enemies, bless them that curse you, do good to them that hate you, and pray for them which despitefully use you, and persecute you; 45 that ye may be the *huios*/children (*mature ones*) of your Father which is in heaven: for he maketh his sun to rise on the evil and on the good, and sendeth rain on the just and on the unjust. 46 For if ye *agape*/love them which *agape*/love you, what reward have ye? do not even the publicans the same? 47 And if ye salute your brethren only, what do ye more than others? do not even the publicans so? 48 Be ye therefore perfect (*mature, complete*), even as your Father which is in heaven is perfect (*mature, complete*)."

A Glossary of Terms

How you act, as a function of the condition of your heart, is also to be called a son or children of some way of thinking or doing. John 8:44 "Ye are of your father the devil, and the lusts of your father ye will do. He was a murderer from the beginning, and abode not in the truth, because there is no truth in him. When he speaketh a lie, he speaketh of his own: for he is a liar, and the father of it. 45 And because I tell you the truth, ye believe me not. 46 Which of you convinceth me of sin? And if I say the truth, why do ye not believe me? 47 He that is of God heareth God's words: ye therefore hear them not, because ye are not of God." John 12:35 "Then Jesus said unto them, Yet a little while is the light with you. Walk while ye have the light, lest darkness come upon you: for he that walketh in darkness knoweth not whither he goeth. 36 While ye have light, believe (*do faith actions*) in the light, that ye may be the *huios*/children (*sons*) of light. These things spake Jesus, and departed, and did hide himself from them." Eph 5:8 "For ye were sometimes darkness, but now are ye light in the Lord: walk as *teknon*/children (*sons*) of light: 9 (For the fruit of the Spirit is in all goodness and righteousness and truth;) 10 proving what is acceptable unto the Lord." [NOTE: Mirroring modern English, the KJV does not draw a distinction between *huios* and *teknon*, so both are translated as either children or sons, to our loss, with no attempt to include the deeper meaning of the words.]

In the New Testament, the word for son also implies a condition. Much like a prince or princess, it is still up to the individual to fulfill the promise of the position. Gal 3:26 "For ye are all (*become and operate as*) the *huios*/children (*sons*) of God by faith (*actions*) in Christ Jesus. 27 For as many of you as have been baptized into Christ have put on Christ. 28 There is neither Jew nor Greek, there is neither bond nor free, there is neither male nor female: for ye are all one in Christ Jesus." Gal 4:6 "And because ye are *huios*/sons, God hath sent forth the Spirit of his *huios*/Son into your hearts, crying, Abba (*Daddy*), Father." 1 John 3:1 "Behold, what manner of *agape*/love the Father hath bestowed upon us, that we should be called the *teknon*/sons of God: therefore the world knoweth us not, because it knew him not. 2 *Agape*/beloved, now are we the *teknon*/sons of God, and it doth not yet appear what we shall be: but we know that, when he shall appear, we shall be like him; for we shall see him as he is."

In the new creation, we are born again, recreated anew. Now it is up to us how we walk in it. John 1:12 "But as many as received him, to them gave he power (*authority*) to become (*and operate as*) the *teknon*/sons of God, even to them that believe (*by faith actions*) on his name: 13 which were born, not of blood, nor of the will of the flesh, nor of the will of man, but of God." 1 Thes 5:5 "Ye are all the *huios*/children (*sons*) of light, and the *huios*/children (*sons*) of the day: we are not of the night, nor of darkness. 6 Therefore let us not sleep, as do others; but let us watch and be sober. 7 For they that sleep sleep in the night; and they that be drunken are drunken in the night. 8 But let us, who are of the day, be sober, putting on the breastplate of faith (*actions*) and *agape*/love; and for an helmet, the hope of *soteria*/salvation."

OK, God, Now What?

You are what you are by birth, but how you accept responsibility to live up to your potential determines what you really "are." A prince or princess may be in the line of royalty, but, by the way they think, speak and act, they define themselves as royal or not.

Sozo; Soteria

Sozo (Strong's' NT 4892, pronounced: sode'-zo) and *soterio* (Strong's NT 4491, prounounced: so-tay-ree'-ah) are Greek words. *Sozo* is the verb *save*, the process through which you become whole and blessed; *soteria* is the noun *salvation*, the state of being whole and blessed. *Sozo* is the process by which all of Earth and human life is made like Heaven on Earth in the fullness of the glory of God, i.e., that which produces the peace of God or the Kingdom of God from now to eternity. Physical healing is just a small portion of the meaning. Salvation has an eternal aspect, that of eternal life with God. The present life aspect is producing Heaven on Earth in your life and in those you are responsible for. Salvation means to be made prosperous and successful to the level of God Himself, in every way possible. So nothing related to the full potential of human life in Christ is left out for this life or the next.

The root word for salvation means "open, freedom of restraint." Sickness, poverty, danger, lameness, infirmity, weakness, etc., are all restraints, limits and pressure points. Salvation or wholeness has no restraints, limits or pressure points, and has the full freedom of God's blessings in action.

Spirit; Soul; Body/Bios; Psuche

Man is a three-part being, made up of spirit (the real you), soul (heart, mind, will and emotions and how you interface or function with this world through your body), and body (what operates in this Earth). From Genesis we see that the addition of the spirit to the body created a living soul. Gen 2:7 "And the LORD God formed man of the dust of the ground, and breathed into his nostrils the breath (*spirit*) of life; and man became a living soul."

Your heart is not your spirit, but the heart seems to be that combination of inner life that includes your mind and touches your spirit. 1 Thes 5:23 "And the very God of peace sanctify you wholly; and I pray God your whole **spirit and soul and body** be preserved blameless unto the coming of our Lord Jesus Christ." Heb 4:12 "For the word of God is quick, and powerful, and sharper than any twoedged sword, piercing even to the dividing asunder **of soul and spirit**, and of the joints and marrow, and is a discerner of the **thoughts and intents of the heart**." When you die, your spirit and soul leave your mortal body. James 2:26 "For as the body without the spirit is dead ..." Your heart is to be purified in this life, especially hardness of heart, to God and His Word, by doing the Word by faith actions and expecting God to do His part (Rom 2:4-5, 1 Tim 1:5, Heb 3:10-12, Eph 4:16-18, James 1:6, 2 Pet 2:14).

A Glossary of Terms

We are made righteous by faith in Jesus in our spirits. This is how we are born again, made a new creature in Christ Jesus. We will get a new, immortal body at the resurrection. Our soul is mostly unchanged. Notice all your memories remain the same, before and after being born again. We are made the righteousness of God in Jesus and given *zoe*/life in our spirits, as Holy Spirit comes to dwell in our spirit.

Our goal in life is to renew our mind, heart or soul to think without iniquity, i.e., just like Jesus. 2 Cor 10:5 "Casting down imaginations, and every high thing that exalteth itself against the knowledge of God, and bringing into captivity every thought to the obedience of Christ." This process is called "saving our souls," or "outworked sanctification," and is demonstrated by how much our walk is like Jesus. This renewing process of the soul comes as we grow in the true knowledge of Jesus, not mere mental facts, but actually working with God, so that the fruits of God are produced in the Earth through you. 2 Pet 1:2 "Grace and peace be multiplied unto you through the *experiential* knowledge of God, and of Jesus our Lord, 3 according as his divine power hath given unto us all things that pertain unto *zoe*/life and godliness, through the *experiential* knowledge of him that hath called us to glory and virtue: 4 whereby are given unto us exceeding great and precious promises: that by these ye might be partakers of the divine nature, having escaped the corruption that is in the world through lust." Our mental learning is solidified as we go and do *agape*/love. As we believe by continual faith actions, to releasing *zoe*/life, we do this.

The old man is the un-recreated spirit and way of thinking that produces sin, also called the carnal mind, or the mind of the flesh and lust. An immature Christian thinks like a "mere man" (1 Cor 3:1-3). The old man, the body of sin, is killed in Jesus and recreated into the new man. John 1:12 "But as many as received him, to them gave he power to become the sons of God, even to them that believe (*by continual faith actions*) on his name: 13 which were born, not of blood, nor of the will of the flesh, nor of the will of man, but of God." Col 3:9 "... seeing that ye have put off the old man with his deeds; 10 and have put on the new man, which is renewed (*made effective*) in knowledge after the image of him that created him." The new birth removes the spirit of the old man, but does not necessarily totally change the old-man-trained soul or worldly way of thinking.

While we are made new creations in the new birth, we have to retrain our minds and hearts so we can walk like Jesus in this Earth. Eph 4:22 "That ye put off concerning the former conversation the old man, which is corrupt according to the deceitful lusts; 23 and be renewed in the spirit of your mind; 24 and that ye put on the new man, which after God is created in righteousness and true holiness."

And this new man delights to walk in all the ways of God in *agape*/love. 1 John 5:2 "By this we know that we *agape*/love the children of God, when we *agape*/love God, and keep his commandments. 3 For this is the *agape*/love of God, that we keep his commandments: and his commandments are not grievous." The new man does not have any resistance to God, and none of God's commands are grievous to him.

Psuche and bios: The other Greek words translated in the KJV as "life" include *psuche* and *bios*. *Psuche* is also translated as "soul," which has a different connotation than "life." As translated in the Scriptures, there is much confusion between these words. *Zoe* is used in reference to general life and the *life* of God, implying it is what God gives. *Bios* is a general form of life that all living creatures have. *Zoe* is in reference to that which God alone gives. So He gives life to all things, and then Jesus said He came to give *zoe*/life as opposed to all other kinds of life or life force (John 10:10). This is in opposition to whatever form of life force people were operating in at the time. So He either meant that He came to give a different life force or a great increase of the good life force people already operated in.

The meaning for *soul* is even more difficult, in that many do not recognize what is clearly revealed in the Scriptures as a difference between *soul* and *spirit*. The Greek word *psuche* (Strong's NT 5590) is translated "soul" fifty-eight times, "life" forty times, "mind" three times and "heart" once. This shows a lack of understanding on the part of the translators, not on Holy Spirit's part.

From *Vine's* explanation of *psuche* we have the following:

"The language of Heb 4:12 suggests the extreme difficulty of distinguishing between the soul and the spirit, alike in their nature and in their activities. Generally speaking the spirit is the higher, the soul the lower element. The spirit may be recognized as the life principle bestowed on man by God, the soul as the resulting life constituted in the individual, the body being the material organism animated by soul and spirit ... .

"Body and soul are the constituents of the man according to Matt 6:25; 10:28; Luke 12:20; Acts 20:10; body and spirit according to Luke 8:55; 1 Cor 5:3; 7:34; James 2:26. In Matt 26:38 the emotions are associated with the soul, in John 13:21 with the spirit; cf. also Ps 42:11 with 1 Kings 21:5. In Ps 35:9 the soul rejoices in God, in Luke 1:47 the spirit. (*This confusion between Ps 35 and Luke 1 is a good example in which the modern thinkers translating the KJV did not understand that the soul and spirit are different, yet have, what can be described as, similar features.*)

"Apparently, then, the relationships may be thus summed up 'Soma, body, and pneuma, spirit, may be separated, pneuma and psuche, soul, can only be distinguished' (Cremer)." (NT:5590 Soul from *Vine's Expository Dictionary of Biblical Words*: Nashville, Tn., Thomas Nelson Publishers, 1985).

One way to distinguish the soul is that it is the mind, the heart, the will and the emotions of all men, and constitutes that which receives information directly from the senses of the body and also from the spirit. So, concerning our acceptable

A Glossary of Terms

thoughts, intentions, motives, attitudes of the heart, the soul is the joining and deciding ground between the body and the spirit. Thus, Heb 4:12 takes the Word of God to determine where either the soul or the spirit ends and the other begins. The spirit of the born-again man will always be in harmony with the Word of God. The soul of the born-again or the natural man may or may not be in harmony, agreement and commitment with the Word of God. This latter is more a function of an individual's experiences, culture and training. What one actually does and says is the result of the status of truth in their soul and, thus, the word *psuche* is often translated as "life." What is in your soul or heart is displayed in the life you live.

So when a person is in the spirit, their soul is mostly controlled or in cooperation with the thoughts and attitudes of a spirit being. This is seen when a demon speaks through a person, or Holy Spirit, as in biblical prophecy (also see the meaning of *zoe*). The life force exhibited is a function of whatever unity the soul has with that particular spirit being (life or *zao*). For example, when one uses the name of Jesus to raise the dead, this is an action in unity with Holy Spirit. When one accepts the death of a person, especially a young one, they are in unity with their body senses, and the person is buried and not raised. In both cases, the soul is the deciding ground of "whose report will you believe by faith actions?" The resulting behavior is then called the "life " of that person, as seen in the action of either raising the dead or burying them.

This understanding of the difference is seen in both the Hebrew and Greek texts, but not in the KJV and most other modern translations. For example, look at the Hebrew and the Greek and then the English translations relating to these important scriptures. Isa 53:11 "He shall see of the travail of his **soul,** and shall be satisfied: by his knowledge shall my righteous servant justify many; for he shall bear their iniquities." Matt 20:28 "Even as the Son of man came not to be ministered unto, but to minister, and to give his ***psuche***/life (*soul*) a ransom for many." John 10:15 "As the Father knoweth me, even so know I the Father: and I lay down my ***psuche***/life (*soul*) for the sheep." According to the original Hebrew and Greek, the meaning is clear and consistent, but not in the English translation.

Also here are both Greek words in the same verse translated as life: John 12:25 "He that loveth his ***psuche*/life** shall lose it; and he that hateth his ***psuche*/life** in this world shall keep it unto ***zoe*/life** eternal." Since we know God does not want us to kill ourselves, the meaning is that if your soul is not just like Father God's, work until it is, and when you do, your soul will release the *zoe*/life of God from your born-again spirit. You work on it according to: 2 Cor 3:17 "Now the Lord is that Spirit: and where the Spirit of the Lord is, there is liberty (*to be all Father God made you to be in Jesus*). 18 But we all, with open face beholding as in a glass (*mirror, seeing Jesus manifest Himself in and through me*) the glory of the Lord, are changed into the same image from glory to glory, even as by the Spirit of the Lord." Eph 4:22 "That ye put off concerning the former conversation the old man, which is corrupt according to the deceitful lusts; 23 and be renewed in the spirit of your mind; 24 and that ye put on the new man, which after God is created in righteousness and true holiness." The transformation occurs as you continually see aspects of Jesus that you desire and, in faith, see yourself walking in, first unto thanksgiving and joy, and then Holy Spirit will transform your inner man according to your faith, and it will be seen in your outer man or walk. Rom 1:17 "For therein is the righteousness of God revealed from faith to faith: as it is written, The just shall *zao*/live (*miracle power*) by (*continual*) faith (*actions*)."

As the New Testament describes the heart of the Christian as possibly dead or resistant to God, we do not consider the heart the dwelling place of Holy Spirit. Rom 2:5 "But after thy hardness and impenitent heart treasurest up unto thyself wrath against the day of wrath and revelation of the righteous judgment of God." The heart seems to be better described as that place or part of your soul or subconscious mind that connects to your spirit, and near that place is also the conscience part of your soul (that internal governor that is always judging your actions based on your beliefs and the soul part of your heart). Rom 2:29 "But he is a Jew, which is one inwardly; and circumcision is that of the *kardia*/heart, in *or by* the *pneuma*/spirit, and not in the letter; whose praise is not of men, but of God." The heart and the spirit are different, but closely tied together. A heart fully indwelt by a right spirit is a right heart. Eph 3:17 "That Christ/*Holy Spirit* may dwell (*happily and fully*) in your hearts by (*continual right*) faith (*actions*); that ye, being rooted and grounded in *agape*/love ..."

According to modern science, the cognitive mind is the cerebral cortex, and the unconscious mind is a combination of the rest of the brain and the neural material throughout the body. The term *heart*, as a portion of the soul, implies the part of the soul different than the cognitive mind. The spirit is considered to reside or be centered near the physical heart and the solar plexus (behind the stomach).

For the born-again one, the heart can be corrupted, but the spirit cannot. We understand Holy Spirit to be in our spirits, so our spirit can now always be pure, but our heart is included in the process of renewing the mind and must continually be kept clean. The goal of the Christian life is for the spirit to once again rule your soul and body, though a right heart, and not the pre-born-again condition, in which the body and/or soul rule instead.

Notice the warning not to let your heart be corrupted by sin: Heb 3:12 "Take heed, brethren, lest there be in any of you an evil heart of unbelief, in departing from the *zao*/living God. 13 But exhort one another daily, while it is called To day; lest any of you be hardened through the deceitfulness of sin." James 3:14 "But if ye have bitter envying and strife in your hearts, glory not, and lie not against the truth." James 4:8 "Draw nigh to God, and he will draw nigh to you. Cleanse your hands, ye sinners; and purify your hearts, ye double minded." 1 John 3:20 "For if our heart condemn us, God is greater than our heart, and knoweth all things." Thus the heart is in need of constant maintenance to stay in cooperation with Holy Spirit.

A Glossary of Terms

Your conscious mind seems to be that active part of the way you think and accesses your memory and the events in the physical world by your senses. Below is a model that shows the distinction between the spirit, soul and body for the new-creation, born-again person:

THE BORN-AGAIN CHRISTIAN

THE SPIRIT WORLD	THE MENTAL WORLD	THE PHYSICAL WORLD
Your Spirit-The Real You	Your Soul	Your Body
	Habits, Attitudes, Desires	Flesh
Hunger for God	Conscience, Memory, Intentions	Senses
Born Again: Bible, Word	Heart, Emotions, Will, Mind	Bible: Word of God
Righteousness-Life-Zoe	Imagination, Cognitive Mind	
Holy Spirit>Jesus>Father	Subconscious Mind	

What this table conveys is that the physical world has a boundary, the world of the spirit, and good portions of the soul do not, or are not of the same kind of "stuff" as the physical Universe our bodies inhabit. Note also that automatic responses, such as attitudes, habits, emotions and memory, are highly linked to the physical body in structure and effect. Damage to the physical brain, for example, can have major impacts on these elements of the soul. To be amused means to be without thinking, so the mind is a deeper part of the person, as you may be alive and active while "amused" but not operating in the deeper centers of the mind of critical reasoning and judgment. This also indicates the reason the devil has such a strong focus in our modern world on keeping people amused, mindless and entertained. To open your mind in such amusement means that you are programming your subconscious without knowledge. As you are responsible for the shape or godliness of your soul, you are still accountable for the effects, whether you are aware of it or not.

Jesus is the living Word made flesh. In the diagram, the Word of God is seen under the spirit and the body, as this is the only physical link God has given man to the spiritual world, and all godly definitions of the spirit must be consistent with the Bible. Ps 138:2 "I will worship toward thy holy temple, and praise thy name for thy *chesed*/lovingkindness and for thy truth: for thou hast magnified thy word above all thy name." Ps 119:88 "Quicken me after thy *chesed*/lovingkindness; so shall I keep the testimony of thy mouth. 89 For ever, O Lord, thy word is settled in heaven. 90 Thy faithfulness is unto all generations: thou hast established the earth, and it abideth. 91 They continue this day according to thine ordinances: for all are thy servants." 1 Pet 1:23 "Being born again, not of corruptible seed, but of incorruptible, by the word of God, which *zao*/liveth and abideth for ever. 24 For all flesh is as grass, and all the glory of man as the flower of grass. The grass withereth, and the flower thereof falleth away: 25 but the word of the Lord endureth for ever. And this is the word which by the gospel is preached unto you."

In reality, the spirit world is actually more solid or real than the physical world, as is all that physically exists is made from spirit. As with everything God makes, the soul and probably the spirit, is, in structure and operation, far more detailed and complex than described here. But remember, that thing which we call the soul was made to house God and, with you, to operate the Universe for and with Him, so it is really quite capable and marvelous. The more you operate in this "completeness" of the new birth, the more you and He actively cooperate to do His will in this Universe. The new creation is an instantaneous event of God, by decree at the initial, re-birth faith decision; the renewed mind takes time and human effort, in cooperation and effort with Holy Spirit in the Word of God. The Word of God is so important, as it is the only physical link (in its printed form) that we are given to the spirit world and God. To hear the voice of God all you have to do is speak the Scriptures. If it does not sound like God, the problem is you, not it.

So to be "filled" with the Spirit means to have your soul in agreement with Holy Spirit and your behavior or "life" reflecting that agreement. One way to describe this is that God fully possess your soul, or you are "full of" or "filled with" His Spirit. Here is both a command and a description of what that looks like. Eph 5:18 "And be not drunk with wine, wherein is excess; but be filled with the Spirit [*by faith actions*]; 19 speaking to yourselves in psalms and hymns and spiritual songs, singing and making melody in your heart to the Lord; 20 giving thanks always for all things unto God and the Father in the name of our Lord Jesus Christ; 21 submitting yourselves one to another in the fear of God." See *zoe* for more detail on this.

THE WRATH OF GOD

There are two aspects of the "wrath of God": 1) God is a consuming fire that destroys all not like or of Him, and 2) The devil is unleashed due to sin in the Earth. In general, we now see very little of the first type; most of the evil seen in the world today is of this second type. *Wrath,* as a word, is an intense application of force to achieve an end result. God's wrath is the force that removes corruption and restores His righteousness on the Earth. The restoration spoken of in the book of Revelation, in which all evil is destroyed and God comes to dwell on the Earth, is a demonstration of His effective wrath. Notice that the intended end result is good. In fact, it is Heaven on Earth. The devil's wrath destroys all that is like God, in a manner designed to cause the most evil fear of the devil among men and the most misery for man, and a twisted view of God so that men will distrust God and all that is good.

The negative consequences of violating God's laws are also called His wrath. This is what most people consider His wrath to be. This kind of wrath is the consequences of the violation of His laws, or of following laws that produce evil consequences. It is not as sure as the blessed consequences for rightly working with God's laws, as evil

A Glossary of Terms

is overcome by good, else Jesus never could have healed anyone. If you ignore gravity and jump off a high cliff, the consequences of gravity, the wrath of gravity, will be felt when you hit the ground. God is the one who designed the parachute, as seen in dandelion seeds and the wings of flying squirrels, to show us how to manage the force of gravity and avoid its wrath. He also showed us the law of flight in birds that, with added energy and right activity, can fly, defying the force of gravity. Today we have the same God and the same law of gravity. It is our choice how we deal with it. Just as with gravity, ignorance of God's law is not bliss. Hos 4:6 "My people are destroyed for lack of knowledge ... ." The problem is, first, our not knowing the facts and, second, our not applying them properly. By biblical standards, knowledge that does not cause right behavior (i.e. faith actions) is deception and not true knowledge at all.

The pattern seen throughout the Bible is that, when men sin, the devil is released to perform great evil and misery on men by the law of sin and death. This law says: you sin you die. So we get attacks from the devil when we sin. Rom 5:12 "Wherefore, as by one man sin entered into the world, and death by sin; and so death passed upon all men, for that all have sinned:" Rom 5:21 "That as sin hath reigned unto death, even so might grace reign through righteousness unto eternal *zoe*/life by Jesus Christ our Lord." Rom 8:2 "For the law of the Spirit of *zoe*/life in Christ Jesus hath made me free from the law of sin and death." 1 Cor 15:56 "The sting of death is sin; and the strength of sin is the law." James 1:15 "Then when lust hath conceived, it bringeth forth sin: and sin, when it is finished, bringeth forth death." Rom 6:23 "For the wages of sin is death; but the gift of God is eternal *zoe*/life through Jesus Christ our Lord."

Another type of attack comes when the devil is looking for anyone he can attack, whether they have sinned or not. 1 Pet 5:8 "Be sober, be vigilant; because your adversary the devil, as a roaring lion, walketh about, seeking whom he may devour." So the devil can inflict his wrath, the destruction of anything that looks like God, when we sin and when we do not sin, as long as he is free in this world. So a fuller definition of the law of sin and death is that, when you sin, death comes, in either a fast or slow form, and if you do not sin, because the devil is in the world, he will try to inflict the law of sin and death on you anyway. The less you know about the work of Jesus through the cross, the less you resist the devil in either kind of attack or oppression.

In Exodus 4, God gave Moses two signs to convince the people he was from God. The first was to put his hand under his robe, and it became leprous. Then he put it back again, and it was clean. God does not have leprosy in Heaven, but the devil does appear to have it in Hell. When Moses first put his hand in, what happened looked like a work of the devil. When he put it in the second time and it came out healed, that was Holy Spirit gladly healing him. So we see numerous times in the Bible in which a plague came (God had sent/could not stop it by His laws), and then He was able to heal the people. God is not confused. Just as with Job, for whatever reason, the devil was involved and produced death in some form, and then God was able to step in and heal because of someone's right action.

OK, God, Now What?

Notice, in the case of the man born blind at birth in John 9, neither the parents nor the man had sinned. This was either an attack of the devil or an accident in this world of sin. God certainly did not make the man blind, else Jesus would not have healed him. Where would God get blindness in Heaven? In either case, here is what Jesus said about it. John 9:3 "Jesus answered, Neither hath this man sinned, nor his parents: **but that the works of God should be made manifest in him. 4 I must work the works of him that sent me**, while it is day: the night cometh, when no man can work. 5 As long as I am in the world, I am the light of the world (*in showing what God is really like*)." Like every other healing, this was a judgment of the wrath of God on the devil's work, by a man knowing it was God's will to always heal. Ps 103:3 "Who forgiveth all thine iniquities; who healeth all thy diseases."

According to Isaiah 53, Jesus took the full wrath of God for us in one action forever. Heb 10:12 "But this man, after he had offered **one sacrifice for sins for ever**, sat down on the right hand of God; 13 from henceforth expecting till his enemies be made his footstool." Rom 3:24 "Being justified freely by his grace through the redemption that is in Christ Jesus: 25 whom God hath set forth to be a propitiation through faith in his blood, to declare his righteousness for the remission of sins that are past, through the forbearance of God; 26 to declare, I say, at this time his righteousness: that he might be just, and the justifier of him which believeth in Jesus." Rom 8:2 "For the law of the Spirit of *zoe*/life in Christ Jesus hath made me free from the law of sin and death."

So, before God, there are now no legal attacks of the devil, whether we sin or not. What is missing is our enforcing the law of the spirit of *zoe*/life in Christ Jesus on the works of the devil, as Jesus did. Luke 10:19 "Behold (*consider and make this change your life immediately*), I give unto you power (*authority, commission, pre-permission and responsibility*) to tread on serpents and scorpions, and over all the power (*ability*) of the enemy: and nothing shall by any means hurt you." Don't blame God for your failure to obey this command and to enforce this responsibility from Jesus.

Jesus is the exact way God is in all a man can be. Heb 1:3 "Who being the brightness of his glory, and the express image of his person, and upholding all things by the word of his power, when he had by himself purged our sins, sat down on the right hand of the Majesty on high." Col 1:14 "In whom we have redemption through his blood, even the forgiveness of sins: 15 who is the image of the invisible God, the firstborn of every creature."

In the Gospels, God, through the life of Jesus, is showing His true nature operating in a man. Every act of healing Jesus did was a judgment of God against the devil for enforcing or implementing the law of sin and death. Acts 10:34 "Then Peter opened his mouth, and said, Of a truth I perceive that God is no respecter of persons: 35 but in every nation he that feareth him, and worketh righteousness, is accepted with him. 36 The word which God sent unto the children of Israel, preaching peace by Jesus Christ: (he is Lord of all:) 37 that word, I say, ye know, which was published throughout all Judaea, and began from Galilee, after the baptism which

A Glossary of Terms

John preached; 38 how God anointed Jesus of Nazareth with the Holy Ghost and with power: who went about doing good, and healing all that were oppressed of the devil; for God was with him." Father God used Jesus to destroy the works of the devil. Healing in the name of Jesus is a right act. Like Jesus, we do the ministry; God does the healing by Holy Spirit.

When Adam sinned, he released sin and death into the world. Rom 5:14 "Nevertheless death reigned from Adam to Moses, even over them that had not sinned after the similitude of Adam's transgression, who is the figure of him that was to come." Notice the Law of Moses stopped the free reign of the devil and gave men a way to get *zoe*/life, to counter the law of sin and death until Jesus came. Acts 13:37 "But he (*Jesus*), whom God raised again, saw no corruption. 38 Be it known unto you therefore, men and brethren, that through this man is preached unto you the forgiveness (*remission*) of sins: 39 and by him all that believe are justified from all things, from which ye could not be justified by the law of Moses." John 10:10 "The thief cometh not, but for to steal, and to kill, and to destroy: I am come that they might have *zoe*/life, and that they might have it more abundantly." Rom 5:21 "That as sin hath reigned unto death, even so might grace reign through righteousness unto eternal *zoe*/life by Jesus Christ our Lord."

The devils Jesus cast out thought the Day of God's Judgment against them was far away. Jesus demonstrated that it was within His ministry as the Day of Salvation, which we are, even now, in. Matt 8:29 "And, behold, they cried out, saying, What have we to do with thee, Jesus, thou Son of God? art thou come hither to torment (*judge against*) us before the time? 30 And there was a good way off from them an herd of many swine feeding. 31 So the devils besought him, saying, If thou cast us out, suffer us to go away into the herd of swine. 32 And he said unto them, Go. And when they were come out, they went into the herd of swine: and, behold, the whole herd of swine ran violently down a steep place into the sea, and perished in the waters." By casting out the devils, Jesus judged against them.

This word *judgment* means "a judicial decree for or against someone." The word in Matt 8:29 translated *torment* means "misery as a result of a judicial decree against." Jesus issued a judicial decree against the demons, and in favor of the man controlled by the demons, when Jesus said "Go," in verse 32. So, yes, the devils had the timing wrong, and now is the Day of Salvation, which also starts the Day of Judgment against the devil and his works. 2 Cor 6:1 "We then, as workers together with him, beseech you also that ye receive not the grace of God in vain. 2 (For he saith, I have heard thee in a time accepted, and in the day of *soteria*/salvation have I succoured thee: behold, now is the accepted time; behold, now is the day of *soteria*/salvation.)" John 5:27 "And hath given him authority to execute judgment also, because he is the Son of man. 28 Marvel not at this: for the hour is coming, in the which all that are in the graves shall hear his voice, 29 and shall come forth; they that have done good, unto the resurrection of *zoe*/life; and they that have done evil, unto the resurrection of damnation. 30 I can of mine own self do nothing: as I hear, I judge: and my judgment is just; because I seek not mine own will, but the will of the Father which hath sent me." John 16:8 "And when he is come, he will reprove the world of sin, and of righteousness, and of judgment (*condemnation*): 9 of sin, because they believe not on me; 10 of righteousness, because I go to my Father, and ye see me no more; 11 of judgment, because the prince of this world is judged (*against*)." 1 John 3:8 "He that committeth sin is of the devil; for the devil sinneth from the beginning. For this purpose the Son of God was manifested, that he might destroy (*execute or deliver or enforce the judgment of God against*) the works of the devil."

The full Day of Judgment will be when God finally cleans the Universe of all of Satan's works. We now, by faith in the power of the blood of Jesus, have salvation from the full wrath of God when He cleans the Universe. 1 Thes 5:8 "But let us, who are of the day, be sober, putting on the breastplate of faith and *agape*/love; and for an helmet, the hope of *soteria*/salvation. 9 For God hath not appointed us to wrath, but to obtain *soteria*/salvation by our Lord Jesus Christ, 10 who died for us, that, whether we wake or sleep, we should *zao*/live together with him." Rom 5:9 "Much more then, being now justified by his blood, we shall be *sozo*/saved from wrath through him. 10 For if, when we were enemies, we were reconciled to God by the death of his Son, much more, being reconciled, we shall be *sozo*/saved by his *zoe*/life. 11 And not only so, but we also joy in God through our Lord Jesus Christ, by whom we have now received the atonement (*reconciliation*)."

Even though we are "saved," to be in eternity with God in being born again, we do not have freedom from our works being judged by the wrath of God on that Day. God has decreed Num 14:21 "But as truly as I live, all the earth shall be filled with the glory of the LORD." The Day of Judgment is the final cleansing to allow this to happen. Rom 2:5 "But after thy hardness and impenitent heart treasurest up unto thyself wrath against the day of wrath and revelation of the righteous judgment of God; 6 who will render to every man according to his deeds."1 Cor 3:12 "Now if any [*Christian*] man build upon this foundation gold, silver, precious stones, wood, hay, stubble; 13 every man's work shall be made manifest: for the day shall declare it, because it shall be revealed by fire; and the fire shall try every man's work of what sort it is. 14 If any man's work abide which he hath built thereupon, he shall receive a reward. 15 If any man's work shall be burned, he shall suffer loss: but he himself shall be *sozo*/saved; yet so as by fire." Rom 2:16 "In the day when God shall judge the secrets of men by Jesus Christ according to my gospel ..."

Burn-It-Now Process: Notice that on the Day of Judgment is the all-consuming fire of God, wrath or judgment, for any work of the devil in anyone's life that is not already destroyed by this ten-step renewing process based on Is 53, Rom 6:1-13, 13:11-14, Eph 4:20-32, 6:10-20, Col 3:5-10 and 1 Pe 2:24:

A Glossary of Terms

1. Confessing (agreeing with what Holy Spirit calls sin)
2. Agreeing that Jesus died for it and you are forgiven by His blood in the New Covenant shed two thousand years ago, and then thanking Him and Father God for sending Him
3. Judging that sin and its consequence was put on Jesus' body and remitted and forgiven by His blood and healed by His stripes and when He was raised from the dead
4. Casting out the devil in the situation or yourself
5. Making any restitution or reconciliation
6. Putting on your mental self the new man, made after the image of God in true righteousness and holiness, the real, born-again, new-creation, you
7. Receiving or enforcing any healing needed in Jesus' name
8. Finding specific areas to stop sinning in, confessing that this is not your real nature in Jesus, and seeing yourself no longer doing that same sin, but, rather, acting like Jesus would
9. Thanking Father God that He is changing you into being more like Jesus every day (When you struggle with this, obey Phil 4:6-7.)
10. Going and helping others get free in the same way. You must go and do acts of *agape*/love because that is what Jesus would do and you have "put on Jesus Christ," and should now act like Him (Rom 13:14, Eph 4:22-24, Col 2:6 & 3:12-13).

This is keeping short accounts with God. A contrite heart knows the judgment is there and sure. The only acceptable way to be sorry/contrite for your sin is to acknowledge that the mighty Arm of God, Jesus, bore it for you already, paid for it already and was healed of it already, so that you thank Him for the healing and then expect to receive that healing to walk more like Him.

Keeping your eye on that Day, while knowing your sins are forgiven is a key to Christian growth. 2 Pet 1:8 "For if these things be in you, and abound, they make you that ye shall neither be barren nor unfruitful in the knowledge of our Lord Jesus Christ. 9 But he that lacketh these things is blind, and cannot see afar off, and hath forgotten that he was purged from his old sins."

The Fear of God: There are several kinds of fear described in the Bible. The fear of God is designed to keep us from sinning (whereas the devil tries to enforce the law of sin and death, the curses, and the wrath of the Law), so that men can do righteousness and God's a*gape*/love can fill the Earth. The fear of the Lord can be described on four levels. All are the territory of a humble and contrite heart.

(1) There is a fear that is the absolute assurance that all sin, every evil work, will be destroyed and that we will reap whatever evil we sow which remains unconfessed. We can then agree that Jesus died for it, make whatever restitution on Earth is required and put on Jesus Christ over it. This is knee-knocking, self-preservation, avoid-all-loss fear, and the one most mentioned in the Bible. (Deut 28 has an impressive list of blessing and what to fear when we disobey. See also 2 Cor 5:10.)

OK, God, Now What?

(2) There is a fear that is the awesome reverence that God is great and to be obeyed, for it is to our benefit. This fear is still a form of self-protection (see 2 Cor 7:1 and Deut 10:20).

(3) There is a fear that God is a loving Father and our sins hurt Him by cutting off His love in that area. This is a loving fear in which we are more concerned that God is not receiving all that He wants, and we are the reason. This loving fear does not want to offend Him (see Rev 14:7 and Heb 12:28).

(4) And there is a fear that is walking in *agape*/love in which you are an active agent of God delivering His *agape*/love in every part of life and, therefore, you do not sin and only do righteousness. This is where Jesus and mature Christians walk, as *agape*/love slaves to God, delighting to only please Him by continual right faith actions in holding on to His Word in trouble and setting others free (see 1 John 4:16-19).

Whatever level of right fear keeps you from sin and keeps you doing righteousness is the place to start. There are many scriptures showing each aspect. Here are a few describing these different aspects of the fear of God. 2 Cor 5:10 "For we must all appear before the judgment seat of Christ; that every one may receive the things done in his body, according to that he hath done, whether it be good or bad. 11 Knowing therefore the terror of the Lord, we persuade men; but we are made manifest unto God; and I trust also are made manifest in your consciences." 2 Cor 7:1 "Having therefore these promises, dearly *agape*/beloved, let us cleanse ourselves from all filthiness of the flesh and spirit, perfecting holiness in the fear of God." Deut 10:20 "Thou shalt fear the Lord thy God; him shalt thou serve, and to him shalt thou cleave, and swear by his name. 21 He is thy praise, and he is thy God, that hath done for thee these great and terrible things, which thine eyes have seen. 22 Thy fathers went down into Egypt with threescore and ten persons; and now the Lord thy God hath made thee as the stars of heaven for multitude." Rev 14:7 "Saying with a loud voice, Fear God, and give glory to him; for the hour of his judgment is come: and worship him that made heaven, and earth, and the sea, and the fountains of waters." Heb 12:28 "Wherefore we receiving a kingdom which cannot be moved, let us have grace, whereby we may serve God acceptably with reverence and godly fear: 29 for our God is a consuming fire." 1 John 4:16 "And we have known and believed the *agape*/love that God hath to us. God is *agape*/love; and he that dwelleth in *agape*/love dwelleth in God, and God in him. 17 Herein is our *agape*/love made perfect, that we may have boldness in the day of judgment: because as he is, so are we in this world. 18 There is no fear in *agape*/love; but perfect *agape*/love casteth out fear: because fear hath torment. He that feareth is not made perfect in *agape*/love. 19 We *agape*/love him, because he first *agape*/loved us."

God does not have to actively judge us and force His wrath upon us in this life. The laws that He made, when He created the Earth and pronounced good, do that. Rom 2:11 "For there is no respect of persons with God." Gal 6:7 "Be not deceived; God is not mocked: for whatsoever a man soweth, that shall he also reap. 8 For

A Glossary of Terms

he that soweth to his flesh shall of the flesh reap corruption; but he that soweth to the Spirit shall of the Spirit reap *zoe*/life everlasting." These two scriptures tell us a fundamental truth: It does not matter who you are; if you plant and nurture good seed, you will reap good fruit; if you plant and nurture bad seed, you will reap bad fruit. This applies to anyone on the Earth—everyone, and everywhere. This is a basic law of the Universe that God has put in place. Like gravity, God does not have to do anything to enforce the law of sowing and reaping. So reaping what we sow, good or bad, is not a direct judgment of God, just the normal process of His laws in operation. In contrast, every healing Jesus performed was an example of God actively judging the works of the devil and the application of His wrath against the devil to set people free from either devil attacks, accidents or evil reaping. He gave us that job to continue. Luke 10:19 "Behold (*stop and make this change your life*), I give unto you power (*authority*) to tread on serpents and scorpions, and over all *dunamis*/power (*ability*) of the enemy: and nothing shall by any means hurt you." As Jesus is the exact representation of God, we can know He delights in judging the devil to freedom for the oppressed through men—you and me.

Many people think that the God of the Old Testament is a God of wrath, and the God of the New Testament one of *agape*/love. Well, He is the same God in both, and has always been and always will be the same. He is also a God of forgiveness. Hear the cry of God to the people of the Old Testament, who had sown and nurtured bad seed. Hos 10:12 "Sow to yourselves in righteousness, reap in *chesed*/mercy; break up your fallow ground: for it is time to seek the LORD, till he come and rain righteousness upon you. 13 Ye have plowed wickedness, ye have reaped iniquity; ye have eaten the fruit of lies: because thou didst trust in thy way, in the multitude of thy mighty men (*rather than in God*)."

Look at the example of Job. In Job 1 and 2, we see a throne or courtroom scene where Satan, the god of this world, accuses God and Job. God does not stop the devil, because the devil is working within God's laws, but God does limit what Satan can do. First, God limits Satan to not touching Job's life, and then, second, God limits Satan to not killing Job. Then we see God go to work. First, in Job 32, He sends Elihu to adjust Job's thinking, so that he will quit finding fault with God. Job does well in holding on to God for goodness, no matter what, but he still sins in accusing God of evil, making a mistake. After Elihu gets a little humility into Job, God appears, and Job repents. Here is what God does now. First, He gets Job to pray in an act of the intercessor for his friends, who did not confess. Now Job is thinking like God. And then God blesses Job, and he gets twice as much wealth and a new set of children, and he lives one hundred and forty more years. This is our God at work!

Historically, the people of Israel continually failed to cooperate with God and allow Him to bless them. Thus, their actions produced the curse and not the blessing. God continually sent them prophets, just like He did to Job, to turn them from their sins so they could receive life from Him, but they would not. In spite of this,

OK, God, Now What?

He mitigated or reduced as much as He could to save them. Mal 3:6 "For I am the LORD, I change not; therefore ye sons of Jacob are not consumed." It seems that our unresolved sin builds up, and even though God's hand is around us as a wall, the sin overflows the wall, and we suffer the judgment of the law of sin and death dispensed by Satan as due. God's ultimate triumph is that He can bless the "saved" in Heaven, in spite of their Earth life.

We see this in the numerous times Israel sinned, and yet God showed them a way to stop the curse or judgment. In Numbers 12, Miriam was stricken with leprosy for sinning, but Moses prayed, and she was healed. In the process, Moses had to forgive Miriam for speaking against his wife. This same scene unfolded repeatedly in the Bible. God has always looked for one who would deal with Him so that He could heal. Ps 103:3 "Who forgiveth all thine iniquities; who healeth all thy diseases." When He could find no man, instead, He sent Jesus. Isa 59:16 "And he saw that there was no man, and wondered that there was no intercessor: therefore his arm brought salvation unto him; and his righteousness, it sustained him. 17 For he put on righteousness as a breastplate, and an helmet of salvation upon his head; and he put on the garments of vengeance for clothing, and was clad with zeal as a cloak."

Here is God's attitude toward death in any form—from a small headache or scrape, to the loss of all limbs, to an untimely death, to famine and war. Hos 13:14 "I will ransom them from the power of the grave; I will redeem them from death: O death, I will be thy plagues; O grave, I will be thy destruction: repentance shall be hid from mine eyes." 1 Cor 15:26 "The last enemy that shall be destroyed is death." Rev 1:17 "And when I saw him *(Jesus)*, I fell at his feet as dead. And he laid his right hand upon me, saying unto me, Fear not; I am the first and the last: 18 I am he that *zao*/liveth, and was dead; and, behold, I am *zao*/alive for evermore, Amen; and have the keys of hell and of death." The bottom line is this: anything that anyone needs healed from is an enemy of God. Jesus cast out devils and healed people to show what God delights to do. In this way, He made it clear that sickness is God's enemy and is to be destroyed by any Christian at any time.

God has no desire for us to suffer any of His wraths. Jesus took all the wrath of God due us on Himself, according to Isaiah 53. God sent Jesus to demonstrate His true nature and to "destroy the works of the devil" (1 John 3:8) This word *destroy* could also mean "to exercise wrath," so this could be stated as "God sent Jesus to exercise His wrath against the devil and, thus, destroy what the devil had built on the Earth, so that men could be *sozo*/saved and Heaven come to Earth."

Zoe/Life is the opposite of the effects of sin and evil. John 3:16 "For God so *agape*/loved the world, that he gave his only begotten Son, that whosoever believeth *(does continual faith actions)* in him should not perish, but have everlasting *zoe*/life. 17 For God sent not his Son into the world to condemn the *(people of the)* world; but that the world through him might be *sozo*/saved." In these scriptures, we see God's attitude toward us and the devil: *zoe*/life for us, wrath for the devil and all his works. The

A Glossary of Terms

problem is that if our hearts and minds are in love with the works of the devil, we will suffer the consequences of evil fruit and loss, along with the devil on that Day according to 1 Cor 3.

Consider: How did Adam and Eve turn this world over to the curse? By disobeying God's Word, they gave this Earth to the consequences of sin and the rule of Satan. One of the meanings of the word *god* is "source." When they believed Satan, rather than God, they made the devil their source of life, releasing sin and Satan's anti-life force, death, into the world. Rom 5:14 "Nevertheless death reigned (*as king, with cruel decrees, enforced by the devil*) from Adam to Moses, even over them that had not sinned after the similitude of Adam's transgression, who is the figure of him that was to come." With Moses, God started to deal with sin and death until Jesus came.

Consider: 2 Cor 4:4 "In whom the god of this world hath blinded the minds of them which believe not (*no right faith actions*), lest the light of the glorious gospel of Christ, who is the image of God, should shine unto them." Just as he did with Adam and Eve, Satan, the god of this world, is still blinding people's minds to the *agape/* love of God in Jesus Christ. The Bible tells us that, in the end, Jesus will be established as the rightful ruler of this world and Satan put fully into the Lake of Fire.

The wrath of God is that impartial force of *agape/*love that must clean up sin, all evil that would hurt or hinder God's children. God is light, sin is darkness, and light must dispel darkness until darkness is no more. The darkness then feels the "wrath" of the light. The opposite is also true, if light is extinguished, it has felt the wrath of darkness. John 8:12 "Then spake Jesus again unto them, saying, I am the light of the world: he that followeth me [*as I walk with Father God*] shall not walk in darkness, but shall have the light of *zoe/*life [*as seen in Me in your own life*]." Jesus, as seen in the gospels, was the true Light of what God was and is and delighted to do good when He could find one who would work with Him. True light is to see Jesus as how God really is and what you are capable of being in this life.

Here is the true nature of the God of the Old Testament. Even when Adam and Eve sinned and, thus, unleashed the entire gamut of misery upon the human race, God sought them out, gave them garments to cover themselves and even gave them the promise that one of the woman's seed would "crush Satan's head" (see Genesis 3). Father God could have destroyed Adam and Eve in a heartbeat, but He did not. Instead, He showed them how to live in the mess they had created with the promise of ultimate victory and restored fellowship with Him. In Gen 3, Adam released a curse into the Earth. God mitigated it so that man could continue to live, even though it was by the sweat of his brow. Otherwise the devil would have killed Eve in childbirth and all living men in famine. So even if God must exercise His wrath, His justice, His established consequences for sin, He always makes a way to bless us in the end. He promised One who would "bruise" the devil's head, but, because we all sin and fall short of the glory of God, He had to send His own Son. John 3:17 "For God sent not his Son into the world to condemn the world; but that the world through him might be *sozo*/saved" to finish the work.

Most of what men today commonly call the judgments of God is simply: a) Us getting back what we have done to others, reaping the evil bounty of our own sins or sowing to the flesh, b) Attacks of the devil, or c) Mere accidents in a world cursed by sin. In all of these cases, it is not God at work, but the devil. Ps 34:21 "Evil shall slay the wicked ... ." Ps 18:26 "With the pure thou wilt shew thyself pure; and with the froward thou wilt shew thyself froward." Ps 141:10 "Let the wicked fall into their own nets ... ." Luke 6:37 "Judge not, and ye shall not be judged: condemn not, and ye shall not be condemned: forgive, and ye shall be forgiven: 38 give, and it shall be given unto you; good measure, pressed down, and shaken together, and running over, shall men give into your bosom. For with the same measure that ye mete withal it shall be measured to you again." Ezek 18:30 "Therefore I will judge you, O house of Israel, every one according to his ways, saith the Lord GOD. Repent, and turn yourselves from all your transgressions; so iniquity shall not be your ruin. 31 Cast away from you all your transgressions, whereby ye have transgressed; and make you a new heart and a new spirit: for why will ye die, O house of Israel? 32 For I have no pleasure in the death of him that dieth, saith the Lord GOD: wherefore turn yourselves, and live ye." (Notice that, according to Heb 8:10 and Ezek 26:36, in the New Covenant of Jesus, God gives us a new heart and a new spirit and/or writes His laws on our hearts and our minds. While it is a new spirit, it is a reprogrammed heart and mind.) Again Rom 8:15 "For ye have not received the spirit of bondage again to fear; but ye have received the Spirit of adoption, whereby we cry, Abba (*Daddy*), Father." A renewed mind walks in the fullness of what God has done for us in the new creation.

God holds back His wrath to give us time to repent and to provide a way of escape, for, through it all, God is calling, "Turn to My Son and live!" It is amazing that people can have faith in God's wrath, but not in His blessing. If we confess our sins to God, receive His forgiveness, apply that forgiveness to the consequences of sin and the curse sin brings, and put on the new man in Jesus, all by faith actions, we can destroy the consequences and the curse sin brings, just as Jesus did.

Every healing Jesus did was an example of God's attitude toward evil that hurts men and what He does when He finds someone with His view on His goodness (see Psalm 103). King David knew the truth. Ps 86:5 "For thou, Lord, art good, and ready to forgive; and plenteous in *chesed*/mercy unto all them that call upon thee. 6 Give ear, O LORD, unto my prayer; and attend to the voice of my supplications. 7 In the day of my trouble I will call upon thee: for thou wilt answer me."

As we agree with God, we will enforce the benefits of all the wrath due us falling on Jesus, and resist the devil in any of his works, until he flees. Acts 10:34 "Then Peter opened his mouth, and said, Of a truth I perceive that God is no respecter of persons: 35 but in every nation he that feareth him, and worketh righteousness, is

A Glossary of Terms

accepted with him. 36 The word which God sent unto the children of Israel, preaching peace by Jesus Christ: (he is Lord of all:) 37 that word, I say, ye know, which was published throughout all Judaea, and began from Galilee, after the baptism which John preached; 38 how God anointed Jesus of Nazareth with the Holy Ghost and with power: who went about doing good, and healing all that were oppressed of the devil; for God was with him." Notice, in verse 35, that using the name of Jesus to get people healed is a working of righteousness, and no matter how good or bad at it you are, this makes you acceptable to God. The more you reprogram your heart and mind, with continual faith actions, the better you will be at it. A right heart operates in the fire of God, just like Jesus.

We see many instances in the Old Testament in which men built an altar to make a sacrifice, and God sent fire and consumed it: Gideon (Jud 6:21), David (1 Cron 21:26) and Elijah (1 Kings 18:38). The sacrifice stood for the sin, and God destroyed it by fire, and then He started, through a man, to set things right. When God destroys something, it is all gone. The great flood destroyed all, as did the judgment on Sodom and Gomorrah. Rev 21 and 22 show the Earth fully cleaned and prepared for God to bring Heaven to Earth. Jesus destroyed, purged, and dissolved our sins, once and for all men two thousand years ago. The job was fully and completely accomplished. God does not live in time, and this work of Jesus was timeless, eternal, once for all time. This is what it means when Holy Spirit says Heb 10:10 "By the which will we are sanctified through the offering of **the body of Jesus Christ once for all**. 11 And every priest standeth daily ministering and offering oftentimes the same sacrifices, which can never take away sins: 12 but this man, after he had offered **one sacrifice for sins for ever**, sat down on the right hand of God; 13 from henceforth expecting till his enemies be made his footstool *by us, the Church*. 14 For **by one offering he hath perfected for ever** them that are sanctified. 15 Whereof the Holy Ghost also is a witness to us: for after that he had said before, 16 This is the covenant that I will make with them after those days, saith the Lord, I will put my laws into their hearts, and in their minds will I write them; 17 And their **sins and iniquities will I remember no more**. 18 Now where remission of these is, **there is no more offering for sin.**" The wrath due us fell on Jesus. All of these scriptures that relate to this are in the past tense. It is done! Our job is to now deliver the wrath of God on the devil and get people set free.

Jesus came to the Earth to baptize with Holy Spirit and fire. That fire burns up all the chaff, the useless parts of the Earth, and chaff is a symbol of any work of the devil. Luke 3:16 "John answered, saying unto them all, I indeed baptize you with water; but one mightier than I cometh, the latchet of whose shoes I am not worthy to unloose: he shall baptize you with the Holy Ghost and with fire: 17 whose fan is in his hand, and he will throughly purge his floor, and will gather the wheat into his garner; but the chaff he will burn with fire unquenchable." The final day is the Day of Judgment, and, until then, we are to judge the devil by fire, in setting people free from any oppression of the devil, in Jesus' name. Stir yourself up with God's Word, the Scriptures, till you operate in God's fire, His zeal for deliverance to *agape* righteousness and hate iniquity like Jesus (Heb 1:9).

Jesus, by Holy Spirit, burns with fire the works of the devil in men and makes them whole, thus delivering the wrath of God to the devil, and not to men. Acts 14:3 "Long time therefore abode they speaking boldly in the Lord, which gave testimony unto the word of his grace, and granted signs and wonders to be done by their hands." Mark 16:19 "So then after the Lord had spoken unto them, he was received up into heaven, and sat on the right hand of God. 20 And they went forth, and preached everywhere, the Lord working with them, and confirming the word with signs following. Amen." We are to continue that same Word, the same way, in that same spirit, Word or fire, against the wrath of the devil, by using the wrath, the Word of God, to create peace, just as Jesus did. Acts 10:36 "The word which God sent unto the children of Israel, preaching peace by Jesus Christ: (he is Lord of all:) 37 that word, I say, ye know, which was published throughout all Judaea, and began from Galilee, after the baptism which John preached; 38 how God anointed Jesus of Nazareth with the Holy Ghost and with power: who went about doing good, and healing all that were oppressed of the devil; for God was with him." Let us go and do likewise, in the name of Jesus, knowing: Isa 55:11 "So shall my word be that goeth forth out of my mouth *through you*: it shall not return unto me void, but it shall accomplish that which I please, and it shall prosper in the thing whereto I sent it." Heb 13:8 "Jesus Christ the same yesterday, and to day, and for ever." He is ever the Healer, and He must always heal by exercising the wrath of God, in *agape* love, by our faith actions, on the works of the devil, through us, His Body.

ZAO; ZOE

Zao (Strong's NT 2198, pronounced: dzah'-o) is the verb form, *live*; *zoe* (Strong's NT 2222, pronounced: dzo-ah') is the noun, *life*. As a Greek word *zoe* means the life force of the spirit you are nurturing or releasing by your actual thoughts, words and deeds. In the Bible this word generally means the life, power, enthusiasm, and attitude that only comes from the true *zao*/living God. Bringing God's *zoe* to men was the primary propose of Jesus and the proof that Jesus is from God. All of His actions in demonstrating the *zoe*/life of God in a man in miracles, dying on the cross, resurrecting from the dead and sending Holy Spirit were so that we could be justified unto *zoe*/life, to provide a dwelling place for Holy Spirit within our spirits. This is so that we can do our part in finishing the job of destroying the works of the devil. John 10:10 "The thief cometh not, but for to steal, and to kill, and to destroy: I am come that they might have *zoe*/life, and that they might have it more abundantly." 1 John 5:9 "If we receive the witness of men, the witness of God is greater: for this is the witness of God which he hath testified of his Son. 10 He that believeth on the Son of God hath the witness in himself: he that believeth not God hath made him a liar; because he believeth not (*no or limited faith*

A Glossary of Terms

actions) the record that God gave of his Son. 11 **And this is the record, that God hath given to us eternal *zoe*/life, and this *zoe*/life is in his Son**. 12 He that hath the Son hath *zoe*/life; and he that hath not the Son of God hath not *zoe*/life." This *zoe*/life in our spirit, with Holy Spirit indwelling, is the main mark of a Bible Christian.

God's answer for every work of the devil and the path into God's prosperity is the *zoe*/life of God. According to John 10:10, we see that the opposite of anything that steals, kills or destroys is the *zoe* of God. Jesus bears the title of the Prince of *Zoe*/Life. Acts 3:15 "And killed the Prince of *zoe*/life, whom God hath raised from the dead; whereof we are witnesses." Rom 8:2 "For the law of the Spirit of *zoe*/life in Christ Jesus hath made me free from the law of sin and death." Thus, we see that every work of the devil, in death in any form, is overcome and destroyed by the *zoe*/life of God.

In the Greek understanding, a human operated in the *zoe* of a god or spirit when they thought and acted like that god or spirit. A Greek warrior wanted to operate in the full *zoe* of Ares, the god of war, to prosper in battle and vanquish enemies. To do this, a warrior would fill his mind with thoughts and attitudes of war and train with weapons and physical exercise to make himself excel in war. Thus, with enthusiasm and joy, he would train and fight, breathing, or *zao*ing that spirit of war. While not addressing a specific "god," we see similar actions and effects in a team locker room, where the coach inspires his or her players to get in agreement so that the "in-spirit-dwells," to "pump up" the team or players before the game or at halftime, or in a motivational speaker to any group. They are now filled with that spirit-thinking alike and excited to gird up their minds for courage, strength, endurance and pain to overcome. In fact, the word *enthusiasm* means "joyously one with god," or to be in *zoe*.

This is the same concept for operating in the *zoe* of God. Holy Spirit is within us. According to Eph 4:17-18, it is how we think and then act that releases Him/*zoe* from our spirit into the world to do good. To sin is to operate in the devil's death or darkness (i.e., the devil's anti-*zoe*). 1 John 3:8 "He that committeth sin is of the devil; for the devil sinneth from the beginning. For this purpose the Son of God was manifested, that he might destroy the works of the devil. ... 10 In this the children of God are manifest, and the children of the devil: whosoever doeth not righteousness is not of God (*in his actions*), neither he that *agape*/loveth not his brother." Rom 6:21 "What fruit had ye then in those things whereof ye are now ashamed? for the end of those things is death. 22 But now being made free from sin, and become servants to God, ye have your fruit unto holiness, and the end everlasting *zoe*/life. 23 For the wages of sin is death; but the gift of God is eternal *zoe*/life through Jesus Christ our Lord."

For our own motivation into the *zoe*/life of God: Eph 5:18 "And be not drunk with wine, wherein is excess; but be (*continually being*) filled with the Spirit [*by continual faith actions*]; 19 speaking to yourselves in psalms and hymns and spiritual songs, singing and making melody in your heart to the Lord; 20 giving thanks always for all things unto God and the Father in the name of our Lord Jesus Christ; 21 submitting yourselves one to another in the fear of God." Col 3:14 "And above all these things put on *agape*/charity, which is the bond of perfectness. 15 And let the peace of God rule in your hearts, to the which also ye are called in one body; and be ye thankful (*in continual faith actions*). 16 Let the word of Christ dwell in you richly in all wisdom; teaching and admonishing one another in psalms and hymns and spiritual songs, singing with grace in your hearts to the Lord. 17 And whatsoever ye do in word or deed, do all in the name of the Lord Jesus, giving thanks to God and the Father by him." Notice that right speaking and singing keeps us in God's *zoe*. Obeying these continually, therefore, will cause you to continually operate in the *zoe* of God. This is also a description of what it looks like to operate in the *zoe* of God.

A similar Old Testament word (*sharat* OT 8334), translated as both "worship" and "serve," carries the concept that in all of God-life we breathe and move in Him, thus, echoing the Greek word *zoe*. Thus, every part of life is an act of worship to God or some other god. There is no human action or thought that does not have a spiritual source and impact of one kind or the other. There are only two choices, God or the devil. Doing business deals, planting seed, cooking dinner or raising children are all to be done in total unity with the true and *zao*/living God. So when we sin, we are actually serving or worshiping or breathing sin. 1 John 3:8 "He that committeth sin is of the devil; for the devil sinneth from the beginning. For this purpose the Son of God was manifested, that he might destroy the works of the devil." So when we sin, we are *zao*ing the devil. Jesus destroyed the devil and his works in the spirit realm, and we have the job of doing our part now. This job of destroying all the devil's works is complete on the Day of Judgment. Thus, when we operate in Jesus, to set people free, we are delivering judgment to the devil. We do it as we *zao* God by faith actions on the subject of healing, or for any other answered *aiteo*, for any other part of His salvation.

So, in essence, as part of the Universe and in the Universe, your every thought, word and action is in tune with some level of that Universe. At the top is God; everywhere else is rebellion and the devil. Thus, you cannot think a thought, speak, or do an action of rebellion and be in unity with God, and when you do, you are in unity with the devil, and not God. 1 John 3:8 "He that committeth sin is of the devil; for the devil sinneth from the beginning." You cannot sin in unity with Father God, so, by default, you are in unity with the devil or the god of this world. 2 Cor 4:4 "In whom the god of this world hath blinded the minds of them which believe not, lest the light of the glorious gospel of Christ, who is the image of God, should shine unto them." John 12:31 "Now is the judgment of this world: now shall the prince of this world be cast out." This unity is on a thought-by-thought basis, so each thought must be judged.

Another biblical term for this unity with the god of this world is *iniquity*: Acts 8:23 "For I perceive that thou art in the gall of bitterness, and in the bond of iniquity." Titus 2:14 "Who gave himself for us, that he might redeem us from all iniquity, and purify unto himself a peculiar people, zealous of good (*God-level*) works." Heb 1:9 "Thou hast *agape*/loved righteousness, and hated iniquity; therefore God, even thy God, hath anointed thee with the oil of gladness above thy fellows." 2 Pet 2:16 "But was rebuked

A Glossary of Terms

for his iniquity: the dumb ass speaking with man's voice forbad the madness of the prophet."

The concept described by *zoe* is that you are always in a unity with a spirit of some kind or another. This is very different from most modern Western thinking, where the concept is that you can have a "middle" position, deciding free from either God or the devil. While convenient in this culture, this does not fit the concept of *zoe*, nor does it fit the Scriptures and will lead to great terror on the Day of Judgment. 1 John 5:17 "All unrighteousness (*dis-unity, anti-zoe in thoughts, words or deeds*) is sin .... ."

To allow or follow a spirit is a function of where you are or what you choose. For example, you may choose certain clothes to remind you of what spirit you have decided to let operate through you. This is the meaning and purpose of a talisman and carrying about statues of various gods, or, in a milder sense, team colors.

Whereas, as a Christian, you may have Holy Spirit as one with your spirit, but your thoughts, words and actions need to be consistent with Holy Spirit for you to operate "in the spirit of God." Conversely, if you are not operating in the Spirit of God, you are operating in another spirit. As you operate within the Scriptures, your thoughts, words and actions allow God to operate through you, to His glory. If you are not operating out of the Jesus-like parts of Scripture, you are *zao*ing out of God and in the spirit of the devil, i.e., unrighteousness.

So one way to describe the Gospel is that **God invites you to operate by His *zoe* in Jesus by faith actions, knowing that all your failures to operate perfectly in His *zoe* have been paid for by Jesus through the cross, and you can come to God freely at any time to operate in His *zoe*.** The more you know this the more your conscience is cleansed of thinking that anything was lacking in the work of Jesus through the cross and resurrection. Col 2:10 "And ye are complete in him, which is the head of all principality and power."

God defines this *zoe* as a distinguishing mark of what He accomplished in Jesus. 1 John 5:10 "He that believeth (*by faith actions*) on the Son of God hath the witness in himself: he that believeth not God hath made him a liar; because he believeth not the record that God gave of his Son. 11 **And this is the record, that God hath given to us eternal *zoe*/life, and this *zoe*/life is in his Son.** 12 He that hath the Son hath *zoe*/life; and he that hath not the Son of God hath not *zoe*/life." Gal 2:20 "I am (*have been*) crucified with Christ: nevertheless I *zao*/live; yet not I, but Christ *zao*/liveth in me: and the life which I now *zao*/live in the flesh I *zao*/live by the faith (*actions*) of (*or concerning*) the Son of God, who *agape*/loved me, and gave himself for me."

Because God made Jesus sin for us, He can now dwell in us because of Jesus. As we access His *zoe*/life, in spite of our failures, we proclaim the power of the blood of Jesus. Heb 9:14 "How much more shall the blood of Christ, who through the eternal Spirit offered himself without spot to God, purge your conscience from dead works to serve (*operate by the zoe of*) the *zao*/living God?"

OK, God, Now What?

Here again is a plea to stop operating or serving in the *zoe* of other gods and only operate in the eternal *zoe* of God. <u>1 Thes 1:9</u> "For they themselves shew of us what manner of entering in we had unto you, and how ye turned to God from idols to serve the *zao*/living and true God; 10 and to wait for his Son from heaven, whom he raised from the dead, even Jesus, which delivered us from the wrath to come."

All of this comes under the area of renewing the mind, so, when Holy Spirit prompts with thoughts and words, we respond quickly in agreement and continue to operate in the *zoe*/life of God. God makes it clear that operating any other way does not bring the Kingdom of God. <u>Gal 5:19</u> "Now the works of the flesh (*anti-zoe*) are manifest, which are these; Adultery, fornication, uncleanness, lasciviousness, 20 idolatry, witchcraft, hatred, variance, emulations, wrath, strife, seditions, heresies, 21 envyings, murders, drunkenness, revellings, and such like: of the which I tell you before, as I have also told you in time past, that they which do such things shall not inherit (*produce*) the kingdom of God. 22 But the fruit of the Spirit (*zoe of God*) is (*actions of*) *agape*/love, joy, peace, longsuffering, gentleness, goodness, faith, 23 meekness, temperance: against such there is no law. 24 And they that are Christ's have crucified the flesh with the affections and lusts. 25 If we *zao*/live in the Spirit, let us also walk (*order our behavior in faith actions*) in the Spirit. 26 Let us not be desirous of vain glory, provoking one another, envying one another." Verse 25 is a clear command to walk by continual faith actions in the *zoe* we now have.

For the Christian, the plea is to no longer do those things that are not God's *zoe*, and, instead, *zao* for and through God. <u>2 Cor 5:15</u> "And that he died for all, that they which *zao*/live should not henceforth *zao*/live unto themselves, but unto him (*for or like Jesus*), which died for them, and rose again."

The concept of *zoe* and Hebrew worship or service is that there are no actions independent of the spirit world and a spirit. We are constantly operating in God or the devil, with no neutral ground. This is a major challenge to modern Western thought, where there are typically three possible choices: a) with God or good; b) with the devil or evil; or c) a neutral ground aligned with neither. The Bible calls this third position deception. <u>James 1:22</u> "But be ye doers of the word, and not hearers only, deceiving your own selves." <u>1 Cor 6:9</u> "Know ye not that the unrighteous shall not inherit (*produce*) the kingdom of God? Be not deceived: neither fornicators, nor idolaters, nor adulterers, nor effeminate, nor abusers of themselves with mankind, 10 nor thieves, nor covetous, nor drunkards, nor revilers, nor extortioners, shall inherit (*produce*) the kingdom of God. 11 And such were some of you: but ye are washed, but ye are sanctified, but ye are justified in the name of the Lord Jesus, and by the Spirit of our God." <u>1 Cor 15:33</u> "Be not deceived: evil communications corrupt good manners. 34 Awake to righteousness, and sin not; for some have not the knowledge of God: I speak this to your shame." <u>1 John 1:8</u> "If we say that we have no sin, we deceive ourselves, and the truth is not in us." <u>Ps 10:4</u> "The wicked, through the pride of his countenance, will not seek after God: God is not in all his thoughts."

A Glossary of Terms

In summary: 1 Pet 1:18 "Forasmuch as ye know that ye were not redeemed with corruptible things, as silver and gold, from your vain conversation received by tradition from your fathers; 19 but with the precious blood of Christ, as of a lamb without blemish and without spot: 20 who verily was foreordained before the foundation of the world, but was manifest in these last times for you, 21 who by him do believe (*by faith actions*) in God, that raised him up from the dead, and gave him glory; that your faith and hope (*actions*) might be in God. 22 **Seeing ye have purified your souls in obeying the truth** through the Spirit unto unfeigned love of the brethren, **see that ye *agape*/love one another with a pure heart fervently**: 23 being born again, not of corruptible seed, but of incorruptible, by the word of God, which liveth and abideth for ever. 24 For all flesh is as grass, and all the glory of man as the flower of grass. The grass withereth, and the flower thereof falleth away: 25 but the word of the Lord endureth for ever. And this is the word which by the gospel is preached unto you."

To have the *zoe* of God is mind-boggling potential. To operate in *zoe* is to activate the *zoe*/life of God into the people, situations and activities of Earth, to change from the current state to the will of God. As with most things of God, the static and academic status does not produce godly results, until we activate *zoe* by faith and deliver it where needed. This active and deep knowing is how we grow in God. 2 Pet 1:3 "According as his divine power hath given unto us all things that pertain unto *zoe*/life and godliness, through the (*deep and experiential*) *epignosis*/knowledge of him that hath called us to glory and virtue." We start with recognition, and then move into being and doing, according to our born-again nature. Eph 4:21 "If so be that ye have heard him, and have been taught by him, as the truth is in Jesus: 22 that ye put off concerning the former conversation the old man, which is corrupt according to the deceitful lusts; 23 and be renewed in the spirit of your mind; 24 and that ye put on the new man, which after God is created in righteousness and true holiness."

Any resistance to this means you have an area or areas where you need to renew (*purify*) your mind to the Christ-mind way of thinking, speaking and doing. 2 Cor 10:3 "For though we walk in the flesh, we do not war after the flesh: 4 (for the weapons of our warfare are not carnal, but mighty through God to the pulling down of strong holds;) 5 casting down imaginations, and every high thing that exalteth itself against the knowledge of God, and bringing into captivity every thought to the obedience of Christ." Notice that this is "our war" or our job in this life now.

As you purify your soul, by *phileo*/brotherly love, you move into *zao*ing God in *agape*/love from a purified heart. It is the way you think that controls your actions and determines whether you walk in the *zoe* of God or not. Eph 4:17 "This I say therefore, and testify in the Lord, that ye henceforth walk not as other Gentiles walk, in the vanity of their mind, 18 having the understanding darkened, **being alienated from the *zoe*/life of God** through the ignorance that is in them, because of the blindness of their heart: 19 who being past feeling have given themselves over unto lasciviousness, to work all uncleanness with greediness."

OK, God, Now What?

For a description of how to walk in the *zoe* of God, from one of many in the Bible: Eph 4:20 "But ye have not so learned Christ; 21 if so be that ye have heard him, and have been taught by him, as the truth is in Jesus: 22 that ye put off concerning the former conversation the old man, which is corrupt according to the deceitful lusts; 23 and be renewed in the spirit of your mind; 24 and that ye put on the new man, which after God is created in righteousness and true holiness. 25 Wherefore putting away lying, speak every man truth with his neighbour: for we are members one of another. 26 Be ye angry, and sin not: let not the sun go down upon your wrath: 27 Neither give place to the devil. 28 Let him that stole steal no more: but rather let him labour, working with his hands the thing which is good, that he may have to give to him that needeth. 29 Let no corrupt communication proceed out of your mouth, but that which is good to the use of edifying, that it may minister grace unto the hearers. 30 And grieve not the Holy Spirit of God, whereby ye are sealed unto the day of redemption. 31 Let all bitterness, and wrath, and anger, and clamour, and evil speaking, be put away from you, with all malice: 32 and be ye kind one to another, tenderhearted, forgiving one another, even as God for Christ's sake hath forgiven you. 5:1 Be ye therefore followers (*copycats, imitators, duplicates*) of God, as dear children; 2 and walk in *agape*/love, as Christ also hath *agape*/loved us, and hath given himself for us an offering and a sacrifice to God for a sweetsmelling savour." This faith-action *zoe*/walk description really goes to the root of Eph 6.

To minister healing, or any work of salvation, in the *zoe* of God includes "breathing in" the attitude of God's promises against the devil and his works and, for those who need the blessing, by applying His *zoe* as needed, knowing: John 16:11 "... the ruler (evil genius, prince) of this world [Satan] is judged and condemned and sentence already is passed upon him." AMP Luke 10:19 "Behold, I (*Jesus*) give unto you power (*authority, commission, pre-permission and the resources of Heaven*) to tread on serpents and scorpions, and over all the power (*ability*) of the enemy: and nothing shall by any means hurt you. 20 Notwithstanding in this rejoice not, that the spirits are subject unto you; but rather rejoice, because your names are written in heaven."

So we are to be continually Col 1:12 "giving thanks (*continually*) unto the Father, which hath made us meet to be partakers of the inheritance of the saints in light: 13 who hath delivered us from the power of darkness, and hath translated us into the kingdom of his *agape*/dear Son: 14 in whom we have redemption through his blood, even the forgiveness of sins." Rev 1:5 "... Jesus Christ, who is the faithful witness, and the first begotten of the dead, and the prince of the kings of the earth. Unto him that *agape*/loved us, and washed us from our sins in his own blood, 6 and hath made us kings and priests unto God and his Father; to him be glory and dominion for ever and ever. Amen .... 17 ... And he (*Jesus*) ... *says to us*, Fear not; I am the first and the last: 18 I am he that *zao*/liveth, and was dead; and, behold, I am *zao*/alive for evermore, Amen; and have the keys of hell and of death." Rom 16:20 "And the God of peace shall bruise Satan under your feet shortly (*as shattered glass*). The grace of our

A Glossary of Terms

Lord Jesus Christ be with you [*to know, be and do this*]. Amen." Ps 103:6 "The LORD executeth righteousness and judgment [*through us*] for all that are oppressed." For He says: Hos 13:14 "I will ransom them from the power of the grave; I will redeem them from death: O death, I will be thy plagues; O grave, I will be thy destruction: repentance shall be hid from mine eyes." 2 Tim 1:7 "For God hath not given *you* the spirit of fear; but of *dunamis*/power, and of *agape*/love, and of a sound mind." 1 Tim 6:12 "*So* fight the good fight of faith (*actions*), lay hold on eternal *zoe*/life, whereunto thou art also called ... ." Eph 6:10 "... be strong in the Lord, and in the power of his might [*by faith actions*]" *preaching His Word of grace*, Acts 14:3 "... speaking boldly in the Lord, which *gives* testimony unto the word of his grace, and *grants* signs and wonders to be done by *your* hands [*words and actions*]." Acts 19:12 "So that from *your* body *are* brought unto the sick handkerchiefs or aprons, and the diseases *depart* from them, and the evil spirits *go* out of them. *For* Mark 16:20 "... the Lord *is* working with *you*, and confirming the word with signs following. Amen."

So to *zao* this means to take these Bible truths and operate, like Jesus did, in the *zoe* of God. Phil 2:4 "Look not every man on his own things, but every man also on the things of others. 5 **Let (*make*) this mind be in you, which was also in Christ Jesus:** ... 12 Wherefore, my *agape*/beloved, as ye have always obeyed, not as in my presence only, but now much more in my absence, work out your own *soteria*/salvation with fear and trembling. 13 For it is God which worketh in you both to will and to do of his good pleasure. 14 Do all things without murmurings and disputings: 15 that ye may be blameless and harmless, the sons of God, without rebuke, in the midst of a crooked and perverse nation, among whom ye shine as lights in the world; 16 holding forth the word of *zoe*/life; that I may rejoice in the day of Christ, that I have not run in vain, neither laboured in vain."

Or, as in another direct command to the Christian: 1 Tim 6:11 "But thou, O man of God, flee these things; and follow after righteousness, godliness, faith, *agape*/love, patience, meekness. 12 Fight the good fight of faith [*by continual, right faith actions*], *lambano*/lay hold on eternal *zoe*/life, whereunto thou art also called, and hast professed a good profession before many witnesses."

So, yes, while we are saved by grace, we are required to labor to get our minds to operate in the *zoe* of God, so God can be released by our continual right faith actions into the Earth in this life, now. This is summarized in this expanded translation: Heb 10:38 "Now the just (*those made the righteousness of God in Christ Jesus*) shall *zao*/live (*operate and release the zoe life of God in miracle-working power*) by *pistis*/faith (*actions*): but if any man draw back (*from this lifestyle of continually mixing the word of God unto victory by faith actions, i.e., unbelief*), my soul shall have no pleasure in him."

BIBLIOGRAPHY AND SUGGESTED READING

1. Amen, Daniel, *Change Your Brain Change Your Life* (Three River Press, New York, NY: 1998)

2. Assaraf, John and Smith, Murray, *The Answer* (Atria Books, New York, NY: 2008)

3. Bartmann, William, *Billionaire Secrets to Success* (Brown Books Publishing Group, Dallas, Texas: 2005)

4. Curry Blake, *The Voice of Healing* (KWHB Television broadcast, Episode 1 and 2, Tulsa, Oklahoma: March 2007).

5. Doige, Norman, *The Brain that Changes Itself,* (Penguin Group, New York, NY: 2007)

6. Leaf, Caroline, *Who Switched Off My Brain?* (Switch On Your Brain USA: 2008)

7. Mann, Donald C., *Battle Prayer for Divine Healing – Field Manual 2* (McDougal & Associates, Greenwell Springs, Louisiana: 2011)

8. Mann, Donald C., *Discovering Our Redemption* (McDougal & Associates, Greenwell Springs, Louisiana: 2011)

9. McDougal, Harold, *Speaking in Tongues: Understanding the Uses and Abuses of this Supernatural Phenomenon* (McDougal Publishing, Hagerstown, Maryland: 2000)

10. Robeson, David, *The Walk of the Spirit — The Walk of Power: The Vital Role of Praying in Tongues* (David Robeson Ministries, http://daveroberson.org/books.aspx, Tulsa, Oklahoma: 1999)

11. Scott, K., *Simple Steps to Impossible Dreams* (Fireside, New York, NY: 1998)

12. Vines, W. E., Unger, Merrill F, and White, William Jr., *Vine's Complete Expository Dictionary of Old and New Testament Words* (Thomas Nelson, Nashville, Tennessee:1996)

13. Wuest, Kenneth, *The New Testament, An Expanded Translation*, (Wm. B. Eerdmans Publishing Company, Grand Rapids, Michigan: 1961)

MINISTRY PAGE

You may contact Don Mann in any of the following ways:

Don Mann
3 Crossan Court
Landenberg, PA 19350

www.CovenantPeaceMinistries.com

eMail: Info@CovenantPeaceMinistries.com

Please share your testimonies with us.

FREE BONUS GIFT WITH YOUR PURCHASE:
Get your FREE GIFT of the first Affirmation divided into ten bite-sized pieces for easy use and portability. Go to the Contact Us page at www.CovenantPeaceMinistries.com to request your FREE GIFT.

Did You Borrow This Book? Want a Copy of Your Own?
Need a Great Gift for a Friend or Loved One?

ORDER LIST

☐ Yes I want to invest $24.95* in my future and have a personal copy of this book. For simplicity, go to www.CovenantPeaceMinistries.com. A hardback version and several eBook versions are also available (Kindle, Nook, iBook and Adobe Digital Editions-PDF).

FREE BONUS GIFT: Get your free list of Top 10 Affirmations to get you started. These are the first Affirmation divided into ten separate bite-sized steps to make it easier to start doing the Affirmations. With all 10 on one page, they can be printed for easy use and portability.

For the following items, please go to our book store at www.CovenantPeace-Ministries.com to complete your order.*

☐ Yes, I want the audio books for *OK, God, Now What?* as read by the author unabridged.*

Vol 1, Understanding Mind Renewing and Faith Building
- o _____ 6 CD Set $34.95
- o _____ 1 MP3 $34.95

Vol 2, Affirmations and Glossary
- o _____ 6 CD Set $34.95
- o _____ 1 MP3 $34.95

☐ Yes, for my regular ministry use, I want a special durable edition of *OK, God, Now What?* for $60.00.*

* Prices subject to change without notice. Please see our website for current pricing. Book website: www.CovenantPeaceMinistries.com with special offers

QUANTITY ORDERS INVITED
Info@CovenantPeaceMinistries.com

To request Don to Speak to Your Group, or for more Valuable and Powerful Ministry Tools, please go to
www.CovenantPeaceMinistries.com

Many have been helped by our free materials and videos!

For encouragement and understanding, see: Blog.CovenantPeace.com

Get the Entire POWER TRILOGY
www.CovenantPeaceMinistries.com

OK, God, Now What?
Activating His Ancient Secrets for Success

How to renew your mind for more power with God.

This book shows the Bible principles that are changing top sports, sales, business and Christian leaders, and ordinary people to godly success in every part of life.

Gain peace of mind, clarity, purpose, health, wealth and a better life. In just 21, 40 or 90 days you will see dramatic results. For the new Christian, get started right; for the mature Christian, get revelation, a new fire and peace like you've only dreamed of.

Discovering Our Redemption
How to Be Transformed By the 52 Days that Changed the Universe

Experience the confidence as you know what Jesus did in each step of the critical last 52 days of His ministry 2000 years ago. Feel your faith rise as you take these historical facts and use them for the foundation for your faith, just like the apostles did. This book shows what Jesus did from the Last Supper to the Day of Pentecost and how to apply these historical facts to greater growth in God.

Battle Prayer for Divine Healing, Field Manual 2
Releasing God's Healing Power When You Need It

> This book is a step-by-step scriptural guide on how to pray so God can heal through you.
>
> Use this book as a spiritual first-aid kit in times of trouble, as a tool for a more effective ministry, and as a study guide so you can grow in Christ and the power of Holy Spirit. For Christians at every level, Battle Prayer for Divine Healing, Field Manual 2 is for you!

Where are the answers I need?
They are in the *Power Trilogy.*
Get the complete set today and experience the transformation of your life!

- **Faith-building facts** of our Redemption ➔ *Discovering Our Redemption*
- **How to renew your mind** for miracles and blessing in God ➔ *OK, GOD, Now What?*
- **How to release** your faith for healing miracles ➔ *Battle Prayer for Divine Healing-Field Manual 2*

Go to www.CovenantPeaceMinistries.com to get yours today.

FREE BONUS GIFT: please use the contact form at www.CovenantPeaceMinistries.com to request your FREE Top 10 List of Awesome and Powerful Bible Affirmations and Slogans to get you started renewing your mind and increasing your manifestation of God's great love plan and blessings for your life.

There are numerous ways to renew your mind, but the Christ Affirmations in *OK, God, Now What?* are the best and the fastest way for dynamic results. This Top 10 List is the fastest way to get started. And we want you to have it, FREE.

With this BONUS offer you will now have 10 of the most powerful slogan affirmations on the planet to jump-start to a higher level God's best for you.

They are the first Affirmation (A) in *OK, God, Now What?* broken into 10 bite-sized pieces, and are just a taste of the complete set of 86 full-length Affirmations in *OK, God, Now What?*

To keep it handy all day, you can fold this FREE starter set for your purse or wallet.

IN THE RIGHT HANDS, THIS BOOK WILL CHANGE LIVES!

Most of the people who need this message will not be looking for this book. To change their lives, you need to put a copy of this book in their hands.

Still other seeds fell on fertile soil, and they produced a crop that was thirty, sixty, and even a hundred times as much as had been planted!
Matthew 13:8, NLV

Our ministry is constantly seeking methods to find good ground, the people who need this anointed message to change their lives. Will you help us reach them?

Remember this—a farmer who plants only a few seeds will get a small crop. But the one who plants generously will get a generous crop.
2 Corinthians 9:6, NLV

EXTEND THIS MINISTRY
BY SOWING
3 BOOKS, 5 BOOKS, 10 BOOKS,
OR MORE TODAY
AND BECOME A LIFE CHANGER!

Thanking you in advance,

Harold McDougal, Founder
The Published Word
Since 2004

McDougal & Associates
www.ThePublishedWord.com

Servants of Christ and Stewards of the Mysteries of God
(Your On-Demand Book Publisher and Bookseller)

Visit our newly designed site
www.ThePublishedWord.com

Free Subscription to **M&A Newsletter**

Receive free articles by ThePublishedWord authors, exclusive discounts, and free downloads from our best and newest books

Visit www.ThePublishedWord.com to subscribe

Write to: McDougal & Associates
           18896 Greenwell Springs Road
           Greenwell Springs, LA 70739

Email: orders@thepublishedword.com

For a complete list of our titles or to place an order online, visit www.ThePublishedWord.com

www.ingramcontent.com/pod-product-compliance
Lightning Source LLC
Chambersburg PA
CBHW072008150426
43194CB00008B/1036